Revisioning Stalin and Stalinism

Revisioning Stalin and Stalinism

Complexities, Contradictions and Controversies

Edited by James Ryan and Susan Grant

BLOOMSBURY ACADEMIC
LONDON • NEW YORK • OXFORD • NEW DELHI • SYDNEY

BLOOMSBURY ACADEMIC
Bloomsbury Publishing Plc
50 Bedford Square, London, WC1B 3DP, UK
1385 Broadway, New York, NY 10018, USA
29 Earlsfort Terrace, Dublin 2, Ireland

BLOOMSBURY, BLOOMSBURY ACADEMIC and the Diana logo are trademarks
of Bloomsbury Publishing Plc

First published in Great Britain 2021
This paperback edition published in 2022

Copyright © James Ryan and Susan Grant, 2021

James Ryan and Susan Grant have asserted their right under the Copyright, Designs
and Patents Act, 1988, to be identified as Editors of this work.

Cover image: 1st May, Stalin (1879–1953) Holds a Child in his Arms, 1952 (colour litho),
(© Resetnikov, Fedor Pavlovic (1906–83) / Private Collection / Archives
Charmet / Bridgeman Images)

All rights reserved. No part of this publication may be reproduced or transmitted in any
form or by any means, electronic or mechanical, including photocopying, recording,
or any information storage or retrieval system, without prior permission in writing
from the publishers.

Bloomsbury Publishing Plc does not have any control over, or responsibility for, any
third-party websites referred to or in this book. All internet addresses given in this
book were correct at the time of going to press. The author and publisher
regret any inconvenience caused if addresses have changed or sites have
ceased to exist, but can accept no responsibility for any such changes.

Every effort has been made to trace copyright holders and to obtain their permissions
for the use of copyright material. The publisher apologizes for any errors or omissions
and would be grateful if notified of any corrections that should be incorporated in
future reprints or editions of this book.

A catalogue record for this book is available from the British Library.

Library of Congress Cataloging-in-Publication Data

Names: Ryan, James, editor. | Grant, Susan, editor.
Title: Revisioning Stalin and Stalinism : complexities, contradictions, and
controversies / edited by James Ryan and Susan Grant.
Description: London ; New York : Bloomsbury Academic, 2020. |
Includes bibliographical references and index.
Identifiers: LCCN 2020031007 (print) | LCCN 2020031008 (ebook) |
ISBN 9781350122949 (hardback) | ISBN 9781350229334 (paperback) |
ISBN 9781350122963 (ebook) | ISBN 9781350122932 (epub)
Subjects: LCSH: Soviet Union–Politics and government–1917-1936. |
Soviet Union–Politics and government–1936-1953. | Stalin, Joseph, 1878-1953. |
Heads of state--Soviet Union--Biography.
Classification: LCC DK267 .R44 2020 (print) | LCC DK267 (ebook) |
DDC 947.084/2092–dc23
LC record available at https://lccn.loc.gov/2020031007
LC ebook record available at https://lccn.loc.gov/2020031008

ISBN: HB: 978-1-3501-2294-9
        PB: 978-1-3502-2933-4
        ePDF: 978-1-3501-2296-3
        eBook: 978-1-3501-2293-2

Typeset by RefineCatch Limited, Bungay, Suffolk

To find out more about our authors and books visit www.bloomsbury.com
and sign up for our newsletters.

For Geoff

Contents

Notes on contributors ix
Acknowledgements xii
Note on transliteration xiii

Introduction: Revisioning Stalin and Stalinism
James Ryan and Susan Grant 1

Part One The Controversial *Vozhd'*: Stalin as Leader and Statesman

1 The many lives of Joseph Stalin: Writing the biography of a 'Monster'   *Christopher Read* 21
2 Stalin's purge of the Red Army and misperception of security threats   *Peter Whitewood* 39
3 Stalin and the Spanish Civil War, 1936–1939: The new historiography   *Daniel Kowalsky* 51
4 Brute force and genius: Stalin as war leader   *Chris Bellamy* 63

Part Two Challenging Stalinist Models: Cults of Personality

5 The Stalin cult in comparative context   *Judith Devlin* 81
6 From heroic lion to streetfighter: Historical legacies and the leader cult in twentieth-century Hungary   *Balázs Apor* 93

Part Three New Ways of Understanding the Stalinist System: The Cold War

7 Revisioning Stalin's Cold War   *Caroline Kennedy-Pipe* 113
8 Working towards the *Vozhd'*? Stalin and the peace movement   *Geoffrey Roberts* 127
9 Constructing a confession: The language and psychology of interrogations in Stalinist Czechoslovakia   *Molly Pucci* 141

Part Four In Lieu of an Epilogue

10 Reckoning with the past: Stalin and Stalinism in Putin's Russia
    James Ryan   157

Notes   173
Select Bibliography   219
Geoffrey Roberts Select Bibliography   233
Index   237

Notes on contributors

Balázs Apor teaches East European history in the Centre for European Studies as well as the Department of Russian and Slavonic Studies at Trinity College Dublin. His research interests include the study of propaganda and symbolic politics under Communist rule, and the Sovietization of Eastern Europe after the Second World War. He has a particular interest in the study of leader cults, the invention and dissemination of socialist myths and the functioning of rituals in Soviet-type societies. His most recent publications include a monograph, *The Invisible Shining: The Cult of Mátyás Rákosi in Stalinist Hungary, 1945–1956* (2017), and a co-edited volume, *The Handbook of COURAGE: Cultural Opposition and Its Heritage in Eastern Europe* (2018).

Chris Bellamy is Professor Emeritus of Maritime Security at the University of Greenwich, UK. A specialist in Russian and Soviet military studies, in 2018 he completed a visiting research fellowship on Russian hybrid warfare as part of the Changing Character of War Programme at the University of Oxford. He was the sole author or senior editor of ten major books, including *The Times Atlas of the Second World War* (1989) and *The Oxford Companion to Military History* (2001). In 2007 he published *Absolute War: Soviet Russia in the Second World War*, which won the 2008 Westminster Medal for Military Literature.

Judith Devlin is a Professor Emerita in modern history in University College Dublin. She studied in Dublin, Paris and Oxford and worked for ten years in Ireland's Department of Foreign Affairs. She was seconded to study at the Ecole Nationale d'Administration in Paris, and served in the Irish embassy in Moscow during the Gorbachev reforms. Among her publications are: *The Superstitious Mind: French Peasants and the Supernatural in Nineteenth Century France* (1987); *The Rise of the Russian Democrats: The Causes and Consequences of the Elite Revolution* (1995); *Slavophiles and Commissars: Enemies of Democracy in Modern Russia* (1999); co-edited with Christoph Müller, *War of Words: Culture and the Mass Media in the Making of the Cold War in Europe* (2013); co-edited with John Paul Newman and Maria Falina, *World War I in Central and Eastern Europe* (2018). Her research focuses on Soviet and Russian political culture and in particular the Stalin cult.

Susan Grant is Reader in Modern European History at Liverpool John Moores University. Her research interests are in healthcare history and the social and cultural history of the Soviet Union. She is author of *Physical Culture and Sport in Soviet Society: Propaganda, Acculturation, and Transformation in the 1920s and 1930s* (2012) and editor of *Russian and Soviet Healthcare from an International Perspective: Comparing Professions, Practice and Gender, 1880–1960* (2017). She is preparing a book manuscript on the history of Soviet nursing and currently holds a Wellcome Trust Investigator Award for a project on ageing and gerontology in the Soviet Union.

Caroline Kennedy-Pipe is Professor of International Security & International Relations at Loughborough University. Caroline works in the area of War Studies and has interests in the history of the Cold War, proxy wars and small wars. She is currently working on Arctic security issues as well as examining the legacies of war and conflict on individuals and communities. In this respect her work on IEDs and their impact on war and society is an important part of her research agenda. Caroline was visiting Fellow at the Rothermere Institute at the University of Oxford in 2018 and is currently a specialist adviser to the House of Commons Select Committee on Defence.

Daniel Kowalsky is Lecturer in European Studies at Queen's University, Belfast. He is the author of numerous books and articles on the civil war in Spain, including *La Unión Soviética y la guerra civil española* (2004), *Stalin and the Spanish Civil War* (2004). He was editor, between 2005 and 2010, of *British Documents on Foreign Affairs. Series A: Russia/The Soviet Union. Part V, 1951–1956*. His work has appeared in *Film History, Archivos de la Filmoteca, the Bulletin of Spanish Studies*, the *Journal of Slavic Military Studies*, and *Dictatorships and Democracies*.

Molly Pucci is an Assistant Professor of Twentieth Century European History at Trinity College Dublin. Her current book manuscript, which is published with Yale University Press, examines the creation of communist secret police institutions in Czechoslovakia, Poland and Eastern Germany in the period following the Second World War. Her research interests include the history of communism, legal history and the history of policing in twentieth-century Europe.

Christopher Read is Professor of European History at the University of Warwick. His recent books include *Stalin: From the Caucasus to the Kremlin* (2017); *War and Revolution in Russia 1914–22* (2014); *The Stalin Years: A Reader* (2004) and *Lenin: A Revolutionary Life* (2005). He is an editor and contributor to the *Russia's Great War and Revolution* international publishing project.

Geoffrey Roberts is Emeritus Professor of History at University College Cork. In 2018–19 he was EURIAS Senior Fellow at the Helsinki Collegium for Advanced Studies. He has also received awards and fellowships from the universities of Harvard, Princeton and New York, the Kennan Institute, the Nobel Peace Institute and the Institute for Advanced Studies, Budapest. A specialist in Soviet foreign and military policy, his many books include *The Unholy Alliance: Stalin's Pact with Hitler* (1989), *The Soviet Union and the Origins of the Second World War* (1995), *The Soviet Union in World Politics, 1945–1991* (1999), *Victory at Stalingrad* (2003), *Stalin's Wars: From World War to Cold War, 1939–1953* (2006), *Stalin's General: The Life of Georgy Zhukov* (2012), *Molotov: Stalin's Cold Warrior* (2012) and (with Martin Folly and Oleg Rzheshevsky) *Churchill and Stalin: Comrades-in-Arms during the Second World War*

(2019). His biography of Zhukov won the Society for Military History's Distinguished Book Award. His writings have been translated into more than 20 languages.

James Ryan is Senior Lecturer in Modern European (Russian) History at Cardiff University. His research interests focus on the interrelationship between political violence and ideology in inter-war Soviet Russia; intellectual history; and the politics of history and memory. He is the author of *Lenin's Terror: The Ideological Origins of Early Soviet State Violence* (2012), and he is currently writing an intellectual history of Soviet state violence, 1917–1941.

Peter Whitewood is Senior Lecturer in History at York St John University, UK. He is the author of *The Red Army and the Great Terror: Stalin's Purge of the Soviet Military* and editor (with Lara Douds and James Harris) of *The Fate of the Bolshevik Revolution: Illiberal Liberation, 1917–1941* (2020).

Acknowledgements

This volume has its origins in a special symposium of the Irish Association for Russian, Central and East European Studies to mark the retirement of Professor Geoffrey Roberts, held at University College Cork in May 2018. The papers seemed to cohere together particularly well, ideas flowed and bounced, and the thought of a book soon emerged.

There are good reasons to bring out a volume of essays on Stalin and Stalinism at the present time, as we outline in the Introduction below. But Geoff's retirement provided a very personal impetus, an occasion that deserved to be marked appropriately. For over thirty years he has been a prolific historian of the Soviet Union, especially its foreign policy during the Stalin era, and a biographer of some of its leading personages. A prominent commentator on Russian and diplomatic affairs, he is a foremost public intellectual in Ireland in particular, acknowledged in his election as a Member of the Royal Irish Academy in 2016.

Born in south London in 1952, Geoff earned his PhD in International Relations at the London School of Economics and Political Science. Very active in left-wing British politics, he transitioned to an academic career and moved to Ireland, taking up his first full-time teaching post in 1992 at the Department of History at University College Cork. He would remain in Cork for the remainder of his academic career, with periodic fellowships at Harvard, Princeton, the Nobel Peace Institute in Oslo, and the Helsinki Collegium for Advanced Studies, amongst others.

The subtitle of this book – 'complexities, contradictions and controversies' – reflects the nature of Stalinism, as we see it, but it also captures the significance of Geoff's voluminous body of published work. He has sought to convey the intricacies and paradoxes of his subjects and to renounce any simplistic rendering of historical themes. His conclusions have been carefully constructed (and, we suggest, convincing), but he has not shied away from controversy, as evidenced in particular by some of the reactions to his masterful *Stalin's Wars* (2006). He has also honed the art of combining prodigious and meticulous scholarship with effective communication to a wide audience. And as a teacher, Geoff impressed and inspired and convinced several generations of students, always generous with his time and his library. We are both fortunate enough to have known Geoff as a teacher, a mentor and a friend, and we dedicate this book to him.

At Bloomsbury, our editor, Rhodri Mogford, has been enthusiastic and encouraging from the outset. We thank him and Laura Reeves for their professionalism and attention to detail, but also their friendliness and adaptability. We are also grateful to We are also grateful to Mark Fisher for his meticulous copyediting, and to Susan Certo for her equally excellent index. And very importantly, we thank all the contributors for their diligence and extraordinary efficiency in meeting our deadlines! Finally, but certainly not least, we thank our wonderful families as well as our colleagues at Cardiff and Liverpool for their constant support, and our own students for their enthusiasm.

Note on transliteration

Transliterations from the Russian Cyrillic alphabet into Latin script follow the Library of Congress system, but with slightly simplified use of diacritical marks, and with the exception of certain names commonly anglicized, e.g. Trotsky rather than Trotskii, Moscow rather than Moskva.

Introduction: Revisioning Stalin and Stalinism

James Ryan and Susan Grant

In the early hours of 25 February 1956, Nikita Khrushchev, First Secretary of the Communist Party of the Soviet Union (CPSU), delivered a four-hour speech to a closed session of the party's Twentieth Congress. Addressing delegates in a large hall inside the Grand Palace of the Moscow Kremlin, it was a defining moment in Khrushchev's career. In his speech, a report on the 'cult of personality', the First Secretary launched an impassioned and almost visceral attack on the reputation of his predecessor, Joseph Stalin, the acknowledged *vozhd'* (leader) of the Union of Soviet Socialist Republics (USSR) from 1929 until his death in 1953. The assault was pointedly personal. 'When we analyze the practice of *Stalin* in regard to the direction of the party and the country', Khrushchev remarked, and 'when we ponder over everything which *Stalin* perpetrated ... the negative characteristics of *Stalin* ... caused incalculable harm to our party' (emphases added).[1] The premise of Khrushchev's excoriating dismantlement of Stalin's rule was the latter's alleged departure from the example provided by Vladimir Lenin, the first leader of the party and Soviet state. Whereas Lenin, according to Khrushchev, had ruled with true authority, wisdom and modesty, through collective deliberation and consultation, Stalin displayed 'complete intolerance of collectivity in leadership'. His character was fundamentally flawed – 'capricious and despotic' – as a result of which he practised 'brutal violence' towards everyone and everything that opposed him or stood 'contrary to his concepts'. True, Khrushchev did not pin all wrongdoings on Stalin. But, he reasoned, Stalin's example and type of leadership 'encouraged and permitted' a more general arbitrariness in Soviet rule, 'many thousands' of arrests and deportations, and a climate of fear and insecurity.

Khrushchev took an enormous risk. By denouncing Stalin and the personality cult that had arisen around him, he had unavoidably called into question the very legitimacy of Soviet rule in the minds of party members, and, eventually, the Soviet populace. Stalin had come to personify Soviet power, its supposed benevolence, achievements and promises. He was, after all, the father-figure that had inspired Soviet victory over the terrifying Nazi war machine. Once leaked beyond the confines of the Kremlin, the consequences of the speech proved difficult to control. East of the imaginary 'iron curtain' that divided Cold War Europe, the Soviet-controlled Eastern Bloc witnessed its greatest strains since a popular rising in East Germany three years before. And within the USSR itself, as Polly Jones has explained, the Soviet system was forced to accommodate an unprecedentedly complex narrative of 'guilt, shame, and trauma'.[2]

Khrushchev's speech was designed to foist upon Stalin ultimate responsibility for the transgressions of the Soviet regime during two-and-a-half decades of extraordinary upheaval and transformation, and thereby absolve the very structure of Soviet power and one-party dictatorship. The party would return to Leninist first principles, and all would be well. However, forceful and iconoclastic though Khrushchev's denunciation of Stalin was, it was not unmitigated. Stalin had achieved much. He was praised for his role in defeating oppositional tendencies in the party in the 1920s. He was praised too for the policies of rapid industrialization and 'comprehensive collectivization' of agriculture in the early 1930s. In addition, Khrushchev did not reveal the true extent of Soviet mass violence in the late 1930s. In fact, for all the scorn heaped upon Stalin, just before stepping from the rostrum Khrushchev sounded a tragic note. Stalin, he suggested, was no mere despot. His errors had flowed from his conviction in what was necessary for the party, for the working people, and for 'the victory of socialism and communism'. In Khrushchev's view the 'true tragedy' (*istinnaia tragediia*) of Stalin was that he was a believer in communist transformation, but he had fallen from the path of Leninism. He had conflated the interests of world revolution with his own.

Ironically, Khrushchev's 'secret speech' is one of the most famous of the twentieth century, an extraordinary piece of rhetoric that has become a staple component of the scholarship and teaching of Soviet history. It has also helped shape that scholarship and teaching as well as wider understandings of Stalin's rule. Stalin's 'capricious and despotic character' is recognizable to most. The depiction of a tyrannical dictator has been reflected in scholarly and popular understandings that have frequently elided the man and the political 'system' that bears his name: Stalinism.[3] The speech also harmonizes with another highly influential narrative developed by Stalin's rival, Leon Trotsky, after the latter had been expelled from the USSR in 1929. Trotsky's condemnation was less personal and more systemic than Khrushchev's, but the message of both amounted to the October Revolution's having been 'betrayed' under Stalin's stewardship.[4] The implication – that Lenin and Leninism represented a purer form of revolutionary Marxism – possessed considerable appeal for many left-wing activists and scholars outside the USSR, although it is now divisive even for the political Left.[5]

Stalin is a towering figure of modern history, and his influence on the course of the twentieth century is difficult to quantify. As undisputed leader of the All-Union Communist Party (Bolsheviks), renamed the CPSU in 1952, and ruler of the Soviet Union, he presided over the country's metamorphosis into an industrial superpower. The Stalinist regime was capable of withstanding invasion by Nazi Germany before conquering Berlin itself in 1945. It was under Stalin that the Eastern Bloc in Central and Eastern Europe was established, modelled on Stalinist rule in the USSR. The global Cold War geopolitical and cultural rivalries were also substantially formed with Stalin in the Kremlin, as the Soviet Union attained global influence and leadership through its alternative to American-led liberal capitalist democracy. And it was under Stalin that the Soviet Union became the most violent state in peacetime modern European history. Many millions of Soviet citizens and inhabitants were arrested, deported, executed, starved, or suffered from neglect as a direct or unintended consequence of the actions of the Stalinist state, often at Stalin's command. Indeed the Stalinist 'revolution' in the Soviet Union in the 1930s provides a prime example of 'developmental violence': state-led transformation of a relatively underdeveloped economy and society into a modern industrial country, rapidly, and at enormous cost in human lives.[6] But the 'Stalin question', as Khrushchev pointed out in the often-overlooked passage at the end of his speech, is 'complicated'.

* * *

Revisioning Stalin and Stalinism introduces and intervenes in thematic controversies that characterize the political and cultural-political history of the Stalin period. Our explicit claim to 'revision' Stalin and Stalinism might seem entirely meaningless, perhaps even irritating. All good historical scholarship revises or reconsiders what we understand about a topic of enquiry, and, besides, it has been several decades since there existed a broadly identifiable school of 'revisionism' in Soviet historical studies. Nonetheless, the title is purposeful. It underlines the continuing challenge to recognize and analyse the complex, multi-faceted, and often contradictory nature of Stalin, Stalinism, and Stalinist-style leadership, and their representations. Hence, the volume 'revisions' Stalin and Stalinism in the sense suggested by historian Geoffrey Roberts in his celebrated and controversial *Stalin's Wars* (2006): together, these essays depict 'many Stalins', including the 'despot and diplomat' and the 'rational bureaucrat and paranoid politician', as well as some of the wider complexities of the Stalinist political system.[7] Broadly speaking, three important areas of debate are examined, united by a focus on political leadership. These are controversies of Stalin's leadership role; reconsideration of Stalin, Stalinism and the Cold War; and new perspectives on the cult of personality. This introductory essay provides a brief overview of these topics and the wider trends in anglophone scholarship on Stalinism, in order to situate the volume within the literature.

Stalin's leadership role

Khrushchev was right: the 'Stalin question' is complicated. There were horrific consequences to Stalinism, yet Stalin and his party were convinced that they acted in the ultimate interests of the working people and socialist revolution, and hence for the protection and advancement of humanity as a whole. And, although Stalin and his comrades bear much responsibility for a Cold War that in places turned very hot indeed, they had sought collective security and continuation of alliances with Western powers after the Second World War.[8] More profoundly, what Khrushchev could not acknowledge or admit was that the paradoxes of Stalinist rule were the most graphic manifestations of a more general paradox that characterized the Soviet regime from its foundation. The lofty ideals of human emancipation from the hardships and exploitation of capitalism and persistent warfare were funnelled, through a complex combination of ideological conviction, circumstance and recalcitrant reality, to create a dictatorial regime that parodied socialism more than it represented it.[9]

Complexity, however, is not an accurate description of how Stalin and Stalinism have conventionally been understood in most parts of the world. Stalin is usually found keeping company with Adolf Hitler in the realm of reviled twentieth-century European dictators. But in Russia, the heartland of the former Soviet Union, things are somewhat different. Reputable opinion polls suggest that Stalin's popularity amongst Russians has grown over the past twenty years, and especially since Vladimir Putin's re-election as president in 2012. In fact, Stalin is one of the three most highly rated political leaders in Russia of the past hundred years.[10] Russians' attitudes toward Stalin and the Stalinist past are actually more intricate than bold statistics might suggest, but what is clear is that wartime triumph in the Great Patriotic War – as the Second World War is known in Russia – is of crucial significance. Putin's remarks at a meeting with young historians in November 2014 neatly summarize the conundrum that Russians (and not just Russians) face. 'It's just hard to say whether we could have won the war if the leaders [of the Soviet Union] had not been so cruel', Putin reasoned. 'And what would the consequences have been if we'd lost?' Putin himself was in no doubt: they would have been 'simply catastrophic', because the Nazis 'were going to physically exterminate the Slavic people'.[11] Baldly put, as Geoffrey Roberts has argued, Stalin's methods of rule 'were unpalatable but effective, and perhaps unavoidable if victory was to be secured'.[12] Whether or not one agrees with Putin, or with Roberts, Soviet wartime victory and Stalin's leadership are closely intertwined in the imagination of many Russians. Hitler's genocidal intent towards the Slavic peoples is not lost on a society for which victory in the war has become a core component of collective national identity. And alongside Soviet wartime victory, Stalin's cult of personality has played an important role in keeping Stalin, the man, front and centre in Soviet and Russian history.

Stalin, Stalinism and the Cold War

If the late 1940s and the early 1950s witnessed the omnipresence of Stalin's cult of personality at home, the leader himself was more visibly absent from Soviet public life. The science and culture wars of the age, as well as foreign policy, drew Stalin away from areas of domestic policy.[13] This was also a period characterized by great inconsistency in Soviet life, with policies of coercion and conservatism juxtaposed to hope and zeal in the social sphere.[14] The *Zhdanovshchina* – the post-war cultural restrictions and anti-Western orientation named for Andrei Zhdanov, the party's principal cultural theorist – accompanied by campaigns against 'rootless cosmopolitans' and anti-Semitism, saw Stalin re-emerge at his despotic worst in post-war domestic politics. A turn against the West and all things foreign was designed to reinforce the pre-eminence of socialism and, ipso facto, the Stalinist system. Abroad, Stalin the diplomat jousted with international leaders in power politics over Germany, Korea, Yugoslavia and the so-called people's democracies in Central and Eastern Europe. Apart from victory in the Great Patriotic War, the foremost legacy of Stalinism in global affairs was the Soviet Union's contribution to the Cold War.

Those post-war years may be thought of as 'the lost peace'.[15] A number of events set the scene for a prolonged period of political tension referred to as the Cold War: Churchill's speech in Fulton, Missouri on 5 March 1946 that famously imagined an 'iron curtain' descend on Europe; American President Harry Truman's 'Truman Doctrine' and the Marshall Plan for European aid; and Zhdanov's description in 1947 of a world divided by 'two camps'. The Soviet Union's ability to launch a nuclear war from 1949 – and turn the Cold War 'hot' – simultaneously elevated the status of the Soviet Union and international tensions. This development, and the creation of the Soviet-controlled Eastern Bloc in Europe along with the rise of communism in China in 1949, placed the Soviet Union in a position of geopolitical strength. As the world realigned into blocs and spheres of influence, and with the Soviet Union now a power player, Stalinism moved outside of Soviet borders. In its exported form, Stalinism was then reimagined or, one might even say, revisioned. Policies of Russification and socialist-style politics and culture made their way across the Eastern Bloc, to be applied in the creation of 'own brands' of Stalinism. This fusion of Stalinism and the former political systems in Central and Eastern Europe was further entangled by a complicated web of cross-border relationships.

Transnational activities were influential on a number of levels, and Soviet relations with the 'people's democracies' and countries further afield have helped to shape understandings not only of Soviet foreign policy, but also Stalinism itself. Michael David-Fox has written that 'border crossings had a crucial impact ... throughout the history of Stalinism'.[16] This impact was felt in relations between the Soviet Union and both its Western and Eastern European neighbours, and is 'integral' to understanding Stalinist notions of communism as a 'superior civilization'.[17] The chapters in this volume, especially those that focus on finding new ways of understanding Stalinism in the Cold War period, show that the reshaping of the international order after the war rested on both domestic and international perceptions and interpretations of Stalinism.

The cult of personality

In theory, political leader cults are antithetical to Marxism's emphasis that socialist revolution is an affair of the working people as a whole. Nonetheless, Stalin's name and leadership style have become almost indelibly associated with the cult of personality. In his not-so-secret speech, Khrushchev heaped blame on the Stalin personality cult as the 'source ... of exceedingly serious and grave perversions of Party principles'.[18] In contrast to Lenin, Khrushchev depicted Stalin as the architect of his own cult, curating the production of literature, film, monuments and art devoted to him. Even though the Stalin cult of personality began in 1929, the cult did not really take off until mid-1933, then took a 'hiatus' during the Second World War, before spiralling again in 1945 and 1949, the latter year seeing Stalin's seventieth birthday celebrated in the Soviet Union and Eastern Bloc.[19]

During Stalin's time adulation for the *vozhd'* was portrayed, out of ideological conviction, as springing organically from the masses.[20] Conversely, Khrushchev separated Stalin and the system, rejecting the notion that the former's abuses of power were linked to the structures, practices and psychology of Bolshevik rule.[21] Questions about the *sui generis* nature of the Stalin cult naturally arise, but, as one scholar of Stalinism has recently surmised, in the context of the 1930s 'the Stalin Cult shouldn't be seen as intrinsically exceptional or above normal politics at all, and it certainly wasn't received as such by the population'.[22] The many layers of Stalinism, it seems, have yet to be peeled back fully to reveal how it functioned in practice.

These layers, the subject of much debate and controversy among scholars of the Soviet Union, persisted well past the death of Stalin himself. Although Khrushchev initiated a process of de-Stalinization after his secret speech, this had lost momentum by the 1960s and 1970s. After all, wartime victory, patriotism and superpower status referenced Late Stalinism.[23] The Brezhnev period reflected the celebratory politics of the late 1930s and 1940s, a suitable backdrop for the re-emergence of Stalinist elements. The Brezhnev years (1964–82) were marked by the 'cult of the Great Patriotic War' as opposed to the cult of Stalin, and Brezhnev himself lost no opportunity to build his own cult of personality by boasting about his own past military exploits.[24] But if Lenin and the revolution seemed inseparable in the minds of many Soviet citizens, then Stalin and the Second World War seemed equally inseparable (in spite of Khrushchev's best efforts). As we have seen, disentangling the two has proven difficult.

The meshing together of experiences, ideologies and representations formed a glue to bind Soviet citizens together, and later to connect Soviet and Eastern Bloc citizens. When the Soviet Union ended, the system that Stalin built came unstuck, but some of the gluey residue remained. As countries in Central and Eastern Europe today attempt to shed their links to 'totalitarianism', leaders and communities have sought, with considerable difficulty, to remove the visible vestiges of their countries' connections to communism. This has often been a dramatic, slow and painful process. Power vacuums, political tensions and economic instability have opened up spaces for other cults of personality and despotism to thrive. Replacing one political culture with another is not easily done; the legacies of Stalinism often live on in unexpected guises and forms.

Interpreting Stalinism: Controversies and contestations

It is difficult to define Stalinism. Initially, it represented a 'Great Break' from the relative moderation of the New Economic Policy (NEP) in the 1920s, with its toleration of a limited market economy and profession of a more gradual evolution towards socialism. The Stalin era in Soviet history (1929–53), however, witnessed considerable change and evolution in policy. Furthermore, important elements of the Stalinist 'system', such as a state-planned economy and one-party rule, had existed before 1929 or were firmly in place by then, and persisted until *perestroika* in the late 1980s.[25] Nonetheless, as a compound of multi-faceted and sometimes contradictory ideological tenets, policies, institutions, practices, ethos, values and more general cultural attributes, it should certainly include the following: commitment to achieving a fully socialist, then communist, society; a centralized state-command economy under a single-party regime; enormous though not continual use of mass coercion and violence in the process of rapid economic and social modernization, and social engineering; political repression, and a somewhat pathological suspicion of 'enemies' of the revolution; a 'propaganda state' characterized by the extraordinary importance of communicating with and mobilizing its citizenry in the service of revolutionary social transformation; heavy regulation of information from within and beyond the state's borders; a cult of the leader and a tendency towards patriarchal rule; and a projection of superiority relative to the assumed decadence of the capitalist world.[26]

All of these themes have been explored in considerable detail. Indeed, the volume of available literature on the Stalin era (in various languages) is so daunting that it is comforting to read Oleg Khlevniuk's honest description of this ever-expanding body of work as 'impossibly vast'.[27] Why, then, would anyone want to add to it? It is true, as David Hoffmann has put it, that 'no problem looms larger' for historians of the Soviet Union than explaining Stalinism.[28] Yet the reader would be forgiven for supposing that there is little new – or substantially new – that remains to be contributed.

In fact, original and insightful work that challenges received wisdom, or that illuminates previously unexplored issues, continues to appear. These outputs result both from the availability of previously classified archives accessible only since the early 1990s, and new approaches, questions and methodologies. For example, Lynne Viola's book on individual perpetrators of Stalinist state violence in the 1930s sheds new light on those that populated the apparatus of the Soviet state and carried out its most distasteful work, a study made possible through recently accessible files in the archive of the Ukrainian security services.[29] Jonathan Waterlow draws on jokes and satire to illuminate how ordinary people lived under Stalinism.[30] Cynthia Ruder and Katherine Zubovich have utilized the archival trails generated by Stalinist construction projects, respectively the Moscow canal and the monumental skyscrapers of post-war Moscow, to examine the projection of socialism onto the built environment; Zubovich's work also illustrates the spatial dimensions of Late Stalinist social differentiation, as space was cleared for these new buildings in the city centre through population displacement.[31] And recent works by Sarah Cameron and Robert Kindler, in particular, foreground Kazakhstan (not just Ukraine) in understanding the terrible phenomenon of famine in the USSR in the early 1930s.[32]

It is noteworthy that today's early- and mid-career scholars typically have little or no recollection of the Cold War, or experience of the politically charged atmosphere that often characterized the work of older generations.[33] But whatever the context, important questions about Stalinism – along with public and scholarly interest in it – will remain, and hence the continued value of works that synthesize secondary literature as well as offer new interpretations. In addition, the recent centenary of the Russian Revolution has provided renewed impetus for studies that reflect on the significance and fate of the Revolution, and the origins of Stalinism.[34]

Schools of thought: Totalitarianism

There have been several significant paradigm shifts in post-war Soviet studies. For much of the Cold War, English-language studies of the Soviet Union were dominated by the 'totalitarian school' or 'totalitarian model'. 'Totalitarianism' entered the political lexicon in the early-mid 1920s, as Benito Mussolini and his Italian Fascists boasted about their power and control and appropriated for themselves a word initially coined by their critics.[35] By the late 1950s the term had become conventional for describing such polities as Fascist Italy, Nazi Germany and the Stalinist USSR. Cold War rivalries between the supposedly free Western world and the 'totalitarian' East had taken shape by then, and scholars – primarily in the United States – were, in effect, enlisted in that struggle. It was important to 'know the enemy', or at least to know it as well as anyone could in the circumstances of restricted access to the Soviet Union, its people and its archives. Within that politically charged climate of American academia, in particular, the understanding of the Soviet Union that emerged was of a powerful, all-encompassing state ruled by a single party that had come to dominate its society almost completely.[36] Central to this framework was the contention that the totalitarian state was, to a considerable extent, constructed under Lenin's rule and merely developed further by Stalin. Its power was maintained by a mixture of invasive propaganda and political repression, backed up by the ubiquitous and brutal political police. There was no room for dissension, at least not without terrible consequences. And, according to the logic of Cold War geopolitics, such a system posed an existential threat to the 'free' world.

In effect, the totalitarian model presented the actually existing Soviet regime as a reflection of the ruling party's own projections – powerful, united, in control – but with the values inverted, and without the assumed basis of genuine popular legitimacy. An early if slightly caricatured example is the study of Bolshevism by Nathan Leites, published the year of Stalin's death. Leites was a social scientist at the RAND corporation, an independent thinktank that explicitly served US security interests. What Leites sought to capture was the 'spirit of the Bolshevik elite', assuming that the latter provided an 'operational code' that could decode the workings of the state itself. Leites was explicit about his methodology: he examined statements of the party leadership without seriously attending to the 'complex of conditions' that might contextualize those statements and their development. This was ideology as *doctrine*, largely shorn of uncertainties and adaptations, largely stable in content and function. And even though Leites acknowledged that there were uncertainties, including significant differences between the statements of Lenin and Stalin, he hesitated little to pronounce the party an omnipotent 'monolith' with clear continuity from its inception to the Cold War.[37]

The totalitarian school, though, was neither homogenous nor static. Leites's 1953 book was not well received by other US-based scholars, for whom it was shallow in approach though not misconceived in its underlying premises.[38] Published the same year was Merle Fainsod's *How Russia is Ruled*, a classic study of Soviet totalitarianism that nonetheless illustrates the possibilities for adaptation within the rubric of the totalitarian model. Ten years after it first appeared, Fainsod issued a revised edition that accounted for what he termed a more 'enlightened' totalitarianism under Khrushchev, thereby undermining the suggestion that Soviet power was monolithic.[39] That elasticity in understanding totalitarianism, and willingness to emend one's work in light of both political changes in the USSR and new evidence, Fainsod shared with Hannah Arendt, a prolific and highly influential political philosopher who had immigrated to the United States after fleeing Nazi Germany. In fact, Arendt's classic study, *The Origins of Totalitarianism* (1951), reminds us that even during the Cold War a distinction could be made between 'totalitarianism' as an object of study – albeit the word itself suggested an interpretation of a particular type of political formation – and an identifiable totalitarian 'school' of thought that provided a model, broadly speaking, for such regimes. Arendt departed from that model in important respects. In her 1966 preface, she went further than Fainsod by referring to a 'process of detotalitarization' in the USSR after Stalin's death. More significant perhaps was her characterization of NEP as an 'obvious alternative' to Stalinism; that would later become a feature of 'revisionism' in Soviet studies.[40]

What bound together all descriptions of totalitarian polities was the understanding that they were not merely dictatorial or authoritarian: they were more socially invasive and repressive, more 'total' in dominance. But from where or what did they arise? In the Soviet context the reasons were often attributed to an ideology that sought total transformation of society and complete state control of the economy, while preaching a message of class struggle. For some scholars, the burden of responsibility actually originated with the ideas of Karl Marx and Friedrich Engels.[41] However, not all works in this vein were equally focused on ideology, and hence the nature and source of 'totalitarianism' was open to dispute. Some located the roots of Soviet totalitarianism in the peculiarities of autocratic Russian political culture, others still in the personalities and pathologies of Lenin and Stalin and their ruthless accumulation of power.[42]

Revisionism

The totalitarian school was in large measure a function of political scientists and political science models, with some of its leading exponents (such as Zbigniew Brzezinski and the historian Richard Pipes) even occupying powerful positions in the Cold War-era White House.[43] Until the mid-1970s, Western historians, due to the inaccessibility of sensitive archive material, tended not to venture into or beyond 1917 in Russian/Soviet history.[44] However, the 'totalitarian' approach was never entirely dominant in Soviet studies beyond the borders of the USSR, especially in British and Western European scholarship. Indeed, to read the Cold-war era works of those such as the British-based economic historian R.W. Davies is to belie any supposition that excellent, relatively non-politicized scholarship was not produced long before the archives opened wide their doors.[45] But as a paradigm, 'totalitarianism' was undermined in the 1970s and 1980s. The challenge came from a wave of young and immensely talented 'revisionists', mainly historians, for whom the postulates of the totalitarian model seemed methodologically flawed as well as politically distasteful. This was the era of the New Left and opposition to the Vietnam War. Revisionism had already appeared in American diplomatic history, challenging and reversing the 'orthodox' assertion that Soviet expansionism was primarily responsible for the Cold War.[46] Conservative American Sovietology was soon engaged in a bitter struggle for control of the narrative on the Soviet Union itself. Some of these young scholars benefitted from new opportunities for cultural exchange to spend significant time living and researching in the USSR, forging friendships and learning the ways of Soviet life first-hand.[47] Yet revisionists were no more united than totalitarians. For some, challenging and replacing the narrative was perhaps more important than it was for others, for whom the inherent value of open-minded scholarship was primary and axiomatic.[48] What united them was opposition to the idea that the Soviet regime was a crudely totalitarian, monolithic, inherently and primarily repressive political system.

There were several distinguishing revisionist strands. Most prominent were social historians led by Sheila Fitzpatrick, who moved from Britain (and before that Australia) to the US in the early 1970s. Whereas the totalitarian paradigm largely assumed that what mattered was what happened at the apex of power, and that there was no significant space for social autonomy, historians such as Fitzpatrick saw evidence of something more complicated. As Fitzpatrick herself later reflected, the main thrust of revisionism was 'to show that Soviet society was something more than just a passive object of the regime's manipulation and mobilization'.[49] Furthermore, as Fitzpatrick again has acknowledged, the very topics of research chosen by historians on exchange in Moscow necessarily reflected that which granted them limited access to archive collections in the first place: if they approached the Soviet period at all, social history was much more ideologically acceptable than party politics, and violent purges were off limits.[50] Such limitations and 'bargaining' aside, revisionist social and political historians were able to document, to the ire of totalitarian scholars, that the Stalinist order had a social support basis. They demonstrated, for example, that the so-called Stalinist 'revolution from above' at the turn of the 1930s actually relied upon some popular initiative and mobilization 'from below'.[51] Whereas Arendt, in particular, had stressed the social foundations and popular support of totalitarian rule, she had explained these by reference to what she disparagingly labelled 'the masses' – identified by sheer volume of number, political 'indifference', and the atomization of individuals in societies where identifiable class structures had broken down – rather than by 'common interest' or any articulated 'goals'.[52] By contrast, revisionists such as Fitzpatrick located the foundations of a new Stalinist social order in such things as 'affirmative action' programmes of social mobility, which allowed ambitious workers and peasants to receive education and to staff the Soviet bureaucracy.[53] But the principal theme that animated revisionists was the question of popular support for radical socialist revolution in 1917: social and political historians including Ronald Grigor Suny, Stephen Smith, Diane Koenker, William Rosenberg and Alexander Rabinowitch exposed significant working-class support (and, hence, some degree of legitimacy) for the Bolshevik declaration of Soviet power in the first place.[54]

In addition to pathbreaking social history that asserted the existence of social agency vis-à-vis the state, revisionist research on aspects of elite political history further undermined tenets of the totalitarian thesis. First, it became abundantly clear that the Soviet Union was not ruled by a monolithic party. Khrushchev's reforms might have been clear evidence of that for Fainsod and Arendt, but Rabinowitch was able to delineate the indeterminacy of Bolsheviks tactics in 1917 itself, and scholars such as Stephen Cohen and Robert Daniels convincingly chronicled alternative and oppositionist trends within the party before and during Stalin's leadership.[55] However viable an alternative might have been, Stalinism, it seemed, was certainly not the only, 'irresistible' outcome of Leninism. Second, there was the significance of ideology itself. Whereas totalitarian scholars tended to over-determine its role and define it rather crudely as rigid doctrine, some (but not all) revisionists tended to downplay its import to the point of neglect. Greater emphasis was attributed to the circumstances and political and economic structures within which the state acted.[56] For example, the political scientist Graeme Gill suggested that a necessary component of the functioning of the Stalinist state was personal networks and patronage, what he described as the 'structure of supporters which Stalin was able to place throughout the system'.[57]

Furthermore, new research in the 1980s by historians including J. Arch Getty and Roberta Manning argued that the spiral of violence in the 1930s issued from a weak and chaotic power-structure, and conflict between the centre and peripheries, rather than from the intentions of party leaders enabled by an all-powerful state.[58] With the unveiling of new archival evidence, Getty has more recently suggested that the apogee of violence in 1937–8 was, to a considerable extent, a response of Stalin and the centre to pressures from provincial party leaders.[59]

Post-revisionism

Work written through identifiably 'totalitarian' and 'revisionist' frameworks continued to be published into the 1990s,[60] and some of their features are still discernible. But with the collapse of the USSR and the end of the Cold War, the political stakes lost their immediate relevance for Western historians. A new cohort of scholars relatively free from the ideological struggles of previous generations entered the newly opened former Soviet archives. They brought to their work not just new sources and a fresh outlook but also methodological innovation derived from the more general 'cultural turn' and 'linguistic turn' that had swept the humanities by the 1980s.[61] Emphasis shifted away from notions of structural determinism and the solidity of categories of social analysis such as 'class', thereby departing from the Marxist philosophy of 'historical materialism' that suggested that cultures are constructed upon particular, immanent forms of social organization, that 'being determines consciousness'. Rather, as we have come to realize, 'culture' itself plays a significant role in forming and shaping social structures – fluid and contingent and contestable – and our place within them.

The cultural and linguistic turns have ensured greater attentiveness to language and other symbols, discursive representations, and identity constructions that inform political and social realities and practices, as well as the question how to read 'texts' and the variety of things that can be considered 'texts'. Drawing on the influences of philosophers, cultural theorists, symbolic anthropologists and historians, such as Michel Foucault, Jacques Derrida, Pierre Bourdieu, Joan Wallach Scott, Judith Butler and Clifford Geertz, cultural historians or historians influenced by the cultural turn and poststructuralism have helped 'unpack' interplays of power and meaning, and how dominant narratives and representations are constructed and challenged.[62] Within the field of Soviet studies, cultural history had become dominant by the dawn of the new millennium. Political and social history were rendered relatively out of fashion – or at least political history focused largely on leading men and state institutions, and social history focused on structures and objective processes out of tune with the concerns of the cultural historian.[63] Since then, innovative new research has appeared on social groups identified beyond class categories, and on hitherto relatively unexplored themes around issues of identity, gender and sexuality.[64]

By the mid-1990s it had become possible to speak of 'post-revisionism' in the historiography of the Soviet Union. Like revisionism, this emerged after Western diplomatic historians had produced a post-revisionist 'synthesis' in the 1980s on the origins of the Cold War, more sympathetic to the argument that it resulted primarily from Soviet expansionism.[65] Post-revisionism as a general historiographical tendency typically combines elements of 'orthodox' and 'revisionist' paradigms but in rather intricate ways, and in Soviet historical studies it has resulted in an altogether more rounded picture. It has posed more complex questions and advanced more complex answers. For example, it has helped move us beyond relatively simplistic issues of continuity and change in the inter-war period, foregrounding instead dynamic interactions, exchanges and adaptations of historical agents and cultural models in what Katerina Clark has termed the 'ecology' and 'ecosystem' of revolution, both across the 1917 divide and the Stalinist 'Great Break'. Stalinism, in other words, did not follow an 'unswerving line' from Leninism or pre-revolutionary Russian culture, but, equally, it needed to locate 'some prior ground for ... authenticity'.[66] And one of the most welcome and decidedly necessary characteristics of post-revisionism in Soviet studies has been the 'return of ideology'.[67] In the mid-1990s the increasingly prominent young historians Igal Halfin and Jochen Hellbeck rather bluntly upbraided revisionism for having 'deideologized' the Soviet system.[68] Scholarship in the post-revisionist vein has uncovered and highlighted the unmistakable depth of Bolshevik ideological conviction, aided by archival revelations that what Bolsheviks said to each other behind closed doors retained the unmistakeable imprint of an ideological mentality. But it has also re-conceptualized the relationship between state and society through examination of ideology as discourse rather than just doctrine; that is, the ways in which ideology was transmitted, received contested, and creatively integrated in people's lives.[69]

Perhaps the critical work of post-revisionism was Stephen Kotkin's *Magnetic Mountain* (1995), a brilliant study of the industrial city of Magnitogorsk on the Ural river that explained Stalinism as a particular form of 'civilization'. Going beyond revisionist identification of a social basis of support for the regime, and spurred by the work of Foucault on subjectivities – the formation of a coherent sense of the individual self – Kotkin argued for a rather fundamental rethink of Stalinism. It was not and could not have been merely repressive; it also provided a positive message about socialism that the populace could believe in. The distinctiveness of Stalinism, according to Kotkin, 'lay not in the formation of a mammoth state by means of the destruction of society but in the creation, along with such a state, of a new society'. Stalinism, he continued, 'signified the advent of a specifically socialist civilization based on the rejection of capitalism'.[70] In addition, ordinary citizens learned to 'speak Bolshevik', to negotiate with official bureaucracy in their own interests by speaking through the terms and norms of Bolshevik discourse. This naturally raised the question of the extent to which ordinary people truly believed in the message of 'revolutionary truth' put forth by the party. Kotkin's answer was inconclusive, but he suggested that Bolshevik ideological categories formed at least an inescapable component of how Soviet citizens interpreted the world. They also provided 'something to strive for'.[71]

Kotkin's work helped inspire other scholars, mainly Hellbeck and Halfin, to develop further the formation of Soviet subjectivities. Yet, according to both Halfin and Hellbeck, Kotkin had inadvertently reinforced 'aspects of the state-society dichotomy' by presenting Soviet citizens as subjects *reacting* to the state and its discourses, conforming to them, working around them or resisting them.[72] For Halfin and Hellbeck, what was most impressive about newly available sources such as diaries and other ego-documents is the extent to which the Bolshevik ideal of individual self-transformation as conscious communist citizen was eagerly seized upon by some rank-and-file party members and ordinary citizens of their own volition. Here were revealed the creative possibilities opened by the Revolution – and later by Stalinism – for the development of empowered individuals, albeit within a framework of collective belonging rather than Western-style liberal individuation.[73] Here also was the suggestion that the idealized 'new Soviet person' of the communist future was no mere fantasy.

Interest in Soviet subjectivity and the discourses of Soviet power has not been without controversy. Whilst few scholars would contest the place of this literature in the canon of modern Soviet studies, for some there have been justifiable concerns of a surfeit of theory and discourse at the expense of empirical, context-based historical research.[74] For others, there is the danger that the Stalinist regime can appear altogether too benign. After all, tens of millions of people suffered. In his assessment of the pioneering studies of Soviet subjectivity, Eric Naiman perceptively concluded that the ideal subject for the party was so highly prescribed and difficult to attain that it was less a 'new Soviet person' and more an 'abridged man [sic]'.[75] In more recent years a sort of scholarly consensus has developed around the issue of Soviet subjectivity, one that posits the composite and sometimes contradictory nature of Stalinist society and culture, with multiple and sometimes fragmented identity narratives and experiences available upon which Soviet citizens could draw.[76] As the reader may surmise, this is a view of Stalinist 'civilization' that harmonizes with the thrust of the present volume.

In a collection of essays published in 2000 that took stock of the 'archival revolution' in Stalinism studies, Sheila Fitzpatrick observed that 'it is the specific characteristics of Stalinism rather than its commonalities with other cultural systems that interest the current generation'.[77] However, since then another recognizable feature of post-revisionist research has been the insertion of the Russian Revolution and the Stalinist regime within its contemporary European as well as historically Russian contexts. Reflecting increased awareness within the historical profession of the interconnectedness or 'entanglements' of modern societies, it is now conventional to suggest that the means utilized by and the general ethos of the Soviet state (and its Russian antecedents) should be situated within a broader framework of modernity.

Particularly influential in this regard has been the work of historians such as Peter Holquist and David Hoffman on the recognizably 'modern' outlook and practices of the Soviet state. This includes various measures of state intervention in society to sculpt an idealized body politic, and in particular the use of surveillance and the general mobilization of citizens in the context of the First World War and its aftermath.[78] This 'shared modernity' framework is not intended to suggest that all modern states were equivalent, or that the Soviet experience was not distinctive in important respects. However, some critical historians consider the modernity framework somewhat limited in understanding how a state such as the Stalinist USSR actually functioned. They have instead underlined the decidedly non-modern, 'archaic', 'neo-traditional' personal networks, practices and conceptions of governance that persisted or recurred after 1917.[79] Yet, as Michael David-Fox has perceptively interjected, the necessarily complicated interlacing of the generically 'modern' and the nationally particular, or the multiple variations of modernity, suggest that there is no incompatibility between the 'modernity school' and the 'neo-traditionalists'.[80] This is a theme that will be taken up explicitly below in the essays that examine various cults of personality.

From the present vantage-point, writing on the Russian Revolution and the Soviet Union has left behind the fraught confrontations of 'totalitarians' and revisionists. Western historians of the Stalin era are fully conversant with wider disciplinary and scholarly trends, and many-sided engagement with that era and its personalities has become largely *de rigueur*. However, in the countries of the former Soviet Union and Eastern Bloc, the history of the Stalin era remains – understandably – politically contentious. The ideological constraints within which Soviet historians could write were replaced in the 1990s by the release of much emotionally fuelled work that denigrated the Soviet system and its leaders.[81] In the current climate of increased geopolitical tensions between Russia and the West, and between Russia and its 'near abroad' in former Soviet spaces, the contested legacies of the Stalin era in particular have assumed renewed political significance involving politicians, popular writers and to a lesser extent historians.[82] Nonetheless, historians from Russia, the former USSR, and the Eastern Bloc remain largely free from overbearing state interference in their work. Many of them are fully integrated in and leading figures of international scholarly networks and intellectual trends. Indeed the most impressive publication series devoted to the Stalin era and its antecedents is published by the Moscow publishing house Russian Political Encyclopedia (ROSSPEN), under the general title *Istoriia stalinizma* (*History of Stalinism*). It includes the excellent monographs of young and established Russian historians and social scientists.[83]

Most recently, the field of Soviet studies has experienced a renewed emphasis on political history 'from above'. This might appear a reversal to an earlier era of historical scholarship that remains unfashionable in the wider profession. However, revisionists and post-revisionists in Soviet studies have rarely (if ever) denied the importance of the political centre and the notable politicization of all aspects of life by the Soviet regime.[84] There is now elevated recognition amongst historians of the significance of political leadership in the Soviet system, the challenges of centralized state-building, and political biography as a genre, and indeed one can identify a recent 'biographical turn' in the historical profession more generally.[85] In particular, there is renewed emphasis on Stalin's leadership, with several high-profile new biographies of him appearing since the mid-2010s.[86] Perhaps this trend is partly a response to revisionist studies that stressed the influences of regional leaders and other pressures from below. Perhaps it is due in part to observation of another strong-willed ruler in Russia today, Vladimir Putin.[87] But more precisely, it reflects evidence that the archives have yielded. Oleg Khlevniuk, the foremost authority on the Stalin-era archives, has long suggested that Stalin had 'the final word' on all important matters.[88] Especially noteworthy is the contribution by Sheila Fitzpatrick, the pioneering social historian of Stalinism, who has always stressed the importance of being led by her sources. In a recent book on Stalin's inner circle of power, she acknowledges having been 'struck by how great his [Stalin's] authority was with the rest of the team, and how unchallenged [was] his pre-eminence'.[89]

* * *

It is within this most recent historiographic context that the present volume appears. What is distinctive about *Revisioning Stalin and Stalinism* is the broad lens that it applies to the political significance of Stalin and Stalinism as a study in political leadership, in its domestic, international and representational aspects. The essays below are eclectic but thematically coherent, pushing the boundaries of how scholars understand the complexities of the Stalinist system. Stalinism was a phenomenon of global significance. It has left an indelible mark in particular on the former Soviet Union and Eastern Bloc. However, most studies of Stalin and Stalinism are geographically focused on the Soviet Union itself, and particularly Russia. True, this volume is also anchored on Russia and the Soviet Union, but it adopts a broader consideration of Stalinism as a phenomenon of contemporary Central, Eastern European and Eurasian history, with continued relevance for the present day. A major collection of essays edited by Timothy Snyder and Ray Brandon, *Stalin and Europe* (2014), also expanded focus on Stalinism to include Eastern Europe and Germany.[90] The primary focus of that book, however, is the relationship between the Soviet Union and Europe as ideological framework and geographic space. Dubravka Olšáková's edited collection (2016) examines the impact of Stalinism in Eastern Europe specifically.[91] The present volume complements those works, but it is more broadly identified as a study of Stalinism and Stalinist political leadership. It should be noted that scholarly examination of Soviet Central Asia has much to tell us about the formation and functioning of the Soviet state, but unfortunately specific consideration of Central Asia is beyond the remit of this volume.[92]

In the past three decades, scholarship on the Stalin era in several languages has undergone a transformation under the twin influences of the cessation of the Cold War and, along with the collapse of the USSR, the declassification of much Soviet archival holdings. What has emerged is a more 'historical Stalin' relatively free from the simplified, politicized caricatures of an earlier era, and a much more complicated understanding of the nature of Stalinism as a political and social form.[93] The understanding that Stalin and his comrades were communist idealists rather than mere power-crazy tyrants has become largely accepted amongst scholars. Even though a prominent historian of the era such as Stephen Kotkin continues to see evidence of Stalin's 'sociopathic tendencies', he is nonetheless careful to note that Stalin was a 'zealous Marxist' and skilful statesman.[94] Stalin and his era remain controversial and politically divisive topics, even amongst experienced historians sensitive to the complications of history, but there is now a remarkably rich body of scholarship from which to draw.

Revisioning Stalin and Stalinism both contributes to that scholarship and makes sense of it by addressing some of the most salient and controversial aspects of Stalinism, namely Stalin's leadership, the cult of personality and the Cold War. Essays in the first part speak directly to the volume's overarching theme of 'revisioning' Stalin and Stalinism, and the task of grappling with their intricacies and controversies. How have they been constructed and understood by contemporaries and generations of scholars?

In the first chapter, Christopher Read, one of Stalin's most recent biographers, provides his personal reflections on the challenges of writing the life of one of history's most notorious – and, as Read suggests, misunderstood – personalities. The fundamental question that dogged Read's initial foray into the already saturated sub-genre of Stalin biography was why he should add to it at all. The reason, he explains, was the need to retrieve further the truly 'historical Stalin' from the layers of distortion and politically motivated representation that have characterized scholarly and popular understandings of Stalin and his era, and that still persist today. Read provides a very useful summary of 'what we now know' about Stalin the man, including a historiographical analysis of the literature that complements and deepens that offered in this introduction, and he offers fascinating insights into the task of writing about such a controversial figure.

Peter Whitewood sheds light on one of the most contested aspects of Stalinism. How and why it was possible for the Stalinist regime to take the extraordinarily counter-intuitive decision to purge the Red Army in the late 1930s, on the eve of war? Whitewood expertly pieces together key events and decisions to provide a cogent and convincing assessment of how the Red Army purge came to be, and Stalin's role in bringing it about. He suggests that fears about spies and security threats within the Red Army can be traced back to the 1920s, thereby indicating longstanding unease in Bolshevik circles regarding the army's political reliability, and harmonizing with the recent trend in studies of Stalinist purges to locate these within a relatively more *longue durée* approach to understanding the mentalities and institutional practices that shaped them.[95]

In his contribution, Daniel Kowalsky provides perspective on the changing contours of international writing on the Stalin-era Soviet Union through a masterful and detailed account of the historiography of Soviet involvement in the Spanish Civil War. Increased archival access, he writes, has greatly contributed to a growing interest in the subject. As a result, our understanding of the Soviet role in the Spanish Civil War (and specifically Stalin's role) have dramatically changed. Kowalsky provides a convincing case for revisiting the Spanish Civil War to gain better insight not only into the Soviet role in the Spanish Civil War, but into the Soviet 1930s more generally.

Part One concludes with Chris Bellamy's account of Stalin as a war leader, a chapter that encapsulates much of the complexities, contradictions and controversies surrounding Stalin discussed above. Bellamy traces the origins of Stalin's forays into military leadership and his earliest instances of 'brute force' and 'genius'. In the context of revolution and civil war, these traits did not seem out of place. Was Stalin simply a product of his time? Bellamy suggests so. He was not 'brought up to be a war leader' but became one. Focusing on the Great Patriotic War, Bellamy refutes any notion of a nervous breakdown on Stalin's part following Operation Barbarossa – the Nazi invasion of the Soviet Union – and he focuses instead on Stalin's resilience during the war's most difficult moments. Stalin as war leader, it seems, will continue to provoke debate and discussion.

Chapters in Part Two focus on the construction of leader cults, providing comparative analyses that question the origins, purposes and particularities of the Stalin Cult. Do historians need to reassess the 'Stalinist' nature of Stalin's cult of personality? Judith Devlin focuses on the rise of political personality cults in Europe after the First World War in order to underline the *unexceptional* nature of the Stalin cult, but also to identify what was actually unique about it. Based on exhaustive analysis of the literature on the cults of such political luminaries as Tomáš Masaryk, Józef Piłsudski, Paul von Hindenburg, and Mustafa Kemal Atatürk, Devlin identifies the important function that personality cults played in processes of identity-formation and state-building in the aftermath of the political and socio-economic destabilizations wrought by the war. They were designed to communicate powerful narratives about the state, its origins and purposes, and they provided models for the interaction of rulers and ruled through their ritualized and heavily curated mechanisms. Did the Stalin cult have any truly exceptional, defining features? Devlin provides a clear and concise answer: its 'inflation and extravagance' after the mid-1930s, a consequence of the spiral of violence within the regime as well as society more broadly, a dynamic that contributed to political and cultural elites competing to 'signal their loyalty' to the *vozhd*'.

In his chapter on historical legacies and the leader cult in Hungary, Balázs Apor argues that the various legacies of past regimes in Hungary reflect 'the interaction between persistence and change'. Apor offers an overview of the cults of Emperor Franz Joseph, Miklós Horthy, and Mátyás Rákosi, and Viktor Orbán today, with a particular emphasis on common themes and techniques of representation that survived or were revived in cult building practices after major historical ruptures (1918, 1945, 1956, or 1989). A cultic layering of sorts took place, and Apor situates his analysis in the historiography of 'multiple modernities' – an idea espoused by Schmuel Eisenstadt, and debated by historians of the Soviet Union in the 2000s. Apor argues that the leader cults in Hungary reflect aspects of modernity, but also depict 'the irrational adulation of certain individuals'. We may have moved to a post-socialist and social media age, but, as Apor shows, the leader cult is still with us.

Essays in Part Three of the volume engage with controversies related to the origins of the Cold War and Stalinist influence on the Eastern Bloc. The various factors that motivated Soviet foreign policy at the outset of the Cold War are discussed in Caroline Kennedy-Pipe's contribution. In a notably honest reflection on her own earlier work on Stalin's role in the origins of the Cold War, written in the mid-1990s, Kennedy-Pipe provides an overview of the more recent historiography of the Cold War. She holds firm to her earlier view that the Soviet Union was a 'fragile superpower' that sought cooperation with the West rather than confrontation. However, she amends her own earlier arguments through stress on three inter-woven themes that can usefully be extracted from the differing schools of historical thought on the Cold War's origins. First, the novelty of the situation in international relations that political elites faced after 1945. Second, the moralism of American foreign policy in particular, a moralism that reversed the Westphalian consensus that the enemy other was a political 'opponent' to defeat rather than an existential threat to be destroyed. And third, considerations of geopolitical realpolitik and 'spheres of influence'. Stalin, Kennedy-Pipe remarks, could be avowedly 'anti-imperial' yet also demonstrate 'a keen appreciation of colonial politics'.

One of the paradoxes of the Stalinist regime, that most violent of peacetime states, was its support for and indeed instrumental role in the post-war international peace movement. Geoffrey Roberts's chapter examines this phenomenon as a means of exploring the concept of 'working towards the *Vozhd*'', thereby drawing comparisons with Ian Kershaw's well-known suggestion that functionaries in Nazi Germany 'worked towards' Hitler. Roberts argues that a not altogether dissimilar process was underway in the Soviet Union. Examining post-war politics and Soviet interactions with the outside world in the late Stalin period, Roberts suggests greater continuity with the post-Stalin era than hitherto acknowledged. Stalin, Roberts argues, was genuinely interested in seeking international agreement to end the burgeoning Cold War and prevent it from turning hot.

Molly Pucci broadens the Stalinism vista to the Czechoslovakia of the 1950s and 1960s, and to its interrogation techniques in particular. Drawing on a variety of fascinating and extraordinarily insightful sources, Pucci highlights the inner workings of the methods and ideology behind Stalinist interrogations, tracing the footprints of how the Stalinist style of confession was transposed to Czechoslovakia. Pucci's chapter raises questions about accountability and complicity, and it engages with Lynne Viola's recent work on Stalin-era perpetrators in the USSR itself. How and when are cogs in the Stalinist machine, such as interrogators, considered perpetrators? What commonalities of the exported/imported Stalinist system existed across East-Central Europe, and what do these tell us about Stalinism more generally? Pucci reminds us how Stalinist bureaucratic power structures, in this case the relationship between the interrogator and the accused, could become so intimate and personal, so forceful and dependent.

The volume concludes in Part Four with a consideration of the present-day legacies of Stalinism. James Ryan examines the place of Stalin and Stalinism in Russian collective memory, and how Russia has – or has not – come to terms with its Stalinist past. The key question addressed here is whether or not a distinct 'rehabilitation' of Stalin and Stalinism is underway in Putin's Russia, which itself bears some of the hallmarks of an authoritarian regime. Ryan suggests that this is not really the case, emphasizing the ambiguities and inconsistencies in elite and popular attitudes towards Stalin and Stalinism. In so doing, he reflects more broadly on the normative basis and validity of dominant assumptions about the need for public reckoning with, 'working through', and 'overcoming' the past; how that should be conducted; and its consequences for a society's progression.

Part One

The Controversial *Vozhd'*: Stalin as Leader and Statesman

1

The many lives of Joseph Stalin: Writing the biography of a 'monster'

Christopher Read

There are many lives of Joseph Stalin already published. Why add another? I was invited by a publisher to add to the pile.[1] The first steps were harsh. I mentioned to a colleague in the Soviet field that I was writing a Stalin biography to which she snorted in response 'What! Another one!' I asked which of the supposed plethora available she used with her students and she replied 'Deutscher', which cheered me up somewhat since, magnificent though Deutscher's book is, it had been written in the late 1940s. A great deal had been revealed since then which I believed needed to be incorporated. The present chapter is a survey of approaches to Stalin, which occupies the first half, followed by some personal reflections on the particular challenges presented by adding to this formidable collection. If journalism is the first rough draft of history then any account of Stalin needs to start with the first rough draft of his life – the cult of personality.

The first draft: The Stalin cult

From the 1930s and during the Cold War there were two dominant discourses about who Stalin was. In the Communist movement within the USSR and beyond, the so-called cult of personality ruled. Beginning with Lenin the custom emerged for leaders of communist-governed countries to be surrounded by a discourse of their personal greatness. Lenin had been reluctant to allow such a thing to develop in his lifetime and it was Stalin who did as much to promote it, and the associated idea of Leninism, around the time of Lenin's death (21 January 1924).[2] But as Stalin's own leadership emerged from around 1927 onwards, so the cult of his personality grew at the instigation of his entourage. His significant birthdays – fiftieth (1929); sixtieth (1939) and seventieth (1949) – were celebrated with increasing extravagance, even though the date celebrated was a year later than Stalin's actual birthdays. The terms in which Stalin was described became ever more fulsome. 'Great', 'wise', 'leader', of 'the Russian', 'world', working class and 'father of the Russian/Soviet people' who were his 'children' were terms used in an endless variety of combinations. He was praised as the leading worker, thinker and revolutionary strategist of the communist movement.

The phenomenon spread across all cultural media. Journalism, academic writing, novels, poetry, painting, poster art, music, film, theatre, ceramics, textiles and so on bore witness to the cult. During the war, soldiers went on the offensive with the words 'For Stalin' on their lips. One poster said, 'Thank You Stalin for a Happy Childhood'. Others reflected the supposed gratitude of workers and peasants for the benefits Stalin had brought them. In party posters the figure of Stalin moved from being a lesser acolyte of Lenin to becoming his equal and eventually the dominating figure. The trinity portrayals of Marx, Engels and Lenin soon became a quartet. The cult raises many issues beyond our scope here but it may be worth mentioning that Stalin himself did not appear to subscribe to it and on a number of famous occasions distanced himself from it. Of course, that may have been a subtle way of reinforcing it by portraying himself as too modest to go along with it. But maybe not. Perhaps it was simply a useful tool. It is also the case that the term 'Stalinism' was not part of the regular Soviet ideological vocabulary while Stalin was alive. His enemies, notably Trotsky, used the term in a disparaging sense from around 1936/7 but it was only after his death that the fount of ideological orthodoxy, The Institute of Marxism-Leninism, briefly became the Institute of Marxism-Leninism-Stalinism just as Khrushchev was about to denounce the cult of Stalin's personality in his speech at the Twentieth Party Congress in February 1956. For the Stalinists there was no 'Stalinism', it was simply the orthodox version of Leninism.

Where Stalin's many supporters and admirers subscribed to the cult, in the capitalist and imperialist world a counter-cult reigned, which expressed itself in almost directly opposite language. The terms 'dictator', 'monster', 'psychopath', 'power-hungry', 'cruel', 'brutal', calculating', 'treacherous', 'talentless', 'ill-educated', 'deceptive', 'manipulative', 'byzantine', 'unintellectual' flourished in a mirror-image version of the cult. Stalin was the source of all that was rotten in the Soviet Union. Where the cult followers saw his invincibility and infallibility, his Cold War critics saw evil personified. He was, it was frequently stated, an intellectual and social mediocrity, a psychological misfit marked out only by a lust for power, a deep sense of revenge and a barbaric streak of cruelty, often assumed to be the result of childhood beatings at the hands of his alcoholic father. Perhaps the only point the two versions of Stalin had in common was that he was a leading agent of history for good or ill. Ironically, both sides gave him a vast range of effectiveness and impact beyond any other force. Indeed, one of the points Stalin personally criticized about the cult was that it over-attributed influence to him as an individual, an approach he once claimed belonged to romantic, populist, hero-seeking thinking rather than the true Marxist acknowledgement of the role of deep historical forces beyond individual control.[3]

Perhaps ironically, many of the card-carrying anti-communist cold warriors were probably unaware that the source of most of the negative stereotypes of Stalin was none other than the ardent Marxist and revolutionary Leon Trotsky, Lenin's comrade-in-arms of October. Trotsky was, for decades, one of the most influential sources of information about Stalin and, indeed, still is to the present day. He worked alongside him and knew him well, so his testimony is very valuable. The problem, however, was that Trotsky saw Stalin as a bitter political rival, an attitude Stalin eventually reflected back on Trotsky. If one considers other political rivalries, even the less bitter and less deadly disputes of liberal democracies, it is customary to use a politician's views of her or his rivals with extreme caution. Trotsky's views were, however, taken up without criticism since, in the words of Adrian Jones: 'As any celebrity or astrologer knows, the laurels in games of soothsaying and renown do not necessarily go to those who have things right; they go to those who confirm whatever their audiences most want to hear'.[4] Trotsky's hostile story fitted perfectly with the cold warrior outlook. It was also backed up by other sources, much of it accounts by defectors – which can be useful and informative but also need careful analysis and a balanced critique, which they were not given in the atmosphere of intense ideological warfare. Western academic works of the post-war to 1970 period tended to subscribe, with a greater or lesser degree of scholarly sophistication, to the Trotsky-sourced version.[5] Ironically again, the greatest work separate from this tradition was by the Polish socialist and Marxist Isaac Deutscher, himself a great admirer of Trotsky rather than Stalin, so his interpretation also repeated much of the Trotsky-based discourse.[6]

It should be noted that not every account fitted the pattern. Ian Grey wrote a controversial, pioneering and largely ignored biography, arguing that Stalin was a 'strong' ruler in the Russian tradition of Ivan the Terrible, Peter the Great and lesser autocrats. It was, in many respects, a 'defence' of Stalin as, like his predecessors, a ruthless but 'necessary' tough guy who built up Russia's strength and saved it from invasion.[7] Grey was one of the first to criticize the overwhelming reliance on Trotsky in Western interpretations of Stalin. It was arguments of this kind that led Alec Nove, over a decade earlier, to produce his famous essay 'Was Stalin Really Necessary?' as part of an examination of alternatives to Stalin that might have had comparable economic results.[8]

Breaking the Manichaean binary

Quite unexpectedly it was in Moscow that the Manichaean binary of Good Stalin/Evil Stalin began to break down. At the Twentieth Party Congress in February 1956, Khrushchev opened up a critique of aspects of Stalin's rule, in particular that he had illegally turned the repressive apparatus (mainly the NKVD secret police) against the party and substituted the cult of personality (essentially, his personal rule) for the authority of the Communist Party. The critique was quite limited, however, and only in the Gorbachev era did the critique within the USSR extend to all aspects of his rule, while the works of Bukharin, Trotsky and other repressed authors began to circulate openly in the final years of the USSR.

The Twentieth Party Congress caused turmoil in the communist world. Non-ruling parties split and those in power were riven with uncertainty about the direction of policy that had seemed so certain before Khrushchev's speech. Some parties, with the Chinese Communist Party in the forefront, rejected Khrushchev's line and denounced him as a heretic, a 'revisionist' in communist terminology. Scattered Trotskyite sects received a new lease of life as many disillusioned communists in Western Europe and the Americas took Khrushchev's denunciation as a validation of the Trotsky view of Stalin after all. There was a new interest in Trotsky's ideas, especially his critique of the 'bureaucratization' of the revolution, as efforts were made to analyse what had gone wrong in Russia. The tendency was quickly known as The New Left. Lenin remained exempt from blame in the eyes of much of the left and a Good Lenin/Bad Stalin dichotomy became widespread in New Left and other leftist circles. In any case, a new energy was given to the critique of Stalin and the Stalin era.

In the new situation, the lives of Stalin began to multiply and diversify. No serious historians took on a defence of Stalin in the West or in the USSR, but a number of shades of interpretation nonetheless emerged. These were all in the West because, after Khrushchev, Soviet scholars and politicians went into a long period of silence about Stalin and his era, which continued until February 1987 when, at a meeting with Soviet journalists, Gorbachev proclaimed that there should be 'no blank pages' in Soviet history.[9] Again, taking major contours rather than detail, Western scholarship was divided into a totalitarian school and a group of critics who were deemed to be revisionists (in a different sense from the term applied by the Chinese to Khrushchev). Often totalitarians focused on the personality of Stalin. Building on the Trotsky discourse, they constructed a Stalin who was psychopathic from childhood and driven by a desire for power and domination. The driving force of his career was ambition for personal power. The purges were a personal revenge-taking against those who had slighted him. The 'totalitarian' element was related to the degree of control the centre, in this case usually meaning Stalin personally, had over society.

The doyen of the totalitarian school was the English poet and political commentator Robert Conquest, who spent decades picking over the horrors of the 1930s so that, for the right, what he called 'the Great Terror' became the acme and defining moment of Communism, and, even now for some commentators, of any left-wing politician or movement. Here is one extreme but not unique example, from the Conservative-inclined British broadsheet, the *Daily Telegraph*, in 2015:

> Here is a simple corrective for any gullible youngster you know who has fallen for Jeremy Corbyn's socialist siren song. Buy them a copy of *The Great Terror* by Robert Conquest, the wonderful historian of communism who died this week. It won't cure them of the Left-wing virus, but discovering the full horror of life in the Soviet Union in the Thirties and Forties may at least jolt them out of their ideological stupor.[10]

Conquest also popularized the now dogmatic (in many quarters) assertion that the famine of 1932–3 was a deliberate genocide aimed at the people of Ukraine. This is not the place to debate the issue, but it is far from certain that this interpretation is correct. Be that as it may, Conquest did not write a biography of Stalin as such, but in his writings Stalin's power was the source of almost all political events. Those around him were portrayed as talentless minions and flatterers, themselves often portrayed as psychopathic. Major biographies of Stalin that built on this kind of thinking, though in a much more sophisticated fashion , were written by leading historians such as Robert Tucker, Robert McNeal and others.[11] Though he did not much venture into the Stalin era, Richard Pipes was another intellectual force behind this view of Soviet Communism and, by association, attempted to tar much of the Left with the same brush.[12] The school still has life in influential but controversial writers, with Timothy Snyder in the forefront with his book *Bloodlands*.¹³ Not only does he resurrect the Cold War style of attributing almost everything in Soviet politics to 'Stalin', but he also goes even further than his predecessors, arguing Stalin was the stimulus for Hitler. This repeats a view with a long provenance but most closely associated with the German historian Ernst Nolte, who claimed in the 1980s that without communism Germany would have avoided Nazism, a stance his critics said verged on a defence of Nazism.

The totalitarian interpretation came under critical pressure as the Cold War itself was receiving a more penetrating scrutiny. One of the first contested points was the number of victims of famine and repression. Conquest had arrived at a figure of twenty million deaths. Stephen Rosefielde calculated higher numbers than Conquest for the executed and imprisoned. He and Conquest entered into a long-running dispute with the statistically gifted demographic historian Stephen Wheatcroft, who pointed out that, if Rosefielde's figures had been accurate, an impossibly large percentage of the active (18–60) male population would have been either prisoners or guards.¹⁴ No part of society would have been free from a deep impact in number of marriages, natality, economic production, taxation, culture, family experience and so on. In fact, Robert Thurston attacked the 'totality' of totalitarianism by showing that many aspects of life continued relatively normally. People worked, changed jobs, fell in love, married, celebrated special occasions, and visited cinemas without being in a state of constant fear of arrest as Conquest and others had implied. The purges did impact widely. That was not being denied. But there is a difference between, on the one hand, many families having at least one member arrested and almost all social structures (workplaces, education establishments, the security apparatus, the party etc.) losing multiple members, and, on the other, the assertion that the purges may have involved, as victims and guards, up to 40 per cent of their active male personnel.

Reducing the victim count also stimulated questions about the famines and purges. Early interpretations were shaped largely by the astonishing show trials of former leaders like Kamenev and Zinoviev who had been Lenin's closest associates and friends before 1917. They had even continued to be senior figures despite having attempted to sabotage the October Revolution by leaking the decision to start the armed uprising. At a time when historians were not fully aware of the massive extent of arrests and executions, the widespread assumption was that the purge was a personal policy of Stalin to assert his power and destroy his enemies. Unsurprisingly, this was underpinned, as so much else, by Trotsky's view of these macabre events of which he became a belated and distant victim. However, as Conquest broadened the number of victims, this interpretation no longer fitted such apparently large numbers. It was here that the theory of totalitarianism most applied. The aim was now construed to be the total submission of society to the will of the central government, even of Stalin personally. The works of totalitarian school historians were filled with portraits of a lugubrious, vengeful, mentally sick individual exerting power for its own sake. One of the most thorough and deeply-researched biographies of the late totalitarian era, written by Robert Tucker, felt it necessary to toy with concepts of the dubious field of psychohistory to explain its picture of Stalin.¹⁵ In his fiction and factual writings, the dissident writer Alexander Solzhenitsyn described a brooding figure locked away in his

Kremlin and dacha (country house).[16] In such works, Stalin was a malevolent, byzantine imperial figure with inhuman qualities of cruelty and vengefulness.

The revisionist reduction in the number of victims also required a less 'total' interpretation of the purges and of Soviet society more broadly. Some early accounts were over-revisionist in calculating the number of victims. One of the most assiduous revisionists, J. Arch Getty, appeared to underestimate the numbers when he referred, in an early work, to 'tens of thousands' of purge victims. He and others nonetheless pointed to important mechanisms behind the purges like utilization of the situation by unscrupulous individuals for their own benefit. For example, one such practice was denunciation of a neighbour in the hope of acquiring their superior flat. A 'snowball effect' was added to by local chiefs, whom Getty brilliantly referred to as 'Little Stalins' going beyond their orders.[17]

So far, although they exhibited deep levels of scholarly research and analysis, the above-mentioned historians and schools all shared one major difficulty. Many crucial sources were unavailable to anyone and reliance on limited information opened up the path to speculation and ideologically loaded imagination. This handicap began to lessen rapidly after Gorbachev came to power. In February 1987, at a meeting of journalists and writers, Gorbachev called upon the historical profession and society at large to ensure there would be 'no more blank pages' in Soviet and Russian history. Stalin and his era were key subjects of a wave of unprecedented scrutiny and widespread revelation from the archives. Documents from the highest levels of government, which had been virtually unobtainable before 1987, were even published within ten years. In more recent times a vast range of sources have been made available online. Initially, there was a brief period of simply adding new information. For the record, it should be added that in addition to serious scholarship, an avalanche of pseudo-scholarship on Stalin and his era based on mystical 'insights' and far-fetched conspiracy theories, apologia, and even exaggerated hagiography, have come to dominate the shelves of Russian bookstores.

In the perestroika years (1985–91) the lead role in Stalin biography was taken by Dmitrii Volkogonov, whose four-volume biography was crammed with new information, some of it anecdotal from people who knew Stalin well and worked or fought alongside him.[18] This added a much-needed personal dimension to the, in many cases, caricatural figures that had dominated the field, though, as with all anecdotal history, care is needed to evaluate truth and fiction, memory and imagination. There had been a significant predecessor to this in the form of the dissident historian Roy Medvedev. To simplify greatly, he produced a well-informed study built around the Lenin good/Stalin bad thesis in a work published abroad in the early 1970s.[19] Volkogonov's approach was more pragmatic than ideological in simply pioneering new, more evidence-based opinions about Stalin's role in great events. It took a somewhat Khrushchevian line but was quicker to acknowledge Stalin's abilities. Remaining supporters of Stalin, a constantly diminishing but still surprisingly large group, tended to put his wartime leadership in the forefront of their Stalin-worship. Nonetheless it was clear that, despite the continuing paucity of sources, between 1970 and 1991 the binary discourse had broken down and a multiplicity of interpretations was emerging.

Retrieving the historical Stalin

By the end of 1991 the USSR had dissolved itself and a new era began. As far as archive sources in particular were concerned, this inaugurated a few golden years of wide access and ambitious publication plans which lasted until 1996, before being inhibited by the establishment of a new, closely controlled Presidential Archive that gathered in much of the most sensitive political material and set up a strict code of access favouring approved Russian historians over outsiders. But where information had been scarce it was now drowning scholars in its teeming torrents. What was the outcome?

Perhaps the best way to approach what is still, in effect, the current phase is by adapting Lars Lih's stimulating 2003 exhortation to 'retrieve the historical Lenin'. In recent decades, especially since the millennium, the focus has been on retrieving the historical Stalin, meaning establishing representations based less and less on ideologies and biases of communists and cold warriors, and more and more on information and evidence. Writing in the new era was not on a blank sheet. However, a revolution in the availability of reliable source materials meant that the imaginative theories and speculations had to be tested against a much more unforgiving basis of facts. A process of lessening the ideological presuppositions and replacing them with more objective views deeply rooted in sources had begun. But the old habits and assumptions of the past were to prove tenacious, largely because they remained useful to the anti-socialists and the establishment, but also because they had lodged deeply in the collective consciousness. As Marx had written in another context: 'The tradition of all dead generations weighs like a nightmare on the brains of the living.' His less well-known continuation of this sentiment also applies: 'they anxiously conjure up the spirits of the past to their service'.[20]

The sequence identified in this discussion was not neat and clear-cut. Forerunners and outliers were common. Even in the depths of the Cold War polemic there were historians who attempted to put the evidence first, but there were vital pockets of crucial information that were marginalized in the prevailing discourse. Perhaps the most significant relates to diplomatic and international relations personnel from the West who met Stalin on a regular basis especially during and after the war. The picture painted by many such figures, including Churchill, reveals a Stalin much more intelligent and on top of his brief, especially during the war, than the Trotsky-based analyses allowed. He could be sharp and polemical but also robustly hospitable. Many Western visitors, again including Churchill, believed they had built up a rapport with and understanding of Stalin. Even in his 'Iron Curtain' speech at Fulton, Missouri in 1946, Churchill continued to refer to Stalin in something considerably less than hostile terms. Immediately beforehand, Churchill stated 'I have a strong admiration and regard for the valiant Russian people and for my wartime comrade, Marshall Stalin'. He also seemed to imply that agreement was possible, despite communist machinations all over the continent, since he expressed the view that 'the safety of the world . . . requires a new unity in Europe, from which no nation should be permanently outcast'.[21]

However, such views tended to be marginalized in the rush to speculative psychobabble and myth-creating in the public mind. Perhaps the leading historians who put the facts first were the British scholars E.H. Carr and his later collaborator on his monumental, multi-volume *History of the USSR*, R.W. Davies. Carr wrote little about Stalin personally, but he loomed larger in the works of Davies. It was Davies's Centre for Russian and East European Studies at the University of Birmingham, UK that nurtured many revisionist and pragmatic scholars of the Soviet era, including Arfon Rees.[22] Mark Harrison also produced deeply researched, archive and source-based studies of the Soviet economy especially in wartime, though he did later come to reinterpret the era in neoliberal 'totalitarian' terms after the collapse of the USSR.[23]

A number of historians took advantage of the new conditions to write biographies of Stalin, and there was a deep revision of attitudes to the Stalin years. There was also, after around 1985, a tendency to turn attention away from the Revolution towards the Stalin era. Taking full advantage of living in Moscow where the main Russian archives are located, the young Oleg Khlevniuk began an extraordinary trawl through the archives in the years when they were at their most accessible. The result was a revelatory series of studies of Stalin's day-to-day activities and his interactions with his closest colleagues in the critical years from his rise to the top to the beginning of the war. So rich were the sources that one read many of Khlevniuk's early works with the feeling that, like the *Vozhd'* (Leader) himself, one had been claustrophobically confined to Stalin's Kremlin office, following a day-to-day schedule of meetings, writings and a great deal of reading. For the first time it was possible to become immersed in the world Stalin actually inhabited rather than the one imagined by former members of his staff, like Boris Bazhanov. Letters between Stalin and his close associates, notably Molotov, his closest ally and unofficial deputy, not to mention transcribed minutes of meetings of the Politburo (the Soviet cabinet), took us as a matter of routine into areas that had seemed unimaginable to historians accustomed to piecing together scraps of information of unverified accuracy from a variety of sometimes unreliable sources. The raw materials for the emergence of an historical (soundly based in evidence and with the highest degree of objectivity possible) Stalin was now firmly on the agenda. Khlevniuk himself was one of the first to expand the scope of his research into a full-scale biography of Stalin.[24]

It might seem incredible today to a younger generation of historians but one of the most important conclusions to emerge from the torrent of sources was that the leaders were true believers in the ideology. During the Cold War there was often an underlying assumption that ideology was simply a façade, manipulated to conceal crude machinations of power for its own sake. Geoffrey Hosking, in a review of Naumov and Getty's *Road to Terror*,[25] commented that one of the surprising features the documents reveal is that 'even when writing to each other in private, they [the Soviet leaders] used the same language and articulated the same thoughts as they did in their public utterances. Whether it is right to deduce from this that they actually believed most of what they said is less clear'.[26] The new evidence also began to show that, although no philosophical genius, Stalin was not, as Trotsky claimed, a mediocrity but a sharp and incisive reader and analyst of ideas, people and situations. Pathbreaking books like Eric van Ree's *The Political Thought of Stalin* analysed the works in his personal library and the multitude of annotations he made in the margins, which reflected his reactions to the wide range of material of all ideological persuasions that he read.[27] Geoffrey Roberts is also producing a detailed study of Stalin's reading to outline his ideas and show a person who believed in the power of the word and of ideas, which might be considered ironic as he is usually seen as one of the major architects of fake news.[28] A very detailed study by David Brandenberger of the production of the key ideological text book of the period, the so-called *Short Course* history of the party, showed that Stalin's input was substantial and went far beyond the self-serving vanity-based intrusions he was thought to have made in Cold War interpretations of the topic.[29]

As well as Khlevniuk, a number of other major biographies of Stalin have appeared which took advantage of the new information. In the forefront were items by Robert Service and, twenty-five years on from the collapse of the USSR, the mammoth study by Stephen Kotkin. Service tends to stay within traditional parameters of a somewhat psychopathic Stalin who was motivated by power rather than revolutionary zeal.[30] Kotkin's triology of volumes, still incomplete at the time of writing, has taken upon himself the task of gathering together more evidence on Stalin than any previous account. He has gathered an unbelievable amount of material and followed up numerous leads, many of which take him away from his central character.[31] Another account of Stalin's early years, by Simon Sebag Montefiore, followed a similar approach, including many eye-catching but speculative musings on Stalin's romances, suggestions he was a tsarist agent, and his involvement in bank raids to boost party funds. Perhaps tellingly, given the lack of hard information, two of the most valuable scholarly items on Stalin himself have taken the form of articles rather than books, by Ronald Grigor Suny and Alfred Rieber.[32] However, for Kotkin, Stalin's early life was simply an hors d'oeuvre, and the remainder of the volume was a blockbuster covering Stalin's rise to power in microscopic detail, a formula in which the forest risks being concealed by the trees. Kotkin, however, is not one to let that happen, Kotkin's account is generally refreshing in moving away from the Trotsky template to tell us that Stalin was an intellectually oriented person who read widely; that he was a committed revolutionary; and that his drive for power was politically, rather than personally, motivated. He created a bureaucracy of party and state to implement the Bolshevik project. All the more interesting, then, that Kotkin feels the need to go back to rather far-fetched speculation based on flimsy sources, that the Lenin Testament, in which Lenin criticized not only Stalin but also the other contenders to take over after his death, was probably a fake. He then goes on to make it a major component in his structure of interpretation of Stalin in the 1920s.

Kotkin joins a wider effort at tracing a more historical Stalin, and a more realistic, nuanced and evidence-based view of the Stalin era. There are too many fine contributions to mention them all, and only four will be used to provide a taste of these new approaches. In the highly politicized and therefore deeply contentious field of international relations and foreign policy, the work of Geoffrey Roberts, notably *Stalin's Wars 1939–53*, stands out in its desire to bring out the sources and not the myths. Roberts argues convincingly that Stalin was an excellent military leader respected by those around him, who made a positive contribution to the war effort. Perhaps most controversially he points out that, far from being the architect of the Cold War, Stalin foresaw a post-war world of continued cooperation and condominium among the victorious allies. He also appeared to fight for compromise between East and West and for the control of nuclear weapons.[33] Roberts shows us that the old myths are being replaced by more detailed and better-supported analysis rooted in source materials rather than hearsay and subjectivity.

While it focuses on the era rather than the personality of Stalin, the same is true of the pioneering study of mentalities by Jochen Hellbeck who, as the centrepiece of his work, produced an in-depth analysis of diaries of the 1930s, especially that of Stephan Podliubnyi. In the diaries, Podliubnyi presented his enthusiasm for the Soviet cause and immersion in socialist construction.[34] The point of this and a growing number of studies was that the population was not simply a grey mass, trembling with fear at the threat from their rulers, but a varied and self-acting entity which, to a wide but yet unmeasured degree, supported the regime and its goals. This was enough to undermine the most tenacious assumption of the totalitarian view that the regime was an external imposition uniformly hated by and feared by the populace. More recently, the mammoth *House of Government* by Yuri Slezkine shows, in great detail from memoirs and contemporary sources, that the great entrepreneurs who inhabited the giant house opposite the Kremlin and turned the policy initiatives of the leaders into actual goods, services, infrastructure and military strength, were enthusiastic singers in the Soviet choir, not enforced victims without any choices.[35] Once again the stark Cold War and totalitarian binary was shown to be nuanced, and many myths were undermined. We now have a much more subtle and varied palette of colours making up the broad picture. The emerging portrait is far from definitive. There is still a long way to go. Old myths still die hard, especially in the public imagination, but many major strides have been made. This might be thought of as revisionism, and is sometimes referred to as such, but that may not be the best terminology. It is not a process of overturning a deeply researched conventional view, which is what revisionism usually is, but rather the preliminary establishment of an evidence-based view detailing the contours of Russia's experience of so-called Stalinism and the emergence of a better-grounded interpretation of Stalin. This must not be confused with a whitewash or a form of Stalin-denial, although old Cold War hawks were not slow to suggest that. There is no suggestion in the new historiography that the cruelties did not matter. To establish an archivally based figure approaching 700,000 for executions, rather than many millions, is not denial; it is writing history.

Personal reflections on writing a biography of Stalin

Personally, I am not a natural biographer. I enjoy an anecdote as much as anyone else but am only too well aware that close study of trees conceals the forest, and it is the various forests that have disappeared in some recent historical fashions for identity and culture, crucial though those subjects are. Biography risks being a respectable version of the current cult of celebrity with all its limitations. Individuals are what make up human society, of course, but even the strongest individual has limited agency over the flow of history. 'The masses' and other collectivities exert much more, though not necessarily according to the will of the individuals who make them. The waves and ripples on the surface of the sea appear to be random but each one is the outcome of the interaction of specific forces such as current, tide, depth, wind. To study a wave one doesn't just try to capture each one individually; it is necessary to look at the determining factors. In a sense, 'history', like the state of the sea, is the resultant of multiple forces pulling in many directions. That resultant may not necessarily be to the taste of many, or even any, of the components. In other words, structures, though unfashionable, do exert themselves. However, individuals are still important, and biography can bring 'impersonal' technical history down to the more easily perceived level of the individual, that is, the level at which we all live our own lives. It can also bring out the development and outcome of forces greater than the individual under consideration, since identity and personality are themselves constructed by circumstances, though to what degree is hotly debated. The seventeenth-century English poet John Donne rightly said that no person is an island, we all depend on others and they on us.

In addition, the genre of biography has its own intrinsic expectations and limitations. A reader expects certain things – a narrative of the life lived; a response to key questions about why the subject became who they were; an analysis of their personality and of their accomplishments such as they may be. Not infrequently, hagiography or demonology are not far from the surface. The stages of a biography are beyond the writer's control in that background, birth, upbringing, personal development, career progression, life stages (close family; childhood; parenthood; romantic relationships; personal tastes; leisure activities and others) impose themselves where appropriate. In other words, where an historian can often pose her or his own questions to answer, the biographical genre has a foundation of questions the author must address. It is more difficult to hide and it is often more obvious to the reader of a biography that, through lack of material for example, certain aspects or periods of life are being skated over. 'Lost' years cannot be recovered if there is no evidence and such gaps are more obvious than the omission of, say, consideration of certain provinces in a national history. In some ways historical study is a kind of reverse *matrioshka* (Russian doll) where the smaller the doll the larger the content. Arriving at an individual, one faces the inevitable fact that one cannot ever know everything or represent it in a book or whatever medium. One cannot enter the subject's head on any particular occasion but only analyse the evidence as to what might have been going on in it. Molly Bloom's stream-of-consciousness soliloquy in Joyce's *Ulysses* is a solemn warning for us all; sometimes it seems easier to analyse the causes of a war than the thought processes of an individual.[36] However, for present purposes I want to set these considerations to one side and look at particular problems associated with writing about Stalin.

There are several major considerations. First is moral repugnance followed by a deeply interpenetrating set of tangled skeins, comprising polluted sources, extensive politicization, persistent myths, Cold War remnants and a hypocritical gaze. In addition, there is the associated issue of dehumanization and a persistent tendency to resolve the great complexity of Soviet (and post-Soviet history) into cliché-ridden personalization. To arrive at the historical Stalin, it is necessary to slash through this set of complex knots. How can we do that?

First, let us deal with the thorny issue of moral repugnance. To the lay person this consideration is paramount in stories of great horror and tragedy like the Holocaust and Soviet terror. Sometimes, but not often, it intrudes into consideration of the conduct of war – not atrocities, which do attract moral repugnance – but the morality of war leaders and their approach to fighting or the morality of politicians willing to sacrifice troops for their own political gains. There has been some criticism of First World War allied generals on these grounds and also of Stalin for 'wasting' lives in intensive offensives, but on the whole, war is seen to be war. Mass bombing of German and Japanese cities and the use of nuclear weapons are more often defended than criticized. Stalin, by contrast, is often viewed solely through the optic of terror. Moral judgements are complex and often look arbitrary. In particular, casualties of war are usually seen to be inevitable or understandable.

Applying the moral framework of warfare to Stalin's policies would modify the argument. In the eyes of Stalin and the leadership they were at war with capitalism and its agents within the USSR (from Trotskyites to supposed rich peasant kulaks) identified as an enemy. As in many wars, the end result of victory justified the cruellest of tactics in the minds of leaders. Of course, the atrocities and massacres on which 'victory' was often based are not exempt from moral judgement, but such judgements are seldom evenly balanced. The production of *The Black Book of Communism* in the 1990s, which gave a suspiciously rounded 100 million 'victims of communism' globally, attracted wide attention and the figures are still quoted despite even the disengagement of at least one key contributor from the final result. The 'victims of imperialism', which were calculated in a series of responses to *The Black Book*, have attracted little attention and many former imperial countries, with Britain in the forefront, bathe in a glow of imperial nostalgia which, at the non-specialist level, simply ignores or marginalizes the atrocities and other crimes on which empire was founded.

In the face of these difficulties, the response of some is to exclude moral judgement from historical analysis on the grounds that the task of the historian is to discuss what and why events happened. By and large, this is a useful guide in that, given how frequent ghastliness is in history, the historian would barely stop engaging in moral criticism. Indeed, in the nineteenth century this was often how they operated. However, to totally exclude moral judgement on mass terror is inhuman. The historian cannot reasonably stand aside from morality altogether. She can also point out that morality is often used selectively for polemical purposes, and this will be considered later. So, what is the solution? It is useful to avoid over-emotive and unspecific terms – 'monster' and 'psychopath' spring to mind – but make one's moral position clear. However, dwelling on it excessively, even indirectly, suggests polemic is overwhelming scholarly analysis. Then one can proceed to writing historically about the subject, including probably, the moral optic (or lack of it) through which the subject, in this case Stalin, saw their own actions and policies. By and large the Stalinists saw what they were doing as the equivalent of a war, and applied military-style morality to the situation. Enemies had to be uprooted at any price. In the 1970s Molotov still argued the situation was such that they had to ensure no guilty person was left untouched even if innocent people suffered. It was the morality of an aerial mass bombing campaign. It also had overtones, for Stalin personally, of a mafia-style culture of honour, revenge and feud of a kind that persisted in his native Georgia at the end of the nineteenth century and beyond. Of course, it is possible that dwelling on the morality and horror of the worst of the purges has diverted analysis from perhaps their most significant feature, that they were totally unnecessary and destructive and weakened rather than strengthened the country.

Second, there is a deeply intertwined set of problems arising from polluted sources, persistent myths, extensive politicization, and a hypocritical framework of analysis, many of which arise from the Cold War. As we have seen, the result can often be crude over-personalization and demonization (or hagiography, for admirers), which reduces a very complex reality to stale clichés. And yet refusing to go along with those received opinions lays an historian open to the charge of supporting, even whitewashing or denying, an evil reality. Many revisionists like Robert Thurston, Arch Getty and Sheila Fitzpatrick have been accused of coming close to being apologists for Stalin. Pollution of sources is endemic in this subject area. It emanates in part from Cold War ideology and its predecessors and also from the official Soviet propaganda and information control systems. Memoirs and even forged items were produced by Western disinformation.[37] The Soviet side did the same and selectively released source materials supporting its own positions while denying access to key archives and even doctoring some released documents. As a result, in the Cold War era, each side tended to take what fitted its point of view as valid and denounced what did not as fabrication. As we have already seen, scholars who tried to maintain a balanced view were few and far between. Even though many myths have been dispelled from the minds of careful scholars, many still linger in the public imagination, such as exceptionally high numbers of victims and the view that Stalin ran a Byzantine personal empire based on universal fear and threat.[38] Happily, since the 1980s, the floodgates of sound source material have opened and the scholarly world is much better informed. However, the deep-rooted myths have not dispersed. A key reason for adding a new biography to the pile is to try to correct this situation, to reclaim Stalin for history rather than ideological polemic.

Third, one of the most enduring discourses of the Cold War era lies in the simplistic personalization of Russian politics, which attributes – in the case we are looking at – all decisions and developments to 'Stalin' without reference to others or to other shaping historical forces. While such simplifications are not unique to analysts of Russia, they seem to hold more weight, since the general ignorance of Russia and its past in the outside world is very widespread. At one time, something similar was true of 'Hitler', but even then the roles of others – Himmler, Goebbels, Goering, Heydrich, Hess – were well known. Scholars even came to the view that Hitler was a lazy dictator who left a great deal to his subordinates. However, presumably to plaster over the ignorance gap, much of Russian history is attributed to Stalin, Lenin, Gorbachev and, today, Putin, with little reference to those around them or to wider circumstances. It is not possible for one individual to exert the power and responsibility attributed to them in this kind of discourse. Happily, this syndrome has already been subject to powerful assault. More attention has been paid to Stalin's senior associates – Beria, Molotov, Zhukov and others – referred to by Sheila Fitzpatrick as Stalin's team.[39] This is a refreshing change from the 'gang' or 'cronies' so frequently used. For Stalin and for the Soviet project we are much more aware that, even though Stalin had immense influence, many others contributed to the continuum of history.

With these considerations in mind, let us move to a conclusion summarizing how the historical Stalin differs from his highly ideologized predecessors. Perhaps the most important feature that needs to be recognized concerns Stalin's fundamental motivation, the underlying drive behind what he did. In his own eyes and the eyes of all those around him, he was first and foremost a dedicated revolutionary who associated himself with Marxism and with Lenin from very early in his career.[40] The controversies and criminal errors in his career, including the purges and man-made if unintentional famines, and the achievements, such as the survival of the revolution and the modernization of Russia, including the massive expansion of education, were all driven by revolutionary zeal, by a detestation of capitalism, and by hope for the betterment of the world for the working people of the world. The fact that he often used crude, inefficient and counter-productive methods to achieve these aims does not alter this fundamental fact. Nor is it an excuse for the ruthless excesses and dictatorial nature of his rule. It tells us what he thought he was doing – promoting world revolution – not that he chose the best way to achieve it.

Many observers then and now would baulk at the idea of his concern for world revolution but it is clear that, for Stalin and many Stalinists, 'socialism in one country', a concept he derived from Lenin in 1918 and 1919, was a step towards world revolution, the foundation of world revolution.[41] The strategy that it was necessary to defend the Soviet Union first to preserve the platform from which the anti-imperialist struggle could be waged might be the subject of debate but the point is that, for Stalin, world revolution began with the defence of a Soviet Union encircled by hostile capitalist powers. Such was the strategy Lenin put forward to justify the Treaty of Brest-Litovsk (March 1918) when he turned away from an immediate gamble on revolutionary war which the left of the party wanted to undertake in favour of defending the revolution at all costs. Even retreat 'as far as the Urals' was better than risking all in a romantic gesture of spreading the revolution.[42] Whatever Stalin did, right or wrong, he did because he believed it would promote the revolution. Even the notorious August 1939 agreement with Germany – the 'Nazi-Soviet Pact' in Cold War terminology – was consistent with this. It may be that in his later years, especially around and beyond 1950, his judgement was more clouded as old age took its toll and his behaviour became more arbitrary than ever, but overall this assumption of revolutionary conviction holds good.

The second part of the foundation for constructing a view of the historical Stalin is to accept that his personality falls within the parameters of what is thought of as normal. There are no special morbidities discernible in the more reliable parts of the historical record. Circular tales of violent childhood abuse by his father, creating a monster whom we know was a monster because of violent childhood abuse by his father, have to be discarded. At least into the 1930s and probably beyond, we know that Stalin could exude charm, friendliness and hospitality that not only engaged comrades like Bukharin in the 1920s, but were also in evidence to Winston Churchill and Harry Hopkins who met him in the war years and beyond. He maintained close relationships with his succession of wives including Nadezhda whose suicide was given wild interpretations in the Cold War years but appears to have succumbed to tragic mental instability rather than political protest against her husband. He was not a philanderer. His main friendships were with men of his political circle cut from the same tough political cloth. He was not cruel in the conventional sense. Episodes such as his refusal to make a special allowance for his son to get him out of a German camp can be seen as either cruel or heroic. For Stalin it was simply a decision in conformity with

Bolshevik values. Apocryphal or not, the statement that all Soviet prisoners were his sons fitted the bill. Personal advantage was an abuse of power, as he insisted in discussion with his daughter Svetlana. He is not known to have personally participated in cruel acts though he was a frequent signatory of lengthy lists of people for execution. Impenetrably, he pursued actions against people he had liked, trusted and worked alongside, such as Bukharin, whom he pursued to death via show trial. Lesser cases also showed the dark side of his mind, for example, testing Molotov by arresting his wife in December 1949 because of her links with Israel and taunting him not simply to abstain but to vote in favour of the move. The source of these darker episodes, like that of his son, is more likely to reside in Bolshevik values than in any personality disorder (assuming one can set aside the Cold War view that the Bolshevik mindset is not in itself a mental disorder) and is seen as an extreme form of justifying means by ends, not unlike a military planner or official who gives an order for a mass bombing of Dresden or a nuclear attack such as Hiroshima or Nagasaki.

Moving on from the view that Stalin was not a twisted psychopath as a result of early malign influences does not mean his early years were not influential. They were, but in other ways. As argued by Alfred Rieber and Ronald Suny,[43] his background in Georgia and elsewhere in the Caucasus exerted a strong shaping element. The culture of honour and revenge and of strong, potentially overwhelming hospitality seem to have lasted throughout Stalin's life. His revolutionary codename – Koba – was that of a character in a famous North Georgian novel by Aleksandr Kazbegi who fights for Georgian independence, justice, honour and the defence of women from predatory males, and it easy to see how Koba's relentless and self-sacrificing pursuit of freedom and justice appealed to the young Stalin and remained with him, in part at least, for the rest of his life. Also, obsessing with Stalin's 'banditry' and marginal association with party expropriations, including the massive Tiflis bank robbery of 1907, which netted some $4 million, has led most biographers to miss the obvious – that Stalin was more a kind of Che Guevara, fighting and risking his life to organize early trade unions in the wild west atmosphere of Tiflis and, especially, the British-owned oilfields of Baku. This experience of raw, imperialist exploitation of disposable and ill-paid workers by the rich oil companies stayed with him. It may well have been a source of his deep scepticism at the hypocrisy of the imperial liberal middle-class of London, Paris and New York whose wealth and position were constructed on the basis of thuggish power and violence against which the young Stalin led the early, heroic stages of resistance. He was jailed many times for his actions and engaged in some memorable escapes.

Ironically, the frequency of the escapes have fuelled the other favourite Cold War legend about these years that he was, in fact, a police spy. Suffice it to say no real evidence has ever been presented and peripheral evidence, like his escapes, can be better explained by other factors – notably that escaping tsarist police was not that difficult for politicals who enjoyed privileged forms of detention. When the authorities got serious and confined him to the deepest wilds of Siberia, Stalin did not escape. It may be, though we have frustratingly little firm evidence, that these may have been Stalin's finest years when he personally engaged in life-threatening combat with employers who hired gunmen to attack labour organizers. His positions of moderation, calling for peaceful and organized collective bargaining, also seem untypical but it is the old stereotypes we need to discard to accommodate such evidence, not the other way round. Stalin was practically the only one of the leaders of October who had extensive experience of this kind of class struggle. Most of the rest, including his archcritic Trotsky, contented themselves largely with speeches and theories. Stalin was also capable of those and spent much time in Baku, Batumi and elsewhere following the Leninist principle of setting up and writing for a party newspaper. These obscure years are often forgotten and only when he is absorbed into the central party apparatus do his biographers of the pre-1991 generations really begin to pay attention to him, apart from the bandit and police spy obsessions.

Connected with 'normalization' of Stalin's personality, it is also necessary to remove Trotsky's depiction of Stalin as a mediocrity. Given how much counter evidence there is to this, not least encounters with Western politicians and military people of the highest level during the war who admired Stalin's grasp of events, it is surprising how long this myth has survived and how widespread it still is. According to Trotsky, Stalin was the embodiment of the values of the middle-level bureaucrats whom he accused of taking over the party in the 1920s as part of the process of bureaucratization. Stalin came to power, Trotsky argues, because the despised administrators supported him because he was cast in their image. It is not our aim here to say why Trotsky came to this conclusion, presumably through deep personal antagonism and a refusal, shared by Lenin, to recognize that the undemocratic, elitist nature of the revolution itself was largely responsible for its bureaucratization. After all, if the point is to take control of a country and guide it to a utopian future, someone has to do the practical heavy lifting. In the case of both Lenin and Trotsky, the formidable analytical powers of both failed to penetrate when confronted by the problem of the bureaucratization of their revolution. Lenin blamed the bureaucrats themselves and the lack of true revolutionary consciousness, Trotsky blamed Stalin. Of course, to say Stalin was not a mediocrity is not to support the flattery of some of his followers who proclaimed him to be a genius. He was neither. He was a man of strong personality with a keen but not overwhelming intellect. As we have seen he read widely, deeply and perceptively. He was intelligent and had a capacity for analysing situations. He had been, to some degree, a man of action in his youth, while in middle age he was office-bound but remained very well-informed and on top of his brief. The supposed wobble in the face of the outbreak of war, when he is said to have retreated to his dacha and gone into denial, even partial breakdown, in the face of the situation, has been revised to show that he was, in fact, highly active in his days of withdrawal. Indeed, he took the first steps to adapt the government apparatus to the task of total war.[44]

The last points that I want to mention that need revising relate to his power. Stalin is often thought of in non-specialist discourse as a kind of 'off with their heads' ruler, a type of absolute monarch whose will was carried out without question. Certainly, Stalin was very powerful, but he was never all-powerful. He relied on and consulted with others over many of the crucial decisions. In the end, he would be the one that chose the path, but not in the arbitrary way of personal impulsiveness. He often got the decisions wrong. Hindsight shows how badly he judged Hitler's intentions in 1941 and prevaricated over the prospect of a pre-emptive strike against the German forces as they were massing. In fact, the real critique of Stalin is that so many policies were either misguided and damaging, like the terror and the purges, or conducted in such a way that they were far from reaching the success they might have had by more moderate methods. Industrialization and collectivization are the most important issues that come to mind here, though we should also bear in mind that he did not have a well-oiled machine to carry his policies out. The Soviet state was still a ramshackle institution in the 1930s with a multitude of inefficiencies. In many ways, Stalinism is the methods almost as much as the policies, though it also has to be admitted that he did turn the Soviet Union round from being a backward agrarian power to become an industrial and urban society. It is also likely that Stalin may have underestimated his own power. In the last years of his life he reorganized the highest levels of government but did so in a series of cautious and guarded steps rather than in a great dictatorial sweep of his hand.[45] In fact, again contrary to received opinion, caution was one of his enduring characteristics, though it did not always prevail.

There are many other aspects of Stalin's rule that need to be revised, although, as we have seen, items like the film *The Death of Stalin* show how ingrained the myths are. Key policies, notably his approach to the post-war world, show, again, a cautious approach geared to avoiding ultimate confrontation. He set great store by the United Nations and was deeply involved with designing its carefully balanced structure – with a Security Council having a mixture of permanent and transient members and a General Assembly open to all countries accepting and obeying the UN charter– since he seems to have seen it as an embryonic world government in which the wartime alliance would have turned into a joint condominium over the globe. Only when the West started to consolidate its zones and exclude the USSR from influence, notably by setting unacceptable conditions for it to join the Marshall Plan for European reconstruction, did Stalin ramp up the same approach to consolidate exclusive Soviet control in the East.[46] However, such issues are too complex to deal with in the confines of the present item. One writes a biography in order to do that! The possibility of giving more attention to such burgeoning discussions was the main reason for adding another volume to the many lives of Stalin. That is why it was written.

2

Stalin's purge of the Red Army and misperception of security threats

Peter Whitewood

In June 1937 Iosif Stalin sanctioned an extensive purge of the Red Army that was not brought to a halt until November 1938. In total, approximately 35,000 army leaders were discharged from the ranks and tens of thousands of officers were arrested. Several thousand people were executed.[1] Even though over 11,000 military personnel were soon returned to the ranks, this was a shocking attack on the institution vital for Soviet defence. Indeed, the announcement of the most high-profile executions – that of Marshal of the Soviet Union, Mikhail Tukhachevskii, and seven other senior officers from the high command – sparked international scandal. Tukhachevskii and his co-defendants, Iona Iakir, Ieronim Uborevich, Boris Fel'dman, Robert Eideman, Avgust Kork, Vitalii Primakov and Vitovt Putna, were executed immediately after a closed military trial on 11 June that found them guilty of organizing a 'military-fascist plot' inside the army. The group was said to have coordinated sabotage and espionage to ensure Soviet defeat in wartime. Another central member of the supposed conspiracy, Ian Gamarnik, first deputy People's Commissar for Defense, committed suicide before the sentences were announced, after it became clear that he too would be arrested. This group of officers was publicly presented as the nexus of a wider conspiracy in the Red Army that the military purge was intended to root out.

In reality, there was no foundation to these charges. There was no 'military-fascist plot' to weaken the Soviet state in a future war. Evidence supporting these accusations was secured by the NKVD using violence and torture. Moreover, the accompanying wave of denunciations that exploded from summer 1937 – netting countless additional victims – was the result of officers and soldiers denouncing one another under intense pressure. Some Red Army personnel undoubtedly denounced their comrades to save their own skins. Others were almost certainly taken in by press reports that their superiors were dangerous subversives and action had to be taken. The roles of naked careerism or personal animosity cannot be ruled out either. In any case, the damage caused to the Red Army by the military purge would not have been as extensive without this combination of pressure from above (from the NKVD) and from below (from denunciations).[2]

What impact the military purge had on the Red Army's disastrous performance in 1941 continues to generate debate, but nevertheless it remains remarkable that Stalin would attack his army in 1937 when it was increasingly clear that major war was on the horizon. Numerous explanations have been put forward to explain why Stalin undermined his military strength so precipitously. Most common is the view that Stalin launched a premeditated attack on the army simply to further increase his power. The argument goes that the military was the one institution that could have potentially curbed Stalin's insatiable lust for power and thus needed to be neutralized.[3] Central to this explanation is the NKVD's fabrication of a dossier of evidence (on Stalin's orders) showing a military conspiracy implicating the Tukhachevskii group. Yet the dossier story is based upon unreliable memoir accounts. Stalin also never once referred to such a dossier in any key meeting when the 'military-fascist plot' was discussed at length. It seems strange that he would go to such lengths of having evidence fabricated with the express aim of giving credibility to planned executions in the army and then not bring this up.[4]

On the other end of the scale, some have claimed that a real plot existed inside the high command, but these arguments are difficult to take seriously and lack evidence.[5] More broadly, in general works on the Great Terror, the military purge is often presented as another manifestation of the wider tide of political violence that swept over the Soviet state during 1937–8. The Red Army, in this sense, was collateral damage; another institution into which a wave of terror spread.[6]

None of these explanations, however, provides a convincing explanation for Stalin's attack on the army. None sufficiently considers deeper motivations behind the military purge specific to the Red Army and its longer-term roots. Indeed, historians have typically explained the military purge and wider Great Terror by underlining the importance of proximate and contingent events. These include the assassination of Sergei Kirov in December 1934, which stunned the leadership and set in motion a chain of arrests of former oppositionists.[7] Dramatic events abroad, such as civil war in Spain, have also been pointed to as fomenting concerns in Stalin's mind about a 'fifth column' in the Soviet Union.[8] Not discounting the importance of such central events of the 1930s to the Great Terror and military purge, this chapter points to other – and more longstanding – security anxieties that pre-date the 1930s and are as critical to explaining why Stalin attacked his army in 1937.

Moreover, the often-neglected point about the military purge is that it put Stalin's power and position at risk. There was a real prospect of him going to war with much-weakened defences. Any explanation of the military purge has to account for that risk.

This chapter will show that the key to understanding the purge of the Red Army is to see this as the culmination of longstanding security anxieties that surrounded the Soviet military from its very formation and that suddenly came to a head during the Great Terror. Equally important are Bolshevik perceptions of a threatening international environment throughout the 1920s and 1930s, which only exacerbated concerns about the reliability of their army. Security threats identified by the early Soviet and then Stalinist regimes could easily be exaggerated or entirely misperceived. As we will see, this frequent pattern of misperception had devastating consequences for the army. In the final analysis, the chapter will show that Stalin attacked the Red Army because he and those around him misperceived an extensive spy infiltration of the military in the summer of 1937 – what was taken to be a fifth column – in the context of looming war.

Radical action was the only possible option. Stalin did not purge the army to further consolidate his personal power; this was a reactive decision to a misperceived threat, taken at the last moment. In this sense, this chapter will underline that even though Stalin had consolidated enormous levels of power by the 1930s, the events of the military purge demonstrated the weakness of his position.

Determining how a perceived military conspiracy emerged during the Great Terror and was taken seriously by the leadership raises questions about the limitations of source material. Specifically, political police interrogation transcripts and reports on confessions are some of the sources used in this chapter to show how the Red Army was identified as compromised by 'enemies'. There is a risk in assuming that such transcripts are nothing but fabrications of the NKVD and useful for little more than seeing the ideas imposed on victims by interrogators.

However, interrogation transcripts can help reveal more than just the agenda of the NKVD. When examined in conjunction with other materials, this can shed light on the dynamics inherent in the evolution of conspiracy theories. Notably, the same types of conspiracy theories are found in the public speeches and private correspondence of Stalin's inner circle. There was almost no difference in the manner in which Stalin and his associates communicated in public and in private. In his personal correspondence Stalin regularly detailed conspiracies where they did not exist.[9] In this way, as much as the leadership was influenced by the material results and confessions and conspiracies emerging from political police investigations, the conduct of the latter was heavily shaped from above. Recent research has laid bare the complexity of motivations and behaviours among local NKVD officers; their levels of belief in the various plots and conspiracies underpinning the Great Terror; and the importance of overwhelming pressure placed upon them to achieve results.[10] The evolving conspiracy theories underpinning the Great Terror were a product of mutually reinforcing interactions between a leadership and political police both predisposed towards seeing 'enemies' in their midst. Moreover, the charges against the senior officers in the supposed 'military-fascist plot' were not merely inventions of the NKVD. The charges were grossly exaggerated, but often based on real events then framed in conspiratorial terms. Even though there was no conspiracy in the Red Army, by 1937 the NKVD had a great amount of material to work with when putting together the 'military-fascist plot'.

Civil war and military vulnerabilities

To understand how Stalin could so badly misjudge the threats facing the Red Army in 1937, we need to begin with the circumstances of its formation in 1918. After the revolution, the Bolsheviks, critically, never wanted a standing army, which they saw as a tool of oppressive capitalist powers. A people's militia was seen as a more suitable means of defence for a socialist state. At the same time, however, the Bolsheviks were not blind to the need to protect the revolution and moves were made towards creating a new 'socialist' army in early 1918.[11] These efforts were set on a more conventional course as the realities of war sunk in. Unsuccessful peace negotiations with the German government in early 1918, the renewed advance of its armed forces and the signing away of vast expanses of territory in the Treaty of Brest-Litovsk, were difficult lessons for Vladimir Lenin. As well as underlining that salvation would not arrive in world revolution, humiliation at Brest-Litovsk provided further evidence that the nascent socialist state would not survive without a proper means of defence. As the former Imperial Army had been dismantled before the revolution, the Bolsheviks' new socialist army – the Workers' and Peasants' Red Army – would require serious reform.

The evolution of the Red Army into the mould of traditional standing army was highly controversial in party circles on ideological grounds. A deep and ongoing problem was the composition of the officer corps. The Bolsheviks were revolutionary – not militarily – minded. Lacking expertise in warfare they were forced to turn to former imperial officers – so called 'military specialists' – to staff leading positions in the army (some of whom had to be coerced into serving). As a result, the majority of Red Army officers in the civil war had previous service in the former Imperial Army. This was still approximately 30 per cent by the war's end.[12] This large number of military specialists created an immediate security problem because of questions about loyalty. Looking back on the civil war in 1923, Trotsky recalled:

> Of the old officer corps there remained with us either the more idealistic men, who understood or at least sensed the meaning of the new epoch (there were, of course, a very small minority), or the pen-pushers, inert, without initiative, men who lacked the energy to go over to the Whites: finally, there were not a few active counter-revolutionaries, whom events had caught unawares.[13]

There were clear problems with employing military specialists who might switch sides or feed intelligence to the Whites. Trotsky, as a result, sanctioned punishments for the families of military specialists who betrayed the Bolsheviks.[14] Each military specialist was flanked by a Bolshevik political commissar, establishing a system of dual command. However, these safeguards failed to mollify objections from within the party, which came to a head at the Eighth Party Congress in March 1919. Here Lenin was forced to defend the use of military specialists from the so-called Military Opposition, a group of party members concerned that, while necessary for the war, the former officers were ideologically closer to the Whites than Bolsheviks.[15] The Military Opposition's position gained support at the Congress and Trotsky was forced to give further assurances that more controls would be introduced over military specialists and that political commissars would receive expanded powers. Even so, the principle of employing military specialists was not altered, doing little to ease distrust of the bourgeois outsiders. For Lenin, however, there was no other choice. As he remarked a few months later, 'If we do not take them into service and they were not forced to serve us, we would not be able to create an army.'[16]

The civil war did see significant mutinies by military specialists, such as by commander of the eastern front, Mikhail Murav'ev. However, in general terms there is evidence that former officers were in fact less likely to desert than communist red commanders.[17] Class prejudice was a central driver of suspicion towards military specialists. In April 1919 Commander-in-Chief of the Red Army, Ioakhim Vatsetis, complained to Lenin about hostility towards the General Staff: 'Former officers who are serving on our General Staff do not deserve this unjust attitude [...] Every commissar has a secret desire to catch our staff officers out in some counterrevolutionary attitude or treachery.'[18] A few months later, Vatsetis was falsely accused of working for the Whites.[19]

While Lenin and Trotsky were cautiously supportive of military specialists, other Bolsheviks like Stalin held similar attitudes to the political commissars that Vatsetsis claimed were harassing the General Staff. During the so-called Tsaritsyn Affair of 1918, Stalin (who had been tasked to improve grain shipments from the North Caucasus to Moscow) rounded on the commanding military specialist Pavel Sytin. Partly a challenge to Trotsky's central military leadership, Stalin (supported by his two allies Kliment Voroshilov and Sergei Minin) dismissed Sytin and requested that Voroshilov be put in charge. Over the course of summer and autumn, Stalin made clear his distrust of military specialists, referring to their incompetence and unsuitability for civil war combat.[20] Stalin called for limits on Trotsky's 'erratic commands', claiming that these risked 'giv[ing] the whole front into the hands of those deserving full distrust, the so-called military specialists from the bourgeoisie'.[21] In a letter to Lenin in October, Stalin and Voroshilov again criticized Sytin as 'a man who not only is unneeded at the front, but who is not worthy of trust and is therefore damaging. We of course cannot approve of the front going to ruin as a result of an untrustworthy general'.[22]

Outside tussles in the party leadership over military specialists, the Bolshevik political police, the Cheka, made a priority of keeping an eye on former officers now occupying commanding positions. The struggle against counterrevolutionaries in the military was one of the Cheka's main priorities.[23] Cheka leaders, Feliks Dzerzhinskii and Genrikh Iagoda, complained about White counterrevolutionaries using positions inside the Red Army to damage the war effort.[24] Cheka operatives launched investigations into treacherous military specialists, uncovering strings of supposed plots.[25] The Cheka's involvement with the army only grew throughout the civil war. The number of Special Departments (*Osobye otdely* [OO]) tasked to monitor the Red Army increased, as did their budgets.[26] And it was not only infiltration of the army by White agents and treacherous military specialists that alarmed the Cheka, but also its subversion by foreign spies – a more pressing issue in the later 1920s and 1930s.[27] From the Cheka's point of view, the Red Army faced a risk of infiltration during the civil war irrespective of military specialists. Their mass employment only made matters worse.

The 1920s: Dangers in peacetime

Bolshevik victory in the civil war should have eased security anxieties surrounding the Red Army. The White armies were defeated and the immediate military threat to the Soviet state much reduced. Yet serious concerns about the army continued unabated. This was for several reasons. Most importantly, world revolution had not erupted as anticipated by the Bolsheviks in 1917. Because of this, they came to view their socialist state as surrounded by capitalist powers committed to its destruction. The unexpected economic stabilization of the West following the First World War and what the Bolsheviks took to be the fundamental incompatibility between capitalism and communism, for them, meant that a final war was inevitable. The Bolsheviks also never forgave the assistance given to the Whites by Western powers in the civil war and were alert to the continued hosting of their forces abroad and the financial support provided to them. All of this helped sustain a sense of siege mentality and encouraged the misperception of existential threats to the Soviet Union in the inter-war period.[28] In this context, it is easy to understand why the Bolsheviks continued to fear that their central means of defence – the Red Army – would be subverted by hostile forces.

Increasingly stringent controls were placed on the Red Army in the years after the civil war to protect it from the threat of subversion. In 1922, Trotsky prohibited soldiers from having contact with foreigners without first notifying a political commissar.[29] In 1926, under Voroshilov's military leadership, the families of soldiers were banned from having any contact with foreigners.[30] Supposed spies were discovered in the Red Army throughout the 1920s.[31] For the most part these arrests were at relatively low level, yet the danger could easily ratchet up. In 1926 when Jozef Piłsudski returned to power in Poland, the OGPU reported an increase in Polish espionage and attempts to recruit within the Red Army.[32]

Security concerns common to the civil war continued in this climate of insecurity, especially the risk that unreliable military specialists might be recruited by foreign powers to subvert the army from within.[33] Indeed, despite efforts to replace military specialists with red commanders, they still occupied a sizeable number of commanding positions in the 1920s because of a skills shortage in the army.[34] The perception of the class enemy working within remained difficult to shift, especially as the Whites in exile held on to hopes of one day reversing 1917. The GPU/OGPU reported on various White schemes to infiltrate the Red Army and other Soviet institutions during this time.[35] Red Army personnel were likewise concerned about military specialists and possible connections to the exiled White movement. For instance, fourteen officers raised their fears in a letter to the Central Committee in February 1924 (which Stalin had distributed more widely).[36] Moreover, amnesties of White officers, running through 1920–3, while seen as a way of depriving the Whites of soldiers, in turn created further concerns for the GPU that subversives would infiltrate the Red Army under the guise of returning soldiers. A GPU circular from March 1923 noted that the activity of exiled White general Wrangel's intelligence and counterintelligence organs had increased on a large scale. A number of new intelligence institutions had opened, the main aim of which was the collection of information about the Red army's condition and armament, as well as breaking down the morale of the latter through planting agents in commanding positions.[37]

The persistent climate of distrust towards military specialists in the 1920s had important consequences for the later 'discovery' of the 'military-fascist plot' in 1937. It reinforced a perception of the 'enemy within', which was seriously escalated during the Great Terror. However, it is important to stress that certain military specialists attracted more attention than others during these years. Tukhachevskii, the future leader of the supposed military-fascist plot, was the subject of feverish speculation in White émigré circles in the 1920s. Many Whites harboured hope that the young military specialist might become a 'Red Bonaparte' and unseat the Bolsheviks.[38] Evidently these rumours did nothing to halt Tukhachevskii's rapid rise in the Red Army. He reached the position of deputy chief of staff by November 1925. At this point, rumours of Tukhachevskii's disloyalty were simply seen as rumours (however much the Whites were taken in).

Another reason for the dismissal of rumours about Tukhachevskii was that many of these first originated with the GPU/OGPU and were used to entrap White counterrevolutionaries. For instance, in the long-running Trust Operation, coordinated by Soviet counterintelligence in the 1920s to gather information on White organizations in exile, Tukhachevskii's name (along with other senior officers) was circled among White emigrés as a potential candidate for a military dictator. By trading on the speculation surrounding Tukhachevskii – and through creating a fictional counterrevolutionary organization called the Monarchist Union of Central Russia – Soviet counterintelligence hit upon an effective way to make contact with White organizations to gather important intelligence. The Trust Operation was one of the most striking successes of Soviet counterintelligence before its final unmasking in 1927.[39]

Despite the obvious intrigue of the Trust Operation, it is important to stress that rumours about disloyalty in the high command were never entirely forgotten. Intelligence reports were produced about White hopes of a military coup against the Bolsheviks and the faith they placed in Tukhachevskii.[40] Paperwork was filed in the usual way. Even if these reports were not taken seriously in the 1920s, there were two major consequences. First, they gave no respite to ongoing speculation about loyalties at the top of the army. Second, when the Great Terror erupted years later, long-filed reports of disloyalty in Tukhachevskii's circle added fuel to the fire at a time when the most tenuous of accusations achieved common currency.

A final threat identified to the Red Army in the 1920s was domestic: the minority of officers and soldiers who supported Trotsky's political opposition to the party majority. As Trotsky was head of the Red Army until he was pressured to resign in January 1925, it is unsurprising that he attracted a number of military supporters who also shared his objections to the restrictions on democratic practices and the so-called bureaucratization of party life overseen by the party majority. This small group of Trotskyist officers was by no means a threat to the stability of the army and was presented as a lower-order danger. Reports from the Political Administration of the Red Army (PUR), for instance, frequently described Trotsky military supporters as representing only a small minority and estimated their impact on the ranks as limited.[41]

PUR was of course accountable for political reliability in the Red Army and had a vested interest in presenting a harmonious picture. There were some who disagreed with their assessment. The OGPU was more concerned about the dangers posed by Trotskyist officers in the second half of the 1920s. In the peak year of the United Opposition's activity, for instance, in November 1927, head of the OGPU, Viacheslav Menzhinskii, sent alarmist messages to Stalin warning about a potential Trotskyist coup d'état with military involvement. Menzhinskii claimed that officers were working with Trotsky to overthrow the party majority. Indeed, the OGPU had arrested a group of men operating an illegal Trotskyist printing press only two months before, one of whom, when interrogated, claimed that he was part of a military group planning a coup inspired by Piłsudski.[42] In his November letters to Stalin, Menzhinskii ramped up the drama, claiming that the opposition's 'secret combat organization' was carrying out propaganda in the Red Army, which had been 'partly contaminated and […] the commanders now are often not reliable in the full sense of the word'. Menzhinskii was clearly pushing for a crackdown on the army in his appeals to the General Secretary.[43] But Stalin rejected the OGPU view and favoured restraint. In his reply to Menzhinskii, Stalin argued that the countermeasures already taken had made it difficult for the opposition to make inroads into the army.[44] There would be no military crackdown.

Menzhinskii may have failed to convince Stalin of the threat in 1927, but the OGPU continued to pay close attention to Trotsky's sympathizers in the army. Even after Trotskyists were brought back into the party fold, after recanting their 'political errors' at the end of the 1920s, the OGPU maintained observation nonetheless. A surveillance file, for instance, was opened on future 'member' of the military-fascist plot Vitalii Primakov in the early 1930s, which expressed doubts about the sincerity of his break with Trotsky.[45] The OGPU continued to make arrests in the army on charges of Trotskyism throughout the early 1930s as it did across other Soviet institutions.[46] Trotskyism in the Red Army, in this sense, remained a live issue for the political police, even if former Trotskyist officers were now making their way back into central party and military positions, some with glowing endorsements from Voroshilov and Stalin.[47] It is highly likely that some military Trotskyists simply went along with the requirement to recant past political affiliations without fundamentally changing their views. There is evidence that former Trotskyist officers continued to meet in secret in the years before the terror.[48] The OGPU did not entirely imagine underground Trotskyist activity in the early 1930s.[49] However, it was only after the murder of Sergei Kirov in 1934 that Trotskyism in the Red Army became an increasingly pressing issue.

The Great Terror and military purge

For many in the party and political police, the Red Army had proved itself vulnerable to internal subversion on several fronts in the years after the civil war. 'Unreliable' military specialists continued to staff senior positions; there was a risk of infiltration by foreign agents; a core of hostile Trotskyist officers had raised fears in some quarters about a military coup. In reality, while these security threats existed on a certain level, they were magnified by the isolated position of the Soviet Union in the world and by a shared understanding among senior Bolsheviks about the dangers of capitalist encirclement. With the political police already pushing conspiracy theories about potential coups emanating from the military in the 1920s, this foreshadowed exactly how the political violence of the 1930s would be justified.

At the same time, it would be wrong to see a rising wave of repression in the Red Army that culminated in the military purge of 1937. Arrests came in peaks and troughs. Despite the security anxieties surrounding the army in the 1920s, there were few arrests of supposedly subversive infiltrators.[50] During the early 1930s, the situation was very different. The collectivization drive sparked major instability in the lower ranks as peasant soldiers discovered how their families had been dispossessed of their lands.[51] At the same time, the OGPU 'unmasked' what it said was an extensive military specialist conspiracy in the officer corps during 1930-1, with apparent ties to the British and Polish governments. This subversive organization was supposedly planning a coup. At the upper end of estimates, 10,000 people were arrested as part of the investigation, given the name Operation Springtime.[52] Notably, Tukhachevskii was interrogated about his possible role in the conspiracy after his name was mentioned during the interrogation of another military specialist. Tukhachevskii was said to be sympathetic to the Right Deviation and – reminiscent of the rumours about him abroad – the leader of a conspiracy planning a military takeover.[53] Menzhinskii wrote to Stalin in September 1930, urging immediate action against the 'whole insurgent group', yet Stalin once again showed restraint, waiting two weeks to act and delaying discussion for a meeting of the Politburo in October.[54] Following a face-to-face meeting with Tukhachevskii in the same month, Stalin dismissed the allegations, later pronouncing him '100% clean' in a letter to Molotov.[55]

Too much emphasis should not be put on Stalin's dismissal of the accusations against Tukhchevskii. He still accepted the premise of the wider military specialist plot in the Red Army uncovered by the OGPU. Several thousand military specialists were arrested and charged with working with foreign powers and carrying out sabotage. Moreover, these exact accusations would reappear in 1937 with the key difference that they would be levelled not at the distrusted military specialist outsiders, but at the bulk of the officer corps, including its upper establishment. A radical increase in political tensions inside the Communist Party was responsible for initiating this shift in focus.

* * *

When Leningrad Party Boss, Sergei Kirov, was gunned down outside his office in the Smolny Building on 1 December 1934, the Red Army, like other Soviet institutions, was subjected to increasing scrutiny. As is well known, Kirov was killed by a lone assassin – disgruntled party member Leonid Nikolaev – but Stalin pointed the finger at the former political opposition, sparking an investigation that would later culminate in the show trials of the 1930s. For the army, this meant growing OGPU attention on the small number of former Trotskyist officers in the ranks. However, alongside a steady number of arrests in the military from this point on, connections emerged between some former Trotskyist officers and the senior oppositionists arraigned at the August 1936 show trial.[56] This group of former Trotskyist officers – including future 'members' of the military-fascist plot, Putna and Primakov – was rounded up and arrested in the summer of 1936 and accused of participating in a counterrevolutionary military organization connected to the alleged main oppositionist conspiracy soon to be publicized by the first show trial. But momentum did not stop there. Under the leadership of Nikolai Ezhov – a dyed-in-the-wool conspiracy theorist – the NKVD turned increasing attention to the military in the aftermath of the first show trial. Ezhov was clear in personal communication to Stalin in September 1936 that there were undiscovered Trotskyists in the army. Later in December, at an NKVD conference, he remarked: 'I think we have still not fully investigated the military Trotskyist line. [...] We opened a diversionary-wrecking organization in industry. What grounds are there to believe that it is impossible to carry out diversionary acts in the army? There are more opportunities here anyway than in industry, not fewer.'[57]

Ezhov's growing interest in the Red Army (alongside calls from senior officers themselves to investigate more closely) saw rising numbers of arrests going into early

1937.[58] In this way, the arrest of the small group of former military Trotskyists in summer 1936 was a key moment for the later military purge. Yet a question remains: how did these arrests spread to Tukhachevskii and the other senior officers soon to be accused of coordinating the military-fascist plot? Tukhachevskii had not supported Trotsky in the political struggle after Lenin's death. There was little to tie him to the arrests among the former military Trotskyists. Moreover, while he certainly had a strained personal relationship with Voroshilov, Stalin had personally vouched for Tukhachevskii in 1930 when he could easily have had him arrested.

What left Tukhachevskii fatally exposed was a shift in the parameters of the conspiracy narrative that was driving forward the Great Terror in 1937. At the outset of the growing arrests from the Kirov murder, former oppositionists were accused of participating in secret opposition networks and planning terrorist attacks. In the first few months of 1937, however, the investigations and associated conspiracies underpinning the terror took on a stronger international dimension. The former opposition was now said to be working hand-in-hand with foreign powers, particularly Germany and Japan. This shift was likely a consequence of Ezhov's conspiratorial thinking. Before taking over leadership of the NKVD, Ezhov had invested efforts in safeguarding the Soviet Union from espionage and had been closely involved in scrutinizing Soviet citizens working abroad.[59] His expanded powers as NKVD head gave him more influence from 1936. Ezhov put more resources into investigating political and counterrevolutionary crime than his predecessor Iagoda, who had paid more attention to policing the social order.[60] Outside of Ezhov's efforts, threatening international events such as formation of the Rome-Berlin Axis in October 1936, the signing of the Anti-Comintern Pact in November 1936 and the ongoing risk that the Spanish Civil War might become a flashpoint for world conflict, undoubtedly contributed to this shift in emphasis in the terror. All of this put the wider Red Army in danger. Arrests could now quite easily spread beyond circles of former Trotskyists, and a narrative quickly emerged that the army was under threat from foreign agents. Clear indications of this shift can be seen in the second show trial of January 1937, when the defendants were accused not simply of being dangerous former oppositionists, but also of working for fascist powers.[61] One month later at the February–March Plenum of the Central Committee, Stalin pointed to a wide array of dangers posed by fascist agents, supposedly working with Trotsky and his supporters.[62] At one point at the plenum Stalin chose to underline the danger with a telling military reference:

> In order to win a battle during war, this may require several corps of soldiers. But in order to thwart these gains at the front, all is needed are several spies somewhere on the staff on the army or even on the staff of the divisions, who are able to steal operative plans and give these to the enemy.[63]

Ezhov echoed Stalin's comments about the threat from spies and saboteurs, arguing that not enough was being done to expose them. He also made reference to a possible palace coup or military plot in the upper ranks.[64] Yet head of the army Voroshilov struck a markedly different tone. Downplaying the danger to the military, he claimed that very few enemies had been revealed in the army, which only accepted the 'best cadres'.⁶⁵ Voroshilov was certainly right on the numbers. It was only in April that the NKVD's investigation into the military started showing real dividends.⁶⁶ But Voroshilov was clearly striking the wrong tone and his efforts to downplay the perceived threat to the military did not succeed. Indeed, Molotov was most clear in calling for a thorough checking of the army, even though there were, as yet, only 'small signs' of sabotage. For Molotov, it was natural to scrutinize the military: 'If we have wreckers in all sectors of the economy, can we imagine that there are no wreckers in the military? It would be ridiculous. The military department is a very big deal, and its work will be verified very closely.'⁶⁷

The presentation and acceptance of a subversive threat to the Red Army at the February–March Plenum had immediate impact. Soon enough, senior military leaders were openly talking about spy networks. Voroshilov also quickly scrambled to change his line. Dropping any effort to shield his institution, he now argued in a speech in March, given to the Red Army *aktiv*, that not a single enemy could be permitted in the army and that it needed to be 'utterly and completely clean'.⁶⁸ At the same meeting, his deputy Gamarnik proclaimed: 'the Japanese–German Trotskyist agents, spies, and wreckers are in a full range of our army organization'.⁶⁹

It was only a matter of time before the investigation swung towards the high command. As we have seen, Tukhachevskii had already been subject to rumours about his disloyalty and similar hearsay circled again in early 1937. Soviet intelligence agents and diplomats reported conversations abroad of plots and military conspiracies, of supposed connections between the Soviet high command and the Nazis.⁷⁰ Old and newly emerging rumours would appear more credible than they once did in light of the growing security concerns surrounding the army. Moreover, as we have also seen, Tukhachevskii had narrowly avoided arrest as a counterrevolutionary back in 1930. It is no wonder that he fell under the NKVD's gaze in spring 1937 when the parameters of their Great Terror broadened beyond the former political opposition.

However, the key moment that explains the timing of Tukhachevskii's arrest in May 1937 and the subsequent explosion of the military purge was the 'discovery' of a supposedly extensive spy infiltration in the army that same month. On 10 May Voroshilov reported to Stalin about a serious infiltration, admitting that the army had been significantly compromised by foreign agents at all levels. Sabotage and espionage were widespread. According to Voroshilov, serious damage had already been done and urgent action was needed, particularly the scrutiny of all officers in all areas of the army.⁷¹ This report coincides exactly with the first action taken against Tukhachevskii and the group of senior officers who would be presented as the leaders of the military-fascist plot one month later. Tukhachevskii was demoted the very day that Voroshilov sent his report to Stalin. In this way, it is likely that the unearthing of this supposed 'spy infiltration' gave Stalin the push he needed to have Tukhachevskii arrested and launch a devastating purge of the Red Army. And the spy scare itself was an extension of the rising security concerns surrounding the Red Army evident from earlier in the year. Moreover, Stalin seems to have had espionage firmly on his mind at this time, having written a long article for *Pravda*, published also in May, which underlined the threat from fascist agents to the Soviet state.⁷² But still, it was a major risk to launch a destabilizing purge of the army when the country was gearing up for war. Stalin had exercised restraint in the past when he rejected Menzhinskii's call to crack down on the army in 1927 and when he let Tukhachevskii off the hook in 1930. Stalin would not attack his army without good reason. During the first months of 1937, he probably waited to see what came up in the NKVD's investigation into the military, but as soon as Voroshilov reported on an extensive spy infiltration in May – affecting all levels of the army – there was no other choice but a mass purge. How could he go to war with an army compromised in such a way? The gamble of a purge could not be avoided.

* * *

Stalin attacked his army because of a spy scare in the military in summer 1937. This spy scare was given credibility because the Red Army had been judged as vulnerable to subversion for nearly two decades. Longstanding security concerns had circled the army since its formation: from 'unreliable' military specialists to spies, foreign saboteurs and domestic Trotskyists. Supposed 'military conspiracies' of different stripes had been 'exposed' in the twenty years before the 1937 purge. There was rarely a moment from its formation in 1918 that the Red Army was not subject to questions about its reliability. These longstanding security concerns came to a dramatic head during 1937. In the aftermath of the Kirov murder, the arrests of a small group of former Trotskyist officers in 1936 swung attentions more firmly towards the army. This gave the NKVD an opening to scrutinize the military more deeply. As the parameters of the terror widened in 1937, this then provided the opportunity and momentum for arrests to move beyond the danger of Trotskyism. In this respect, the Great Terror alone was not enough to spark the military purge; nor were longstanding security concerns that had trailed the army since 1918. It was a combination of persistent anxieties about the reliability of the military and the sudden eruption of political violence in the Great Terror that left the Red Army fatally exposed.

This explanation of the military purge has implications for how we understand the nature of Stalin's power. From the late 1920s, Stalin spearheaded a radical transformation of Soviet military and industrial power in anticipation of major war with the capitalist world. However, at the same time, Stalin and his circle could easily exaggerate or totally misperceive security threats to the Soviet state, causing the regime to lash out in unpredictable ways. As this chapter has shown, the Red Army fell victim to such misperceived conspiracies in 1937, doing much to severely destabilize the institution critical for defence. Stalin exercised vast control over the Soviet state by the 1930s but did much to undermine its strength through misperceiving the nature of security threats. In this way, Stalin's ability to build with one hand and destroy with the other defined the nature of his power.

3

Stalin and the Spanish Civil War, 1936–1939: The new historiography

Daniel Kowalsky

The Spanish Civil War, which began on 18 July 1936, quickly attracted the attention of the Great Powers. The fascists were the first to show their hands, Adolf Hitler and Benito Mussolini delaying only one week before decisively coming to Franco's aid. A fortnight into the war, the British and French proposed the Non-Intervention Agreement, to which twenty-seven European states would eventually adhere. General Secretary Joseph Stalin quickly committed to Non-Intervention, though the Soviet position would continue to evolve in the months that followed. Events in Spain presented a quandary for Moscow. Soviet diplomacy since 1934 had promoted collective security and the postponement of world revolution, yet the global left was galvanized by Spain and looked to the USSR for leadership in the cause of anti-fascism. This dilemma was never resolved, but in mid-September 1936, as Republican fortunes waned, and the fascist powers brazenly violated the terms of Non-Intervention, Stalin approved 'Operation X': an unprecedented projection of Soviet power into Western Europe.

The history of 'Operation X' was long obscured by Cold War bias and archival inaccessibility. On either side, combatants and their supporters vilified Soviet participation. The Nationalists fabricated a patent lie about Soviet influence in Spain as the pretext for their rising, a Cold War-type 'red scare' *avant la lettre*. The Republican camp demonized the Soviets for heavy-handed Stalinist policies that allegedly crushed the spirit of resistance. In brief, the right used communist intervention as its *casus belli*, whereas the left blamed communist intervention for defeat.[1] Roundly denounced, Soviet policy long remained poorly understood, and documented with scant empirical evidence. As late as 1998, the leading British historian of the internationalization of the conflict could write that, on the Soviet role 'there is no work ... which quotes original material'.[2]

This chapter not only addresses that lacuna, spectacularly corrected through recent publications, but revisits both the role of the Soviet Union and Stalin in the Spanish Civil War, and the role of Spain in late-1930s Stalinism. On the one hand, Soviet policy in the civil war was more wide-ranging, and subject to contradictions, than earlier narrowly construed or monocausal explanations have claimed. On the other hand, Spain was significant in determining the course of pre-war Soviet domestic and foreign policy, and influencing Stalin's worldview. This chapter will show that, quite apart from the Soviet Union's influence on the nature and length of the Spanish Civil War, for Stalin, Spain mattered.

Historiographical currents, East and West: 1936–91

Publications in the USSR

Though barely noticed in the West, Soviet-era publications on the Spanish Civil War constituted an impressive array of scholarship, memoirs and document collections. Eventually comprising over one thousand individual works, this corpus would be the subject of annotation in numerous edited bibliographies, beginning in the early 1960s.[3] The key figure in early efforts was M.T. Meshcheriakov, who would dominate the field of Soviet Hispanism throughout the 1960s and 1970s, and examined new scholarship on Spain as well as recently published memoirs of Soviet participants in the Spanish Civil War. The author paid homage to the efforts of Ivan Maiskii, the Soviet ambassador to the Non-Intervention Committee, who, following the war, had encouraged Hispanic studies and facilitated the publication of memoirs.[4] The 1966 *Istoriia zarubezhnikh stran (Bibliografiia russkikh bibliografii)*, or *History of Foreign Countries*, was a valuable update, and included annotated summaries of memoirs and fictional accounts of the Spanish Civil War as well as historical monographs.[5] More significant was L.M. Iurieva's 1973 bibliographic study on the 'national-revolutionary war' in Spain and world literature. Iurieva analysed the literary output of Republican sympathizers throughout the world, including little-known accounts of eyewitnesses who had travelled to Spain from the USSR.[6] In 1975, the most complete list of Soviet scholarship to that point on all areas of Spanish History appeared in *Problemy ispanskoi istorii (Problems of Spanish History)*,[7] whereas the fiftieth anniversary of the Spanish Civil War in 1987 was marked by S.P. Pozharskaia's exhaustive survey, 'Sovetskaia istoriografiia antifashistskoi voiny v Ispanii (1936–1939)'.[8]

Simultaneous to the steady production of historiographical studies, Soviet researchers frequently published documentary collections, the first of which appeared during the war itself.[9] A different category of publication on Spain were those issued internally by the Defence Commissariat. These volumes, whose access was heavily restricted, assembled after-action reports from the advisory staff, together with battle plans, maps and general assessments of Soviet and enemy hardware.[10] Beginning in 1946, the Soviet Foreign Ministry published volumes of general documents on foreign policy, four of which were relevant to events in Spain.[11] Despite their neglect by Hispanists in Europe and North America, these volumes were invaluable, assembling key official letters and memos on the Spanish war. In 1975, the Institute of Marxism-Leninism published a selection of materials from the VII Comintern Congress, including letters, telegrams and speeches on the Spanish war.[12] Earlier, the official Soviet history of the civil war in Spain, *Voina i revoliutsiia v Ispanii, 1936–1939*, reproduced other original documents.[13] In 1988, the Soviet Academy of Sciences published original materials relating to Ukrainian popular support for the Loyalist cause.[14]

Of the approximately 2,200 Soviets who would eventually serve in the Spanish war, around one hundred published accounts of their experiences. This literature reflects the varied backgrounds of those involved in the Spanish struggle, who included journalists, diplomats, filmmakers, translators, officers, pilots and general military support staff. Mikhail Koltsov was the first Soviet representative dispatched to Madrid after the 18 July rebel uprising, and his weekly articles in *Pravda*, published between August 1936 and November 1937, were assembled in what would become one of the key documents of the entire war, the two-volume *Ispanskii dnevnik*, or *Spanish Diary*.[15]

Ilya Ehrenburg, meanwhile, was sent to Spain as *Izvestiia*'s war correspondent. Arriving just weeks after Koltsov, Ehrenburg's activities in Spain, like those of his colleague, ranged well beyond the work of a reporter. Though supplying his paper with regular dispatches, he took up projects oriented towards propaganda, including agit-prop tours with mobile cinemas offering Soviet feature films. Before the arrival in Catalonia of Consul General Antonov-Ovseenko, the journalist also prepared detailed reports for the Soviet military attaché in Madrid. Ehrenburg published his reflections on the Spanish war in several works, including his multi-volume autobiography, *Liudi, gody, zhizn*,[16] and *Ispanskie reportazhi*.[17]

A largely untapped resource is the corpus of reminiscences by Soviet men in uniform, including the general staff adviser Meretskov; war commissar adviser Nesterenko; chief artillery advisers Voronov and Goff; chief naval advisers Kuznetsov and Piterskii; Central Army advisers Malinovskii and Shumilov; Twelfth International Brigade adviser Batov; Eleventh International Brigade and Fifth Communist Regiment adviser Rodimtsev, commander of mechanized regiments Krivoshein, fighter pilots Iakushin, Osipenko, Puzeikin, Smirnov and Gusev; bomber pilot Prokof'ev; tank commander Krivoshein; mine specialist Starinov; intelligence specialists Vaupshasov and Vasilevskii; and many others.[18] Memoirs of Soviet participants in the Spanish war were first published in 1959 in a collection of short essays and eyewitness accounts, edited by Maiskii.[19] In 1962, he published his own memoirs of the Spanish war, *Ispanskii tetrady*, or *Spanish Notebooks*, a work of considerable humour and irony, if at times deceptive on Soviet policy. Despite its flaws, *Spanish Notebooks* would become one of the best known and most widely used Soviet sources on the war available to Western scholars.[20] Finally, the year 1965 saw the publication of *Pod znamenem Ispanskoi respubliki* (*Under the Banner of the Spanish Republic*), the last collection of reminiscences issued under Maiskii's direction, and one that includes a number of strikingly critical assessments of Soviet effectiveness in the war.[21] Meanwhile, the Leningrad veterans section issued *Leningradtsy v Ispanii* (*Leningraders in Spain*), a work of considerable popularity and one that appeared twice again with revisions.[22] Other works of collected memoirs include the 1976 Ukrainian publication of *Vmeste s patriotami Ispanii* (*Together with Spanish Patriots*), which underwent two additional editions, and the popular, usually reliable *My internatsionalisty* (*We Internationalists*), a work that first appeared in 1969.[23] Meanwhile, a perennial favourite up to the present day remains the memoirs of Nikolai Kuznetsov, chief Soviet naval adviser to the Republic and commander-in-chief of the Soviet navy during the Second World War.[24]

Other Soviet memoirs shed important light on oft-neglected subthemes. Take, for example, the 1972 work of Roman Karmen, *No Pasaran!*[25] Karmen was one of two official Soviet cinematographers who shot footage in Spain and edited newsreels for screening in the Soviet market. After Koltsov, he was among the first of Stalin's men to reach Spain in

August 1936, arriving ahead of the diplomatic corps and military advisers. His account, barely included in the most recent historiographical boom, well illustrates the day-to-day activities of a non-military representative of the Stalinist regime. Of equal value, though even less known in the West, is the account of journalist Ovadei Savich, *Dva goda v Ispanii* (*Two Years in Spain*), a work of considerable popularity in the USSR and one reprinted several times.[26] Paulina and Adelina Abramson's *Mosaico Roto* gives us the only memoir of the Soviet linguistic team sent to Spain.[27] The Abramson sisters, who emigrated from Argentina to the USSR in the 1920s, provide a unique impressionistic pastiche of the familial atmosphere among Moscow's personnel on the ground in Spain.

Among Soviet secondary studies of our topic, the 1972 work released by the Academy of Sciences of the USSR, *International Solidarity with the Spanish Republic, 1936–1939*, is a reliable account of official Soviet policy towards Spain as expressed in the press. This work does not, of course, provide any sense of the Kremlin's largely concealed strategic and political motivations for the intervention in Spain, but it is invaluable in its reproduction of official Soviet announcements and press accounts of Moscow's relationship with the Republic.

Three important works from the 1970s consider the impact of the Spanish war on Soviet domestic society. V.A. Talashova's 1972 dissertation on Komsomol solidarity with the Spanish Republic was the first to document how the war was received among the Soviet public. The emphasis of V.V. Kuleshova's book on Spain and the inter-war USSR is on the cultural exchanges initiated between the USSR and Spain in the years leading up to and during the civil war.[28] Finally, A.A. Komshukov's article concentrates on the myriad manifestations of Soviet interest in and solidarity with the Republican cause.[29] Especially useful in Komshukov are references to the archives of the Soviet agency charged with overseeing the upbringing of the 3,000 Spanish children evacuated to the USSR in 1937 and 1938, later to become the foundation for a flurry of scholarship on the *Niños de Guerra*.

Western scholarship, 1936–1991

Beginning in the mid-1950s, American scholars produced several ground-breaking studies on Soviet activities in Spain. Among these was the young political scientist David Cattell, whose first volume, *Communism and the Spanish Civil War* (1955), considered the role of the Comintern and the CPUSSR in the events of the first half of 1937.[30] Cattell suggested that the Spanish Communist Party (PCE) had many opportunities to seize power, such as in May 1937, but Moscow held them back. He followed on with *Soviet Diplomacy and the Spanish Civil War*, the focus of which was Moscow's participation in the oxymoronic Non-Intervention Committee (NIC). Cattell's thesis was that the Soviets were betrayed by Britain and France, both in the proceedings of the NIC and over the course of the war. Furthermore, Moscow's disenchantment with the possibilities for an anti-fascist alliance, coupled with the Munich accord, led Stalin to sign the Russo–German pact of August 1939. Munich's message to Stalin was that Chamberlain assumed that England and France could appease, outwit and eventually outfight the Axis without Soviet support. This proved, in Cattell's words, 'almost fatal for both democracy and communism'.[31]

Appearing at the same time were two doctoral dissertations, never published as books: Robert Lee Plumb's 'Soviet Participation in the Spanish Civil War' and David E. Allen's 'The Soviet Union and the Spanish Civil War, 1936–1939'.[32] Plumb succeeded – in an era of total archival inaccessibility – at collecting important material on Soviet activity in the civil war, and he accurately traced the basic outline of the intervention. Allen's great achievement, meanwhile, was his use of the Soviet press. The work is the account as presented officially by the Kremlin, though the author lets nothing pass without a required qualifier.

From the late 1960s, singularly influential was the work of Burnett Bolloten, whose studies on the Republic's wartime government progressively revealed a great deal about Soviet policy and activities in Spain.[33] In Bolloten's *oeuvre*, Soviet published sources – long neglected in the Western historiography – began to be incorporated into a revised understanding of the war. Bolloten was concerned with the net impact of Soviet intervention on the functioning and ideological direction of the Republic's government. For Bolloten, the USSR's intervention was the basic source of the Republic's inability to quell the internal rebellion and turn the tide of the war. Yet in his treatment of Soviet involvement, Bolloten neglects many of the distinct facets of Moscow's interaction with Republican Spain, some of which, it should be pointed out, might cause him to revise his conclusions. One of Bolloten's influences was George Orwell's *Homage to Catalonia*, first published in 1938, but a work that achieved prominence only from 1952, after which it remained a basic document of the war.[34] Orwell's novel-cum-memoir is the ur-text for the Left's broadly negative interpretation of the Soviet role in Spain. Orwell wrote how the war triangulated between fascism, communism and democracy, but his overall thesis was that Soviet destruction of the non-Stalinist POUM (Workers Party of Marxist Unification) sabotaged the Republic's military fortunes. The Bolloten–Orwell thesis, which roundly vilifies Stalin, remained, for the balance of the twentieth century, an article of faith for many students of the civil war, but it has now seen considerable revision.

In the 1980s, a handful of Western secondary works dealing mainly with Soviet foreign policy also did much to illuminate the Kremlin's activities in the civil war. Jonathan Haslam's *The Soviet Union and the Struggle for Collective Security in Europe: 1933–1939*, and Jiri Hochman's *The Soviet Union and the Failure of Collective Security* exemplified the two sides of the historiographic debate as it stood in the mid-1980s.[35] Haslam represented the traditional interpretation, emphasizing that the Soviets were committed to forging collective security with the West and that, when it failed, the West was largely to blame. Hochman, on the other hand, stands for the radical and minority interpretation, arguing instead that the Soviets never looked at Germany as a mere second choice, but sabotaged agreements with the West in order to effect an alliance with the Nazis. Haslam views Foreign Minister Maxim Litvinov as a tireless lobbyist for collective security; Hochman regards him as the reason why collective security failed. In short, Haslam blames both the West and those forces within the Kremlin working against an alliance with the West, while Hochman places nearly all the blame on the Soviets – especially Litvinov – for leading a duplicitous foreign policy that never committed strongly enough to either the West or the Nazis to form a lasting coalition that might have prevented the war.

Haslam's thesis is not new; it has been espoused by the earlier authors discussed above (Cattell, Plumb, Allen), and is the logical conclusion if only the Western diplomatic records are considered and Litvinov is deemed the sole arbiter of Soviet foreign policy. Haslam defends Litvinov and the Soviets' sincerity throughout. He claims that Stalin was driven by the West to a policy of 'fortress Russia' and ultimately into the Germans' hands. What was new and compelling in Hochman's book was the suggestion that the primary motivation behind Soviet foreign policy was never the continuity of Russian imperialism nor the desire for world revolution, but rather the 'concern of the elite to maintain power'.[36] Thus, internal security drove external policy, which was based on realpolitik, short-term necessity, and above all the self-preservation of the ruling elites. Apropos of Hochman's thesis, it should be noted that one of the conclusions of this study is that, in the case of the Spanish Civil War, the Soviet leadership was presented with opportunities to promote external security while also buttressing support for the regime. This is especially evident in the many activities organized within the Soviet Union, whose main purpose was to reinforce the notion that the Spanish rebels were part of a larger international fascist plot that threatened Soviet sovereignty.

A different tack is pursued by Geoffrey Roberts, who is loath to link Soviet policy in Spain with a single strategic theory, arguing instead that Moscow's reaction to events on the Iberian Peninsula 'was informed by various strategic purposes – anti-fascism, collective security, popular frontism [and the] priority of defending and building socialism in the USSR'.[37] While Roberts admits that all of these were at play to varying degrees in the Kremlin's Spanish policy, none was more important than the defence of socialism at home and the advancement of Stalinist ideology. At times, Roberts argues, the immediate needs of the Spanish Republic more or less meshed with Moscow's ideological goals. When they did, Soviet assistance was invaluable to the Republic, and Soviet actions were largely altruistic. At other times, when the Soviet commitment to ideological purity imperilled the Republic's military viability, Moscow did not hesitate to sacrifice the latter for the former.[38] Roberts's most compelling argument is to reject the earlier thesis that Moscow was entirely motivated in its Spanish policy by the pursuit of collective security with Britain and France. He argues instead that the USSR was in 'an isolationist mood' by the summer of 1936.[39]

Given the geographic centrality of the Iberian Peninsula to the problem of Soviet intervention in the civil war, it is perhaps surprising that Spanish scholars have until recently contributed relatively little to the literature on this topic. Until the death of Francisco Franco in 1975, there were, of course, daunting obstacles to academic freedom in Spain. Scholars wishing to study official Republican government records had to wait for a comprehensive reorganization of state archives, a process not completed until the 1990s. The Franquista interpretation held that the July uprising was a direct response to a Communist plot to take over the Republic. This historiographic trend, though based largely on right-wing propaganda that pre-dated the war, resulted in a series of Western academic responses whose principal goal was the disproving of Franquista theories of pre-war Soviet intervention.[40]

Meanwhile, only unreconstructed Spanish communists took a favourable view of Moscow's involvement in the civil war. The most senior Spanish communist to take up residence in Moscow was Dolores Ibárruri, aka *La Pasionaria*. Indeed, the principal

Spanish Communist interpretation of the war, the four-volume 1966 *Guerra y revolución en España 1936–1939*, which appeared simultaneously in Spanish and Russian, was ghost-written by Ibárruri.[41] The thesis of *Guerra y revolución* is identical to official Soviet accounts of the war: the rebel uprising was part of a fascist takeover of the peninsula, and the Republican defence a 'national-revolutionary war' of liberation. Soviet military assistance is not acknowledged.

In addition to the Nationalist and PCE versions, two other Spanish interpretations bear mentioning. The first is the anti-Stalinist Marxist version – in effect, that of the POUM – which blames the defeat of the Spanish revolution in 1936 and 1937 on Moscow's anti-Trotskyist crimes in the Republican zone. The chief proponent of this theory, Victor Alba, argued that the main Soviet motivation for entering into the Spanish conflict was to wage war on non-conformist international communists.[42] Meanwhile, the thesis of Left Socialist Luis Araquistáin, and Republican ambassador to France, was that Soviet intervention was highly cynical, extracting maximum profit from the Republic while sending outdated hardware.[43] Following the death of Franco, Stalin's intervention in the civil war became a topic for armchair historians, and many poorly documented pieces appeared in popular magazines, including *Historia 16* and *Tiempo de Historia*, but all were speculative articles that relied heavily on disputed Republican memoir accounts.[44]

Historiography since the end of the Cold War

Russian-language studies

Since the demise of the USSR, the supposed chasm between Western and Soviet scholarly production has gradually faded away, and Russian historians have been at the forefront of opening up the field.[45] Appearing in the last year of the Soviet regime, Vladimir Tolmachaev's work was the first to use extensive archival evidence.[46] A post-Soviet study of greater breadth is M.V. Novikov's study of the USSR, the Komintern, and the Spanish Civil War, the first Russian monograph based largely on recently declassified materials.[47] A work that went further still, and revealed for the first time the wealth of untapped archival collections, was the study of Colonel Iurii Ribalkin, a research historian at Moscow's Institute of Military History. Ribalkin's account appeared as a dissertation in 1992, as a monograph in 2000, and in a Spanish translation in 2007.[48] His study focuses on the military intervention, planned by the Defence Commissariat with great precision, and executed with no little invention, and despite considerable hurdles, by the Red Army naval forces. The sale of arms to the Republic is depicted as fair and equitable, in contrast to conclusions reached in Cold War-era Western accounts. But Ribalkin does not shy away from highlighting the problems Soviet forces faced on the ground, many of which they created themselves. A measured assessment of Soviet terror in the Spanish theatre is dealt with dispassionately, but Ribalkin treats it as a consequence of, rather than the impetus for, Stalin's involvement in the civil war.

The last twenty years have seen the appearance of important Russian document collections that have brought to light many hundreds of state records previously hidden from public view. The first of these, edited in 2001 by Svetlana Pozharskaia, presented important Comintern files related to the civil war. An equally historic release was the 2013 set of 474 declassified documents selected from the Presidential Archive, and organized chronologically. Some of these had already been available in duplicate, in declassified funds in the Military or Party archives, but many others had never seen the light of day. Of special interest are those files that trace the Soviet leadership's responses to outbreak of the war, the intervention of the fascist states, and the organization of the Non-Intervention Committee. The informational appendices are also invaluable resources, and themselves constitute impressive research on the topic. Most recently, in 2019, it was the turn of the Defence Ministry to publish the first volume of reprinted after-action reports produced by Soviet advisers and technicians from the war years. Previously, only Ribalkin had quoted this material. It is difficult to overstate the sea change that has resulted, over the past two decades, with the publication of these documents.[49] Given the centrality of Soviet involvement not only to the prosecution of the war, but the peculiar way that the global historiography of the civil war developed, it is not hyperbolic to state that almost all of the general narratives of the war, written before the new millennium, are now obsolete. More to the point, this shift in the historiography of the war coincides with the publication of new biographies of Stalin, many of which are discussed elsewhere in this volume. Taken together, this new research sheds light on Soviet involvement in that conflict and deepens our understanding of Stalinist policies in the 1930s.

Since the publication of Ribalkin's seminal monograph two decades ago, research by Russian historians has continued apace, a response to wide interest in the subject among both scholars and the reading public. So rich and varied is this production that it would be impossible to cite all the literature that has appeared, but some works deserve special mention. Among these are research monographs exploring the engagement of Soviet military personnel, including specialized studies of the aviation, armour, and the advisery apparatus, but also broadly conceived re-evaluations of Operation X in all its dimensions, based on trenchant research across the archives of the Russian Federation.[50] A work that places Soviet military assistance to the Republic in the larger international context is the 2011 monograph by V.V. Malay.[51] More ambitious still is the 2015 two-volume set of reminiscences of Soviet personnel mobilized to Spain, a worthy update to the spate of similar anthologies of first-person eyewitness narratives popular during the Soviet period.[52] The exploration of the roles played in the Spanish war by non-aligned Russian emigrants – such as Alexander Kerensky – has finally been treated in a book-length account.[53] Even more invaluable is the appearance of a collection of new research into all areas of our question by Russian scholars working in many subfields.[54]

Apart from this impressive corpus, one must draw special attention to two major publishing events that have further advanced the state of the field. Appearing in the end of 2018 was a bi-lingual, Russian–Spanish edited volume that assembled the work of an international team of forty-six scholars, whose mission was to trace and flesh out the history of Russo-Spanish relations since the time of Peter the Great.[55] Professor Angel Viñas has played a key role in the project, himself authoring many of the articles that cover the period of the civil war. Richly documented with facsimiles of declassified archival materials, photographs, interpretive essays and an exhaustive bibliography, the sections on bilateral ties in the twentieth century are peerless. When this book was released, even the casual observer would have had difficulty imagining it being superseded at any point in the near future, yet several months later, in early 2019, an even more stupendous scholarly bombshell was announced: the publication of an invaluable trove of over two-dozen specially commissioned research articles in the ever-expanding history of the Soviets in the Spanish Civil War.[56] The organization of this special issue of *Istoriia* (*History*), edited by Ekaterina Grantseva and Georgy Filatov, proposes understanding bilateral ties through multiple, discrete lenses: from the perspective of Soviets and other Russians sent to Spain; in terms of how the Soviet presence fitted into the larger internationalization of the civil war; and as a problem of scholarship, historical memory and public history, whose resolution lies in part through further mining of archival funds in the Russian Federation. Applying principals of cubism to historical inquiry, the assemblage abandons outdated approaches to the USSR and Spain and seeks to broaden the parameters of the theoretical and narrative landscape of this unique confluence of the Slavic and Hispanic worlds. Indeed, the scholarly breakthrough evident in the 2019 special number of *Istoriia* is mirrored in the fragmentary advances of the broader field of Stalinism over the past two decades.

Anglo-American, French and German scholarship

Outside of the early Russian contributions exploiting recently declassified post-Soviet records, the first important works of scholarship included the British historian Gerald Howson's *Arms for Spain*, principally concerned with reconstructing the Soviet supply of arms to the Spanish Republic, and based narrowly on a set of documents obtained from the Military Archive (RGVA),[57] but also the first of Rémi Skoutelsky's research monographs on the International Brigades, which finally clarified the Comintern and Stalin's role in their creation, based on documents in RGASPI.[58] The following year, the last of the millennium, saw the door to hidden post-Soviet riches cracked open slightly more. Steven Zaloga's ground-breaking study of Soviet tanker operations in Spain, exploiting extensive Red Army after-action reports, allowed the author to conclude that armour performance in Spain was handicapped by poor planning and support, and the inability to coordinate combined infantry and armour operations.[59] In Spain, the same year saw the arrival of Antonio Elorza and Marta Bizcarrondo's comprehensive account of Comintern activities in Spain from 1919 to the end of the civil war.[60] This monograph was the first book to appear in Spain that sought to revise, with post-Soviet declassified documentation, several generations of unsubstantiated anti-communist propaganda, including the *ur*-lie of the Nationalist camp, i.e. that the July uprising was a response to Comintern activity in Spain.

In the first decade of the twenty-first century, research proceeded on multiple fronts. Mary Habeck and Ronald Radosh's jointly authored work, *Spain Betrayed: The Soviet Union in the Spanish Civil War*, was a fascinating development, but in the intervening two decades it has not withstood scrutiny.[61] The volume is an annotated set of eighty-one translated declassified documents, mostly from the Military Archive, but also from RGASPI and a few other archives. Their interpretation is heavily influenced by the outdated, anti-communist works of Orwell, Araquistáin, Bolloten and others, who argue that Soviet intervention doomed the Republic's war effort, and that Stalin sought the establishment of a People's Republic-style satellite in the Western Mediterranean. None of the major interpretive works that have appeared in the intervening two decades have in any way confirmed the conspicuous bias evident on every page of this book. Indeed, the author of this chapter positioned his work largely as a rebuttal to *Spain Betrayed*, beginning with monographs appearing in English and Spanish, and later in specialized articles or chapters. Arguing, broadly, that Stalin's support of the Republic was a response to Western abandonment and fascist aggression and that it was often altruistic.[62] Not dissimilar conclusions were simultaneously being reached by the German Sovietologist Frank Schauff, whose meticulously researched monograph appeared first in German, then Spanish and, most recently, in a Russian translation.[63] Schauff's strength and weakness is the Comintern, the study of which, in relation to Spain, forms the core of his book. However, Schauff overstates the Comintern's influence in Spain, at the expense of Stalin, who oversaw not only major decisions vis-à-vis the Republic but quite often rather trifling ones.

Yet the most important and in-depth study yet produced in any language is Angel Viñas's trilogy, published between 2006 and 2008, a work of towering scholarship and erudition.[64] Through his mobilization of unpublished material from Moscow, mastery of the Spanish and French source base, and minute historiographical analysis, Viñas succeeds in laying to rest dominant Cold War-era myths about the Spanish Civil War. He refutes allegations that Stalin intended to create in Spain a Soviet satellite and that Soviet advisers in the Republic were actively involved in the events of May 1937 – the centrepiece of Orwell's novel and thus the heart of the Englishman's case against Stalin. In Viñas's account, the Republic was destroyed by fascist aggression; its betrayal came at the hands of the Western democracies, not the USSR. Further, according to the author, the Soviet Union offered the Republic its best chance of survival; Stalin's leadership, together with a professional advisory staff and equipment of the highest quality, served the Republic well.

Building upon Viñas' authoritative scholarship, new research has appeared year after year, further contributing to the rolling sea-change in civil war historiography. Two decades into the thaw, and ten years after the first spate of publications appeared, specialist conferences were now organized to assess the state of the field. In autumn 2009, the Fundación Pablo Iglesias organized an exhibition in Madrid entitled 'Los Rusos en la Guerra de España'. This was a singular scholarly event without precedent up to that moment, for it not only created a multi-media installation of all aspects of Soviet participation in the Spanish Civil War, but the accompanying catalogue served as a summative monument to ongoing collective research by an intrepid group of international scholars.[65] Nor was this the only such event occurring in those years. In February 2011, William Chase brought eight scholars to Pittsburgh for a colloquium entitled 'The Spanish Civil War's Impact on Spanish and Soviet Political Cultures'.[66]

After Madrid and Pittsburgh, it became clear that the Soviet–Spanish relationship forged during the war had given rise to unique socio-cultural consequences. These were now pursued through additional research projects that sought to examine specific components of the bilateral ties. The fate of the Basque children evacuated to the USSR in 1937 and 1938 became a rich subfield in its own right, whereas other researchers took up separate aspects of the cultural exchange.[67] Both in Russia and in Spain, the last few years has seen the publication of important new research on Stalin's deployment of Soviet journalists to the Republic.[68] And whereas diplomacy between the Republic and the USSR had seen no new monograph since the 1950s, in 2018, Madrid's long-suffering ambassador to Moscow, Marcelino Pascua, found his biographer.[69] Overall, the vistas of the field have greatly expanded, not only thematically but chronologically. North American Russianists, not least Stephen Marks and the late Richard Stites, who had not earlier sought to explore Slavic–Hispanic relations, now began to reimagine those connections, going back to the early modern period.[70]

Similarly, the most recent book-length studies of Stalin became a barometer by which to measure the state of play. In the seminal biographies by Isaac Deutscher and Dmitri Volkogonov, events in distant Iberia were relegated to a footnote. In the more recent studies of Oleg Khlevniuk and Stephen Kotkin, Spain looms large, and the Spanish Civil War become an event on a par – indeed intertwined – with the Purges and the Pact.[71] Khlevniuk's assessment is less that Soviet policy shaped the war in Spain than that the war in Spain shaped Stalin's domestic policies in the USSR. Observing Spain's descent into anarchy, guerrilla warfare, sabotage and extrajudicial justice (e.g. the general consequences of 'total war'), 'Stalin ... became further convinced of the need to purge the homeland in the interests of military readiness'.[72] For Kotkin, on the other hand, Stalin was drawn into the Spanish Civil War principally to hunt his ideological enemies: '[t]he specter of Trotskyites capturing a physical redoubt in a real country would seize Stalin like the proverbial red cape in front of a bull'.[73] This thesis had some currency during and after the war; it originated with Orwell. But had Stalin wished to only undermine or exterminate the non-aligned, renegade revolutionary left in Catalonia (e.g. the CNT anarchists and the Marxist POUM), could he not have sent sufficient agents to the Republic to do this? Why, in addition, rush authorization of the logistically challenging 'Operation X', despatching over five dozen heavy vessels, from a distance of three-thousand kilometres, and over a period of twenty-six months, in order to supply the Republic with the latest Soviet fighters, nor empty Russian armour parks of the finest tank then produced anywhere in the world, the T-26, nor indeed support that matériel through the organization and funding of a vast army of volunteer fighting men, drawn from cadres in fifty-three countries?[74] Why, furthermore, admit three thousand Basque children into the Soviet Union, evacuated from the northern front, in 1937, to be housed and schooled in palatial Black Sea accommodation, entirely at Soviet expense? Why import to the USSR every variety of tactile Spanish cultural artefacts, and put these on display in the Museum of the Revolution? Why export to the Republic Soviet film products, arranging screenings in cities and at the front of classic pictures that included the *Battleship Potemkin*, *We of Kronstadt* and *Chapaiev*?

Part of Kotkin's work is informed by discredited Cold War-era research and Franquista propaganda, and he ignores key scholarship: not only the magisterial trilogy of Angel Viñas, but, for example, Josep Puigsech, who, over the past decade, has meticulously documented relations between the Soviet consul general in Barcelona and the Catalan government throughout the civil war. Puigsech's starting point is the long-held assumption, reiterated in innumerable books and articles dating from as early as 1938, that it was through the Soviet consulate that Stalin attempted to exercise military and ideological control over both the Generalitat and, more broadly, the whole of Republican Spain. The author demonstrates that Moscow never achieved dominance nor even undue influence in either axis, and that, furthermore, the Kremlin neither sought nor desired such a dominance in Spain.

Parallel conclusions have been reached by Jonathan Sherry, who has investigated the Soviet-style October 1938 show trial of the POUM leadership in the Republican zone.[75] Whereas this trial was hitherto held up as an example of Stalinist oppression in the Republic, Sherry's thesis is much the opposite: the accusations of sabotage and collusion with the fascists were not plausible, and the accused were acquitted.[76] In the same vein, Boris Volodarsky tackles the topic of NKVD repression in Loyalist Spain. In contrast to the Orwellian myth of swarms of Soviet illegals carrying out assassinations and sapping the Republic's moral, Volodarsky's sobering revision concludes that the Stalinist purges were exported to Spain on such a small scale as to have barely made a ripple: at most twenty kills, perpetrated by fewer than ten men, and this in a war where over three million men were mobilized, and well over three hundred thousand men and women were murdered extra-judicially.[77]

* * *

Overall, recent scholarship on Stalin and the Spanish Civil War has clarified three key components of the topic. First, Soviet motivation in entering the Iberian imbroglio can now be reliably attributed to the defence of Popular Frontism and the broad cause of anti-fascism. Second, new research into the multiple facets of Soviet engagement with the Spanish Republic flesh out a broadly imagined, epic encounter between the Slavic and Hispanic worlds. Third, and finally, Stalin's highly engaged, personal role in the planning and execution of Operation X supports the wider thesis of this collection that the *Vozhd'* would involve himself in the minutiae of state and party policy, interested as much in the details as the larger picture. In Spain, Stalin was a quick study, able to quickly take the measure of the rolling crises of politics in the Republican zone, as well as the tactical exigencies of the war effort itself. Where supply to the Soviet ally was concerned, Stalin never hesitated to adjust this way or that the shipment dockets of matériel bound for Spanish ports. Even on the rhetorical strategies of the Republic's propaganda initiatives, Stalin expressed strong opinions. He objected, for example, to the Loyalist slogan *No Pasarán!*, condemning it as too passive, and reflective of a defensive, rather than offensive, military struggle.[78]

To sum up, in less than a generation the narrow canon that dominated this field for half a century, one that incorporated no unpublished Soviet-era documentation, has now been eclipsed by a strikingly diverse, multi-lingual and international set of monographs, anthologies and articles, with more appearing all the time. Pockets of dogged and stalwart adherence to outdated paradigms, and resistance to this new scholarly revisionism, are not difficult to locate, although they are less significant with each passing year. The remarkable story of the Soviet Union and the Spanish Civil War is finally being told through a richly documented, new historiography. The new canon is not only important to our understanding of the war and Soviet involvement in it, but also in helping historians re-envision Stalinism in the late 1930s.

4

Brute force and genius: Stalin as war leader

Chris Bellamy

'It is hard for me to reconcile the courtesy and consideration he showed me personally with the ghastly cruelty of his wholesale liquidations', wrote Averill Harriman (1891–1986). He continued:

> Others, who did not know him personally, see only the tyrant in Stalin. I saw the other side as well – his high intelligence, that fantastic grasp of detail, his shrewdness and his surprising human sensitivity that he was capable of showing, at least in the war years. I found him better informed than Roosevelt, more realistic than Churchill, in some ways the most effective of the war leaders ... I must confess that for me Stalin remains the most inscrutable and contradictory character I have known – and leave the final word to the judgment of history.[1]

Harriman was US Ambassador to Moscow from April 1943 to 1946 and had previously accompanied Churchill to Moscow in 1942 to help explain why the Allies were operating in North Africa rather than opening the second front in France. As Ambassador he also took part in the summits between the 'big three' – the US, UK and USSR – at Tehran in November–December 1943 and at Yalta in February 1945. He therefore knew Stalin as war leader as well as any foreigner. But his opinion was echoed by others, notably President Harry S. Truman, who took over from Franklin D. Roosevelt (1882–1945), on the latter's death. Truman first met Stalin on the first day of the victorious Allies' Potsdam (Berlin) Conference at the Cecilienhof Palace on Tuesday 17 July 1945. Truman's biographer, David McCullough, wrote: 'Harry Truman, like nearly everyone meeting him for the first time, was amazed to find how small he actually was: "A little bit of a squirt", Truman described him, as Stalin stood 5′5″.'[2] However, Truman soon wrote 'I can deal with Stalin [...] He's honest but smart as hell'.[3]

Stalin's contradictory characteristics and extraordinary personality and intellect are widely covered in the other chapters in this volume. As Geoff Roberts wrote, in *Stalin's Wars*, he was 'despot and diplomat, soldier and statesman, rational bureaucrat and paranoid politician. They add up to a complex and contradictory picture.'[4]

Stalin's unique qualities meshed with the three cardinal components of fighting power. His ability to inspire through a counter-intuitive combination of charm and terror, and his memory for people, made him a master of the moral component. His ability to master detail and to sense, almost instinctively, the values and limitations of military technologies made him master of the physical. So, it must be said in the Soviet context, did his utter disregard for human life. And his astuteness and attention to detail, wide knowledge and retentive mind made him master of the conceptual. Of grand strategy – the politics of alliances. Of strategy – the use of battles to win wars. Of operational art – the planning and conduct of large-scale, coordinated campaigns and operations. And even of tactics – how individual battles, now linked in a common design, are fought. These aptitudes did not all coalesce at once, and not fully until the 1941–1945 Great Patriotic War was well underway, and past its 1942 crisis, but they were there.

Overture at Tsaritsyn

Stalin had no formal military education but he had a razor-sharp intellect and read voraciously. His early experience was extraordinarily varied, as a trainee priest, sometime meteorologist at the Tiflis observatory, fugitive, gangster and bank-robber and then revolutionary politician. These unlikely strands coalesced, as his friend and colleague Kliment Voroshilov (1881–1969) said, 'by chance', in 1918.[5] In May that year Lenin sent Stalin as Director-General of food affairs, to Tsaritsyn (later named after him as Stalingrad) to get food from the south east. In spring 1918 the Bolshevik-controlled area, and particularly Moscow and Petrograd, were starving. Stalin arrived with 450 armed men on 6 June.[6]

The Bolshevik Revolution had taken place on 7 November 1917 [new style[7]] and the regime was only seven months old. The administrative organization, indeed the apparatus of Government, was in flux and many key enterprises – including fuel – were still in private hands. In order to grip the existential food problem, plenipotentiary powers were required. This serendipitous chance gave Stalin his first experience of military as well as political command. However, the 'official' account of Stalin's achievement at Tsaritsyn, by his colleague and later friend and publicist Voroshilov, differs widely from others. In 1937 N. Markin, a pro-Trotsky émigré writer, said that 'not even a single line' in Voroshilov's account was true.[8] The comment about 'chance' is.

On 7 June Stalin cabled Lenin saying that he was about to send eight trains full of food and that his agents were 'pumping out' the grain of the Kuban.[9] On 11 June the Government declared a 'food dictatorship', a somewhat unlikely beginning to Stalin's career as a senior military-political commander.[10]

Stalin was clearly fully aware of his plenipotentiary powers and of the opportunity that the largely uncontrolled space of the wild east offered him to make his mark with Lenin. Tsaritsyn was also where the White counterrevolutionary forces were likely to deliver their main attack. Its capture would have cut off the Bolsheviks from the oil of Baku, and would have enabled the counterrevolutionaries in the Don region to join forces with Kolchak and the Czechoslovak Legion, which had moved east along the Siberian railway, for a general advance on Moscow. Stalin could see that Tsaritsyn had to be retained at all costs. Meanwhile, almost immediately, a turf-war over jurisdiction had erupted. The first victim was K.A. Makhrovskii, an official in the fuel industry. Stalin accused Makhrovskii of criminal dereliction of duty, allegations reviewed at a 12 July 1918 session of the Council of People's Commissars (Sovnarkom) in Moscow. Stalin's allegations were rejected, and Lenin noted that he thought Stalin – already clearly a 'bad boy' – had made them in a fit of temper.[11] A series of accusations and counter-accusations followed, until Makhrovskii was released on 21 September.[12]

It is already clear how Stalin's rebellious instincts towards higher authority, especially given Lenin and Trotsky's tendency towards a more 'collegial' style, and Stalin's authoritarian instincts towards anyone below him in the system might coalesce. And then there was fierce competition with anyone at the same level.

Stalin's later instincts and actions as Soviet dictator and supreme commander first appeared at Tsaritsyn. Given plenipotentiary powers over multiple civil and military agencies, Stalin resented but acknowledged and then disregarded instructions from above. It is a formula common in military command structures and sociology: 'consent and evade'.[13] Trotsky, exasperated by Stalin's frequent disobedience, referred to the 'Tsaritsyn opposition'.[14]

Stalin had a particular hatred of the so-called *voenspets* – the 50,000 former Tsarist officers recruited by Trotsky to provide professional military expertise under political direction. Some genuinely believed that the new regime offered the best hope for Russia: others were probably recruited at gunpoint. Many of them seem to have hated each other more than they hated their former colleagues who had sided with the Whites. Within about a month Stalin had, according to Voroshilov, 'cleared the city of White Guard plotters', and had anyone suspected of being one shot.[15] Stalin's hatred and suspicion of former Tsarist officers was to persist, with the execution of some of the most able who had managed to survive until the late 1930s in the great purge from 1937.

In July 1918, the White general Pëtr Krasnov's (1869–1947) Don Army launched its first attack on Tsaritsyn. Defending Tsaritsyn was a matter of life and death for the revolution. The Whites knew that, and Stalin knew that.

Opposing Krasnov were some 40,000 men of the Red Army, but they were made up of uncoordinated detachments. On 22 July the Military Council of the Northern Caucasus Military District was established, with Stalin as chairman, along with Voroshilov and S.K. Minin. The White forces were pushed back but launched a second offensive on 22 September. By this time the defences of Tsaritsyn had been augmented to include 13 armoured trains, a favourite device in this often one-dimensional war, and a favourite nostrum of Stalin's.[16] The Soviet Southern Front, to coordinate operations against the Whites, was formed in the same month.

On October 3, the Soviet forces on the Kamyshin and Tsaritsyn axes were incorporated into the Tenth Army, under Voroshilov's command. The following day Trotsky telegraphed Lenin:

> I insist categorically on Stalin's recall. Tsaritsin [*sic*] front in a bad way, despite the abundance of troops ... In so far as Stalin and Minin remain in Tsaritsin, they, in accordance with the constitution of the Military Council, possess only the rights of members of the Military Council of the Tenth Army ...[17]

Stalin's disregard for orders from Lenin and Trotsky did have a positive effect, however. In defiance of direct orders, Stalin ordered the transfer of Dmitrii Petrovich Zhloba's 'Steel Division' from the Northern Caucasus. It arrived after a legendary trek of 800 km in 16 days, and on 15 October 1918 attacked the White Cossacks from the rear. Zhloba (1887–1938) was a young Cossack mechanic from Southern Ukraine who had been made an NCO in the Imperial Army during the Great War. This action turned the tide of the battle in the Bolsheviks' favour. Zhloba had saved Stalin, but Stalin repaid him with a bullet in 1938, during the Great Purge.[18]

Stalin went on to supervise the defence of Petrograd in May 1919, to counter the Polish attack in summer 1919, and to supervise development of Ukraine in May 1920. Although Stalin's 'genius' during the Russian Civil War was clearly exaggerated by his Soviet acolytes, he was very effective and did gain a great deal of experience. Most of that was directly applicable to his subsequent performance as perhaps the 'most effective' of the 'Allied' war leaders in the Second World War. His ability to coordinate multiple agencies stayed with him. So did his hatred of former Tsarist officers, his passion for armoured trains and trains in general, an awareness of the value of attacks in the enemy rear. He was a 'fireman', arriving to take matters in hand and coordinate unruly army and front commanders. This probably influenced his use of *Stavka* representatives – special representatives of the Supreme High Command – much to his front commanders' annoyance – in the Great Patriotic War. He was not born or brought up to be a war leader, but, by nature, nurture, chance and opportunism, he now had the makings of one.

Geopolitics and geostrategy

Stalin knew that Tsarist and Provisional Government Russia had lost in the First World War because it lacked the industrial capacity to fight a protracted industrial war and stay ahead of the latest military scientific and technological developments. Therefore, he initiated the Five-Year Plans from 1929, to industrialize the country and provide it with the means to fight and win a modern industrial war. In 1924 Stalin had initiated 'socialism in one country' with Nikolai Bukharin (1888–1938), another of his later victims in the Great Purge. The big question about how Stalin behaved in international relations and security policy is how far he stuck to this and how far he retained his – and Lenin's – commitment to fomenting world revolution. He did both.[19]

The latter is clear from the activities of Comintern, known also as the Third International. Comintern was founded in 1919, and finally dissolved in 1943. Its aim was 'struggle by all available means, including armed force, for the overthrow of the international bourgeoisie and the creation of an international Soviet republic as a transition stage to the complete abolition of the state'.[20] In spite of the announcement of 'socialism in one country' in 1924 and its implementation from 1928, Comintern and Soviet intelligence services continued to try to undermine and destabilize Western capitalism. Although their attempts to do this in Europe largely failed, they enjoyed more success in the European powers' Asian colonies.[21] Lenin's attack on Poland in 1920 had been part of a drive to spread world revolution, which failed because of military defeat and because the Western proletariat did not show much enthusiasm.[22] Although 'socialism in one country' appeared to mark a move away from Trotskyist international ambitions to unite the world's workers, it was only an 'operational pause', probably reinforced by a need to publicly separate Stalin himself from the exiled Trotsky. His moves from 1939 marked a re-engagement with Lenin's legacy. Then, once the Red Army started moving west from 1943, opportunity reinforced motive.[23]

Stalin and the pre-war development of the Soviet armed forces

Stalin stayed largely aloof from the intense and voluminous debates on developments in military art and science in the 1920s and 1930s. He was clearly aware of them, and the close cooperation between German and the Soviet militaries in the late 1920s and early 1930s, both pariahs on the international stage, could not have taken place without his knowledge and approval. Two of the most prominent thinkers, Mikhail Tukhachevskii (1893–1937) and Aleksandr Svechin (1878–1938), were former Tsarist officers and both were killed in the Great Purge. Tukhachevskii (also discussed by Peter Whitewood in this book) had been a hero of the 1920 Polish war, wrote extensively on land-air operations, and was behind the large-scale development of paratroops and other air-landed forces including flying tanks, as part of his vision of deep operations.[24] He was made one of the first five Marshals of the Soviet Union in 1935. Tukhachevskii attended the funeral of King George V on 28 January 1936. Some seventeen months later, on 12 June 1937, he was shot for spying for a foreign power, presumably Germany. Svechin produced the blueprint for the Soviet conduct of the Great Patriotic War in *Strategy* (1926), in which he forecast and demanded the mobilization of the entire nation and the disappearance of the distinction between 'front' and 'rear'.[25] Svechin's book was the last to bear the title *Strategy* until Marshal Vitalii Sokolovskii's *Military Strategy* in 1962 – the blueprint for nuclear war – and that may be significant in analysing Stalin's role in the development and definition of Military Doctrine.[26] In the late 1920s, for example, the Soviet Union adopted the German-derived term operational art to refer to the higher conduct of military operations, which would previously have been referred to as strategy. Although it reflected the emergence of a new level of warfare, it could also have been, in part, because Stalin increasingly reserved 'strategy' – the higher conduct of war and the most important measures of high command – for himself.

Stalin was more interested in the practical lessons of conflicts. Up to 3,000 Soviet combatants and advisers served on the Republican side in the 1936–9 Spanish Civil War. The latter included senior officer Nikolai Voronov, later Chief Marshal of Artillery. Voronov recalled that immediately on their return they were summoned to report to Stalin. It was late and they were tired, but Stalin said: 'do not put off until tomorrow what you can do today', and questioned them intensely.[27]

Although there is little direct evidence of Stalin's involvement in pre-war procurement decisions, it is likely that any major decision would have to be passed by him. One was the important and fortuitous decision to fuel future Soviet tanks with less-flammable diesel, which also has a lower freezing point, rather than petrol. At the Battle of Khalkin-Gol (Nomonhan) in August 1939, the Japanese set fire to many of the petrol-fuelled Soviet BT-5 and BT-7 light tanks, which had been operating in temperatures of more than 38 degrees celsius on the Mongolian plains, with Molotov cocktails. The victorious Soviet commander Georgii Zhukov, later Stalin's deputy, noted that his 'BT tanks were a bit fireprone'.[28] Stalin would undoubtedly have been informed and, well-advised, probably made the final decision.

Stalin's direct influence is most evident in the naval field, but that makes sense. Soviet air-land strategy was clearly defined and had been endlessly debated by numerous experts. Until 1935 the Soviet Navy was a predominantly coastal and 'brown water' force, heavily influenced by the French *jeune école* and strong in submarines. But at the end of 1935 Stalin ended all debate and demanded a rapid shift from a 'small war at sea' strategy to one centred on capital ships and 'mastery of the sea'. Stalin had attempted to build a blue-water navy and, according to the *US Naval War College Review* in 2001, 'Stalin took naval strategy into his own hands but never divulged any strategic precepts or plans to his naval leaders'.[29]

By 1939 an immense programme had evolved to build twenty-four powerful battleships by 1947. With the onset of the Great Patriotic War, all long-term projects were suspended. Only submarine and light surface projects continued, as circumstances allowed.[30] But such were the circumstances of the outbreak of the Great Patriotic War on 22 June 1941. Stalin clearly saw, as had Ivan the Terrible and Peter the Great, that Russia's position on the world stage would ultimately depend on mastery of the sea. Stalin's personal preoccupation with naval matters was further fuelled by the Soviet experience in the Spanish Civil War. The Soviet Union's assistance to the Republicans in Spain was frustrated by Franco's German and Italian allies' control over maritime access to the Iberian peninsula.[31] Like a later important announcement, Stalin left it to Viacheslav Molotov (1890–1936) – later, from May 1938, the Foreign Minister – to announce that 'a mighty Soviet power must have a sea and oceanic fleet corresponding to its interests, adequate for our great task'.[32]

Two 59,000-ton battleships were laid down in 1938 in Leningrad and Nikolaev, and two battlecruisers in 1939. Stalin liked battlecruisers but not aircraft carriers. Work on the first battlecruiser, believed to be called *Strana Sovetov*, was suspended in late 1940. This led to one of the notable intelligence errors that emanated from Stalin's habit of keeping his cards so close to his chest. German air photographs showed the incomplete cruiser before the pointed bow and stern sections had been added, giving the squared-off appearance of the classic 'flat-top'. This led photographic interpreters to think it was an aircraft carrier, an error that persisted after the Second World War.[33]

Among very few primary source documents directly proving Stalin's undoubted interest in naval affairs and his role in signing off major projects is a remarkable note from 1935–6, which came up for auction recently.[34] Two officials signed a top secret (ss) minute, entitled simply *Raport*, and addressed to 'Central Committee Comrade Stalin'. The two-page minute, of which there were four copies, was received by the Central Committee on 19 December, 1935, and signed off by Stalin on 13 January 1936. It was about a thermal direction-finding device – *tëplopelengator* – which could allegedly find warships in the dark, out to 20 or even 25 kilometres from its shore installation, with an accuracy of 0.5 degrees Naval workshops could start producing these thermal direction finders quickly and they could also be developed to be fitted to naval and merchant ships. Stalin scribbled a note to Defence Minister Voroshilov on the top-left of the first page in the green coloured pencil of which he seems to have been fond. 'Comrade Voroshilov. What does this mean?'.[35] Because Stalin's signature on documents available to the public is so rare, this very slender indication of his direct involvement in the procurement of new technology was offered for $25,200. Stalin might have been amused that his signature on a relatively insignificant document was so valued in the capitalist world, nearly a century on.

The purges from 1937 killed the principal senior commanders who had been associated with the schema of massed armoured attacks and the 'deep operation', notably Tukhachevskii. But another, less well-known development at this time clearly bears Stalin's personal imprimatur. From 1932 Red Army operational plans had included provision for partisan and deep-penetration operations up to 100 km from the Soviet frontier to penetrate enemy fortified regions and to destroy railways and other communications. Other partisan units were assigned to operate on Soviet territory in the event of enemy success, remaining in position behind the enemy to disrupt his advance and launch diversionary attacks – what the British call 'stay-behind' parties. The senior officers involved in these plans included Tukhachevskii, a Marshal from 1935, and Army Commanders First Rank (Generals) I.P. Uborevich and I.E. Yakir.[36] All three were killed in the purge. In 1932 three centres were set up to train partisan warfare specialists: two for the IV (Reconnaissance and Intelligence) Directorate of the Red Army (later the GRU), and one for the OGPU (the 'Joint State Political Directorate' (*Ob"edinënnoe Gosudarstvennoe Politicheskoe Upravlenie*), the new name that had superseded the Cheka in Tsaritsyn since 1923, and would become the NKVD from 1934.[37]

Some of these trained specialists in 'diversionary' tactics were sent to Spain. By November 1937, XIV Partisan Corps had been established in the Spanish Republican Army with about 3,000 combatants, operating in small groups about a dozen strong.[38]

The development of Special Forces and diversionary tactics, including the pre-positioning of large weapons stocks either in neighbouring countries near Soviet borders or within Soviet territory did not fit comfortably with Stalin and his cronies' paranoia. As a result of the 'repression' of 1937-8, the diversionary cadres so carefully and expensively trained were annihilated. All the partisan detachments were demobilized and the secret stocks of weapons and explosives apparently decommissioned, although that must be debatable. Even the terms 'diversion', 'diversionary action' and '*diversant*' – a person doing diversionary operations – were banned.[39]

This little-known aspect of the purge went further. In 1928 the deputy chief of the Intelligence Directorate of the Ukrainian Military District General Staff, P.A. Karatygin, had written a book called *Partizanstvo – Partisan Warfare*. Unfortunately, it has so far been impossible to find the book although it clearly reflected a big problem the Russians had – and arguably have – with partisans in Ukraine. It was one of a number of books listed for destruction in the People's Commissariat for Defence of the USSR's Order Number 147 of 10 August 1937, 'Concerning the Commission's determination on the removal of *politically dangerous and outdated military and military-political literature*' [emphases added].[40]

Orders of this nature could only have emanated from Stalin, albeit perhaps over-enthusiastically, implemented by his subordinates. The idea of preparing 'stay-behind parties' to counter the enemy penetrating Soviet space would have been anathema to Stalin, especially given the overwhelming dominance of the Red Army's commitment to attack. However, almost immediately, experience in the 1939–40 Russo–Finnish winter war led the Leningrad Military District's Intelligence Directorate to resume experiments with 'reconnaissance-diversionary sub-units' (presumably small groups on the dozen-or-so man model), to operate in the enemy rear.[41] In spite of the determined attempts to eliminate all record of doctrine and training for 'diversionary operations', the fifth 'Specialist Diversionary Department of the General Staff's Intelligence and Reconnaissance (*Razvedivatel'ny*) Directorate was reformed. In May 1940 Marshal Semën Timoshenko was appointed to the People's Defence Commissariat and noted that 'there was no operational war plan'.[42] Therefore, there were no plans for conducting a 'small war' with partisan or regular formations, even in the opening period of a war. In December 1940 to January 1941 some 270 senior Red Army commanders and political staff gathered for war games. However, diversionary and partisan operations did not feature. Only on 16 June 1941, less than six days before the German attack on the Soviet Union, was the People's Commissariat for Internal Affairs (NKVD) and its head of diversionary, reconnaissance and intelligence operations from the 1930s to the early 1950s – P.A. Sudoplatov – brought in to cooperate with the frontier Military Districts to organize 'diversionary' action. But even then there was no appetite for revisiting the ideas validated in the Spanish Civil War and then erased. The Commander of the Belorussian Military District, which morphed – as Soviet Military Districts did – into the Western *Front*, on the outbreak of war, Dmitrii Grigor'evich Pavlov (1897–22 July 1941), showed no interest.[43]

Only after the German attack, which made outstandingly successful use of these very techniques, were the Soviet forces – Red Army and NKVD – galvanized into resurrecting the ideas that had been ruthlessly erased, almost certainly on Stalin's direct orders. On 10 July, in a meeting with Voroshilov, Timoshenko and Budënny, Stalin signed Order GKO-83 ss of the State Defence Committee (*Gosudarstvennyi Komitet Oborony*), authorizing:

> Commanders-in-Chief, as soon as possible [*pochashche*], to use aircraft to launch pamphlets with my own signature summoning the population to threaten the rear of the German armies, destroy bridges, tear up railway tracks, burn woods, join the partisans and continuously stress the German invaders. In this summons, underline, that the Red Army will soon come and liberate them from the German invader.[44]

Stalin had failed to anticipate the situation, had deliberately erased not only the means but even, as far as was possible, the thinking behind the solution to which he now turned, and had to order the wheel to be reinvented. And the words of the order contained a Stalinist menace. The inhabitants of the areas overrun by the Germans had probably thought the Red Army and the NKVD were long gone. But Stalin's message was as much threatening as reassuring: 'We'll be back'. This particular case – writing off the value of irregular, partisan and 'hybrid' forces – epitomizes the bigger picture. Stalin had made a catastrophic misjudgement. But he would recover and bring his nation back from the brink and lead it to victory.

The cruel romance with Germany: Stalin's motives

Stalin was a master of deception and intrigue and he kept other great powers and commentators guessing as to what he was really about. In 1995, R.C. Raack judged that 'socialism in one country' was a necessary formula for creating a powerful new type of socialist state and, as such, a preliminary to resuming Lenin's quest for global revolution. Then, Stalin's shorter-term (1939–40) international endeavours to regain Soviet control over areas that were all formerly parts of the Russian Empire were, first, a necessary defence and, second, a preliminary to a wider world ambition.[45] This author agrees. But Stalin was also an opportunist, although many of his best laid schemes '*Gang aft agley*'.[46]

The Molotov–Ribbentrop Pact of 23 August 1939 suited both Stalin and Hitler.[47] It bought Hitler time and security to launch his invasion of Poland, in concert with Stalin, and then to turn west against France, the low countries, Denmark and Norway. It also gave Hitler access to the vast natural resources of the Soviet Union, which he would need to fight the British Empire and eventually the United States. Between 23 August 1939 and 22 June 1941 the Soviet Union poured grain, coal, cattle, lead, zinc, manganese, petroleum products, phosphates and nearly a tonne of platinum into Germany.[48] The additional secret protocols to the Pact partitioned Poland between Hitler and Stalin, giving Stalin 'western Belarus' and 'western Ukraine'. It also assigned Bessarabia (modern Moldova), Estonia and Latvia to the Soviet Union but left Lithuania in the German sphere. The later secret protocol, signed on Ribbentrop's visit to Moscow on 28 September, gave Lithuania to Stalin as well.[49] It is now clear that Stalin expected – and wanted – a protracted war of attrition of First World War dimensions to occur between Germany and the British–French entente.[50] That would exhaust all three, possibly leading to insurrection, toward which Comintern had been working in the 1920s and 1930s. Then Stalin could move relatively easily into and across western Europe.

But then Stalin's well-laid plans went awry.[51] The mighty French army, which had played the lion's share on the Western front in the First World War, was swiftly defeated, surrendering on 22 June, and the British were expelled from the continent. The events of June 1940 were a major shock to Stalin. First, because Stalin's undoubted dream of seeing the Western capitalist powers and National Socialist Germany bleed each other to death evaporated. And second, because the German armed forces' stunning and surprising victory showed it to be even more competent and formidable than Stalin would have thought. However, Britain's stand, supported by its overseas Empire and Dominions and the support it was receiving from the United States made Germany aware that, in order to sustain the now global struggle, it needed the resources of the Soviet Union. For the moment, they were being traded for German technological expertise.

Shock and denial

Much recent scholarship has focused on Stalin's refusal to acknowledge the German plans to attack the Soviet Union in breach of the Pact, and on whether he was in fact planning to launch an offensive against Germany when the Germans pre-empted him.[52] Stalin saw and acknowledged receipt of first-class intelligence reports from agents in Berlin. The most shocking example is the report from *Starshina* – 'Sergeant-Major' in the Air Ministry in Berlin, forwarded by Vsevolod Merkulov (1895–1953), the head of the NKGB (Foreign Intelligence)[53] to Stalin and Molotov on 17 June, four days and a few hours before Barbarossa. *Starshina* reported that 'preparations for an armed attack on the USSR are fully complete and an attack may be expected at any moment'.[54] Stalin wrote on the top left, again in his beloved green pencil:

> To Comrade Merkulov.
> You can tell your 'source' from the German Air Headquarters he can go and fuck his mother. This is not a 'source' but a disinformant.
> I.St.

From this brief comment the historian may deduce what sort of person Stalin was and that this was clearly not what he wanted to hear. Stalin had been receiving indications of German intent for months, all of which are widely reported in the literature. He was in denial. But so vicious was his reaction to any suggestion that the Germans would soon attack that his advisers desisted. Three days later, on 20 June, Merkulov decided not to forward a summary of all the Berlin agents' reports to Stalin. There would have been no point. Timoshenko and Zhukov had been trying to get Stalin to put the armed forces on full alert since 9 June, and tried again at a recorded meeting on 18 June. 'Germany on her own will never fight Russia. You must understand this', Stalin said, and then:

> He opened the door and stuck his pock-marked face round it and uttered in a loud voice: 'If you're going to provoke the Germans on the frontier by moving troops there without our permission, then heads will roll, mark my words', and he slammed the door.[55]

The other big debate, which started in 1990, was triggered by a former GRU officer, Viktor Suvorov (real name Rezun) who had defected to the West in the 1970s. His 1990 book *Icebreaker: Who Started the Second World War*, provoked ridicule and anger, but the circumstantial evidence is compelling.[56] Not only had Stalin long harboured the ambition to spread communism across Europe, but in the same year as Rezun's book appeared, details emerged of the 15 May 1941 plan for a pre-emptive strike against the German forces now ensconced in western Poland. The fifteen-page plan, developed by Zhukov, but handwritten by Aleksandr Vasilevskiĭ (1895–1977), then Deputy Commander of the Operations Directorate of the General Staff, was addressed to Stalin. It was marked 'Top Secret. Very Urgent. Exclusively Personal. The only copy.'[57] In his role in the Operations Directorate, Vasilevskii worked with Stalin, who appeared to have liked him. Vasilevskii later recalled that Stalin had asked him about his family.

Zhukov's 15 May 1941 plan was a development of three earlier plans of July and September 1940 and 11 March 1941. However, whereas all the earlier schemes had been for an immediate counter-attack in the event of invasion, the 15 May 1941 plan was undoubtedly for a pre-emptive strike against German forces. It was presented to

Stalin that day, who acknowledged he had seen it, and therefore implied approval, though not necessarily for it to be implemented immediately.[58]

Although the 15 May plan lends additional credence to the idea that Stalin was thinking of an attack on Germany, and that, like any professional General Staff, Zhukov and his team were working on one, it does not provide any firm evidence that Stalin planned to attack the Germans in 1941, and certainly, as Rezun suggests, as early as 6 July. However, the fact remains that when the Germans attacked in the small hours of 22 June, they crashed into a military deployment that was neither configured for attack or defence, and showed many of the signs of deploying for the former. There are three options. If we disregard the imminent Soviet attack, that leaves the contingency plan for a pre-emptive attack, and then, probably most likely, and in accordance with the prevailing Soviet military doctrine at the time, preparedness for an immediate counter-attack. Having moved the Soviet frontier forward into the middle of Poland in September 1939, the so-called 'Stalin Line' – prepared fortifications on the former Soviet border – had been uprooted and new defences were still not in place.[59] I would argue that Stalin might well have been planning to attack in 1942, or even 1944. As it was, he was taken by surprise and, according to the evidence of the unexpurgated memoirs of Marshal Konstantin Rokossovskii (1896–1968), may have ordered the counter-attack plans – or Zhukov's pre-emptive strike plan – to be implemented because there were no others.[60] The results were cataclysmic.

Penitence and resilience

H-Hour for Operation *Barbarossa* was 03.30 German summer time, 04.30 Moscow time on 22 June 1941, pretty much the longest day. The Soviet land and air forces were receiving an alert sent out by Zhukov, the Chief of the General Staff, just after midnight, warning of 'a sudden attack' by Germany, probably the night after, but to resist 'provocations'. Admiral Nikolai Kuznetsov, (1904–74), People's Commissar for the Navy, asked Zhukov if use of weapons was authorized. Zhukov, with that charm for which he is well known, snapped 'yes!'. So Kuznetsov put the entire Navy on full alert at 02.40, about 20 minutes before the first German air strikes along the 1,800 km land border from the Baltic to the Black Sea. At 04.13 Moscow time, H-17, the mighty fortress of Sevastopol in the Crimea switched on its searchlights as German bombers approached. They opened fire a few minutes later, while the land forces fumbled in the dark trying to unfathom a confusing and ambiguous order.

As the first reports came in, Kuznetsov, Timoshenko, Voronov and Zhukov attempted to contact Stalin at his Kuntsevo *dacha*. Stalin was woken and, after a delay of a few minutes, he told Zhukov to bring Timoshenko to the Kremlin. It was war – the biggest and worst war in history.

Stalin was humiliated, shocked and, understandably, depressed. But he had been warned and maybe he had been anticipating this all along. He was in his office by 05.45 and joined by Molotov, Zhukov, Lavrentii Beria (1899–1953) the head of the NKVD, Marshal Semën Timoshenko (1895–1970), the People's Commissar for Defence, and General Lev Mekhlis (1889–1953), Timoshenko's Deputy.

The details of these meetings are well recorded. On the Sunday morning, 22 June, Stalin was probably still in a form of denial. He may still have thought that the German attack, as far as it could be deciphered, might have been a wayward action by renegade German generals. The first People's Commissariat for Defence (NKO) Directive, signed by Timoshenko, Zhukov and Georgii Malenkov, Secretary of the Party's Central Committee and to be a member of the State Defence Committee (GKO) formed on 30 June, was issued at 07.15. It was careful to avoid labelling the German 'air attacks' and troops 'crossing the border' as a full-scale attack.[61]

Stalin had probably expected some sort of ultimatum from the Germans, and initially thought there might be room for negotiation. The speed with which he now swung into action was impressive. Molotov was tasked to write the announcement to the Soviet people, and to the world, while Stalin immediately focused on organizing the evacuation of industry. Molotov made the speech at 12.15. It gave the British and Americans what they needed to hear: that 'fascist Germany' was the aggressor. It referred to the 'patriotic war' against Napoleon in 1812, and said there would be a 'new patriotic war' for the motherland. The last words were insanely optimistic but, after 1,418 more days, proved to be true. '*Nashe delo pravoe. Vrag budet razbit. Pobeda budet za nami*' – 'Our cause is just. The enemy will be beaten. Victory will be with us'.[62] Whether these words were Molotov's or, perhaps, Stalin's own is unclear. But they worked.

A few blocks away from the studio on Gor'kii street, Stalin ordered Lazar Kaganovich (1893–1991), people's commissar for railways and transport, to evacuate factories and 20 million people from the frontline areas. Nikita Khrushchëv, who later denounced Stalin, was behind the story that Stalin 'lost it' for ten days, until he was able to address the Soviet people on 3 July. Evidence that became available in the 2000s shows that this was completely untrue. On 22 June Stalin had twenty-nine meetings with senior people, some of them two or three times. His last appointment was with State Security chief Beria, who had been with him on three occasions. Khrushchëv was in Kiev at the time, meeting Zhukov who had flown to assess the situation for himself. Stalin was back in his office to see Molotov at 03.20 the next morning. In the next three hours he saw seven more people: Beria, Timoshenko, Nikolai Vatutin (1901–44), Chief of the Operational Directorate of the General Staff, Kuznetsov, Kaganovich and Pavel Zhigarev (1900–63) the commander of the air forces. He then had a twelve-hour break before seeing most of them again plus Merkulov and Vlasik, chief of the NKGB's First Directorate.[63] Stalin clearly did *not* suffer a nervous breakdown.

On the contrary, Stalin took a number of critical and far-reaching decisions. He had already ordered Kaganovich to begin the evacuation of industry. After some sleep, on 23 June he ordered the creation of a supreme military-political command with an old Russian name. *Stavka* – a warrior chieftain's encampment. Timoshenko was nominally in charge although, in reality, Stalin was. The other members, in order of precedence, were Zhukov, the Chief of the General Staff, Foreign Minister Molotov, Marshals Voroshilov and Budënny and Navy Minister Admiral Kuznetsov. It was designed to 'effect the most centralized and flexible command of the Armed Forces in the conditions of the war which has just begun'.[64] On 30 June Stavka was complemented by the creation of a War Cabinet, comprising Stalin as President, Molotov as Deputy President Voroshilov, Malenkov and Beria. Stalin had wanted Mikoyan and Voznesenskii as well, but not all agreed, and they were not formally brought in until 3 February 1942. The GKO continued in operation through the war, until 4 September 1945, two days after Japan's surrender. Then, on July 1941, Stavka was renamed the *Stavka Verkhovnogo Komandovaniia* (The Stavka of the Supreme High Command).[65] On 24 June Stalin had set up the Evacuation Soviet, to 'decide the most important strategic and war-economic task, re-basing powerful human and economic resources from the threatened regions [in the west] to the east, to the rear of the country'.[66]

So far, Stalin had handled the situation extremely well, but he appears to have been severely discomfited by the capture of Minsk on 28 June. His frenetic schedule of meetings peaked with twenty-nine on 25 June and twenty-eight on 26 June.[67] Another prudent order came on 27 June – the evacuation of state reserves of precious metals, precious stones, diamonds and the treasures of the Kremlin. Tempting though it is to ascribe some cultural sensitivity to this decision, the Ministry of Finance was to be given an estimate of the artefacts' value as jewels, ingots and scrap. The hard currency value that the state might need. The treasures were to be taken to Sverdlovsk and Cheliiabinsk, well behind the ultimate German objective of the Archangel–Astrakhan line, which the Russians knew from their intelligence.

On 29 and 30 June Stalin broke his normal routine. He and his political colleagues – Malenkov, Mikoian and Beria stormed round to the General Staff building to see what was going on. They had lost contact with the Western Front – in Belarus – and on the shortest route to Moscow.

The creation of the State Defence Committee (GKO) on 30 June provided the opportunity for the crucial test of Stalin's ability to lead the country. That afternoon, Molotov called Mikoian, who had Voznesenskii with him. He asked them to join him, Beria and Malenkov. They proposed the creation of the GKO, with Stalin as Chairman. That would avoid the need to make Stalin 'Commander-in-Chief', which would saddle him with responsibility for the unfolding disasters. They decided to visit Stalin, who was now ensconced in his 'nearer' dacha at Poklonnaia Gora. Mikoian recalled:

> He looked at us quizzically and asked 'Why have you come?' One could sense that he was worried, but that he was taking care to appear calm. Molotov, as our spokesman, said that it was necessary to concentrate the power into one organ that would be called upon to decide all the questions of operations and to organise the mobilisation of all the country's forces for resistance against the occupiers. That kind of organ had to be headed by Stalin.
> Stalin looked somewhat astonished but after a short pause said:
> 'Very well'.[68]

Stalin had probably expected a coup. If anyone had wanted to launch one, that would have been the time. No wonder Mikoian could 'sense that he was worried'. Stalin now looked surprised and relieved. Or maybe Stalin had been testing his Politburo members' and military commanders' loyalty. The critical moment, for Stalin and his leadership, had passed. Stalin's hold on power was secure – against a palace coup, at least. Now, there were the Germans.

The next step came on 3 July. Late on 2 July the editor of the armed forces' newspaper *Krasnaia Zvezda* (*Red Star*) received a phone call, telling him to 'hold the front page'. He did not have to ask what for. After the absence of twelve days, his whereabouts known only to the close circle of the Politburo, Stalin spoke to his people on 3 July.[69] His 3 July speech is extraordinary but it probably needed twelve days to cushion a complete change in the way Stalin's relationship with the people was portrayed, although in reality it had not changed at all. 'Comrades! Citizens! Brothers and Sisters!! Fighters of our Army and Fleet! I address you, my friends!'[70] The new portrayal of the Soviet Union as a 'family' was linked with a renewed emphasis on traditional Russian patriotism.

During the ensuing four years, Stalin's sharp mind and eye for detail made him a superb war leader, notwithstanding his tyranny and paranoia. In Zhukov and the other generals who survived, including Vasilevskii and Rokossovskii, he had first-rate professional military support. The armed forces improved by leaps and bounds when the Voroshilov reforms, which resulted from the lacklustre performance in Finland, began to take effect in 1942 to 1943. At first, the Red Army and air forces, with Naval units largely used as infantry or in close support of land operations, were committed – almost continuously – to the counter-offensive. Stalin and his commanders were committed to the pre-war military obsession with the offensive, and enormous casualties resulted. But the continuous aggressive fight-back cost the Germans and their allies dearly too. Only in 1943 was Stalin persuaded to allow the Germans to attack the Kursk salient, which had been created by very costly Soviet counter-attacks to north and south, to be turned into a giant fortress.

As the Germans approached Moscow, most of the Government, Party apparatus (including Beria) and foreign embassies were evacuated to Kuibishev, modern Samara, under an order dated 12 October 1941. However, Stalin, astutely and bravely, decided to remain in Moscow. There were no serious air-raid shelters, so when air-raid warnings sounded Stalin would descend to the Kirov metro station where a plywood compartment was constructed for him to shield him from the passing trains, which he insisted should be kept running.

On the international stage Stalin's obvious priority was to engage and charm his co-belligerents – they were never formally 'Allies' – Britain and the United States. He managed this superbly. When Churchill first travelled to Moscow on 12 August 1942, he was not quite sure what to expect in the land of the workers and peasants, and brought some sandwiches. He also brought bad news. The second front – the re-invasion of France – would be delayed. He told Stalin about the British and American landings in North Africa, which Stalin, perhaps surprisingly, recognized as contributing to taking some of the pressure off Russia. The second front question remained at the forefront of Stalin's agenda until the Western Allies finally landed in France on 6 June 1944. But by 15 August Churchill and Stalin were acting like old friends. At about 20.30 Stalin suggested they retire to his apartment for a drink. Churchill was there until 03.00 the next morning.

Stalin also took an informed and extremely intelligent interest in all aspects of military-technological development. The two most startling occurred in 1942. The Russians were aware of the UK and US Manhattan project through the NKGB agents, particularly John Cairncross who was Private Secretary to Lord Hankey, who had access to most of the Manhattan project papers. But Stalin's decision to proceed with the development of nuclear weapons in 1942 was triggered by an unusual source. A nuclear physicist, Georgii Flërov, who had been shortlisted for the Stalin Prize in 1940, had joined the Red Air Force and found himself stationed at Voronezh, south of Moscow. The University had been evacuated but the library was intact. Flërov checked out the latest physics journals that the University had received before June 1941. All the top American nuclear physicists had stopped publishing articles. The gap in the peer-reviewed literature could only mean one thing. The work was now classified and the Americans were developing an atomic bomb. In April 1942 Flërov wrote to Stalin – a rather brave thing for an Air Force lieutenant to do. Stalin summoned his top nuclear physicists including Sergei Kaftanov, the Minister of Education and also Chief Scientific Adviser to the GKO, and asked their opinion. After some hesitation, according to Kaftanov, Stalin said 'we should do it'.[71]

The other example is from the other end of the scale, and concerns a weapon individually far less lethal than the atom bomb, but which has killed far more people collectively. In October 1941 a tank commander, a young sergeant, had been badly wounded and burned in the V'iazma–Briansk encirclement battle. His story underlines the capricious nature of Stalin's Russia and the war effort. He was evacuated to Siberia and spent six months recovering – an extraordinary investment in one young man in a country that was often so profligate in squandering lives. He started drawing designs for guns and was assigned to the well-known designers Georgii Degtiiarev and Georgii Shpagin. On 23 September 1942 there is an entry in Stalin's diary. At 21.30 the 'Boss' saw the young tank sergeant for five minutes. His name – Mikhail Kalashnikov.[72]

* * *

Stalin met the British and American leaders, Churchill, then Attlee, Roosevelt and then Truman – at the 'big three' conferences at Tehran in November–December 1943, Yalta in February 1945 and Potsdam in July 1945. The very fact that the democracies had changed their leaders (albeit in America's case because of Roosevelt's death), whereas Stalin was still there, suggests why he was so effective. At Tehran and Yalta the three powers were still cooperating to ensure the defeat of Germany, but Potsdam took place in a different environment (although Japan still had to be defeated). The three powers' differences now surfaced. Truman told Stalin about the new atomic bomb but Stalin, who had been thoroughly briefed on the bomb before travelling by train to Potsdam did not seem very interested, since he knew all about it. Merkulov had reported to Beria on 10 July and it is likely that Stalin saw the report before travelling on 16th.[73]

Churchill and Stalin, for all their differences, clearly liked each other as people and had many characteristics in common. The Soviets had a great respect for Churchill, notwithstanding his background, but did not think much of Attlee. Churchill liked Stalin and admired his vicious sense of humour. Truman also liked him. In spite of the stress and frustration that came from dealing with Stalin and the Russians, according to Truman's biographer, David McCullough, 'Truman liked him.' Leading up to the end of the Conference Truman wrote to his wife, Bess, 'I like Stalin. He is straightforward...' Even when he got back to Washington, he told former Vice President Henry Wallace that Stalin was a fine man who wanted to do the right thing.[74] The Great Patriotic War had turned Soviet Russia from a pariah state to a space-bound superpower. For all his many faults, Stalin had led it effectively, not only in defence against the most professional and advanced military power in Europe, but then in attack, to seize it as far as the Elbe.

Part Two

Challenging Stalinist Models: Cults of Personality

5

The Stalin cult in comparative context

Judith Devlin

The Stalin cult was once explained by reference to the leader's pathological personality power and understood to be a key feature of totalitarianism. It has also been adduced as an instance of Russian exceptionalism.[1] However, a burgeoning literature on leader cults suggests otherwise.[2] Although there were precedents in the nineteenth century, the real heyday of leader cults came in the aftermath of the First World War when a crisis of authority was precipitated by the shattering of the old political order. Neither victory nor defeat seems to have determined their development. Countries that could claim to be beneficiaries of victory (such as Czechoslovakia and Poland) as well as those that emerged from defeat (like Turkey and the Weimar Republic), and those whose victory or defeat in the war was reinterpreted (Italy and the Soviet Union), all witnessed leader cults. They developed not only in so-called totalitarian regimes, dictatorships and authoritarian orders, but also in (albeit fragile) democracies.

Despite the differences between them, these regimes had one thing in common: they operated in unstable and fissiparous or destabilized states that had emerged from the ruins of the old monarchical order of Central and Eastern Europe. As republics, our case studies claimed legitimacy from popular sovereignty but, despite adopting or invoking, at least initially, some of the practices and institutions of democracy, giving functional expression to the popular will remained problematic in the face of internal conflict and poverty. These new dispensations developed a personalized symbolic politics out of a common need to forge from a diverse, disputatious or indifferent population a united and committed nation on which to stabilize the state.[3] This study will focus not so much on the totalitarian leader cults that are the usual point of comparison for the Stalin cult but on those surrounding Piłsudski, Atatürk, Hindenburg and Masaryk.[4] It will examine not what the Stalin cult owed to exceptional aspects of Soviet political culture and Russian tradition, but what it had in common with cults in the new states of the post-war order, where it differed and what light this sheds on it. Rather than emphasizing the singularity of Stalinism, this approach attempts to explore some of the ways in which it shared in and was shaped by broader trends and forces of the period.

Forms and functions: Iconography

One common feature was the widely disseminated iconography of the leaders, which was carefully cultivated, not least by the leader himself. The leader (invariably male) was commonly imagined and depicted in quasi-military vein. Aleksandr Kerenskii is thought to have initiated this fashion,[5] while another obvious example of the influence of the First World War on this type of iconography is furnished by Hindenburg, in liberal eyes the acme of Prussian militarism in his *Pickelhaube* helmet. A cult grew up around him as early as Autumn 1914, thanks in part to his role in the defeat of the Russian army at Tannenberg and partly due to a symbolic vacuum the Kaiser was unable to fill.

Hindenburg was to emerge as a symbol of national unity and as the figure to whom the German public looked for reassurance both during the war and thereafter.[6] He bore a striking resemblance to Bismarck (a man whose myth was still potent in the 1920s),[7] and this was exploited in the many portraits of him in uniform which circulated during the war. According to Wolfram Pyta, a boom in Hindenburg painting and portraiture took off after his promotion to Field Marshal in November 1914, and Pyta estimates that by the end of 1920, portraits of Hindenburg had been made by about five hundred painters. Initially, unlike Stalin,[8] he allowed some artists to paint him from life but gave them only one sitting – a concession he allegedly made only if the portraits were to raise money for war charities. Hindenburg was not indifferent to his image, as this tactic suggests, and was in fact a political general, increasingly aware of the power of the media and interested in self-promotion, but at this stage he did not try to influence how he was depicted. As time went on, however, popular depictions made him even taller than he was (6′), turning him into a colossal figure. He resisted photography and, according to Pyta, only rarely and unwillingly admitted photographers. Stalin, too, retreated from photography, even though (as David King has shown) it was prone to drastic censorship. *Pravda* printed fewer photographs of him after the mid-1930s, and in the post-war period he seems to have preferred the press to reproduce paintings of him, often in marshal's uniform. Photographs were too close to reality (they showed his age), while painting allowed the imagination to play. Hindenburg's portrait hung in people's homes beside that of the Kaiser and religious pictures. During the war and in the mid- to late 1920s, his image was reproduced in a wide variety of media from paintings and postcards to posters, the illustrated press and even to cups, plates, teacups, and card games. A mass of kitsch appeared after Tannenberg with mouth-organs and Hindenburg cigars especially popular. During his Presidency, his image was used to sell luxury goods and his office did not usually object, being less censorious than those of either Hitler and Mussolini (or indeed the Soviet authorities, in the case of Lenin).[9] Leader cult kitsch developed in market economies, and if it posed the threat of symbolic devaluation and iconoclasm, it suggests there was a demand for such artefacts and, thus, that the cult helped to promote the leader's popularity.[10]

Hindenburg was typical of inter-war leaders in emphasizing his military exploits. One reason for this was the formidable challenge faced by inter-war regimes in establishing or stabilizing the political and social order. The leader had to be able to inspire his nation in the struggle to overcome the difficulties that beset the path to the ultimate victory of the national project. Hence, the dominant iconography favoured showing him in military uniform or a stylized version thereof. Hitler, Mussolini and Stalin affected this style and Piłsudski too was partial to being depicted in martial guise (looking vaguely Sarmatian with his big moustache and romantic dashing garb, in deference to Polish tradition). With his title of Marshal (incidentally shared with Atatürk, Pétain and later Stalin), Piłsudski's image emphasized his role in leading the Polish legionaries in the First World War, defeating the Red Army and restoring Polish statehood and independence. This was a trope of his myth, and his iconography served to reinforce it.

A not dissimilar approach influenced Atatürk's monuments, although like Stalin he looked forwards rather than backwards, being concerned with the consolidation and modernization of a new state rather than, like Piłsudski, with the resurrection of an old one. Atatürk commissioned monuments to himself to illustrate his military prowess and victory in the Greco-Turkish war that led to the foundation of modern Turkey, with the aim of ensuring that the public was reminded of this narrative and its meaning for the new nation as they went about their business.[11] In Turkey, as elsewhere, the size and location of monuments (and of portraits and pictures) mattered. Statues and memorials occupied prestigious sites in city and town centres, reflecting the importance of the values and messages they conveyed. They often served not just as a visual illustration of a narrative repeated in other forms, but also during national holidays as ceremonial sites where the powers and the people acted out rituals of loyalty and deference. Unlike Stalin and Hitler, Atatürk cultivated a second, civilian image: much of his official iconography showed him in Western dress and he was regularly accompanied by a team of personal photographers who took carefully staged photographs of him in dinner jackets, golfing trousers, top hats and business suits, and engaged in such modern activities as dancing, drinking alcohol and mixing with women. These images served to present him as the incarnation and symbol of his programme of modernization and Westernization and as the epitome of the new Turkish man the regime wanted to create. If the drive to modernity was not true of Hindenburg and Piłsudski as symbols, it applied to both Lenin and Stalin and was also, but in a more ambivalent manner, part of Mussolini's mythology. Images and statues of Atatürk adorned every city and town centre and laws and regulations directed that his portrait should be displayed in every government and public office and institution, as well as in schools. The State Supply Office, state-funded artists and private businesses furnished the requisite images, which included large building-size portraits for national holidays. This approach is clearly reminiscent of the Soviet one, where it enabled artists to survive but also drew them into active participation in the system and myth-making. After Atatürk's death in 1938, it became in 1951 a criminal offence to insult his memory or destroy images of him, a reprise of the idea of *lèse-majesté*.[12]

Although the first Czech President Tomáš Garrigue Masaryk, like Piłsudski, emphasized his links with the Czech Legionaries, he also cultivated the image of the scholar, hard-working statesman (at his desk) and country gentleman, as befitted an icon of liberalism.[13] Masaryk's image – like that of Atatürk, Hindenburg and Stalin – was very widely disseminated in a multiplicity of forms and locations, including government buildings, shops and schools. His domestic virtues were recalled through photos of the leader with his grandchildren (like those of Hindenburg with his, Stalin's with little Pioneers etc.).¹⁴ Masaryk assisted in the making of his iconography. He never rejected artists' requests for sittings and posed for at least sixty-four painters, according to Orzoff. He permitted himself to be filmed too, as did Atatürk. Like the Turkish leader (and Garibaldi), he was often shown alone, rarely with other politicians, apart from his successor, Edvard Beneš. His mythologized image showed him not only as a statesman and scholar but also as a man of the people, talking kindly to peasants (like Lenin and Stalin).

Biography and history

The leader's graciousness and humility were to be set against his genius (Masaryk, like Stalin, Atatürk and Hitler, was hailed as such). His care for the lowly, his long hours of unremitting labour for the nation, and his self-sacrifice and often martyr-like dedication to the struggle for freedom socialism the nation (in various combinations) were tropes common to most leader cults. It was a theme rehearsed in the cults of Stalin, Hitler, Piłsudski and Hindenburg, not only in iconography but in the leader's biographies and in official histories of the new states.¹⁵ Stalin was thus not alone in tending his image and recent history. Masaryk, according to Orzoff, not only propagated his image through his writings, but also assisted with some of the many biographies published of him. The most famous was Čapek's very popular *Conversations with Masaryk* (1927–35), a quasi-autobiography. Čapek sent his first draft to Masaryk to approve and the President's staff, daughter and Beneš reviewed it too. Masaryk's life story, from his humble origins as the son of a cook and former serf to liberator of the nation and President, was told as though by Masaryk himself and the benevolent image it conveyed disguised the 'aggressive, canny politician' Orzoff claims he actually was. Masaryk helped many other biographers too, by granting them interviews and he personally encouraged and assisted the author of the influential *Building of the State*.¹⁶

Likewise, Piłsudski helped a sympathetic biographer with material. Hein believes that he saw himself as a central character in the modern history of Poland and allowed his followers to establish a historical institute to enshrine this reading. Its main idea, she contends, was that Piłsudski had devoted his life exclusively to the independence of Poland, enduring a form of martyrdom in Siberian exile and that, in assuming the leadership of the Legions, he led the avant-garde of Poland – an itinerary not unlike that of Stalin. He liked to present himself as the enemy of dictatorship and as a good democrat (something that sat at variance with his role in the *sanacja* and his contempt for parliamentarians, opponents and the educated bourgeoisie). Furthermore, he saw himself as the moral leader of the country, a self-image reflected in many of his writings. Like several other leaders he issued tablets of stone, including such suggestively entitled autobiographical works as *My First Struggles* and *Fights* (*Boje*), in 1925. As with Masaryk, Atatürk and Stalin, this heroic saga was reflected in children's literature and school textbooks.¹⁷

Self-sacrifice for the nation was a key theme in the Hindenburg cult, according to von der Goltz, and both in person and with the help of his office he supervised its reproduction in film and fiction in the late 1920s and early 1930s. When *Iron*

Hindenburg, a documentary biographical film about the President, opened in Berlin in 1929, it tried to demonstrate a deep link between Hindenburg and the German people while illustrating key elements of his myth. Following his life from his youthful service in the Prussian army to Tannenberg, his First World War leadership to the presidency, the film was punctuated by shots (some of them staged) of large crowds cheering him, inter alia on his 70th and 80th birthdays. It rehearsed the stab-in-the-back thesis to explain defeat. His staff, von der Goltz tells us, monitored the production closely and Hindenburg personally demanded the removal of a clip where the subtitles showed him proclaiming his weariness, an unwelcome reference to his senescence. Another film which retailed his myth was *Tannenberg*. Released in 1932, it had a very large budget and vast cast. It too was supposedly a documentary, although it included an entire fictional subplot (a combination of genre conventions typical of Stalinism and some famous Stalin cult films).[18] Again, Hindenburg's office and the Interior Ministry monitored the film and censored it heavily (finding fault with the actor who played Hindenburg for 'not doing justice to the Reich President's historical personality'). In 1929, a war novel by the popular right-wing author Werner Breumelberger was vetted in a similar way. Hindenburg supplied a foreword and he and one of his ministers read the entire book, insisting on detailed changes, including in the chapter on the Kaiser's abdication (to make it conform to the Hindenburg myth), the insertion of a long scene about Tannenberg and the reduction of Ludendorff's role (as it was thought he had been given far too much attention).[19]

The analogies with the Stalin cult are obvious, from the personal review and approval of the myth in film and literature and the broader concern with and monitoring of his image to the combination of fact and fiction and the excision from the narrative of rivals and opponents.[20] Hitler too intervened to shape his film image, suppressing Leni Riefenstahl's 1933 film *Victory of Belief* about a party rally, which featured other leaders, including Ernst Röhm. Hitler ordered the destruction of all copies of it and *Triumph of the Will* was made on his orders the following year. He not only devised the title but also ensured that he overshadowed other party leaders, while being depicted as kindly greeting peasants in traditional dress.[21] Atatürk too featured in many documentary films made in the early years of the Republic, including in two made by Soviet directors: *Ankara, Heart of Turkey* (1934) by Sergei Yutkevich and Leo Arnshtam (which, according to Yutkevich used actors and staged scenes to make its point about Turkey's liberation and modernization) and a now lost film by Esfir Shub, *Forward Steps in the Turkish Revolution*. Relations with the Soviet Union were quite cordial until the late 1930s and, according to Özyürek, Atatürk held Soviet propaganda in high esteem, and even wanted Soviet directors to make a film about his life. Rather than have an actor portray him (there was a ban on actors playing him until the 1980s – which reminds us of the ban on an acted Lenin and Stalin between 1928 and 1937), Atatürk proposed playing himself, wearing his old outfits and acting out his earlier exploits.[22]

Few regimes failed to understand the power of the mass media or to use and manipulate them to convey a compelling narrative about the foundation of the state, the regime and its leader. In the early to mid-1930s, when attempts were being made to find a suitably distinguished biographer for Stalin (it was hoped that Maksim Gorky could be persuaded to act in this capacity), the possibility of making a biographical film about him was broached by Henri Barbusse.²³ In the end, neither the film nor a satisfactory biography ever emerged, although Yevgeny Dobrenko has proposed reading the *Short Course* (the Stalinist history of the Communist Party) as an essay in autobiography.²⁴ It was not, however, the desire to create an engaging biographical narrative (whether cinematographic or textual, novelistic or historical) that was unusual; nor was the censorship or manipulation of resultant material, or the involvement of Stalin's acolytes and officials in its production. Trotsky might scoff at the falsification of Stalinist history (and it was certainly blatant) but, as Lucy Riall has observed in her discussion of Garibaldi's partly fictionalized and certainly romanticized biographies and memoirs, they were not intended as autobiography or authentic history but as a 'political act'. The aim, she argues, was to establish a narrative of the Risorgimento, compelling enough to mobilize the population behind it. Garibaldi's memoirs were light on historical detail but enlarged on his childhood, his precocious and single-minded dedication to the cause of Italian liberty and unity. He omitted from his narrative important characters – notably his early sponsor Mazzini – and most living Italians in favour of dead comrades. A number of different versions of his memoirs were published by friends and comrades, including Alexandre Dumas, who recast the text as a set of 'canonical episodes', while adding sensational and personal details.²⁵

The analogy with popular versions of Stalin's biography is clear and affords a more interesting perspective on Stalin's biographies and history than simply rehearsing once again their many inaccuracies. Most of our heroes were involved in the construction of their biographies as leaders who had sacrificed themselves and their private lives to the creation of an order and state that would liberate the people from oppression and open up the prospect of national wellbeing and citizens' self-fulfilment.²⁶ The needs of the regime trumped the requirements of professional history, something not confined to states with leader cults. Despite the active intervention of the leaders themselves in shaping their image, cults were not the product of one man but were promoted by the circles around him, defenders of the regime, its professed ideals and of the powerful interests often vested in it. This was true not only of Lenin and Stalin, but also of Masaryk (and the ruling group around the 'Castle'), Piłsudski (initially the Legionaries and then the colonels who took power with the *sanacja*); Hindenburg (initially the military and government and later the political Right) and Atatürk (the military and ruling circle).²⁷

Rituals and cult practices

The leaders' services, real or imagined, furnished the pretext for the many honours conferred on them. Atatürk, Hindenburg and Masaryk, Piłsudski, Hitler and Stalin (and his colleagues) all had towns, streets and institutions named after them; some had medals, coins and stamps issued to mark important anniversaries.²⁸ In Poland, from 1920, military and combat organizations took the initiative of naming institutions and streets after Piłsudski. A second wave of renaming developed in 1928, on the tenth anniversary of the state, when many prestigious sites adopted his name and after his death, there was a final round of renaming. When Piłsudski was Minister for Defence, his office approved these proposals, just as Stalin's did. In Stalin's case, the adoption of Stalin's name by cities and institutions developed gradually in the mid- to late 1920s, but really took off after 1934, when hundreds of places adopted the name of Stalin or his fellow leaders (especially Kirov). Adopting the leader's name for a locality or organization enabled stakeholders (mayors, party officials, institutions etc.) to pledge their loyalty to the leader and regime and bid for his support and patronage.

These practices also purported to give effect to what Richard Wortman has called (in relation to Tsar Alexander II) 'the scenario of love'.[29] Other enactments of the scenario involved public rituals and ceremonies held in the leader's honour on key anniversaries, such as the foundation of the state or regime and the leader's birthday or name day. Masaryk, Piłsudski and Hindenburg, as well as Hitler and Stalin, were all acclaimed publicly in this way. Piłsudski's name day (on 19 March), although not a national holiday by law, was nonetheless marked by elaborate public rituals. Initiated by officers of the First Brigade of Polish Legionaries in 1915, they quickly developed wide political significance, although remaining until 1926 essentially a form of political demonstration by military circles in honour of their 'Creator, Restorer and Leader'. Thereafter, nationwide ceremonies were organized by a number of ministries, with soldiers, civil servants and schoolchildren given a free day. Official buildings and private houses were decorated with the national flag, and local dignitaries, military commanders and schoolchildren attended religious ceremonies and parades. In 1918, on the eve of independence, Piłsudski had received hundreds of thousands of postcards from the public with good wishes and lists with thousands of signatures, while in the early 1930s, when he was ill and recuperating abroad, the name day committee made strenuous efforts to ensure the widest possible public participation in the celebrations. It organized a postcard campaign, distributing cards with his portrait to institutions whose members were to buy and dispatch them. Schoolchildren too were expected to write cards of congratulations to him, thereby participating in the cult of 'the hero' and 'national genius', and learning to see Piłsudski as the 'Creator of our Morning'. Floods of letters and telegrams were sent to him in 1931 and 1932. The name day celebrations, at their height during his lifetime, were presented by the regime press as a 'school of personal education in the values which contribute to the survival (*Dauer*) and development of the state and the Polish people'.[30]

In a similar vein, Hitler's birthday on the 20 April was celebrated annually from 1933 and sometimes called 'Hitler Day'. Shop windows displayed garlanded busts of the Führer, streets and trains were decorated with festive bunting, Hitler lindens were planted, torchlight processions, parades and religious services were held, all to the accompaniment of the inflated rhetoric of the regime's main speakers.[31] By contrast, Stalin's putative birthday celebrations were marked by major public events only once a decade and took the form of official institutional rituals rather than street festivals before 1949, when his 70th jubilee was celebrated on an unprecedented scale and as a public holiday. Nonetheless, public enactments in the form of floods of telegrams of congratulation – which in 1929 and thereafter were published in the press for days on end – and the later mobilization of schoolchildren and the public, recall the Piłsudski cult described by Hein.³² There was, however, a significant difference in Poland: in the west of the country, there was resistance to Piłsudski's name day celebrations. The National Democrats were powerful in this region and preferred to celebrate his rival Jozsef Haller, whose birthday fell on the same day, while in Czechoslovakia, attempts were also made to compete with the Masaryk cult.³³ This was a significant difference from the Soviet Union, where the Stalin cult was unchallenged.³⁴

Rituals such as these enacted the language of love, which surrounded the leader in the form of political theatre. This 'scenario of love' was reflected not only in ritual but also in language and practices derived from it. The leader was represented, in iconography and rhetoric, as the father of the nation (not unlike the 'Tsar batiushka'). The title of 'Father Turk' was conferred on Atatürk in 1934, while Stalin was hailed as 'Father of the Peoples', and Masaryk as 'Tatiček' (daddy).³⁵ Most of our leaders also received more private and personal outpourings of the people's love (as well as, more practically, thousands of petitions and pleas for help). The idea of an intuitive and emotional bond between leader and people was typical of cults and suggested a more elemental and organic connection between leader and people than a mere transitory or contractual political relationship. Children were expected to sing songs about their love of the leader, learn poems about him and his care for them, while some composed verse assuring the leader of their devotion to him. In the post-war years in the Soviet Union, schoolchildren and adults were sometimes moved to verse on special occasions, offering the *vozhd'* poems, professing feelings of love or inspiration in terms that official rhetoric sought to inculcate.³⁶

In less prescriptive regimes, the leader also received poetic tributes. In 1917, Kerenskii was the subject of poetic effusions. Hindenburg's myth rested, Goltz believes, on genuine popular enthusiasm and during the war was partly shaped from below through brochures, songs and verse composed by members of the public, which were then published in newspapers.³⁷ Orzoff thinks that Masaryk also enjoyed real support or popularity, as ordinary people contributed to the cult through verse and gifts. As in the Soviet Union, professional writers such as Čapek provided the models which the young and naive might copy, as did a self-identified worker, who sent Masaryk a poem entitled 'To our Dear President'. All six verses started 'Our Tatiček, [daddy] Mr. President' and he outdid other versifiers, who had compared Masaryk to Jan Hus and Moses, by finding a parallel between Masaryk and Christ.³⁸ Popular 'love' of the leader was also expressed in gifts. 'Ordinary' citizens sent Masaryk folk art they had made for occasions such as his birthday. In 1930, for his 80th birthday, a worker painted a portrait of Masaryk with his grandson (after a famous photo); a barber made a portrait of him out of coloured hair, and a baker sent a tiny cake with 80 candles and a bust of the President in a bottle. So many offerings came to his office that the Masaryk Institute opened a Museum of Gifts, filled with amateur busts, portraits, collages, pictures, embroidered textiles etc.³⁹ Stalin too received gifts on Party and state occasions, as Lenin had before him, most famously in 1949 when some of the choice pieces were put on display in a special exhibition in Moscow, occupying three museums. In 1939, in honour of his 60th birthday, an exhibition of amateur art on the Stalin theme opened to the public. Although most of the gifts to Stalin were official and from institutions, they were explained as expressions of popular love and support, an interpretation, like the practices involved, which dated back to the early years of the Soviet regime.⁴⁰

Popular love could also be expressed in official settings, such as the leader's birthplace, houses he had lived or worked in, or his mausoleum. In his final years in power, Stalin's revolutionary life was commemorated in dozens of museums and memorial venues, including his birthplace in Gori. On the Georgian authorities' initiative in 1934, the town was spruced up and the family shack enveloped in a temple-like structure, transformed into a tourist attraction visited by thousands of apparently reverent visitors. It illustrated his humble origins, exceptional gifts, precocious dedication to the people's happiness, and, in the adjacent museum, the story of the revolution and Soviet state. Atatürk's birthplace in Thessalonica was handed over by the city to the Turkish government in 1937, allegedly to the leader's gratification, and turned into a museum located in the Turkish consulate. It illustrated the leader's virtuous childhood. Several other houses, some only very briefly associated with Atatürk, became museums, enshrining stylized visualizations of his career and character. His residence in Ankara, now also a museum, presents the President as modest and frugal.⁴¹ Mussolini's birthplace, Predappio, was not only revamped, like Gori, but the village was reconstructed in a more convenient location nearby and soon became immensely popular with thousands of visitors, individuals as well as groups, and a thriving trade was done in Mussoliniana.⁴² The idea of turning Piłsudski's birthplace into what was intended to become 'in eternal times a place of pilgrimage and a symbol of the love of independence and the boundless readiness for self-sacrifice for the Fatherland' was mooted in 1934, shortly before his death, by a group of sponsors who declared themselves inspired by the 'the deepest obligations of our hearts and love of all that is close to the person of the Leader of the Nation'. It was not taken in hand by the state until 1937–8, when its reconstruction was planned and a small museum inaugurated at the ceremonial opening of the site.⁴³ Venues such as these not merely paid homage to the leader, they incarnated the regime's values – often in touching, human terms – and put them on display for consumption by the public. In contemporary Turkey, Glyptis observed the interest displayed by visitors to the museum in Atatürk's mausoleum complex, as they crowded around the exhibits of his personal effects, including his rowing machine, his clothes, his stuffed dog and gifts he received. The museum shop did a roaring trade in Atatürk artefacts of every description (as does that in the Museum to the Great Patriotic War, where a great variety of Staliniana is on sale).⁴⁴

Post-mortem cults

Nothing could be more indicative of the fact that leader cults were not merely, or even primarily, about satisfying the leader's personal vanity and lust for power than the survival of post-mortem cults. The Atatürk cult, which has been more resilient than most, illustrates this: orchestrated by the authorities, it was promoted especially after his death (in this like the Lenin cult) to strengthen the state, communicate its core values and aims and forge a common sense of purpose and identity among the public.⁴⁵

The cult of Piłsudski was promoted assiduously after his death by the ruling colonels due, Hein believes, to their lack of legitimacy and popularity. The quest to mark Piłsudski's death in a fitting manner prompted an enormous number of projected memorials. A mausoleum for his heart, which was to be interred with his mother in a Vilnius cemetery, was envisaged but like some other plans was never entirely realized due to the war. The most bizarre memorial to him was Cracow's revival of the supposedly Slavic idea of an earth mound. Proposed in 1934 for a hill outside the city, the memorial placed earth from all battlegrounds where Poland had fought for its freedom in 3,000 ornate urns in an elaborate ceremony. An explanatory museum, post office and chapel were planned, but did not open before the war, although the mound was completed in July 1937 and opened with great pomp in the presence of the President and government.[46]

The most imposing of these memorials was the vast memorial complex built between 1944 and 1953 in Anitkabir in Ankara, following a competition held in 1941. In Glyptis's analysis (and the memorial's own website) it is a hybrid symbolic narrative in stone, illustrating the various strands of the myth of national unity and the greatness of Atatürk. At his cenotaph in the central building, when the author visited, visitors of all ages and backgrounds filed past solemnly, some leaving flowers, others assuming prayer-like poses, with heads bowed and hands clasped together. Some bent to kiss the steps leading to the crypt and Atatürk's sarcophagus. A tearful elderly man wrote in the visitors' book: 'Great father, thank you'. Leafing through the book, she noted that this message seemed typical: all seemed to be addressed to the 'great father' and spoke of love and gratitude. This resembles Steinbeck's observation of visitors' behaviour at Gori and the tenor of comments in visitor-books there.[47] Not everything about the Atatürk cult was staged by the state: in the 1990s, the inhabitants of a remote poor village claimed to see his profile appear on a local hillside as the setting sun's shadow fell on it and hailed this as a kind of miracle, attesting to Atatürk's greatness. The military (the chief guardians of his myth) and the media took the 'miracle' up and it became a significant and presumably profitable local festival, with several thousand people gathering to witness the phenomenon between 25 June and 5 July annually.[48]

Not all our cults were as enduring as that of Atatürk. Those of Masaryk and Piłsudski were discarded after the communists came to power, as their message of national liberation ran counter to new state narratives. While Stalin too was embalmed and placed in the mausoleum beside Lenin, his heirs rapidly dismantled his cult, despite considerable public confusion and criticism.[49] A number of reasons may be adduced for this: insofar as the cult contributed to his power and hegemony over his colleagues and the Party *nomenklatura*, it was neither needed nor desired by them. Its legitimizing and mobilizing functions were replaced by the culture of war victory, and the figure of Lenin was available to fulfil Stalin's symbolic role in the regime's myth of origins.

Conclusion

The cults that developed around our subjects shared many features: ubiquitous iconography symbolizing the values that the leader incarnated; an authoritative narrative about the leader's self-sacrificing and decisive role in the struggle to save the nation/state and lead it to victory; and finally, rituals that mobilized the public around the regime, its goals and its leader. The Stalin cult shared all these characteristics to a greater or lesser extent but what differentiated it? One aspect of the cult that struck most visitors as exceptional was its inflation and extravagance after the mid-1930s. The Party's political culture (its patronage networks and communication conventions), growing state violence and the prevailing international climate contributed to this. In the politically-fraught context of the Terror and impending war, the political and cultural elites competed to signal their loyalty on the 20th anniversary of the revolution in November 1937 and Stalin's 60th birthday in December 1939 and all lower actors necessarily followed suit. Cult performance was at this point largely a survival strategy, while even inadvertent or light-hearted *lèse majesté* incurred severe punishment. Unlike most of our comparators, the Stalin cult was incontestable: subordinate cults (of Lenin and of lesser figures, such as Kirov) were to some extent constructive of Stalin's and generally permitted, but challenges, real or imagined, were outlawed. Iconoclasm was treated as subversion. If throughout the 1930s, the regime felt insecure and under siege – and was correspondingly savage in its repression of perceived dissent – it was the context of the Terror that lent to the Stalin cult its key distinguishing feature. Nothing comparable was present in Masaryk's Czechoslovakia, Weimar Germany or even in Atatürk's Turkey.[50] In this, Soviet practice was closer to policy in the latter days of Mussolini's Italy and, in particular, wartime Nazi Germany. Yet, even if the political culture and context inflated the cult, it did not account for its inception, main forms and functions over time.

There was nothing exceptional about the fact that the Stalin cult was manufactured rather than spontaneous, promoted in the first instance by powerful politicians and supervised by the leader himself. This was the pattern in all our cases. Playing to the leader's personality and his drive for power also played a role in all these cases, and the cult certainly bolstered Stalin's power and hegemony. Yet the number and diversity of contexts in which these cults developed strongly suggest that they also served broader political purposes. What these functions were emerges from the fact that they used the same techniques: the aim was to communicate a meaningful narrative about the state and regime, its origins and purposes, and to situate the public within this story while inculcating the attitudes and behaviour it was proper to adopt. Cults encouraged the 'common people' to communicate with the leadership within a narrowly defined framework of petitions, letters, gifts etc., to participate in new rituals of belonging and step into new prescribed identities, thereby signalling their loyalty as right-thinking and right-feeling citizens. Our cults emerged in new polities and confirm the growing understanding of cults as a tool in identity-forging and state-building in an age of mass politics and modernization.

6

From heroic lion to streetfighter: Historical legacies and the leader cult in twentieth-century Hungary

Balázs Apor

In his satirical dystopian novel, *Feleségverseny* (*Wife Contest*, 2009), the Hungarian writer György Spíró depicts a scene in which university students and unemployed graduates discuss the most suitable system of government for a future Hungary – in a pub. During the debate the main speaker, Akerál Orkán, argues that in its thousand-year-long history none of the political systems that emerged in the country truly reflected Hungarian customs and the sentiments of the population, as they were all imposed from above. Using historical examples from the twentieth century, Orkán highlights the absurd anachronisms manifested in all three major political systems that were implemented in the country: Miklós Horthy's right-wing authoritarian regime in the inter-war period, the Communist dictatorship in the second half of the century, and liberal democracy after 1989. Horthy's regime is depicted as a 'virtual kingdom', indicating the fact that it was a monarchy without an actual monarch; János Kádár's and the Communist party's claim to equality and puritanism is contrasted with the 'royal cult' around the figure of the party secretary; whilst the anachronistic aspects of the post-1989 Hungarian republic are illustrated by the fact that the new elite chose a monarchical symbol – the royal crown – to decorate the state's new coat-of-arms. Assessing the absurdly interwoven legacies of the past century, Orkán eventually comes to the conclusion that the political system that would be most harmonious with the Hungarian psyche is a communist kingdom.

This scene and the metaphor of 'communist kingdom' encapsulate the main theme of this chapter, the interconnected, multi-layered and entangled legacies of the past and their impact on the present. It highlights the absurd blending of seemingly antagonistic symbolic systems in twentieth-century Hungary with a particular emphasis on monarchical symbols – virtual kingdom, royal cult, crowned crest – and their remarkable endurance despite the comings and goings of radically different political regimes: right-wing authoritarian, communist dictatorial and democratic. The scene also depicts a patrimonial thread in twentieth-century Hungarian political culture: the propensity to perceive politics in personalized terms and a certain belief in the ideal of a strong, but benevolent leader that brings about stability and social harmony.

Although the scene only refers to János Kádár's 'royal cult' in post-1956 Hungary, the cultic veneration of political leaders was a phenomenon that, somewhat anachronistically, resurfaced in all three political systems that Orkán described. From Emperor Franz Joseph through Miklós Horthy to the Stalinist leader Mátyás Rákosi, many political leaders in twentieth-century Hungary were represented in cultic terms, although to a significantly varying degree. Such representations also produced the blending of different symbolic systems and historical legacies. Miklós Horthy, the Regent of inter-war Hungary, was no king, but his cult embraced dynastic elements whilst the Stalinist dictator Rákosi was portrayed as heir to national traditions despite his role in turning the country into a satellite of the Soviet empire. Despite the many paradoxes, inconsistent images and radical ruptures in cult-building practices in Hungary, the leader cult was a recurring feature of the country's recent history, and it has played an important role in the symbolic politics of the respective regimes.

Moreover, the phenomenon seems to have made a reappearance in recent years. One of its manifestations – that echoes Orkán's dystopian vision of Hungarian political culture – was a wooden carving of Prime Minister Viktor Orbán wearing a crown that was spotted at a village fair in Szilvásvárad in August 2018. The timing was probably not accidental: the proximity of 20 August, the national holiday that celebrates the foundation of the Hungarian state, suggests that the artist considered Orbán a worthy successor of Saint Stephen, the medieval king who established the Hungarian kingdom at the turn of the first millennium.[1] The image went viral on social media platforms and triggered a range of responses, from disgust to support. Although the carving is most likely an isolated example of spontaneous cultic adulation and not a government-sanctioned product, it nonetheless signals the return of certain social practices – the irrational veneration of political leaders – that were thought to have gone out of fashion. The absurd fusion of monarchical symbolism, folk art (wooden carving) and iconography indicates that long-term historical legacies of the past – legacies that include communism, the authoritarian regime of the inter-war period, as well as the monarchical/imperial past – continue to exert an influence in present-day Hungarian politics.

This chapter is concerned with the resilience, accumulation and peculiar interaction of different historical legacies, viewed from the perspective of the leader cult. It aims to explore the extent to which the notion of 'historical legacy' can account for the reappearance of the cultic representation of political leaders in recent Hungary. Can the frequent resurrection of the phenomenon be linked to the existence of certain 'deep structures' in Hungarian society, or was it always 'imposed' on the Hungarians, as Orkán suggested? The chapter will also address the importance of specific historical circumstances and the role of novelty and innovation in the construction of cultic images.

Persistence, change, legacy

The historiographical/theoretical assumptions that inform the argument in this chapter emerged in the context of debates on the role of historical legacies in shaping post-Communist development, as well as reflections on the modernity of the Soviet system. Indeed, the study of Communist systems contributed significantly to discussions about the nature of modernity and to debates about the features and functions of historical legacies. Shmuel Eisenstadt's oft-cited notion of 'multiple modernities', for example, was developed, in part, as an attempt to extend the scope of modernity theory to include the Communist experience, and it also fertilized historiographical debates about the modernity of the Soviet state in the 2000s.[2] At the same time, the study of historical legacies, or 'Leninist legacies', grew out of the field of post-Communist transitology in the social sciences that revolved around the institutional transformations that accompanied the dismantling of Soviet-type regimes in Eastern Europe, and the construction of democratic political systems in the region.[3]

The key themes that connect historiographical debates about the modernity of Soviet-type regimes, the study of historical legacies and Orkán's fictional analysis of the Hungarian psyche include the accumulation of historical experience and the dynamics between persistence and change. More specifically, it is the endurance and/or the transformation of certain social, political or economic structures and practices that connect the relevant academic and literary texts. In discussions about Soviet modernity this theme is mainly framed by the modernity versus neo-traditionalism debate that a number of historians of the Soviet Union have contributed to since the early 2000s. Advocates of the modernity paradigm generally argue that the Soviet Union was a quintessentially modern state that created a vast bureaucratic apparatus and pursued a modernizing agenda that transformed social structures, property relations, the educational and health systems, social identities, and so on.[4] Critics of Soviet modernity, on the other hand, while not necessarily questioning the modernizing aspirations of the Russian Bolsheviks, highlighted the persistence or the revival of certain other, more traditional political and social structures and practices. Early critics of the Soviet system, such as Nikolai Berdyaev or Nikolai Timasheff, famously observed the resurrection of pre-revolutionary practices in the fields of religion, education or family life, whilst the neo-traditionalism argument, advocated by a number of historians since the 2000s, holds that while the Bolshevik policies were motivated by modernizing ambitions, the outcome of their actions provoked the return or survival of traditional practices and social identities, sometimes in a new form.[5]

One of the most controversial criticisms of the modernist school came from the historian J. Arch Getty, who argued in his 2013 book, *Practicing Stalinism*, that 'from the angle of practice, it is possible to see Russia as an example not of modernity, but of its opposite: an example of the persistence of apparently archaic practices existing in a particular, ongoing relationship to modern institutions'.[6] The book's primary aim was to analyse the patrimonial features of the Stalinist regime and the specific methods whereby Stalin's personal rule was construed and sustained. The author claimed that Stalin's power rested on personal relations and the careful, albeit often brutal, manipulation of informal political networks or 'clans'. The book contends that this specific aspect of Stalinism was not a novel feature of Russian political life but part of the political toolkit of Russian autocrats since the time of Ivan the Terrible. Getty's detailed analysis of Stalinist clientelism draws frequent parallels between the Stalinist era and various historical epochs, including the present, and claims that the dynamics of oligarchical rule defined and continues to define Russian political culture to a significant extent.

The cult of the leader enjoys a prominent place in Getty's narrative. He reflects in detail on both the cult of Stalin and the cultic veneration provincial party leaders created around their own persona, and argues that the cult was the symbolic cornerstone of Russian patrimonial rule. The book holds that the irrational adulation of certain individuals was a key element in the construction of authority (patron–client) relations in the Russian oligarchical system, and its rituals promoted the norms and values that members of the 'clans' were expected to internalize. Getty claims that:

> Leadership cults at all levels of Soviet society and the manifestations of leader cults after Stalin suggest that something more is at work here than an individual's personality needs; something more than local leaders copying Stalin who had consciously modeled himself on Lenin, or had simply selected a method of rule based on the clan heritage of his native Georgia. It simply will not do to imagine Stalin and his associates rationally choosing rule-by-cult among a menu of available options, or even consciously choosing patrimonial rule. Stalin did not just copy Lenin (or Ivan the Terrible), and regional party secretaries did not just copy Stalin. Because we find this understanding of politics and government from Riurik to Putin, at all levels of the hierarchies at all times and places, it was inescapable. This was the deep structure by which Russia had always been governed. There were no alternative models to contemplate.[7]

Although Getty's book triggered virulent criticisms, the emphasis on the endurance of specific practices of exercising power – patrimonialism, clientelism, nepotism – is not unjustified.[8] The emphasis on the persistence of 'deep structures' in Russian society, in fact, echoes the arguments of Cold War political scientists that analysed aspects of political cultures in the then-communist regimes of Central and Eastern Europe. While Getty focuses specifically on how Stalin constructed and maintained dictatorial rule through patrimonial practices, his argument resonates with the claims of analysts in the 1970s–1980s that highlighted phenomena such as popular distrust for institutions, the personalization of politics, the importance of informal social relations, the popular appeal of a paternalistic state, and a certain mythical perception of the distant political leader ('naïve monarchism') in the relative stability of Soviet-type regimes.[9] Moreover, historians and social scientists whose attention turned toward the long-term impact of communism in Eastern Europe in the past few decades have identified a very similar set of features in the social and political life of post-Communist societies. In works on the historical legacies of Communism there has emerged a tacit consensus about some of the common features of post-Communism that include the continuing importance of corruption, nepotism and informal social networks; weak democratic institutions; ethnic nationalism; a strong distrust with institutions and politics; and the lingering dominance of Communist institutions of control and surveillance.[10]

The cultic representation of political leaders rarely features in such lists, in part due to the fading away of the appeal of strongmen in post-1989 Central and Eastern

Europe. The one notable exception is Vladimir Putin in Russia, whose return to authoritarian leadership methods in the 2000s and revisionist take on the Stalinist past have triggered significant scholarly, as well as journalistic, attention in the past two decades. Apart from the Russian case, however, the cultic representation of political leaders was not considered to be a remnant of the communist past. How, then, can one account for the emergence of blatantly cultic images of political leaders in Orbán's Hungary? How can one explain the return to the symbolic language of patrimonialism after decades of democratization? If the leader cult was not a component of the immediate post-Communist historical baggage in Hungary, can one still claim that its manifestations originate in the ritual practices of the recent past? Can the emerging cult of Orbán be considered a reflection of the persistence of past practices at all?

It is the notion of historical legacies that could assist in coming to terms with the revival of cultic practices after a significant rupture in the realm of symbolic politics. 'Historical legacy' is a term that has gained academic currency since the fall of Communism in 1989, but it remained somewhat under-theorized. One of the most recent systematic theoretical and empirical engagements with the term was offered by Mark Beissinger and Stephen Kotkin in a 2014 edited volume that defined the notion as 'a durable causal relationship between past institutions and policies on subsequent practices or beliefs, long beyond the life of the regimes, institutions, and policies that gave birth to them'.[11] What differentiates a legacy from historical continuities, according to the authors, is the element of rupture between the past and the present that gives rise to new political, social and economic structures. Historical legacies, therefore, embrace change as well as persistence, and often manifest themselves in the revival of enduring institutions, practices, and so on, in a modified form.

At the same time, the theoretical framework of legacies enables scholars to analyse the accumulation, overlap and blending of various historical experiences in specific contexts. The interconnected and cumulative aspects of legacies – Ottoman, Roman, Byzantine, Communist – was discussed by Maria Todorova in the historical development of the Balkans, also highlighting that legacies often remain un-reflected – undetected even – and that they sometimes work at a subliminal level.[12] A similar feature of the interaction between past and present – the unpredictable blending of the legacies of distinct historical epochs – was also analysed by Vladimir Tismaneanu, although he did not specifically address the concept of legacy. In his analysis of political myth after the collapse of Communism, Tismaneanu argued that the ideological remnants of Leninism blended with some elements of inter-war nationalism to produce a hybrid political myth, which he labelled 'Stalino-fascist baroque'.[13] The fusion of elements of distinct historical legacies was made possible by a degree of overlap between the two ideologies (communism and fascism); authoritarianism, collectivism and virulent anti-Westernism characterized both.[14]

The history of the leader cult in Hungary reflects the accumulation of different historical legacies and the interaction between persistence and change. A *longue durée* approach to the subject highlights continuities and ruptures in the development of cultic phenomena in Hungarian political culture, as well as the blending or fusion of seemingly conflicting symbolic systems.

Monarchy, nationalism and the leader cult

The interaction (including the blending of) and conflict between different patterns of leadership representations – old and new, traditional and modern – intensified in the late nineteenth century with the advent of modernity in Hungarian politics. The Compromise of 1867 and the establishment of the Austro-Hungarian empire resulted in the gradual liberalization of political culture, the emergence of party politics and political/social movements, as well as the extension of political franchise in the kingdom of Hungary. Such changes had serious limitations, however, and unfolded in a historical context that continued to be dominated by authoritarian styles of leadership and in which the emperor – Franz Joseph – retained the means to interfere and influence Hungarian political developments. Franz Joseph's leadership, the political culture at the court, as well as the representations of the Emperor reflected the continuing dominance of the absolutist tradition in the Austro-Hungarian Empire. In the context of rapid economic modernization – and the social upheaval it provoked – the symbolic language of absolutism seemed increasingly anachronistic. As historian András Gerő argued, Franz Joseph had become 'a relic of a previous age'.[15] The emperor's attachment to the practices, rituals and myths of absolutism was remarkably consistent and characterized different phases of his rule, despite significant transformations in the political, social and economic dynamics of the empire after 1867. He continued to believe in the absolutist premise that the emperor ruled by the grace of God and that it was the responsibility of his subjects to obey him. He was unaffected by the emergence of mass politics and the notion of popular sovereignty, and therefore he had little concerns about his own personal popularity:

> he remained entirely self-consistent in his belief that there was no need for his Hungarian subjects' approval. All he was aiming for was acceptance. He cared nothing for devotion: he simply did not recognize any intrinsic value in such attachment. The "will of the people" was of absolutely no significance to an emperor reigning by God's grace.[16]

He made very few gestures to appeal to the population – or the Hungarian political elite, for that matter – yet he expected absolute loyalty in return.

Franz Joseph's adherence to traditions of absolutist rule was reflected in the rigidity and formalistic nature of court rituals (audiences, balls etc.), in his postures and public appearances, and in the propagandistic representations of his image in the press and other forms of media at the time. Court rituals and personal interactions with the emperor remained highly formalistic, brief, and ultimately very impersonal and superficial. His public postures and interactions with various people – mostly members of the political elite – also remained dry and formalistic. His close adherence to military style and discipline resulted in the image of the emperor as an individual who lacked any personal charm.[17] Yet representations of the Kaiser endowed his figure with charismatic traits that created a distance between the actual person and his representations. His cultic representations remained rather generic and they were attributed to the office of the emperor rather than Franz Joseph the individual. Official representations of him emphasized the role of the sovereign as a father to his subjects. The image of the father that was linked to the emperor's public persona described him as a stern but benevolent father who protects his children (subjects), but metes out punishment in cases of misbehaviour (uprisings, protests etc.).[18] At the same time, the Kaiser was portrayed as the embodiment of the empire, the symbol of unity in an ethnically and culturally diverse political entity.

Representations of the sovereign as a wise, benevolent, courageous king representing the interests of his Hungarian subjects were promoted and widely circulated on the occasion of his birthdays, official visits, the coronation and its anniversaries, the celebrations of the millennium of Hungarian statehood in 1895–6, and so on. Despite Franz Joseph's role in crushing the Hungarian War of Independence, the retaliation that followed and the creation of the neo-absolutist regime of the 1850s, every effort was made in official propaganda to portray him as a 'national' king. During the twenty-fifth anniversary of his coronation inscriptions decorating Budapest assured the monarch of the unbreakable loyalty of his subjects and declared that 'the king is the first among Hungarians!'[19] At another occasion, during the lavish celebrations of the millennium of Hungarian statehood (in 1896), the gala in the Opera that concluded the events was choreographed in a way to emphasize the symbolic unity of the ruler and his subjects. In the final act, singers representing the various classes of the nation – peasants, soldiers, noblemen etc. – who gathered around the statues of the royal couple on the stage, sang the Hungarian anthem while turning towards the royal box. The king and the queen also stood up and faced their subjects – as well as their own images – while listening to the national anthem.[20] Attempts to portray the Habsburg monarch as a national king were even more emphatic during the celebrations of the king's 70th birthday in 1900. One poem (by Andor Kozma), for example, declared him the heir of the state founder king Saint Stephen, and called him a heroic lion who would remain the 'fortress of Hungarian freedom',[21] whilst one propagandistic article argued that 'since the reign of the great Mathias Corvinus, there has never been a Hungarian king whose virtues could compare with those with our present king'. The article boldly stated that 'it is no exaggeration to say that there is no other nation in the world today which would surround its ruler with a more deeply felt adulation than the Hungarian nation feels for its crowned apostolic king'.[22]

The attempts of the state to promote the notion of a national king who is adored by his subjects remained ambivalent and failed to resonate with most parts of the Hungarian population. It was the leader of the failed War of Independence, Lajos Kossuth whose 'grassroots' cults became all pervasive, and not the king who suppressed the uprising. At the same time, there was a remarkable tendency to look for traces of Hungarianness in other members of the Habsburg family. The growing cult of Franz Joseph's wife, Elizabeth, reflected the popular aspiration to identify with a representative of the royal family who allegedly nurtured pro-Hungarian sentiments.[23] This resulted in significant paradoxes in Hungarian symbolic politics around the turn of the century: there was support for the monarchy, but not for the monarch, and there emerged an unresolved tension in the symbolic space between the official cult of Franz Joseph and popular adoration of his nemesis, Lajos Kossuth.[24] At the same time, cultic representations in general witnessed a certain degree of symbolic devaluation in the late nineteenth century, due to the increasing tendency to describe other prominent political figures in charismatic terms. For example, the mastermind of the Compromise, Ferenc Deák, was also described as the 'Hungarian Moses', similar to the leader of the 1848–9 War of Independence, Kossuth.[25] Hungarian symbolic space was becoming crowded and that also contributed – to an extent – to the growth of popular indifference towards the cult of Franz Joseph.

Franz Joseph's was a cult that was built most intensely in periods of stabilization and it did not spring from an extraordinary or 'charismatic' event. Although he made a good impression on the Hungarian political elite at the time of his coming to the throne in 1848, his role in the suppression of the war of independence ruined whatever reputation he had in the country. His popularity increased to some extent during the upheaval of the First World War, but it was quickly buried under the rubbles of the Austro-Hungarian Empire in 1918. The collapse of the empire and the disintegration of historic Hungary, however, amounted to an extraordinary event that gave rise to the emergence of cultic figures, most notably Miklós Horthy, who came to occupy the position of head of state (Regent) subsequently and stayed in power for over two decades.

The anachronisms that characterized inter-war Hungary have been analysed extensively by historians.[26] While the economy and society continued on the path to modernization, legacies of the past continued to loom large. This was reflected in the survival of semi-feudal – 'neo-baroque' – social structures, the reconstruction of the state as a monarchy (without a monarch), and the diffusion of a political culture that was overloaded with political symbolism. The cult of Horthy represented the interaction of historical legacies and the radically changed political circumstances that were triggered by the dissolution of the Habsburg monarchy, and it was characterized by the blurring of dynastic traditions of representing rulers and novel techniques of depicting military figures after the First World War. The emergence of distinct layers of representation could be – in part – explained by the origins of Horthy's cult. His rise to prominence is linked to a significant historical rupture – the collapse of the Empire and the Hungarian state – but at the same time, his figure represented continuity with the country's imperial past. As a celebrated war hero and a former adjutant of Franz Joseph, he could be portrayed as the embodiment of tradition, but also as a new type of military hero who arose in the midst of chaos to restore order and battle a new enemy: Bolshevism.

The cult of Horthy sprang from radical right-wing military circles that came to play a prominent role in the events that unfolded after the dissolution of the Austro-Hungarian Empire.[27] It was the officers of Horthy's National Army that initially promoted messianic images of the leader at the time of the Hungarian Republic of Councils in 1919, and portrayed him as the saviour of the nation. The metaphors most often associated with Horthy from the beginning reflected his background as a naval officer (admiral) and depicted him as the helmsman who would navigate his ship (the country/nation) on troubled waters into a safe haven.[28] In a country that witnessed the collapse of the state, the emergence of a communist dictatorship, paramilitary violence and foreign invasion, the image of the strong leader who would restore order had a significant appeal. In this historical context, the image of Horthy absorbed messianic features and was enriched by biblical metaphors. The leader was described as a man of providence, and 'the saviour of the country' whose mission was to save 'the crucified Hungary'. In propagandistic depictions of the time it was Horthy's sacred mission to 'resurrect' Hungary that suffered 'martyrdom' and was 'mutilated' as a result of the significant territorial losses ratified by the treaty of Trianon in June 1920. At the same time, he was portrayed as 'the new Árpád' – the Captain of the Hungarian tribes that conquered the Carpathian basin in the ninth century – who was sent by 'the God of the Hungarians' to restore the integrity of historic Hungary.[29]

With the consolidation of the regime in the mid-1920s, the most irrational elements of the cult were toned down, and Horthy's imagery assumed more traditional features. He came to be represented as a head of state who stood above party politics and as the personification of stability, law and order.[30] His status at the epicentre of Hungarian symbolic politics was confirmed by 'the law of gratitude' that was passed by the Hungarian parliament in 1930, which codified Horthy's image as the saviour of the nation and the architect of the country's rebuilding.[31] The rituals of the cult were gradually standardized with their format and style borrowed from the dynastic tradition. Horthy's visits to cities, to the countryside and to the territories that were re-annexed after the Vienna Awards mimicked the choreography of Franz Joseph's visits decades earlier. Similar to the emperor before him, he became the centre of public attention on the occasion of prominent anniversaries, such as birthday celebrations, and his cultic image was promoted by the press through acts of renaming, the erection of busts, the publication of biographies and the creation of works of arts, mostly paintings. Horthy was also portrayed mostly in his uniform to emphasize his military prowess, but his traditionalist depictions included the image of a stern and benevolent father figure ('our dear father') as well. As in the pre-war epoch, representations of the encounters between the leader and the led revolved mostly around the themes of love and gratitude.

While the main rituals, the key tropes and the stylistic features of the Horthy cult were inherited from the past, its content was the product of the specific historical context. The cult was entangled with the cult of irredentism, and Horthy became the symbolic embodiment of revisionist ideology that dominated Hungarian political culture in the inter-war period.[32] As the champion of revisionism, Horthy personified Hungarian aspirations to achieve the revision of the treaty of Trianon and the territorial changes it enforced. Historical parallels were employed excessively to emphasize the Regent's prerogative to restore the integrity of historic Hungary. He was often called 'the first Hungarian man', and his figure was compared to great leaders and state-builder kings and politicians of the past, ranging from Captain Árpád through Saint Stephen, Saint Ladislaus, Béla IV, and János Hunyadi to István Széchenyi, Ferenc Deák and Lajos Kossuth.[33] For example, one newspaper article, published in 1937, claimed that 'since our first regent, János Hunyadi there has not been either a king or a freedom-fighter national leader who was supported in such rock solid unity by this discordant people than Miklós Horthy'. One genealogist went even further and argued – in 1938 – that Horthy was a direct descendant of the first Hungarian royal dynasty, the House of Árpád that died out in 1301.[34] Such historical parallels were supposed to reaffirm the idea of Horthy's historical mission to restore Hungary's historical borders. This idea gained substance and further momentum after the two Vienna Awards, which gave a significant boost to Horthy's popularity and led to the escalation of his cult. He personally visited a number of re-captured cities – riding in on a white horse – and was labelled as 'liberator' and 're-taker of the country' in official propaganda at the time.[35]

The cult of Horthy remained a central feature of Hungarian symbolic politics in the inter-war period, and due to its connection to the trauma of the treaty of Trianon – Hungary lost two-thirds of its former territories – it had a significant appeal to various social groups. As the symbolic embodiment of the nation's revival, Horthy assumed sacrosanct qualities – similarly to Franz Joseph – as demonstrated by the increasing number of *lése-régent* (slander) cases that were related to his name in the 1930s.[36] The dynastic aspects of his cult were further amplified by the election of his son, István, to vice-regent in 1942. At the same time, the cult of Horthy was not a solitary phenomenon in the symbolic landscape of Hungarian political culture at the time. Similar to the pre-war period, there emerged a number of individuals who were represented in cultic terms and attracted a certain following. Such cults arose mostly from radical nationalist circles in the 1930s, but a tendency to represent prominent political figures with the help of irrational imagery was also apparent in the conservative-liberal sphere, as demonstrated for example in some images of prime minister István Bethlen. These representations never challenged the symbolic primacy of Horthy, even if they employed markedly similar rituals, metaphors and images, such as 'leader' and 'father'. Prime minister Gyula Gömbös, for example, who was one of Horthy's close associates in 1919, was depicted as the leader of the nation during his tenure (1932–6), and his premature death in 1936 contributed to the further growth of his cult.[37] As opposed to Horthy, however, representations of Gömbös drew their prime inspiration from militant, radical, right-wing (i.e. fascist) cults, in which the leader played a much more prominent role. Following international – mostly Italian – models, Gömbös's constructed persona was tied to organic conceptions of the nation and to the ambition of creating a whole 'new world' populated by a 'new type of man'.[38] Such a radical attempt at refashioning the human soul was not linked to the symbolic figure of Horthy, which remained more distant and vague in order to appeal to broader sections of the population.

Similar to the official cult of Franz Joseph, the coordinated adulation of Horthy was also ended by a world war. Since the symbolic persona of both leaders was intimately entangled with state- and nation-building efforts and official ideologies (monarchism/nationalism), the cataclysmic collapse of the state in the two wars discredited their cults and destroyed institutions of cult building. Yet, just like after the dissolution of the Austro-Hungarian monarchy in 1918, the historical rupture of 1945 was also followed by the revival of cult-building practices, this time under the aegis of a communist dictatorship.

Hungarian communism and the leader cult

The role of historical legacies in the re-emergence of the leader cult after 1945 is less straightforward than in the context of post-Trianon Hungary. The Horthy regime was conscious and systematic in its efforts to recycle monarchical imagery, nurture national traditions and promote the illusion of national grandeur through the dissemination of romanticized images of the past. Horthy himself was the living embodiment of historical continuity with the monarchy, and he oversaw the resurrection of certain myths and ritual practices of pre-war Hungary. In contrast, the post-1945 period witnessed a complete elite change in society and a radical reconfiguration of the institutional structure of the state. The communists who seized power in 1948–9 were members of a small, illegal party in the inter-war period, and many of them were either in prison most of the time or in exile in the Soviet Union or elsewhere. Although they were familiar with the socio-political and cultural conditions of inter-war Hungary and had a relatively sophisticated approach to national traditions, they had a very limited role in shaping symbolic politics in the country between the two world wars. The historical rupture after 1945 – in terms of myths and rituals – was, therefore, larger than after 1918. In addition, the primary model for the Hungarian communists was Stalinism, including its political symbolism and ritual culture. Their attitude towards the Horthy-regime remained antagonistic and consistently unsympathetic.

Nonetheless, the communist version of the leader cult shared many similarities with its historical antecedents. In fact, a significant proportion of the cult's vocabulary – the non-Marxist segment – and some of its rituals, including the leader's visits to the countryside (which involved raising triumphal arches) and gala performances in the Opera seem to have been borrowed directly from the previous epochs. It appears that despite their general antagonism towards the Horthy era, the communists retained a pragmatic stance towards its symbolic politics. Moreover, there is anecdotal evidence that suggests that the communist leadership's decision to put its leader Rákosi at the forefront in 1945 was, in part, provoked by their acknowledgement of successful cult building under the Horthy regime.[39] Instead of a tsar, the Hungarian communists recognized that the people needed a Horthy.

The communists made a significant effort to emphasize their embeddedness in Hungarian national traditions. They claimed to be the 'true heirs' of the nation's 'progressive' traditions and argued that their historical mission was to realize the unfulfilled aspirations of Hungarian freedom fighters, including Ferenc Rákóczi and Lajos Kossuth.[40] They also recycled the trope of 'the second land-taking', and they likened the construction of socialism and the attempt to create the socialist 'new man' to the feats of Captain Árpád.[41] With sovietization already underway, they were in the position to hijack the centenary celebrations of the 1848–9 war of independence and use the event for political purposes and to legitimize the take-over process. They also relied heavily on national symbolism in their propaganda – sometimes at the expense of Soviet revolutionary symbols – and continued to observe and celebrate national holidays. National imagery was used in the representations of their leaders, too: Rákosi was portrayed as the new Kossuth, whereas the distant Stalin was portrayed as the 'best friend of the Hungarian nation' and the guarantor of its freedom.

The tendency to borrow from the vocabulary and the ritual repository of the Horthy era, and the party's deliberate strategy to represent its leaders in national terms, seem to support the argument that the emergence of the communist leader cult in post-war Hungary was – in part, at least – the result of historical legacies, i.e. the revival of a phenomenon in a new form after a historical rupture. However, it needs to be emphasized that the main reason for the return of cultic leaders to the Hungarian political landscape was post-war sovietization, which included the importation and adaptation of Stalinist rituals and techniques of representation to the Hungarian context. The adoption of the leader cult, therefore, was not (only) instinctual – in contrast to what Getty claims in relation to the Soviet context – but part of a conscious strategy to adopt the Soviet model and recycle techniques of cult building from the Hungarian past at the same time.

Although the national components of the Stalinist leader cult were toned down in Hungary after the Soviet–Yugoslav rift and the stigmatization of 'national deviation', they never disappeared from representations of Rákosi and remained important aspects of his constructed persona until 1956. However, the primary model that was used in cult-building strategies in Hungary in the 1950s was the Stalin cult. The cult of Rákosi emerged as part of a dual cult, in which the role of the distant 'divinity' was reserved for Stalin, whose 'best Hungarian apprentice' Rákosi acted as some sort of 'high priest'.[42] The Hungarian party leader was most often portrayed as a benevolent father figure who was surrounded by the gratitude and love of the people for his contribution to the construction of socialism. Rákosi was also depicted as the leader who directed the country on the road to the socialist future, but in stark contrast with the cults of Horthy and Franz Joseph – and also of Stalin – he was rarely represented as a heroic military figure. At the same time, he was routinely described as the teacher of the nation, whose wise guidance was the guarantee of a happier (socialist) future. This image was related to the central status of Marxist (and Stalinist) ideology in the Soviet-type regimes, and was less prominent in pre-war representation of cultic figures in Hungary.

The peak of Rákosi's 'cult of personality' was the celebration of his 60th birthday in March 1952, which was modelled on the coordinated celebrations of Stalin's 70th birthday three years earlier.[43] The party leader was showered with gifts that were exhibited in a museum, a literary anthology with sycophantic poems and short stories was published on the occasion, and a photo album about his life was also assembled to mark the date. The main event of the celebrations – just like in the case of Franz Joseph – was a gala performance in the Opera that culminated in a joint singing of a fake folk song praising the Stalinist party leader. During the campaign Rákosi was portrayed as a quasi-omnipresent – and hence omnipotent – leader who is surrounded by the love and gratitude of the people. Despite this domineering image, Rákosi's adulation was not a solitary phenomenon, and similar to the cults of Horthy and Franz Joseph, its development was accompanied by the emergence of a number of minor cults in the party elite – such as the one around Defence Minister, Mihály Farkas – and in the provincial party apparatus. While the spread of the cult at the lower rungs of party and state was usually condemned and suppressed, the orchestrated adulation of Rákosi was integrated into a hierarchical system of leader cults at an international level that were all subordinated to the symbolic – and very real – authority of Stalin.[44] The development of cultic practices across post-war Central and Eastern Europe was a core feature of sovietization, the aim of which was to link the satellite states to Moscow through ritual means.

The Stalinist leader cult in Hungary assumed monumental proportions, yet it remained largely ineffective and superficial. Due to the brevity of the cult and its absurd, paradoxical features – the 'cult of personality' was condemned, while the party's leader was glorified – the phenomenon provoked indifference and enjoyed only limited social support. Therefore, the cult could be interpreted as a failure, because – as opposed to Franz Joseph – the communists did care about what people thought about them and their leaders, and invested significant efforts to mobilize the population and engender positive affective responses from the people.[45] They also monitored 'popular opinion' excessively, as demonstrated by the heaps of documents called 'mood reports' that were created at the time. However, due to their teleological worldview, they thought they knew how the population would respond to their policies and assumed that the people would eventually become supportive of the party's goals – they thought history was on their side after all. Their assumptions in relation to the popular reception of the Stalinist leader cult were mostly wrong and were one of the reasons for communist misperceptions of social support in the 1950s.

The cult of Rákosi – and that of Stalin – was moderated and toned down to an extent after 1953, and it came to an abrupt end in 1956. Similar to the cults of Franz Joseph and Horthy, it was violent upheaval and military struggle that terminated the orchestrated adulation of communist party leaders. The burning of Rákosi's books and images, and the physical destruction of his busts – along with the demolition of the infamous Stalin statue in Budapest – were common scenes during the uprising of October 1956.[46] But the revolution of 1956 did not simply mean the conclusion of the Stalinist leader cult in Hungary. It also marked a rupture in the tradition of representing power in personalized (and affective) terms in Hungary. The communist party after 1956 under János Kádár's leadership made a deliberate choice not to revive the practice of emphasizing the role of individual leaders in the construction of socialism in order to avoid 'even the illusion of the cult of personality'.[47] The anti-Stalinist stance that defined the ideology of the Kádár regime – next to the interpretation of 1956 as a 'counter-revolution' – was mostly responsible for the fact that the party leader was not surrounded by cultic veneration during his lifetime. His image was choreographed to a certain extent – he was represented as a humble, puritan and competent leader – but it was bereft of the emotionally-laden vocabulary that characterized earlier cults and there were no excessive rituals organized to celebrate his persona.[48] While Kádár did not have the 'royal cult' Orkán referred to when he was alive, his figure assumed cultic features after the collapse of communism. In the context of economic hardships and the quick-sand politics of the 1990s, Kádár came to represent bygone stability and social welfare, and was associated with growing nostalgic feelings towards the late-socialist regime. To a significant extent, therefore, his posthumous cult was the legacy of communism.

Post-communist legacies: The return of the cult

The collapse of communism in Hungary in 1989 could be considered a rupture from numerous perspectives – political institutions, economic structures etc. – but it did not mark the return of the cultic leader. Post-communist nostalgia did provoke the emergence of cultic perceptions of Kádár in certain circles, but no dominant leader figure emerged in the 1990s, and active politicians were not depicted with the help of irrational, affective vocabulary at the time. The revival of techniques and practices of cult building after a rupture of half a century is therefore all the more startling. The new target of initially uncoordinated and quasi-spontaneous cultic veneration that recycled – to a limited extent – the vocabulary and imagery of both communist and pre-communist leader cults was prime minister Viktor Orbán. The gradual increase in the number of cultic representations of his figure was concurrent with the emergence of authoritarian methods of exercising power since the mid-2010s, the growth of a web of oligarchs and cronies ('the clan'), and the marked reorientation of Hungarian foreign policy, as well as political rhetoric towards Russia since 2014.[49]

The origins of cultic representations of Orbán go back to his first tenure as prime minister between 1998 and 2012. While one cannot identify consistent and centrally coordinated cult-building strategies, his figure certainly assumed symbolic connotations, and there were isolated attempts to represent him in irrational terms. According to one scholar, he emerged as a political celebrity among his followers that led to a degree of 'neo-folklorisation' of his persona at the time.[50] Moreover, it was the turn of the century that witnessed the marked revival of pre-communist historical legacies, including the use of monarchical symbols in political rituals. In order to celebrate the millennium of Hungarian statehood in 2001, the Orbán government removed the Hungarian royal crown from the National Museum, transported it on the river Danube to the city of Esztergom where the first Hungarian king Saint Stephen was allegedly crowned, and then shipped it back to the building of the parliament in Budapest where it was put on permanent display.

The recycling of monarchical imagery did not save the governing party FIDESZ from losing the elections of 2002. When the party moved to opposition, Orbán was removed from day-to-day political battles. He rarely spoke at the parliament or made announcements. His appearances were scarce, staged and strategic. This was to protect his symbolic reputation, which had become a significant asset for the party. The leader was not to be associated with futile parliamentary struggles, mundane political punch-ups or political failures in opposition. It was also the period in opposition during which he consolidated his dominance over FIDESZ, and emerged as the (mostly) uncontested leader in the party.

The political-moral crisis of 2006 and the economic crisis of 2008 paved the way for Orbán's return to power and the intensification of cultic representations of his figure. After the landslide electoral victory of 2010, his figure dominated the communication strategy of FIDESZ.[51] He was represented as the man who would restore order and stability in Hungary after years of crisis and austerity. The shift of his party towards the far right after 2014 furthered the revival of leader-centred politics, and the return of political and symbolic practices that were long thought to have disappeared. The key theme in Orbán's rhetoric – and in government propaganda – since 2010 was crisis. The theme enjoys a prominent role in the new constitution of 2012, which labelled the post-1989 years as 'turbulent', and it became a core element of the government's communication strategy during (and since) the 2015 refugee crisis. As a recent analysis demonstrated, Orbán often uses a language that evokes the themes of fear, anxiety and threat.[52] The trope of a 'nation under threat' is most often evoked with regard to immigration and it continues to occupy centre stage in governmental propaganda despite the fact that the number of illegal border crossings has diminished significantly.

Crisis and threat also inform cultic representations of the prime minister. He is represented as a competent, responsible, decisive and caring leader – the man in charge – during difficult times or extreme weather conditions, such as the snow crisis in March 2013 or the flood of the Danube in June the same year.[53] The image of the caring leader who picks up hitch-hikers whose truck is stuck in the snow is increasingly accompanied by representations that portray him as a father figure. During the 2018 election campaign, for example, there were several representations that portrayed him amongst children. His meetings with children – mostly in kindergartens – were portrayed as 'spontaneous' visits that provoked enthusiasm and joy. Fan pages on Facebook also advance the image of the leader as a father figure. One such page ('Best of Viktor'), moderated by young employees in governmental administration, tends to refer to him as 'apuka' (daddy), which – apart from self-subjugation and self-infantilization in the face of paternal power – indicates the revival of the myth of the father of the nation, a myth that featured the cults of Stalinist leaders, inter-war authoritarian figures, and monarchs before.

Another cultic legacy that has made a return in representations of Orbán is the trope of the 'man of the people' that was the key component of the imagery of communist leaders. This image is supported by videos – often posted on the prime minister's official Facebook page – in which the leader pays a 'surprise' visit to old ladies, 'ordinary' families and kindergartens, or when he is depicted talking to 'the man of the street', in one case a drunken trashman (whose name happens to be Ferenc József, or Francis Joseph).[54] Images of Orbán's approachability and accessibility are accompanied by representations that portray him as a statesman of international reputation, who acts as the main driving force behind the Visegrád 4 group, and who also took on the role to defend Europe, mostly from itself. The trope of the 'defender of Europe' echoes Horthy's image as 'the heroic protector of European civilisation', and is depicted in newspaper articles as well as commercial items, including mugs and t-shirts.[55] During Orbán's annual appearance at the Tusványos festival in Transylvania in 2019, for example, young people were spotted wearing t-shirts with the inscription 'Orbán Makes Europe Great Again' (OMEGA), which serves as an indication of (some) sources of inspiration for representations of leadership.[56]

Although Orbán's physical prowess is rarely put on public display – as opposed to Putin's, for example – war metaphors are used frequently in association with his persona to emphasize his image as a strong leader. National elections, political conflicts with the EU or the IMF are often described as 'battles' and are used to support representations of the prime minister as a decisive politician with fortitude and foresight. Such images are also evoked in Orbán's self-representations. In a video shared on his Facebook page in 2018, which depicts his meeting with martial artist and Hollywood actor Chuck Norris and his wife, he described himself as a 'streetfighter', and somebody who does not come from the elite.[57]

Celebrities like Chuck Norris also furthered Orbán's image as a leader of international reputation. For example, Paul Anka during his visit to Hungary in July 2019 performed his famous song 'My Way' to a special audience with the prime minister as the guest of honour. The famous singer even changed the lyrics of the song and listed 'all things Hungarian' that he liked, including Saint Stephen's day, Lake Balaton and 'prime minister Viktor Orbán'.[58] But the most important celebrity whose reputation has been systematically exploited for cult-building purposes was the legendary football player, Ferenc Puskás who had led the Hungarian national football team to the World Cup final in 1954. It is no coincidence that the football academy set up in Orbán's home village, Felcsút is named after Puskás, but there is also a special ambassadorial position (since 2017) in 'Puskás-affairs', which is currently held by the former communications officer of the academy. The promotion of the dual cults of Puskás and Orbán has been exploited by hopeful politicians to further their careers, as well. One state secretary and president of a football club, for example, gifted a painting depicting Puskás and Orbán to the prime minister in February 2015 – he became head of the tax office the same year.[59]

While it is difficult to foresee the future trajectory of the growing cult around the Hungarian prime minister, some features of the regime and its propaganda indicate that it is likely to grow further. The gradual expansion of patrimonial rule through the establishment of a network of loyal oligarchs – which now includes family and friends – the increasing radicalization and centralization of governmental propaganda, and the continuing reliance on monumentalism and political spectacle – represented in the stadium-building frenzy – suggest the further escalation of cult-building tendencies in Hungary. For example, on 7 April – the day before election day during the 2018 national elections – the large majority of local newspapers (at county level) that are owned by government-friendly businessmen and have since been gifted to a single foundation were published with the same cover page: a photograph of Orbán and a call to vote for FIDESZ.[60] There have also been attempts to adjust historical narratives to promote cultic images of the leader. The video prepared for the celebrations of the anniversary of the collapse of communism – which was played in a loop during a summer festival in June 2019 – identifies only one historical actor of significance in 1989: Viktor Orbán.[61] While history is being remoulded, the style of leadership that the prime minister represents is also being used as a model by state officials – party-affiliated lord mayors mostly – in the localities, which underlines the expansion of paternalist imagery at the local level. At the same time, the affective dimension in Orbán's representations remains restrained, and he is rarely portrayed as a leader who is surrounded by the love and gratitude of his followers. Images, such as a man at a party rally holding up a t-shirt with the prime minister's picture and the inscription 'Orbán is living God' are very rare and are not part of centralized image-building strategies.[62]

Conclusions

The concept of historical legacies offers a useful analytical prism through which the long history of modern leader cults in Hungary could be viewed and interpreted. It embraces the notion of rupture as well as continuity and helps account for the constant re-emergence of the phenomenon in different historical contexts and after marked caesuras in history. The contemporary history of Hungary is spotted with cataclysmic moments, but the cults of leaders in the past 150 years or so show many similarities with each other in terms of representation, rhetoric and ritual practices. The political figures discussed in this chapter were all represented as strong leaders, benevolent father figures, symbols of unity, and embodiments of the values and aspirations of the respective political communities. They were all surrounded by the love of their followers in cultic representations, yet their cults all retained a degree of superficiality and impersonality. The style of leadership they promoted also tended to be mimicked by others, which was reflected in the semi-spontaneous spread of cultic imagery at lower levels of party, state, or government hierarchy. At the same time, all these cults were shaped by the specific historical circumstances in which they emerged, and their trajectory was conditioned by the specific political, social, cultural and ideological context – imperialism, radical nationalism, Stalinism or neo-authoritarianism.

Historical antecedents often informed cult-building practices in the form of either conscious or unconscious borrowing of techniques, rhetoric or patterns of representation. The historical legacy of earlier leader cults, therefore, continued to exert a certain influence on the manufacturing of leader worship throughout the twentieth century, and contributed to the accumulation of diverse layers of legacies – monarchist, nationalist, communist – in cultic practices over time. This accumulation of legacies of cult-building was not always reflected very clearly, partly because of ideological antagonisms between different historical epochs.

While the notion of historical legacy may help to understand broader trends and the long-term developmental features of leader cults, it should not be considered an exclusive factor to explain the emergence of cultic phenomena. Individual agency also had a crucial role in defining the shape and form of leader cults – some leaders promoted irrational representations of their own persona intensely, others were more modest – and it even contributed to the abandonment of cultic practices altogether, as the case of post-1956 Hungary demonstrates. The transnational circulation of ideas and images as well as the importance of international sources of inspiration need to be underlined, as well. Franz Joseph's cult emerged in the age of empires when most of Europe's crowned heads were represented with the help of monarchical and imperial imagery; Horthy's representations were in harmony with the imagery of right-wing military figures – Mussolini, Salazar, Piłsudski, Franco etc. – in the inter-war period; Rákosi's cult was just one example of the spread of Stalinist leader cults in sovietized Eastern Europe; and Orbán's cult fits into the pattern of representing new 'strongmen' – Putin or Trump – in irrational terms. The role of agency and international models in the construction of cultic phenomena casts some doubt on the explanatory value of the concepts of 'deep structures' or Orkán's idea of 'imposition'. While both played a significant role, cult-building in Hungary was also the result of the conscious implementation of various strategies and models – past and present, national and international.

Part Three

New Ways of Understanding the Stalinist System: The Cold War

7

Revisioning Stalin's Cold War

Caroline Kennedy-Pipe

Has Stalin been forgotten? In the summer of 2019, the anniversary of D-Day was celebrated by the US President and several heads of state in Normandy to mark the beginning of the end of the Second World War. The Russian head of state was not invited despite the enormous sacrifices on the Eastern Front throughout the years of war. Indeed, President Putin remarked that this was a snub to the Russian people. The 'snub' was part of a framework of isolationary tactics to punish Moscow after the war in Crimea, its role in Syria, and its use of hybrid war. Stalin and his leadership during the Second World War merited barely a mention – indeed, were 'forgotten' at least in certain political circles.

This is not the case, though, in popular culture. Stalin has been the subject of at least one colourful Western biography,[1] and the object of ironic fun in the British film, *The Death of Stalin*.[2] Martin Amis in his novella 'Koba the Dread' even turned Stalin in to a figure of autobiographical whimsy.[3] There is still an appetite to know more about the dictator, not least because in contemporary Russia Stalin usually appears as a popular and iconic figure.[4] In academic circles the study of Russia has also undergone something of a renaissance, with attempts to understand the historical influences that have shaped the country of Putin.

So, any attempt to 'revision' Stalin is timely and has already been the subject of two 'meetings' in honour of the retirement of Professor Geoffrey Roberts, the distinguished historian of Soviet foreign policy and Stalin.[5] Many years ago, and certainly influenced by Geoff Roberts, I wrote a book entitled *Stalin's Cold War*.[6] I sought to offer a version of the Soviet Union as a fragile super-power with its leader, Joseph Stalin, seeking cooperation not confrontation after the end of the Second World War. That project was naturally a product of its time. I had started studying not during the original Cold War but in the Second Cold War – a period of confrontation that owed rather more to Ronald Reagan than it did to Stalin. The manuscript was produced against a backdrop of the ill-fated Soviet invasion of Afghanistan and the ensuing war against the Mujahedeen backed by the ISI and the CIA. The Iranian Revolution sat as a powerful example of the growing potency of Islam, while the emergence of the 'reformer' Gorbachev and the astounding shifts within the USSR itself led to the unexpected breakup of the Soviet empire. The version of Stalin's foreign policy in that book came directly out of that period and the atmosphere of optimism in the West, which celebrated the 'end of history', the collapse of so-called bipolarity, and the termination of what George Orwell had originally termed the Cold War.[7] A certain degree of nostalgia that lamented the passing of that period also infused studies of International Relations. So, despite triumphalism, more sobering assessments of what might come after the defeat of communism also took root and became the material for not just historians and International Relations scholars but novelists like John Updike, whose character in the Rabbit trilogy wondered what purpose could possibly exist for Americans in the absence of the great confrontation.[8]

The disappearance of the Soviet Union was something not predicted nor foreseen except by a few canny scholars and those like George F. Kennan, the original architect and erstwhile critic of the doctrine of Containment.[9] Some in the International Relations community remained chagrined that the end of the USSR had not been predicted or even anticipated within its academy.[10] Along with many others I sought to make sense of the end of that era: what it meant that the 'fairy-tale' of the long peace in Europe was over, but also I pondered whether we had fully understood the beginning of the Cold War.[11] All those toiling in Cold War studies enjoyed the benefit of knowing how that half century of confrontation ended, even if we could not and did not agree on all its possible outcomes. Historians jostled to see what the Russian archives contained and, even though much of the documentation remained patchy, they sought novel stories and nuggets of knowledge.

Despite this heady atmosphere there was something both striking and rather disappointing because much of the 'new' history that emerged from the 1990s onwards seemed to affirm existing prejudices, whilst ostensibly re-opening debates about who or what had been responsible for the Cold War. Thus, it was not unusual that after scrutiny of some of the Russian documents (and from other archives such as in the former East Germany), the weight of new articles and books published in the English language sought in the main to expound the virtues of the post-1945 trajectory of US foreign policy 'warts and all'. These justifications continued to pervade many assessments of US behaviour abroad in the period after 9/11. Perhaps understandably, commentators asked why, after 'winning' the contest with Communism, the homeland had been the subject of a catastrophic surprise assault by men armed with box-cutters.

Given that historical canvas, and surveying contemporary accounts, this chapter looks back at *Stalin's Cold War* and, in the light of the two and a half decades that have followed its publication, reprises some of its wisdoms, its optimism and its obvious silences and omissions. This essay expands on some themes of Cold War historiography and looks at what I term novelty, moralism and realpolitik (with boundaries) as explanations for why the Cold War began and which explain not just Stalin's Cold War but the conditions that cast him as 'villain'. In doing so it contributes to the volume's effort to re-vision Stalin.

The question whether the Cold War could have been avoided is a rather large one, perhaps better suited to a monograph rather than an essay. But I remain interested in whether there were chances that it all may have turned out rather differently, and why even the newer historiography relies on the idea that with Stalin in charge, a Cold War was preordained. (This neatly side-steps the fact that after Stalin died in March 1953 the shape of the Cold War remained pretty much the same, with the overtures for a détente from the post-Stalin leadership in the Kremlin firmly rebuffed).

My revisioning of Stalin argues that if we 'forget' him there is a chance that we misjudge not just how the Cold War began but also some of the important reasons why the Soviet dictator became the justification for Cold War, nuclear armed confrontation and a series of brutal proxy encounters. Maybe too we can learn some lessons about our challenges with Putin.

Histories

The path of Cold War historiography is well trodden. The various 'schools' or interpretations were firmly established by the 1980s even as the USSR began to falter. Students engaged with the Traditionalist or Orthodox accounts in which Stalin's presence and paranoia lay at the eye of the storm.[12] Many were beguiled by the subsequent Revisionist historians with their dark interpretations of American capitalism, power and ambition. Later, scholars perceived something rather more appealing and convincing in attempts by the Neo-Revisionists (led by John Lewis Gaddis) to offer an ostensibly balanced and more accurate account of the facts underpinning the origins of the Cold War. All these groups must be seen as products of their time. The Traditionalists wrote within the dark belly of a novel nuclear world with a formidable erstwhile ally in the Kremlin and the peoples of Central and Eastern Europe under the yoke of a vastly expanded Communist project. Many of the founding fathers of the Traditionalist view, like George F. Kennan, were bitterly disappointed by the development of Communist politics throughout the Soviet bloc even after the death of Stalin, while certainly in Kennan's case also essentially melancholy and frustrated by American society and US foreign policy.[13] Revisionists reacting not just to the near miss of the Cuban missile crisis as well as the agonies of Vietnam in the 1960s, and the 'tragedy' of US diplomacy as that war faltered, had deep intellectual and ideological roots embedded in the study of the export of American capital and empire. Inspired by the 'New Left' and its critique of the domestic framework of society, considerable academic energy was spent interrogating US conduct in the early years of the Cold War. The doyen of Revisionism, William Appleman Williams,[14] led the charge against any simplistic or one-dimensional account of a turbulent world shaped wholly by Stalin.[15]

The Neo-Revisionists (working in the 1970s) offered a welcome corrective to earlier versions. The rise of China, Soviet assertiveness in the Horn of Africa as well as emerging Japanese economic strength had led Richard Nixon in 1971 to describe a complicated 'pentagonal' world, reflecting a myriad of challenges to the US position as the war in Vietnam stumbled to an end. Against that backdrop of uncertainty and what seemed the very real prospect of a United States in decline, these Neo-Revisionists had the considerable advantage of working through newly released and burgeoning evidence from the US archives and unpicking the documents of the Truman years.[16]

Beguiling accounts of a reluctant American superpower coming to terms with a new world order seemed to answer some of the questions about how the confrontation with the Soviet Union had begun. As Gaddis would have it, more by accident than hostile design a series of 'misunderstandings' over loans, capital, Japan and Eastern Europe dogged and eventually destroyed Soviet–American relations.[17]

Woven through this essentially American story was that of the rapid decline of both Britain and France, leading first to the creation of the Marshall Plan and second to the foundation of NATO: these were both depicted as acts of huge American generosity and indeed sacrifice. We also learned far more about the initial and, as it turned out, fateful American commitment to shore up fading French power in Indo-China, adding to the perspective of a reluctant American superpower. While the archives in Moscow remained resolutely closed, any story was necessarily incomplete, leaving 'doubters' to take up the Revisionist mantle as to whether the Marshall Plan or the foundation of NATO had been entirely disinterested.[18]

Stalin himself was still primarily interpreted through speeches and his interactions with Western diplomats, journalists and politicians. Overall, there was little serious attempt to rehabilitate Soviet Cold War politics. Rather, a justification for and of the US conduct of its national security agenda was framed almost entirely in terms of the cruelty and cunning of the Soviet dictator and his legacy as Neo-Revisionist accounts dominated and justified the emergence of a Second Cold War.[19]

By the 1990s, the collapse of the Soviet regime, the end of Communism, and the emergence of a more pro-Western leadership under a shambolic Boris Yeltsin heralded something of a golden age in Cold War scholarship. Precisely because of some access to the archives in Moscow, more nuanced accounts began to emerge of the early years. The economic and political fragility of the USSR, the peculiarities of the Soviet system, and the complexities provided by other actors in the theatre of Cold War, not least a Mao or a Castro, all provided welcome and versatile accounts of what seemed to have happened.[20]

Historians moved rapidly to build valuable accounts of Communism in Central and East Europe with new interpretations of, for example, Soviet behaviour in Austria, hitherto a rather neglected country in any Cold War story.[21] But it was not just the so-called 'Second World' (a label oozing assumptions of inferiority) that yielded detailed accounts but also that of the so-called 'Third World', as historians began to carve out stories from the complex competitive arena of what many preferred to term a 'developing' world. Outside the descriptions of elite politics, narratives of cultural politics, human concerns and social accounts of living in the Cold War all emerged to provide considerable richness to the historical tapestry.[22]

The idea that 'we now know' became the leitmotif for those Western scholars, led (again) by the redoubtable John Lewis Gaddis. Gaddis's *We Now Know* – a large monograph and an admirable feat of scholarship – gained considerable intellectual traction.[23] In this undoubtedly better informed if still flawed interpretation, some admittedly new evidence was utilized, but again to confirm Stalin as wily villain creating the conditions for the origins and durability of the Cold War. Explanations for the outbreak of the Korean War again seemed to confirm the nature of Stalinist ambition.[24]

So, much of this was not revisioning so much as reconfirming earlier 'truths'. Gaddis, as adviser and friend to President George W. Bush, became a pillar for the advocacy of the pursuit of the US national interest in the troubled times of the post

9/11 world.²⁵ Indeed, in a critique of Gaddis's *The Cold War*, published in 2005, Tony Judt argued that the Gaddis oeuvre was 'a history of America's Cold War as seen from America, as experienced in America and told in a way most agreeable to many American readers'.²⁶ Gaddis, himself no slouch in intellectual jousting, rebutted any such allegation.

However, out of all this more recent scholarship, several themes have emerged and remain important to any revisioning of Stalin in the breakdown of the Grand Alliance and the years of new East–West competition. In reverse order the Neo-Revisionists were correct that what I term 'novelty' was indeed important to the conduct of politics. American decision makers (as well as Stalin) did confront a new world: one which demanded a considerable rethinking of the use of US power abroad especially in the wake of both the collapse of British influence and Communist expansion into Europe.

The Revisionists were correct in thinking about US ideology, its 'moralism', as well as economics and empire, and indeed the impact of its use of nuclear weapons for the first time,²⁷ whilst the Traditionalists certainly understood the 'realpolitik' involved in the wartime discussions of the future disposition of power. The division of Europe was of crucial importance in the creation and maintenance of spheres of influence for Stalin, if also underpinning the Traditionalist concern with the expansion of Soviet power, influence and the abrogation of democratic politics.

Finally, the new (or somewhat newer) history was and remains correct that there was a bigger and wider landscape than simply the politicians and diplomats arguing over the future division of Europe and Asia. In this respect the historian Odd Arne Westad has done much to widen and 'revision' Cold War politics. His collection *Reviewing the Cold War* (2000) provided many fine chapters, which somewhat unusually twined International Relations theory and historical analysis.²⁸

There were of course necessarily many gaps in that volume. Westad himself noted that there was a considerable deficit in work on gender and the Cold War. (This was a somewhat ironic comment from the editor of a book that, as he himself 'deplored', contained not a single female contributor!) The view expressed in that collection that women existed primarily in negative contexts in the Cold War is one that has thankfully been addressed in a contemporary wave of scholarship exploring female agency.²⁹ If not quite a feminist 'turn' in Cold War studies, then we have witnessed a most welcome addition to our understanding of the social and material conditions of both women and men living and resisting under Communism. This may not however be a 'turn' that William Appleman Williams would necessarily have approved of, given his view that women did not have or should not have a history separate to men.³⁰

Novelty

The defeat of Germany and Japan in 1945 created unique conditions for interpreting International Relations and the related challenges for diplomacy and the creation of a post-war settlement. The doctrine of Unconditional Surrender declared by President Roosevelt at the Casablanca Conference in January 1943 meant that, rather than an armistice to end the war as in 1918, fascist states were crushed – in Germany's case primarily by the Red Army on the Eastern Front. In Japan's case defeat was secured after ferocious conventional and naval war by the dropping of a novel invention: atomic bombs.

Many consequences stemmed from FDR's declaration (which was made with direct reference to General Grant's unconditional victory in the bloody US Civil War). One consequence was that the final months of the war were characterized by sustained German resistance as well as the breaching of respect for the protection of civilian populations – on all sides.[31] (General Eisenhower later came to regret Unconditional Surrender, believing that it had meant war had lasted longer than was strictly necessary in Europe.[32])

A second and related consequence was that the strategic bombing of cities by the British and Americans became more permissible if no less controversial as the war wore on. Even if doughty pacifists like the former First World War nurse and writer Vera Brittain protested the bombing of civilians, that strategy was relentlessly pursued against both Japan and Germany. Long before Hiroshima and Nagasaki the line between combatant and non-combatant as targets of war had been crossed, but the decision-making over the dropping of the atomic bombs on Japan has been the subject of much debate.[33] New evidence demonstrates that in pursuit of unconditional surrender, once the Trinity test had been successful it was merely a matter for the politicians (if not the scientists) where and when to use the weapons.[34] The killing of innocents and the creation of dead cities was part and parcel of the eradication of fascism, perhaps underlining the Revisionist argument that bombing (especially atomic bombing) was about more than military necessity perhaps also revenge, punishment and warning?[35]

For Stalin, the destruction of Hiroshima and Nagasaki was indeed a warning about the future constellation of power. The United States had become the first nuclear state. We now know the stories of Soviet espionage, which rendered Truman's oblique reference to his new weapon at Potsdam was merely confirmation not revelation. But we also now know thanks to scholars such as David Holloway that the dictator struggled to ensure the success of his nuclear programme to avoid an inferior position – an inferior and indeed vulnerable one in the immediate months and years after Hiroshima. We will return to the issue of nuclear weapons and relative Soviet weakness, but that initial strategic fragility was and has been ignored by much of International Relations scholarship.

In fact, the Second World War and its outcomes redefined the field of International Relations. Such seemed to be the overwhelming power of all the members of the Grand Alliance that commentators struggled to define and categorize this novel condition of states that were more than simple great powers. The term superpower was devised by William T.R. Fox in 1944 to describe the unique characteristics of the USSR, the US and, quaintly as it may now seem, Britain.[36] These superpowers were expected to dominate the new order. As Fox later explained, when pressed as to why the British had deserved their place in the top tier of power, Britain plus its empire had manpower, reach and mobility.[37] As he admitted, it was not so easy for an American observer to note how much of Britain's apparent resilience was the strength that Canada, Australia, New Zealand, South Africa, India and the rest of Empire-Commonwealth had provided.

If Fox misread the future, so too did Stalin. The dictator fully expected Britain and its empire to play a crucial role in the post-war years and perhaps even act as a counterbalance against the US. The rapid decline of the British empire set up a 'direct' competition with the Kremlin. But that occurred later, not in 1945 and early 1946 when the British seemed still powerful, even if Churchill (much to Stalin's astonishment) had been dismissed by the electorate.

Here too we must also be careful with the imposition of the bi-polar 'tag' for the conditions that prevailed not just in 1945 and 1946 but for the wider Cold War.[38] The Anglo-Saxon world of course dominated much of our understanding of the Cold War and my early work was, alongside that of Geoff Roberts, the product of essentially ethnocentric concerns. That label of bi-polar was in retrospect incorrect, not just because the non-European worlds and peoples had their own dynamics but because so-called peripheral politics were intimately connected to and affected the core politics of a Britain, a France and later a United States in Vietnam.

But both the inaccurate descriptors of superpower and bipolarity became embedded in the lexicon of International Relations and underpin many understandings/misunderstandings of the Cold War. In his incisive critique of the failures of IR to really understand the early Cold War, William Wohlforth has argued that the problem with bi-polarity or any balance of power theory is that it does not stand the test of examining the 'new' evidence of the Soviet position after the war. Thus, he explains:

> On balance, this evidence shows a Soviet Union with a much more tentative grasp on superpowerdom than nearly all observers imagined until recently. In short, Moscow's Potemkinism worked in misleading everyone, including scholars about Soviet power and hence the overall balance of power. Thus, the new evidence renders one of the central puzzles of the Cold War for balance of power theory – the imbalance of power between the main protagonists – even more puzzling.[39]

Quite so. Perhaps, as Wohlforth has argued, commentators struggled to find descriptors of the new politics post-1945 and so both superpower and bi-polar remained (incorrectly) as descriptors. This is understandable as novelty can breed uncertainty and victory heralded a new situation: the end of the war was a unique moment when the United States moved permanently (or so it seemed) away from the guiding principles of the Monroe Doctrine and Washington's Farewell address to an entangling association with the fading European powers. This needed both justification and legitimation. Domestically, Truman had to overcome significant obstacles to ensure a new global role could be undertaken and isolationism rejected – all this with the shadow of Wilson's failure with the League of Nations hovering over hopes for a renewal of his presidency.

Originally signalled in Kennan's long telegram, the substance of US policy was forged in the Containment Doctrine of 1947. The economic and military commitment through the Marshall Plan and the subsequent foundation of NATO in 1949 bolstered Western Europe, creating conditions for peace on one side of the continent and a testy contestation in the other. The division of Europe as 'we now know' meant on one side a democratic and economically vibrant West (albeit a West dependent on US economic strength and political good will) and a darker more sombre version of alliance in the East. Two empires: one by invitation and one by coercion.[40] One world that was nuclear armed and a 'second' world that was not. But this was not, as Geoff Roberts and I have separately argued, the world that Stalin had sought.

To repeat, the issue of atomic monopoly was a crucial one. What the advent of nuclear power heralded was something that Bernard Brodie, the American military strategist, understood clearly. The morning after nuclear weapons had been dropped on Japan, Brodie learnt of the event from his morning newspaper: 'Everything has changed' he stated. What he understood was that an enemy could now be defeated whilst leaving standing armies intact in the field. Stalin too understood that the world had been transformed after Hiroshima. The hard-fought gains to defeat Germany could be/were nullified by the US nuclear advantage. It was indeed a 'world shaken'.

I skimmed over the importance of this vulnerability in my original work. This was odd because it would have strengthened the case I made for a weak and compliant Soviet state, at least in 1945–7, one of the central premises in my book. At least part of my thinking was that the elite around Stalin and the dictator himself had proved keen on cooperation and a continuation of the Grand Alliance after the war was won. This was in no way whimsical. That view was based on the discussions during the wartime conferences. Stalin envisaged a great power condominium certainly for the future occupation of his most troublesome neighbour – Germany. The discussions on the future of Germany were exhaustive, for FDR as it turned out exhausting, and for Stalin an absolute key to any post-war settlement.

The movement of Soviet troops throughout 1944 and in the initial months of 1945 demonstrated this point. The Army pushed as far West as possible and entered Berlin after brutal urban warfare, and finally subdued the country at immense costs to the military and the civilian population. Note here the scholarly and public fascination with the defeat of Germany and the new histories surrounding its final days.[41] It was of vital importance to Stalin to crush the Germans and hold the capital. General Eisenhower did not contest the Soviet course for Berlin. Thereafter Germany was divided, and the capital subdivided between the victors. Even France, which had collapsed ignominiously in the face of invasion, was permitted to hold a zone. There is scant evidence that division was a negative outcome for Stalin. (There were, however, other concerns, not least that as troops advanced through Europe, they became exposed not just to the dangers of battle, but higher living standards and a way of life denied at home).

Stalin famously remarked to Milovan Djilas that he who occupies a country imposes his own social system upon it. Sometimes. As the war in Europe reached its conclusion, Soviet troops took as much territory as possible in areas of strategic, political and economic interests. This included the hunt for uranium to help the Soviet atomic programme. The race for Berlin (which turned out not to be so much a race as a bloody Soviet assault on the city) has been described elsewhere as has Stalin's brooding anxiety that his Western allies might yet deceive him by pushing on to take the German capital.[42] This despite assurances to the contrary provided by General Eisenhower and the 'goodwill' demonstrated by Western troops during the invasion and ceding of Czechoslovakia to Soviet ambition.[43]

Realpolitik

For Stalin, what was crucial was the realpolitik requirement for a security buffer to prevent a revanchist Germany and ensure predominant Soviet influence in Poland and the Baltic states at the very least. In this respect any idea that Stalin had exhibited disingenuity or duplicity with his Western allies over that geopolitical agenda is incorrect. Soviet objectives were in Poland and the Baltics perfectly clear and ultimately respected, however reluctantly, on the American and British sides.[44] If we revisit Stalin's attitude towards the Baltic States, there seemed no option but to yield to his insistence on dominance in a key geo-strategic location. The Baltic states were sacrificed to a Soviet 'sphere' despite the avowed resistance of 'the people'. Konigsberg (now Kaliningrad) too had been placed into Soviet control on the spurious premise that it would legitimately provide Stalin with his long-held ambition to have a warm water port in the north. That issue had been raised on a repeated basis by Stalin. George Kennan in his memoirs was scathing about the idea that Konigsberg was ice-free year round, but the city was yielded. In fact the future of Finland as sitting not exactly in the Soviet camp but under its influence gave rise to yet another novel phrase – that of Finlandization to describe its unique position at the beginning of the Cold War.

So, in my earlier work I pointed to the fact that at the end of the war Soviet troops pushed as far West and North West as they possibly could, precisely to ensure that influence would be guaranteed, and a buffer established. A security buffer that after the summer of 1945 potentially could be breached by atomic weapons – a Soviet Union made vulnerable again simply weeks after victory in Europe by the advent of nuclear weapons. And in that original narration of Soviet vulnerability and cooperation there were also cases of retreat from its hard-fought outposts. Stalin did not insist on a position in mainland Japan despite the repeated promises made by US leaders before the successful atomic test. He later came to regret that decision, instead holding on to the Kurile islands, a space of less strategic value. Certain aspects of Soviet occupation and then withdrawal perplexed Western policy makers. One such was from the Danish island of Bornholm in early 1946 and another in that same period from Northern Iran. In those troubled months of early 1946, when Kennan was penning his Long Telegram and Churchill had declared an iron curtain to be descending over Europe, the curious case of Bornholm demonstrates both Soviet cooperation in terms of the admittedly somewhat fading Grand Alliance but also compliance with the wishes of its much smaller neighbour – Denmark.[45] There is now a considerable body of work by Scandinavian scholars which has addressed the issue of Norway, Sweden, Denmark and indeed on the margins, the island of Bornholm in relation to Soviet ambitions in the region during the end and aftermath of the war.[46]

At the Yalta Conference it had been agreed that the dividing line between East and West would lie along the River Elbe. Bornholm itself lay well east of the Elbe. From the Soviet perspective the island was clearly in their 'sector' or sphere of control. Berlin fell to the Russians on 30 April. A race then took place to 'capture' Danish soil. (Denmark was ultimately liberated by the Americans in Greenland, the British in the centre and the Russians on Bornholm). The Soviet Army occupied Bornholm for almost a year with a quiet withdrawal in the spring of 1946. The one condition of Soviet withdrawal was that only Danish forces would be stationed on the island. While Bornholm may have been a small feature of that post-war scenario, the very fact that in early 1946 it was evacuated alongside the Soviet withdrawal from Northern Iran points to a complex pattern of politics in these early months.[47]

While newer accounts have been written by scholars in Denmark of the Bornholm episode, pointing again to the very valuable addition of regional studies to Cold War studies, it is the Iranian case that has engendered more notice. This is understandable as that crisis, when Stalin maintained troops in Northern Iran beyond the agreed deadline, has led to much speculation about the role of Harry Truman in the crisis and a fascinating new set of claims about actions and threats. In his rather overworked memoirs, the former President relates that he had threatened to give it to the USSR with both barrels over the Iranian crisis.[48] Soviet troops did in fact withdraw from Northern Iran.

Was this in fact the first case of nuclear blackmail? The US was, despite the paucity of nuclear weapons in the arsenal, the world's only nuclear state. It had therefore a decided military advantage and one of which Stalin was keenly aware. His Cold War was one in which, despite the military sacrifices of his country and the fact that he believed that the Second Front had been deliberately delayed (ensuring that the bloodletting occurred on the Eastern Front), he found himself 'vulnerable' even as a victorious power. He was in fact vulnerable twice over – in technological terms having essentially lost the contest to become the first nuclear weapons state, and then for a four-year period aware of the potential for the US to unleash nuclear weapons on his own homeland.

What David Holloway amongst others has demonstrated is the urgency with which Stalin pursued a Soviet atomic programme.[49] While there could be no resting – even after the successful test of 1949 had been accomplished – until a delivery capability was achieved, those four years of American nuclear monopoly skewed Soviet behaviour including in 1946 the obvious avoidance of a confrontation over Iran. Hence my view in that earlier work that the Soviet Union did not in fact behave like a superpower.

So, to return to the Iranian crisis. The story of Truman and nuclear blackmail fits perfectly with malign accounts as narrated by the Revisionists. It is actually a good story, but the problem is that it is not a true one. Meticulous recent scholarship has revealed that US diplomacy during the crisis was careful and cautious to avoid any military confrontation, a judicious mix of coercion but also conciliation: the classic carrot and stick![50] According to accounts that have appeared in regional studies journals, no overt nuclear ultimatum had to be issued such was the strength of the US position.[51] Soviet troops were in fact withdrawn with a consequent and costly loss of Soviet influence in the region. As the seasoned Soviet watcher Isaac Deutscher noted, it was instructive how many humiliations Stalin had to swallow not least because of the Iranian question. 'Russia was in the dock' at the first regular assembly of the UN.[52]

But even if new materials point to a relatively weak Soviet Union, there were of course multiple novel challenges for the United States. The most formidable was how to deal with an expanded USSR that had gobbled up peoples, territories, resources and threatened to reach still further into Western Europe through the force of arms and ideology. To meet the challenge decision-makers invoked a moralism long present in the American psyche.

Moralism

For Truman the Cold War was a military, political, economic, but also moral challenge. In many versions of American foreign policy its actions are cloaked in the language of democratic ideology. The country itself had during the war years undergone an economic revolution – in part Revisionists argue that this 'economic miracle' was one reason why after the end of the war American politicians aggressively pursued new European markets – to keep employment high and prevent another post-1929-style domestic depression. New markets meant an expansion of credit and finance into Europe and beyond. Protection of those interests from communism became vital. So far – so persuasive. Yet it was not just the opening of markets that drove Washington but the imperative to reorder the world in a democratic mould. These features were of course linked. Capitalism and free trade were engines of democracy.

For the Truman administration to reject isolationism, jettison the Monroe Doctrine and go hunting 'monsters abroad' there had to be justification. This manifested itself in what Noel O' Sullivan has termed a moralization of both politics and the Cold War itself.[53] What had marked out the Westphalian system from 1648 down to the First World War was the 'qualified' overcoming of a moralistic barbarism by a willingness to regard the 'political' other as an 'opponent' rather than as an existential 'foe'. The return to moralism in 1918 was characterized by the American demand to 'hang the Kaiser'. Thereafter the US grew into the supreme proponent of 'moralism'. After 1945 the meta-narratives of crude power politics became wrapped up in the 'demonization' of the other – Stalin and his – as Kennan would have it – abnormal state. The USSR could not be treated normally in diplomatic, economic and social terms so it had to be contained in Europe and Asia and then constrained across the globe.

A broader landscape

This broader landscape was missing from my original assessment of Stalin's Cold War. True enough the subtitle did contain 'Europe' to signal a narrow intent, and the Cold War game throughout the developing world only really gained urgency after Stalin's death in March 1953. Nevertheless, I should have made more of Stalin's fascination with empires: his own experience corralling the Central Asia republics into the newly formed USSR, as well as his views on the future of India, for example. Stalin saw a world in which there were many reasons after the defeat of fascism to see communism flourish across the globe, not least after decolonization. His avowedly anti-imperial discussions with Roosevelt were all wrapped up in a keen appreciation of colonial politics.

Those discussions with FDR were ones that allegedly infuriated Churchill, who preferred the realpolitik of a 'spheres of influence' agreement. The point here though is that Stalin did have a wider view. Most notably, the shaking of the world that occurred on the morning that Hiroshima was bombed meant that Stalin was indeed cut out of the occupation of Japan, despite all promises of that precious foothold in Asia. The balancing between West and East in the mind map of Stalin meant that the incitement of the Korean War was a chance to obtain some leverage in the region even if fatefully he misread the Western reaction.

And then there were the colonial wars of empires, a Malaya, an Algeria, which sapped British and French strength. Here too we see nuclear weapons leading to the development of 'proxy' wars. These conflicts, for example, witnessed the US underpinning French interests in Indo-China. Such wars, rooted in the broadening of the Cold War beyond Europe, are important because they cast long shadows – the imposition of the Shah in Iran or the later backing of the Mujahidin in Afghanistan fostered a broader Cold War. The militarization of the Cold War outside of Europe may have occurred primarily after Stalin, but the ambitions of the great powers are rooted in the ideology and moralism of the early years.

The costs of 'losing' territories or peoples became heightened in the context of a global competition. The rapid evolution of technology meant that wars became barbarous. Nowhere was this more apparent than in Vietnam when the extensive use of high-end combat against Soviet forces/proxies as well as against Vietnamese fighters meant that US aircraft dropped 7.6 million tonnes of bombs on South East Asian countries. The Allies had dropped a mere 3.4 million tonnes in the Second World War, 2.7 million tonnes on Germany. Laos formally neutral was hit by approx. 2.5 Million tonnes of high explosives – one ton of bombs for every person.

Throughout the Cold War endemic violence was perpetrated by states, proxies and sub-state groups.[54] What was curious in my early work – and there has subsequently been much fine scholarship by the likes of William Reno and Odd Arne Westad – was the absence of a Cold War from the ground up. In my account and many others 'the people' were missing. I did not deal with agency or the actors on the ground doing the work supposedly of communism or capitalism. (Big business was also absent). This is rather odd as the idea of 'the people' was central to Soviet and US claims about sovereignty, politics and the exercise of power. In US ideology the exercise of power has routinely been justified if conferred from below by the people. Hence in the post-1945 period the emphasis on the importance of elections and nation building after armed confrontation whether it be in a Germany, a Japan or later and disastrously an Iraq.

Villain

At the heart of contemporary debate is the thorny issue of Stalin. It is curious just how often positive assessments of the man were lost or rewritten after the end of the war. The preoccupation with FDR as Stalin's dupe, albeit an ailing dupe, has pervaded the literature: the apparent naivety that personal diplomacy could win over a canny ally his Achilles heel. While it has been fashionable for social scientists and historians alike to dwell on the personal qualities of leaders, much certainly of the Traditionalist accounts did in fact centre on the dangerous and untrustworthy qualities of the Soviet leader. While there is still a tendency to debate whether President Roosevelt had the full 'measure' of his Georgian ally,[55] or whether things could have been different if it had not been for Mr Truman, there is still something discordant and at odds in Traditionalist versions with the accounts of, for example, a 'beaming' Stalin as he met FDR for the first time,[56] or the descriptions of the scholarly, serious and bookish young Stalin. In those versions that took seriously psychological interpretations, Stalin himself was bestowed with a more human texture as personal relationships came under the spotlight. Eden's view that it was difficult having met Stalin to think of him 'dripping' in blood is but one of the assessments of wit, charm and charisma of the dictator.[57]

I started this chapter by asking whether Stalin had been forgotten. Certainly, the achievements of Stalin's Russia in defeating fascism seems to have been put to one side in contemporary Western politics, as does indeed the successful construction of the Grand Alliance and the pursuit by Stalin of cooperation with his Western allies after the war. Stalin rarely appears in current historical or political discourse except as villain, and usually a paranoid, damaged, brutish villain; if not forgotten, then certainly unsavoury. Comparisons have been raised between Stalin and some modern populist leaders. This matters because the wholesale use, abuse or interpretation of a historical figure affects contemporary politics. Stalin has long been dragged off his metaphorical and real pedestals in Western imaginations and historiography,[58] but he exists on multiple plinths in Russia.

Reflections

It may be, perhaps should be, impossible to rehabilitate Stalin, but in the current age of anxiety over Putin it is not a task that could be undertaken lightly. Given the new Cold War that characterizes East–West relations, positive assessments of Russia are unlikely to be welcome. Yet we may do well to reflect on how the original Cold War lasted for over two generations and the costs imposed not just on the Soviet peoples themselves but on other sites of contestation. As at the beginning of the Cold War the United States is richer, strategically superior and part of a successful military alliance – NATO. Russia is contained physically and economically. Oil and gas provide Moscow with some leverage over European states but a declining population, Chinese assertiveness and issues over who will succeed Putin render Russia vulnerable. But here there is something curious that takes us back to the early days of the Cold War: Putin remains optimistic that Russia will prevail and is on the right side of history, in contrast to a declining capitalist neo-liberal system. From the standpoint of the West this appears delusional but ignoring and containing contemporary Russia may mean repeating some of the errors of the original Cold War.

8

Working towards the *Vozhd*'? Stalin and the peace movement

Geoffrey Roberts

In his famous essay on the nature of Hitler's dictatorship, 'Working towards the Führer', Ian Kershaw highlighted a series of contrasts with Stalin's regime that help explain the cumulative and violent radicalization that led to the destruction and mass murder of the Nazi *Vernichtungskrieg*:

- The charismatic basis of Hitler's power, the bureaucratic basis of Stalin's
- The ordered and rational nature of Stalinism compared to the chaotic functioning of Nazi politics and bureaucracy
- The activism and interventionism of Stalin compared to Hitler's laziness and passivity as a decision-maker
- The indispensability of Hitler to the Nazi system, Stalin's replaceability within the Soviet system

As Kershaw points out, while there were very violent episodes of Stalinist radicalization – the collectivization of agriculture, breakneck industrialization, the Great Terror – these were transitory. After the dictator's death the Soviet system rapidly evolved into a conservative authoritarianism that functioned perfectly well without Stalin, his personality cult or his propensity for mass repression. In Hitler's case, the momentum of destructive radicalism was unstoppable because the Nazi regime was, in effect, system-less, and the Führer's mode of charismatic rule unleashed forces that he could not and, indeed, did not want to control.

One of the key dynamics was the opacity of Hitler's decision-making and efforts by people and officials at every level of the Third Reich to discern and anticipate their leader's wishes by a process of 'working towards the Führer': through the implementation on a trial-and-error basis of what they thought he wanted or would allow them to do.

Hitler's willing executors were not completely in the dark. 'Time after time', wrote Kershaw, 'Hitler set the barbaric tone, whether in hate-filled public speeches giving a green light to discriminatory action against Jews and other "enemies of the state", or in closed addresses to Nazi functionaries or military leaders where he laid down … brutal guidelines for the occupation of Poland and for "Operation Barbarossa".'

Hitler's charisma-based regime could never function normally, argues Kershaw, because the pursuit of national redemption through racial purification, war and conquest was inherently destructive and self-destructive. In sharp contrast to Soviet socialism, a peaceful evolution or end to the Nazi experiment was inconceivable.[1]

Implicit in Kershaw's treatment is the idea that Soviet officials did not need to work towards their boss or *Vozhd'* because Stalin's desires and intentions were readily apparent and formalized in resolutions, decrees and statements. Moreover, Stalin took many decisions himself, intervening frequently to shape the political and bureaucratic behaviour of those below.

Kershaw published his essay in the early 1990s, before scholars had a chance to work in the Russian archives and examine the internal functioning of Stalin's system. Decades of subsequent research have revealed that Kershaw's depiction of the Stalinist system was not far off the mark. Indeed, new researches have revealed the Soviet system as more bureaucratic and Stalin more of an activist decision-maker than anyone imagined. Equally, the archives have also revealed the limits to Stalin's activism and the surprising passivity with which he sometimes presided over his system of power, particularly after the Second World War.

Soviet decision-making under Stalin was based on explicit and detailed written policy directives. Every decision of political weight – in practice a very wide-ranging category – was the subject of a Central Committee or Politburo resolution, usually accompanied by extensive documentation. While the *Vozhd'* ruled, all the important decisions – and many trivial ones, too – were referred to him personally and processed by his office. This practice of referral to the top leader continued after Stalin's death, though with a more collectivist hue that brought other Politburo members into the picture.

This highly formalized process of decision-making clarified what Stalin and the Politburo wanted and expected from those below them in the hierarchy. Detailed reporting back by officials meant that what they did in response to directives could be subject to detailed scrutiny. The paper trail recording decisions and actions precluded any significant deviation from the party line, at least in theory.

While it was clear in general terms what Stalin wanted and expected, the details and specifics of the implementation of policy were often opaque, at least to middle-ranking officials, such as those who mediated the Politburo's relations with the international peace movement. In particular, the boundaries of what was permissible within the prescribed line were often unclear. This was especially true when Stalin was passive in relation to a particular policy area. Stalin's office processed proposals for action in relation to the peace movement on a weekly basis, but the boss was generally silent, rarely intervening directly or even making his background presence felt. Much like Nazi officials in Hitler's Germany, Soviet representatives to the peace movement had to guess how far they could go.

The general party line in relation to the international peace movement was crystal-clear: the Soviets wanted to create and sustain a mass, broad-based peace movement that would exercise influence favourable to the USSR and its foreign policy. But how broad-based would the movement be allowed to become? Was any deviation by the peace movement from the Soviet party line permissible? Could there be a degree of divergence between Soviet interests and peace movement interests? To what extent should the peace movement pursue its own agenda and forms of struggle for peace?

Above all, what was the trade-off between the political dividends that might result from a powerful but independent and diverse peace movement and the danger of losing control of its policies and politics?

The Soviet interlocutors in the peace movement also faced a further set of complications: they had to work with a foreign (mostly Western) leadership, which had its own ideas about policy and strategy. Peace movement leaders were loyal to Moscow – many of them were communists – but they saw themselves as critical friends of the Soviet Union who were entitled to express their own views. They did not always go along with the messages emanating from Moscow. They saw their relationship with the Soviets as a two-way process of lobbying, negotiation and compromise. While Moscow controlled the purse strings and exercised powerful ideological leadership, Soviet hegemony within the movement was based on consent, not coercion. It was the job of Moscow's representatives within the peace movement's leadership to win that consent and sometimes during the course of discussion they had to amend Soviet policy in order to do so.

In the case of the peace movement, 'working towards the *Vozhd*' entailed efforts to shape as well as to discern Stalin's preferences. Helpful in this respect was the fact that peace movement issues were dealt with by a Politburo Foreign Policy Commission, established in March 1949 to handle relations with foreign communist parties and associated movements and organizations. The commission was headed by Molotov, who had stepped down as Foreign Minister following the arrest of his wife, Polina, because of her association with members of the purged Soviet Jewish Anti-Fascist Committee.[2] But Molotov's close working relationship with Stalin continued and his presence in the decision-making process made it unlikely that anything to which the *Vozhd*' might object would reach the dictator's desk. It also meant that peace movement leaders could lobby Stalin through Molotov as well as by direct, written communication with him.

Like Hitler, Stalin was a powerful enabler; his support, passive though it might be, was essential to the priority and resources the peace movement received from Moscow. Certainly, peace movement leaders did not doubt Stalin's supreme importance as decision-maker. Their reports, proposals and entreaties were often addressed to him personally, especially at critical moments in the development of the peace movement. In effect, peace movement leaders sought to work through as well as toward Stalin to achieve their goal of a mass independent and influential peace movement that would, in their view, help prevent war, avert nuclear annihilation and preserve world peace.

Post-war Soviet foreign policy

Stalin's relations with the peace movement must also be viewed against the backdrop of broader trends in post-war Soviet foreign policy. Ted Hopf has identified three phases of Soviet foreign policy in the 1940s and 1950s, each associated with a distinct discourse about international politics. First, the discourse of collaboration during the period of the grand alliance with Britain and the United States (1941–7). Second, the discourse of danger during the early years of the Cold War (1947–53), which were dominated by

Soviet fears and perceptions of acute external and internal threats. Third, the post-Stalin era's discourse of difference – the idea that the socialist system was not under existential threat and that the Soviet Union could and should tolerate a degree of difference at home and abroad.[3]

As I have argued elsewhere,[4] the lacuna in Hopf's analysis is that between the discourses of danger and difference there was an intermediary or transitional phase in which the peace movement played a predominant part. While the peace movement grew out of the discourse of danger, its broad-based politics anticipated the post-Stalin discourse of difference. Indeed, by the early 1950s the discourse of danger – associated with the Cominform and Zhdanov's two-camps doctrine – had been largely superseded by a discourse that revolved around the possibility of constructing a coalition of diverse political forces that could mount a successful struggle for peace. In effect, the peace movement provided Stalin and the Soviets with an alternative foreign strategy to the confrontational policy enunciated by Zhdanov.

Crucially, the Soviet struggle for peace was waged at home as well as abroad. Within the USSR there developed a mass popular peace movement that articulated and reinforced Soviet state self-identity as fundamentally peace-loving. The mobilizational success of the peace movement internationally also gave the Soviet leadership hope that war with the West could be averted and the Cold War ended by political means. This peace struggle discourse emerged, developed – indeed came to the fore – while Stalin was still alive. Although Stalin was not particularly active in this discourse's development and was somewhat sceptical about prospects for ending the Cold War, he allowed the peace movement strategy to run its course.

After Stalin's death the Soviet leadership launched a so-called peace offensive calling for a negotiated resolution of Cold War differences. Often seen as a new departure, it was, in fact, a continuation of Soviet peace campaigning during the late Stalin era. This was the starting point for the radical changes in post-Stalin Soviet foreign policy and for the rise of the discourse of difference.

The idea that Stalin began to step away from the Cold War as early as the late 1940s was the theme of Marshall D. Shulman in *Stalin's Foreign Policy Reappraised*, published in 1963. However, Shulman's book was perforce based on public Soviet and communist sources and as a result he tended to exaggerate the extent to which the peace movement directly reflected Moscow's will. With the aid of Russian party, state and foreign policy archives it is now possible to tell a more nuanced story not just of the relationship between the peace movement and Soviet foreign strategy, but the particular role played by Stalin.

Emergence of the peace movement

The progenitor of the post-war communist peace movement was the World Congress of Intellectuals for Peace, held in Wroclaw in August 1948.[5] The staging of the congress is commonly attributed to the Soviets. In fact, the event was initiated by the French and Polish communists in February 1948 when they established a preparatory committee of twenty-five important cultural figures from France and Poland. The Soviets were not represented on that committee. Not until July did the Poles send an emissary to Moscow seeking Soviet participation in the congress. The Polish delegate also sought Moscow's advice on a number of policy and political issues. As Soviet officials noted in their report on the conversation with the Pole, this Franco–Polish initiative had been undertaken 'without the prior agreement of the [Soviet party]'. Among the questions discussed was a proposal to establish an annual Peace Prize as an alternative to the Nobel Peace Prize. But the officials in the Foreign Policy Department (a predecessor of Molotov's Foreign Policy Commission) considered such an unnamed prize inadvisable – advice that presaged the creation of the Stalin Peace Prizes a couple of years later.[6]

In the event the Soviets sent a large delegation to the congress, led by Aleksandr Fadeev, head of the Soviet Writers' Union. Another prominent participant was the writer and journalist Ilya Ehrenburg, destined in the 1950s to became one of the peace movement's best-known leaders internationally. Together with Fadeev, Ehrenburg was the main Soviet representative in the higher echelons of the peace movement. Importantly, the two men did not just passively receive orders from Stalin and the Politburo. They helped frame policy and compose the texts of the resolutions that contained the directives they were mandated to carry out. What they proposed in Moscow often reflected prior discussions at international meetings with their fellow peace movement leaders.

Before departing for Poland, the delegation was issued with a directive on Soviet policy for the congress: its role was to mobilize the progressive intelligentsia against the aggressive policies of the United States and American plans to 'enslave' Europe. Soviet delegates were instructed to highlight the leading role of the USSR in the struggle for peace, democracy and national independence, and to speak out against the persecution of progressive intellectuals in Western countries.[7] These proposals, it should be noted, were no different from those put forward by the French and Polish communists.

The Wroclaw congress was a big success. Some 500 delegates from forty-six countries attended, including a dazzling array of famous Western scientists, artists and intellectuals. Albert Einstein sent a message of support as did Henry Wallace, former Vice-President of the United States and Progressive Party candidate in the 1948 US presidential election. In his speech Fadeev claimed the USSR was supported by the world's intelligentsia, citing names such as Anatole France, Henri Barbusse, Pablo Neruda, Frédéric Joliot-Curie, George Bernard Shaw and Roman Rolland. The British historian, A.J.P. Taylor spoke in favour of intellectual freedom on both sides of the iron curtain, while a scattering of delegates (including Taylor) voted against a manifesto calling for national cultural congresses in defence of peace, the creation of national peace committees, and the strengthening of international links among pro-peace intellectuals. To further these aims the congress established an International Liaison Committee of Intellectuals for Peace (ILC) with headquarters in Paris. Among its members were Fadeev and P.N. Fedoseev, the chief editor of the Soviet party theoretical journal, *Bolshevik*.

At the end of December 1948 Molotov sent Stalin a resolution proposing the organization of a broad-based 'international congress of partisans of peace', to be held in Paris or Geneva in February or March 1949. The congress would rally support across the world for Soviet proposals on arms control and the prohibition of nuclear weapons. A gathering of 1,500–2,000 delegates was envisaged and it would cost the Soviets a subsidy of 50,000–100,000 dollars.[8] In the next iteration of this resolution, dated 6 January 1949, the reference to supporting Soviet policies was omitted – possibly at Stalin's behest – and replaced by a general campaign for a 'lasting peace'. Fadeev and Fedoseev were instructed to put this proposal to the ILC.[9]

Like many of Moscow's initiatives in relation to the peace movement, the Soviet position evolved during the course of discussion. Fadeev's proposal for an international congress was accepted but the date put back until April and there was a request for a Soviet delegation, including Ehrenburg, to attend a peace congress in New York in March. The participation of 'bourgeois' politicians in the Paris congress was also raised. Molotov agreed to this but said they should not have a leading role in the organization of the congress and insisted that Moscow should be consulted about who was invited onto the organizing committee. These communications, and many others about the preparation of the congress, were conducted via cypher telegrams to and from the Soviet embassy in Paris.[10]

The Soviet delegation to the World Congress of Partisans of Peace was led by Fadeev, with Fedoseev acting as secretary.[11] The directives setting out Soviet policy for the congress stated that the main aim was to ensure the peace movement involved as many people as possible, irrespective of national, political and religious differences.[12]

Attended by nearly 2,000 delegates claiming to represent 600 million people in 72 countries, the Paris congress was graced by even more luminaries than the Wroclaw gathering. It was opened by Frédéric Joliot-Curie, the French nuclear scientist and Nobel laureate, who told his fellow scientists that 'it is our duty to prevent the use of atomic energy for destructive purposes, to prevent this abuse of science and to support the efforts of those who propose to outlaw atomic weapons'. Another notable speech was given by Pietro Nenni, the leader of the Italian Socialist Party, who implicitly contradicted Zhdanov's two-camps doctrine when he said: 'Our Congress does not place before the nations of the world the dilemma of choosing between the Soviet Union and the United States of America. To have to make this choice would mean that we are already at war and that we already consider the struggle for peace lost.'[13]

Resolutions were passed condemning the establishment of NATO, opposing the rearmament of Germany and Japan, and calling for the prohibition of nuclear weapons. A hundred-strong Permanent Committee of Partisans of Peace (PCPP) was elected with representatives from 50 countries and international organizations. After the congress, national meetings were organized in countries across the world by peace committees supporting the PCPP.[14]

Fadeev and Fedoseev reported to Stalin on the results of the congress in early May. The meeting demonstrated, they wrote, the broad basis of the Partisans for Peace. Fifty to sixty per cent of delegates had a communist perspective but there were a range of participants from diverse social, democratic, cultural, religious and political organizations. Women's organizations had played an important role in the congress as had left-wing socialists from Britain, bourgeois liberals from France and Italy and delegates from Africa and the Far East.[15]

Stalin: Man of peace

Symbolically, Stalin loomed large in the peace movement. In 1951 Soviets launched their alternative to the Nobel Peace Prize – the International Stalin Prize for Strengthening Peace among Peoples. Several such prizes were awarded each year to prominent peace movement leaders, activists and cultural figures.[16] Stalin's death in 1953 was mourned as the loss of a great man of peace and his successors pledged to continue the Stalinist peace offensive that had begun in the late 1940s.

Yet while he was alive Stalin had little to do directly with the peace movement. He did not even attend the conferences of the Soviet peace movement and rarely met with the leaders of the international movement. Publicly, he made general noises in support of the struggle for peace but said little or nothing specific about the peace movement and its activities.

Stalin was just as passive and silent behind closed doors. His only known intervention in the practical affairs of the peace movement came on the eve of the Paris congress. In March 1949 he exchanged a series of telegrams with Terabin, the Soviet representative to the regions of China controlled by the Chinese communists. Stalin was keen for the Chinese to send 20–30 delegates to Paris, including Soong Ching-ling, the third wife of the late founder of the Chinese Republic, Sun Yat-sen. (In 1951 Soong Ching-ling was awarded one of the first Stalin Peace Prizes.) Unfortunately, Soong Ching-ling was sick and, in any case, living in territory controlled by Chang Kai-shek's nationalists. However, the Chinese did send a large delegation to Paris and Stalin took a detailed interest in the arrangements for their transit across Soviet territory.[17]

There were 44 Chinese delegates to the Paris event, four of whom made speeches and four were elected to the permanent committee set up by the congress. In October 1949 – after the communist victory in the civil war – a peace conference in Beijing attracted more than a thousand delegates. Subsequently, there was considerable Chinese engagement with the international peace movement. Hundreds of millions of Chinese signed the movement's anti-nuclear petitions, more than from any other country, including the Soviet Union.[18]

In 1952 Stalin made what could be construed as an indirect intervention in the politics of the peace movement. In his last published work, *Economic Problems of the USSR*, in a section entitled 'The Inevitability of Wars Between Capitalist Countries', he took issue with 'comrades' who 'hold that, owing to the development of new international conditions since the Second World War, wars between capitalist countries have ceased to be inevitable'.[19] It is not clear which comrades Stalin had in mind. It might have been peace movement politicians like Nenni or people closer to home such as Mikhail Suslov, Zhdanov's successor as Soviet ideology chief, who at a meeting of the Cominform Secretariat in April 1950 criticized fatalistic talk about the inevitability of war and emphasized the 'Lenin–Stalin thesis on the possibility of peaceful coexistence between capitalism and socialism'.[20] This theme was taken up by an editorial in the Cominform newspaper, *For a Lasting Peace, For a People's Democracy!*:

> One of the main propaganda theses of the Anglo-American imperialists is that of the inevitability of war. This thesis is the basis for the war hysteria which they are

fomenting ... We must be firm in the knowledge that war is not inevitable ... it depends on the partisans of peace ... That is why the exposure of the thesis of the fatal inevitability of war ... is the most important task of the communist parties.[21]

By contrast, Stalin sought to reaffirm traditional Marxist doctrine that the contradictions of capitalism and imperialism inevitably led to wars between capitalist states. Theoretically, that remained true, insisted Stalin, but in practice the peace movement – if it was strong enough – could prevent each and every particular war threatened by capitalism. This crucial qualification of traditional doctrine could not but underline the importance of the peace movement. Hence Stalin's formulation may perhaps be seen as his arcane way of accepting the peace movement's rhetoric on the question of the inevitability of war without ditching traditional doctrine.

Economic Problems of the USSR appeared on the eve of the 19th party congress in October 1952. Stalin did not make a major speech at the congress but he did edit heavily the Central Committee report, which was drafted and presented by Georgy Malenkov. However, Stalin made little or no change to the section in which Malenkov spoke about the struggle for peace and the Soviet Union as a peace-loving state.[22]

The PCPP held its first meeting in Rome in October 1949. By the time it met, the Stalin–Tito split was at its height, as was the purge of so-called Titoites from the communist movement. Anticipating Soviet wishes, peace movement leaders resolved to exclude Yugoslav representatives from the Rome meeting and to dis-affiliate Yugoslavia's national peace committee.[23] This display of fealty to Moscow was not without cost. It strengthened the peace movement's identification with the Soviet Union and undermined its claims to independence and diversity. Some left-wing socialists broke with the peace movement because of the anti-Tito campaign. A prominent example was Konni Zilliacus, a British MP, one of the stars of the Paris congress, who had been expelled from the Labour Party because of his support for the peace movement. Soviet attitudes towards Zilliacus were curiously contradictory. He was shunned by the Soviets because of his support for Tito's Yugoslavia and depicted as an imperialist agent and spy. In September 1949, for example, the Soviet embassy in London was warned by Moscow that Zilliacus was a 'cunning agent of British intelligence' who pretended he was left-wing as a cover for intelligence activities in the people's democracies.[24] Yet, as we shall see, they continued to cultivate relations with him in the context of the peace movement.[25]

The Stockholm Appeal

The peace movement's first big public campaign was the Stockholm Appeal, launched at a PCPP meeting in the Swedish capital in March 1950. The Soviets supported this initiative but the idea came from the French.[26]

The PCPP campaign was fronted by its Chair, Frédéric Joliot-Curie, who had headed France's nuclear energy programme until he was sacked by the French government in April 1950. Joliot-Curie supported the peaceful use of nuclear energy but was implacably opposed to its militarization. He was also President of the World

Federation of Scientific Workers, which sought to mobilize scientists against the nuclear danger.[27]

The Stockholm Appeal called for the prohibition of nuclear weapons. While the Soviets had tested their own nuclear bomb in August 1949, they continued to support universal prohibition as long as the Americans gave up their bombs and there were international controls to ensure that no other country went nuclear.

The success of the Stockholm Appeal campaign exceeded all expectations: by the end of the year half a billion people – a quarter of the world's population in 1950 – had signed the petition. When the petition was launched, however, there were concerns the campaign would not take off. On 10 June 1950 Ehrenburg wrote to Stalin personally with his observations on the progress of the campaign. In East Germany people did not know what they were signing, while in Belgium there was little sign of any campaign. In Sweden the communist party leadership did not understand the campaign and claimed it was of little interest to the Swedish people. In France the movement had failed to broaden its base by including supporters of neutrality. The movement's journal *Partisans of Peace* was weak and had little circulation. In conclusion Ehrenburg wrote: 'Forgive me dear Joseph Vissarionovich for taking up your time with this letter but it seems to me that urgent measures are necessary. Partisans for Peace needs to expand if the (next) congress ... is to be as broad and influential as that in Paris.'[28]

There is no record of a reply by Stalin but on 4 July the Politburo passed a resolution, 'Measures for the Further Development of Partisans for Peace', noting, as had Ehrenburg, that while the Stockholm Petition had evoked a popular response, the campaign was weak in countries where there was no serious commitment to it. The most important task of the peace movement, the resolution stated, was to strengthen its mass base.[29] In a plenary address to the staff of the Politburo's Foreign Policy Commission in mid-July 1950 Ehrenburg noted that while the USSR's domestic peace campaign rightly emphasized the peace-loving policies of the Soviet Union, the Soviets should not publicly claim leadership of the international peace movement.[30]

In August 1950 Stalin's officials sent him a report on a conversation that they had conducted with Ehrenburg about his recent trip to Britain. According to Ehrenburg the British Peace Committee (BPC) was too communist, quite weak, and split over whether to collect signatures for the petition or to organize strikes in war factories. In Britain he met members of the pacifist National Peace Council (NPC), including Zilliacus, who told Ehrenburg that the NPC was willing to collaborate with the PCPP but not with the BPC because it was 'insignificant'. When Ehrenburg objected, Zilliacus agreed there could be some cooperation between the BPC and the NPC. In Ehrenburg's view cooperation with the NPC was very important, especially in relation to the Stockholm Appeal. Ehrenburg also saw possibilities for cooperation with the left-wing of the Labour Party, with progressive scientists, and, perhaps more surprisingly, with British Baptists. He thought it important – organizational and political difficulties notwithstanding – that the next world peace congress be held in London or a city in another capitalist country.[31]

In the event the WPC decided to stage the second World Peace Congress in Sheffield in November 1950, but when the British authorities refused entry to a number of delegates the venue was hurriedly changed to Warsaw, a contingency for which the Soviets were prepared organizationally.

The Soviets were pleased with the success of the Stockholm Appeal but thought the movement needed to campaign more generally against war and in favour of peace. They also thought the Warsaw congress should pass a resolution condemning prominent Western warmongers such as Winston Churchill, Charles de Gaulle, John Foster Dulles and Dwight D. Eisenhower. To broaden its political basis the movement needed to attract more women and young people and conduct a more active campaign in countries such as the United States, Canada, Britain and Australia. Moscow expected the congress to attract 2,500–3,000 delegates and allocated the hard currency equivalent of half a million roubles to defray expenses.[32]

The World Peace Council

By the time the congress took place the Korean War was in full swing and delegates passed a motion urging peace in Korea, as well as resolutions calling for a meeting of Britain, China, France, the Soviet Union and the United States and for 50 per cent cuts in the armed forces of the great powers. The congress also decided to replace the PCPP by a 220-strong World Peace Council with representatives from 58 countries.

In relation to the warmongers resolution there was a minor hiccup when Fadeev reported to Moscow that some delegates at the congress did not want to name names. To maintain a united front, Fadeev asked for authorization to omit names from the resolution, and was duly authorized to do so by Stalin and the Politburo.[33]

After the congress Fadeev, Ehrenburg and others sent Stalin a long report. More than 2,000 delegates from 81 countries attended the congress. It was a relatively youthful congress with three-fifths of the delegates aged under 40. A good number of the delegates were from the arts, sciences and professions, and a fifth of them female. There were 59 parliamentarians present (fewer than at the Paris congress) and representatives from 13 international organizations, though most of these were from other communist-led fronts. A total of 722 delegates were communists.[34]

In their covering letter to Stalin, Fadeev et al. argued that the congress showed the peace movement had developed into a mass movement. To develop further the movement needed to broaden its appeal to cultural, religious and pacifist organizations. Among the next steps should be a meeting of the WPC in Berlin or Vienna to discuss the German question and Western plans to remilitarize West Germany, a meeting that should include representatives of organizations that did not want to be part of the peace movement but were willing to cooperate with it on some issues.[35]

This broad front approach to the development of the peace movement – which revived the communist popular frontism and anti-fascism of the 1930s and 1940s – was fine in theory, but in practice the Soviets and their closest supporters were intolerant of any dissent or opposition. O. John Rogge, an American leftist delegate to the Warsaw congress and a member of PCPP, received a very hostile reception when he criticized Soviet foreign policy and rejected the demonization of Tito and the

Yugoslav communists.[36] In the report to Stalin, Rogge was dismissed as a paid agent of Tito's who had received no support from other congress delegates.

The first meeting of the newly created WPC was held in Berlin in February 1951 and it decided to organize a new petition campaign calling for a peace pact between the five great powers (Britain, China, France, the USA and the USSR). The call for such a pact had been a central plank of Soviet foreign policy since 1949.

Just before the Berlin meeting Stalin answered some questions from a *Pravda* correspondent. Asked if a new world war was inevitable he answered that no, it was not, at least for now, notwithstanding the aggressive plans of reactionary governments who were trying to hoodwink their peoples into believing that peace-loving countries were aggressive. The reactionaries had turned down Soviet proposals for a peace pact, for reductions in armaments and the banning of atomic weapons because they were afraid of the campaign for peace. 'Peace will be preserved and prolonged if people take the cause of peace into their own hands ... As for the Soviet Union, it will stick to its policy of preventing war and preserving peace.'[37]

The Berlin Appeal, as it was called, amassed 100 million more signatures than the Stockholm petition but it took two years to do so. As Nenni said: 'to gain 500 million signatures to the Stockholm appeal it was enough to appeal to the emotions'.[38] The peace pact campaign was a much more political and clearly pro-Soviet endeavour. It also ran counter to peace movement efforts to broaden its identity by reaching out to independent peace campaigners. But Moscow accorded the peace pact campaign the highest priority and this was reflected in numerous instructions given to Ehrenburg and Fadeev in 1951–2.

Vienna peace congress

Peace movement leaders acceded to Soviet wishes for a sustained campaign for a peace pact but with dwindling enthusiasm. Increasingly, their attention turned to the character, timing and location of the movement's next world congress. What they had in mind was an attempt to break out of the isolation – reinforced by the Korean War and the intensifying Cold War – that resulted from the peace movement's close identification with the Soviet Union and the communist bloc. Hence the decision to convene in Vienna at the end of 1952 a Congress of Peoples for Peace. The idea was to reach out to non-aligned peace campaigners and involve the representatives of a wider range of social, political, cultural and trade union organizations, together with an increase in the number of parliamentarians present. Invited to attend the congress were all those committed to negotiations to resolve international problems.[39]

This was an important but politically hazardous initiative by the peace movement, and the spectre of a repeat of the Rogge affair haunted preparations for the congress. These concerns were heightened when, in November 1952, Stalin took a personal, albeit indirect, interest in the congress via his private secretary, A.N. Poskrebyshev, who asked for a report on pre-congress preparations. Soviet officials in the Foreign Policy Commission spoke to Ehrenburg, who warned them that because of its broad-based character the Vienna congress would not be the same as the Paris and Warsaw congresses. Decisions taken by the congress would be consensus-based and it might not even be possible to reach agreement on the peace pact campaign, though the Soviets should continue to push for its prioritization. It might even be necessary to set up new organizational structures – distinct from those of the WPC – to implement congress decisions. But Ehrenburg's main message was that the congress should be seen as an opportunity to significantly broaden and strengthen the struggle for peace.[40]

Ehrenburg's approach was reflected in the directive to the Soviet delegation to the congress. In deference, perhaps, to Stalin's sensibilities the directive noted that because of its open character the congress might be 'penetrated by elements with provocative aims'. The delegation was instructed to do all it could to ensure that progressive, non-communist elements rebuffed any such provocations.[41]

The Vienna congress was similar in size to its predecessors in Paris and Warsaw (1,857 representatives from 85 countries) but its composition was more diverse and its discussions more open. Among the attendees was Giuseppe Nitti, the liberal chair of the Italian parliament's peace group, and the French philosopher Jean-Paul Sartre. In his speech Nitti paid tribute to the openness of the congress's deliberations, while Sartre described the congress as an 'extraordinary experience', one that for him was on a par with the Popular Front of 1936 and the Liberation of France in 1944.[42] Resolutions passed by the congress were less strident versions of existing WPC policies but included the demand for a five-power peace pact. There was also an important new discursive theme at the congress: the need to create conditions conducive to the reduction of international tensions.

After Stalin

After the congress the Soviets wanted to continue the five-power pact campaign but peace movement leaders such as Pietro Nenni were increasingly resistant, arguing instead for a more broad-based approach. By the time these discussions took place in mid-March 1953, Stalin was dead. Coincidentally, the last foreigner to meet him was Dr Saifuddin Kitchlew, the head of India's peace committee. Kitchlew was in Moscow to receive his Stalin Peace Prize and on 17 February he had an hour-long meeting with the *Vozhd'* in the Kremlin.[43]

At a meeting of the Supreme Soviet on 15 March, Malenkov, the new Soviet Premier, declared 'there is no disputed or unresolved problem that cannot be resolved on the basis of mutual agreement between interested parties'.[44] Malenkov's remarks gave Ehrenburg the scope to support a call by Nenni for a broader peace campaign. When the WPC Buro met again in May he argued that recent improvements in the international atmosphere meant that a campaign in favour of negotiations to reduce international tensions had a real chance of success, and that the achievement of a peace pact should be the culmination rather than the spearhead of such a campaign. Ehrenburg's remarks signalled the end of the peace pact campaign. When the WPC returned to petitioning a year or two later it was to anti-nuclear petitions like the Stockholm Appeal.

At its meeting in Budapest in June 1953 – an enlarged forum attended by the representatives of a number of religious, pacifist and non-communist political organizations – the full WPC decided to launch a world campaign for negotiations aimed at lessening international tensions. As Ehrenburg reported to Molotov (reinstated as foreign minister after Stalin's death), the campaign for negotiations would take different forms in different countries, depending on local issues.[45] In August Suslov proposed a major Soviet domestic campaign in favour of the negotiated resolution of international problems.[46] Subsequently, this became a major theme of Soviet foreign policy, with the added ingredient of a call for the restoration of trust in international relations. This was the beginning of a substantial campaign by the Soviets in 1953–5 to end the Cold War and begin nuclear disarmament.[47]

Like the new Soviet collective leadership, peace movement leaders felt liberated and empowered by Stalin's death to push the boundaries of permissible policy in a direction that suited the needs of their domain of struggle. Ehrenburg, in particular, became ever bolder in his efforts to make the peace movement more independent of Moscow. Indeed, by 1957 – in the aftermath of the Hungarian crisis – he had persuaded the Soviet leadership to issue an edict that the peace movement should no longer be treated as an adjunct of Moscow's foreign policy.

While Stalin's background presence had constrained efforts by peace movement leaders to unshackle themselves from Moscow, it did not stop them from trying. Their greatest success was in persuading Stalin and the Soviet leadership to accept the political risks entailed by the Vienna peace congress. Three years later, at the Helsinki World Peace Assembly of June 1955, they staged an even more diverse and open event. According to Soviet analysts nearly a quarter of the members of the World Peace Council elected by the Assembly were representatives of 'bourgeois political parties'. In his report to the Soviet leadership on the assembly Ehrenburg was frank about delegates' criticisms of the WPC and the USSR but highlighted, too, the enthusiastic support for the peace-loving policies of the Soviet Union and the 'evidence of the great turn among broad sections of international public opinion in favour of negotiations and the reduction of international tensions'.[48]

Conclusion

As Ian Kershaw noted, while Hitler's leadership was pivotal to the functioning of the Nazi regime, it was also inimical to rational decision-making. Stalin was similarly pivotal in the Soviet system but his regime displayed a high degree of operational rationality. The rational-bureaucratic nature of the Soviet system both restrained and enabled peace movement leaders. Their actions were constrained by Politburo resolutions and decisions but they could use the same mechanism to articulate and further their own goals. The system itself provided the means through which they could influence Stalin.

The analogy with Hitler's regime should not be pushed too far, but Kershaw's 'working towards the the Führer' hypothesis can help illuminate how the Soviet system under Stalin sometimes worked in surprising ways.

Stalin was both pervasive and passive in relation to peace movement policy-making but that did not impede the movement's development into an increasingly pluralistic political force. Peace movement leaders were highly successful in interpreting Stalin's wishes and furthering their own agenda within the Soviet political bureaucracy. Stalin's silence in relation to peace movement affairs allowed its leaders to take seriously the stated Soviet commitment to an inclusive struggle for peace. There is no evidence that Stalin resisted the direction in which Ehrenburg and others wanted to take the movement. On the contrary, he was buoyed by the success of the peace movement and drawn towards the voluntarist rhetoric that Western warmongers could be defeated politically and war averted.

9

Constructing a confession: The language and psychology of interrogations in Stalinist Czechoslovakia

Molly Pucci

For two weeks, day after day, for twenty hours on end, I had to tell the interrogator my life history, from my childhood up to 28 January 1951, when two cars drove up and I was kidnapped in the middle of Prague. I had been in the hands of State Security for six months, but I had not yet realized that I had entered a world of fastidious repetition, protocol, reports, paperwork and signatures. I was not aware of the stage I had reached. It was an apprenticeship, in a way, my apprenticeship in an absurd, evasive, destructive activity – the fabrication of my confessions.[1]

This passage was written by Artur London, a defendant in the show trial of Czechoslovak Communist Party General Secretary Rudolf Slánský and his thirteen alleged co-conspirators in late November 1952. In his 1968 memoir, *On Trial*, London described the process of writing his confession during months of battles against tireless Czechoslovak interrogators and mysterious Soviet advisers. As his account attests, confessions were a cornerstone of Stalinist political violence. Torture, sleepless nights, food deprivation, and threats were all used to force defendants to sign them. And they became a symbol of the excesses and arbitrariness of Stalinist violence after the leader's death in 1953. In his 1956 'secret speech', Nikita Khrushchev placed confessions at the centre of the universe of arrests, executions, and show trials that shattered the communist movement during the Great Terror in the late 1930s:

> The only proof of guilt used, against all norms of current legal science, was the 'confession' of the accused. As subsequent probing has proven, 'confessions' were acquired through physical pressure against the accused. This led to glaring violations of revolutionary legality and the fact that many entirely innocent individuals who in the past had defended the Party line became victims.[2]

But it remains a puzzle why a regime that provided no legal protections for the accused and vastly expedited the process of convicting prisoners bothered to attain confessions at all. As historian David Hoffman put it, 'The question is not so much why purge victims confessed – the use of torture by the secret police is well documented. Rather, the question is why such elaborate confessions were necessary.'[3] Some historians have argued that confessions were attained to spread an orthodox view of communist ideology. One account argues that confessions forced communists to come face-to-face with their ideological shortcomings.[4] Others contend that they were used to convince the regime's enemies of the righteousness of Marxist-Leninist ideas.[5] Still others perceived them in terms of administrative practices. According to one interpretation, there was simply no other evidence to prove the guilt of the people Stalin wanted to destroy.[6] Another suggested that confessions provided easy forms of evidence during periods of mass arrests since they were 'mass produced' by reiterating party jargon and revealed little about the people they purported to describe.[7]

This chapter considers both ideological and administrative interpretations to understanding the place of confessions in Stalinist political violence. It also seeks to explain why confessions were emphasized yet again during the Terror in East European communist parties between 1949 and 1954. The recreation of the Terror inside communist parties – albeit at a far smaller scale than in the Soviet Union – suggests that we cannot explain the issue by looking only at contingencies specific to the USSR in the 1930s.[8] This chapter takes Czechoslovakia in the late 1940s and early 1950s as the main case study. It argues that confessions played an important role in creating and training the interrogation department and its agents in Stalinist administrative practices and orthodox beliefs. The party trials, then, were not only a period of repression or attempt to destroy Stalin's enemies (a term that did not describe any defendants in the Slánský trial), but also an integral part of building and expanding the Czechoslovak police state.

To understand why this was so, it is necessary to explore the role of confessions in the Stalinist legal system more broadly. After all, as historian Edward Peters has pointed out in his study of torture from medieval to modern times, confessions have for centuries been considered the 'queen of proof' in the legal systems of continental Europe. And legal cultures in which confessions hold a prominent place rely more extensively on the use of torture during pre-trial investigations than those that do not.[9] How was the Stalinist system particular? First, confessions were only used as evidence in political cases.[10] As legal scholar Peter Solomon has pointed out, the restriction of confessions to political crimes was perceived as an advance over Tsarist practices in which confessions were considered the best evidence in all cases.[11] The emphasis on confessions was introduced to Czechoslovakia in late 1949 when many judicial protections and procedures were suspended after the announcement that enemies had infiltrated the KSČ. This legal state of exception, which lasted until the end of the Stalinist period, shaped the ethos and methods of the interrogation department and its newly recruited staff. Second, confessions in the Stalinist system were often attained with the goal of staging public trials of the defendants. Defendants in show trials, particularly former communists, were to be morally and psychologically broken to the point that they would both memorize the confession and repeat it in a public forum. In this way, confessions had a didactic function. They were a lesson for the public and a way to demonstrate the power of the state to destroy its enemies.[12]

The Soviet advisers, who arrived in Prague at the end of 1949, played a significant role in shifting the emphasis of Czechoslovak legal procedure from the investigation of crimes to the attainment of confessions. A study of the interrogation department in Prague therefore sheds light on the micro-processes underpinning the Sovietization of the Czechoslovak secret police and judiciary. Differences between Czechoslovak and Soviet systems, this chapter shows, were evident not only in questions of ideology – the idea that the Czechoslovaks would pursue a "national road to socialism" after the Second World War – but also in administrative practices. Such issues included the structure of the interrogation department, the information interrogators received about defendants, the purpose of interrogations, the standards of evidence required to attain convictions, and the methods of recording information (in the Soviet system, a key question was which information was *not* recorded – namely, anything attesting to a suspect's innocence).

The chapter reconstructs the process of writing confessions from the perspectives of the interrogators and the defendants. It focuses closely on a few documents to reveal the theories and practices of interrogations. Like most accounts of Stalinist Terror, it draws on the defendants' memoirs, in particular Artur London's memoir, *On Trial*. For the purpose of cross-country comparison, it contrasts London's account with that of Hungarian defendant, Béla Szász, who was arrested in the same period, and Aleksander Solzhenitsyn, who was arrested in the Soviet Union in 1941. As in other memoirs written by victims of the Stalinist Terror, interrogators feature as central figures in these accounts. They represented the most visible face of the regime's brutality and violence. Unlike secret police operative agents, who conducted surveillance on suspects covertly (or through hidden informer networks), interrogators confronted prisoners on a daily basis over the course of weeks, months, or even years. The accused were convinced that the interrogator decided whether a prisoner would be freed, fed, starved or executed. But it is necessary to approach this perspective critically, since interrogators sought to convince prisoners of their power, influence and omnipotence precisely in order to attain confessions.

The chapter therefore also examines the interrogators' documents. How much power did they have to influence the outcome of a case? Did they believe the charges against the accused? What, in their view, was the purpose of the confessions? How did Czechoslovak interrogators interact with their Soviet advisers? To study these issues, I examine a 1951 training manual for interrogators and the testimony of former Czechoslovak interrogator, Bohumil Doubek, *StB o sobě*. The latter was written after Doubek's arrest in 1955 (before Khrushchev's speech in 1956, when it became widely known that the regime had extracted confessions through torture). While clearly written to justify his actions in the interrogation department, Doubek's account contains remarkable details on what Czechoslovak interrogators were told to do, the information they were given, and their interactions with the Soviets.

The first part of the chapter recreates the structure and goals of the interrogation department during the party trials in Czechoslovakia in the late 1940s and early 1950s. The second examines how interrogators were trained by achieving confessions through torture, psychological pressure and the manipulation of language. The role of Soviet advisers, who helped reorganize the interrogation department and train its newly recruited officials in Czechoslovakia, is addressed throughout.

The interrogation department: Powers, structure, purpose

The interrogation department was created in communist Czechoslovakia in 1951. From the communist takeover of power in February 1948 to the creation of the department in 1951, the same agents who carried out surveillance operations had also conducted interrogations on suspects. It was a system, one agent explained, in which 'everyone did everything'.[13] For this reason, security agents entered the interrogation room with knowledge of who a defendant was, the charges against him, the evidence collected on him and the reason he had been arrested. None of these assumptions was true of the special department dedicated to interrogations in 1951. Interrogations were carried out after suspects were identified, subjected to surveillance operations and arrested. All of these steps were the purview of the operative department of the secret police. Operative agents decided who to target and why. Interrogators were responsible only for attaining confessions and compiling the materials sent to court for a public or secret trial.

When the Soviet advisers arrived in Prague in September 1949, they pushed forward the shift toward these new methods. Soon after their arrival, much of the correspondence collected by local interrogators was translated into Russian. As London described:

> Important reports were translated into Russian. This was the version that counted. The advisers made the necessary changes and corrections before passing them to the group leaders whose job it was to force the defendant to sign them. This system enabled the advisers not only to follow the interrogations step by step but also to establish the direction of the 'confessions' and organize competitions between each group and between interrogators within the group [on who could attain the greatest number of confessions].[14]

Although the Soviet advisers followed the work of Czechoslovak interrogators closely, they also allowed them to develop their own methods of attaining confessions. According to London, 'Our interrogators bragged about their formulations between themselves with as much vanity as bad poets.'[15] Doubek, who headed a group of interrogators at the time, confirmed that each had 'his own way of doing things'.[16] The 1951 training manual stressed the importance of 'personal initiative' (*vlastní iniciativa*) in achieving success.[17] Officials were rewarded with promotions and privileges for their initiative and activism in attaining confessions.

Since the interrogation department was separate from other investigative stages, interrogators only received minimal information about defendants. This reality shaped their perception of guilt and innocence. In short, from the early 1950s, interrogators were told that if a defendant had been arrested, this meant that enough evidence had been collected on him by the operative department to prove his guilt. In the formulation of the training manual: 'A person is not arrested or interrogated because he did something good, but because he engaged in enemy activity.' In a conversation with Doubek, a Soviet adviser made a similar point: 'Everyone who is arrested is an enemy and it is necessary to treat him in this way'.[18] Since guilt had been established at the moment of arrest, the interrogator was told to ignore pleas of 'not guilty' or attempts to prove innocence when questioning the defendant. As their manual made clear: 'The interrogator should be vigilant against attempts by the defendant to subtly sneak a defence into the protocol'.[19] They were to leave information attesting to a defendant's innocence out of the protocol entirely (in the interest, supposedly, of 'brevity').

The task of the interrogator was not to uncover evidence or the facts about a case, but rather, in their words, to 'break' prisoners' will [*zlomit*], 'push them to confess', [*přimět k doznání*] or 'uncover' their enemy faces [*odhalit skutečně neprátelské tvaře*].[20] As Béla Szász described, agents could be given the following instructions: '*X.Y. Imperialist Agent. Establish this!*'.[21] And guilt by association was accepted as evidence of enemy behaviour. Interrogators mapped defendants' social and personal connections to find more people to implicate in the final 'plot' and sought to establish incriminating links between defendants.[22] While interrogators had the power to expand the conspiracy or push for more arrests, they could not establish innocence or pardon a person after he or she had been arrested.

Information inside the secret police, including its interrogation department, was circulated on a need-to-know basis. Chief interrogators and Soviet advisers were the final collection points for the disparate parts of the 'conspiracy' formulated over the course of several months to link defendants' testimonies in preparation for a show trial.[23] Rank-and-file interrogators were given only limited information about each case. Often, they were assigned small tasks, such as forcing a defendant to confess to a particular charge or involvement in a small part of the conspiracy. As London explained: 'Each interrogator knew only one aspect of the elaborate charges formulated against us by his chiefs. He had to obtain a confession on this point whatever the price. Then he was given another point, and so on.'[24] Some points that interrogators were told to establish seemed at first glance innocuous, such as determining whether a defendant was acquainted with a person who had been arrested or had taken a trip abroad at a particular time. In some cases they collected information that was factually accurate, but interpreted actions as having been undertaken with malicious intent (and the 'intent' of an action was far more difficult for a defendant to disprove than the facts).

The distribution of information on a need-to-know basis was combined with the practice of 'uninterrupted interrogations'. In this approach, multiple interrogators worked one after the next to break prisoners. At the beginning of a shift, an interrogator received only a short report about what the prisoner had said in the previous session. As London noted: 'The new interrogator received a slip of paper containing one or two questions and the answer he was to obtain when he relieved his colleagues and continued the interrogation.'[25] Along the way, each interrogator recorded no evidence suggesting a defendant's innocence. Over time, information proving guilt was amassed and information suggesting innocence was removed from the protocol. When the materials were handed to the next interrogator, only evidence of guilt remained.[26] The final narrative was stitched together by Soviet advisers who rarely conducted interrogations themselves and often did not speak Czech, but who nevertheless set the line for the general conspiracy and the methods used to attain confessions, whether through torture, psychological pressure, or the manipulation of defendants' language.

The interrogator's task was depicted as determining absolute truth. Absolute truth was dictated more by ideology than what the prisoner said (which was assumed to be either self-interested or false). The Soviet advisers were convinced that defendants would disguise their true selves and cover up their enemy activity during interrogations [*přetvářka*].[27] This assumption was not unique to the Stalinist system. A theory of confessions developed in Chicago in the 1950s, the Reid Technique, posited that the aim of interrogations was to uncover deception.[28] It urged interrogators to manipulate defendants and persuade them to accept the interrogator's version of events.[29] A more recent policing manual likewise suggests that police should collect information in different ways depending on whether they believed that a suspect was guilty:

> ...the interrogator has only one purpose: to obtain a confession from a guilty individual.... The interrogator is only seeking confirmation of information he already knows or highly suspects.... Therefore, the interrogator makes sure that a '95:5' conversation mode is maintained, in which the interrogator speaks 95% of the time, and the suspect only 5% of the time.[30]

The interrogator approached interactions with the prisoner as a contest of wills. In the *Gulag Archipelago*, Aleksander Solzhenitsyn described how an interrogator's ego could make him obsessed with obtaining confessions, regardless of charges or evidence:

> They felt no mercy, but, instead, an explosion of resentment and rage toward maliciously stubborn prisoners who opposed being fitted into the totals, who would not capitulate to sleeplessness or the punishment cell or hunger. By refusing to confess, they menaced the interrogator's personal standing. It was as though they wanted to bring *him* down.... If it's to be war, then war it will be![31]

The interrogator of course held overwhelming advantages in this contest: power, information and the ability to write the final record of the encounter (the 'true' version of events).

The structure of the department influenced interrogators' incentives, outcomes, and goals in other ways. From 1949, two chief interrogators led teams that competed against each other to attain results. Each pressured the other to attain more confessions and interrogate prisoners longer. These incentives were part of a system of 'socialist competitions' (evident in all parts of the Stalinist party, state and economy) aimed to increase outputs. In the interrogation department, 'outputs' were the number of confessions written and number of hours defendants were interrogated. Some interrogators, such as Bohumil Doubek, received the title of 'shock worker' for obtaining confessions or interrogating suspects for the most number of hours. The system exploited personal hatreds as well as institutional incentives. Outspoken anti-

Semites were assigned to interrogate Jewish prisoners. The Soviet advisers rehired officials who had previously been fired to interrogate those who had fired them.

It is difficult to say with certainty whether the interrogators believed in defendants' guilt. Doubek suggests that they suspected that the charges were false, in part because they helped write them. He explained that young interrogators recruited in the late 1940s, often from militia units or factories, expressed the most doubts. Doubts were expressed in the form of innuendos or jokes rather than outspoken protest.[32] Other sources suggest that interrogators believed the charges. As Szász observed, given their limited information on cases and the atmosphere of widespread propaganda vilifying defendants at the time, it was possible that rank-and-file interrogators believed in what they were doing.[33]

There were several reasons for this. For one, defendants' guilt was loudly proclaimed in party speeches and newspapers even before the interrogations took place. As Doubek noted: 'After an arrest, news was spread that an enemy had been uncovered and that suspicions and charges against him were proven facts. [...] In interrogating former party functionaries, we used the argument that it was not possible for them to contest the outcome of the case because the party had already revealed them publicly.'[34] After the news of a defendant's 'criminal activity' was published, denunciations from the public, so-called 'resolutions', were received from across Czechoslovakia in which lower-level party organizations, average citizens and others demanded harsh sentences, including the death penalty, for the accused. Interrogators showed these letters to prisoners to break their will.[35] Public support for the interrogators' work was asserted in their training materials: 'we are strong because we are right. Our struggle is correct. The working class and all respectable citizens stand behind us.'[36] The interrogator may have approached an investigation bolstered by the conviction that a guilty verdict was supported by the Party, the press and the public.

On attaining confessions: Between torture, psychology, and language

Although interrogators clearly used torture to extract confessions from defendants, neither local officials nor the Soviet advisers appear to have issued written orders on the matter. As Lynne Viola has pointed out in the case of the Great Terror in the Soviet Union, the only written evidence by the regime on the use of torture was produced when such methods were being retracted. Viola gives the example of a telegram issued by Stalin in early 1939 expressing the view that it was acceptable to use 'physical methods' against 'obvious enemies of the people'.[37] For lower-level officials, directives on torture were given orally or spread through imitation of superior officers.[38]

In Czechoslovakia (the practice was likely copied from the Soviet Union), the protocol that the court finally received consisted of a basic, narrowly defined formula. It contained the questions the interrogators asked, the answers they reported being given, and the admission of guilt with the prisoner's signature at the bottom. Evidence that physical violence had been used to attain confessions was removed from the materials handed to the court. Doubek described his experience writing *svodky*, or daily progress reports ('summaries' in Russian). At first a Soviet adviser chastised him for writing them incorrectly:

> I had written that a suspect had confessed to something after an uninterrupted interrogation. [The Soviet adviser] said that I should not write that. No one reading the report was concerned about the methods used to attain the confession or had time to read long reports. It was necessary to write only the outcome, not how the outcome had been achieved. [...] I was told in the future to just write that the defendant had confessed.[39]

In spite of the fact that evidence of torture was erased from official documents, witness accounts contain ample descriptions of the forms of torture used during interrogations. Most frequently, these included beatings, verbal abuse, sleep deprivation, threats and solitary confinement.[40] In Czechoslovakia, the main forms of torture seems to have been sleep deprivation and extended interrogations. According to the manual for interrogators: 'If we want to break the accused and force a confession, it is best to do so by means of extended, exhausting interrogations.' Short interrogations were considered less effective since they gave the prisoner time to think through his responses: 'if we interrogate someone for a short time, we allow him to think through his situation, find a way out, or think up tricks to deceive the interrogator.' It was recommended that interrogations last long enough to exhaust a prisoner.[41] Since interrogations could last many hours, or well into the night, they structured the lives of interrogators as well as prisoners. As Doubek related:

> It was determined that if the interrogation was to have any result, it must last at least 14 to 16 hours per day.... The Soviet advisors set the working day to between 8 in the morning and 4 in the afternoon, then a break, and then between 8pm to 12am. The interrogator was allowed to rest between 10pm and 6am. Throughout the day, the prisoner could not rest, even when he was in his cell, since he was not allowed to sit and was forced to walk continually.... The prisoner could be woken in the night by guards. When he awoke for the interrogation, he was physically and psychologically exhausted, so it was not as difficult for the interrogator to convince him of things.[42]

After such treatment, a prisoner was more likely to sign anything put in front of him: 'He was completely apathetic. He didn't care about anything except when he would be allowed to rest.'[43] As Doubek explained, sleep deprivation gave the interrogator a psychological advantage since the latter, in contrast, could sleep, rest, and 'live in normal conditions'.[44] London describes the impact of sleep deprivation on his ability to respond to questions: 'The lack of sleep for weeks and months on end caused moments of insanity and hallucinations. I was no longer in control of my senses. I thought I was going mad. I would fall into a state of total sottishness and apathy and move like an automaton.'[45] Even when he was alone in his cell he was not allowed to sit down.[46]

As the impact of sleep deprivation on London's mental state showed, there was a thin line between physical and psychological torture. As Hungarian defendant Béla Szász affirmed, physical torture – beatings with a truncheon, threats, or punches – reduced him to a state of indifference that made other methods, such as appealing to his party loyalty, more effective:

> The methods applied in the past three weeks had the purpose of reducing me, the suspect, both physically and mentally, to such an animal condition that my momentary needs would deprive me of human dignity and render me blind; they were aimed at distorting my judgement or falsifying my standards when differentiating between rational and irrational, so an hour's sleep seemed a greater treasure than life itself, and where, in exchange for a little peace or a jug of coco, or to escape from the terror of physical pain, I would confess even to a charge involving the noose.[47]

Although Soviet advisers were present in Hungary as well as Czechoslovakia, methods of torture differed in each country. In Hungary, Szász spoke of beatings and the practice of 'soling', in which a prisoner's soles were beaten with a cane or rubber truncheon.[48] Based on his own experience and conversations with other victims of the Stalinist Terror, Aleksander Solzhenitsyn gives a detailed account of forms of torture used in the Soviet Union, such as immersing prisoners in acid baths and squeezing their skulls with an iron ring.[49]

Interrogators also employed psychological torture. Such methods included instilling a sense of fear, frustration, and helplessness in prisoners, and sowing discord between them. The practice of psychologically manipulating defendants are outlined in modern interrogation manuals as well, such as *The Psychology of Interrogations and Confessions*: 'Persuasion in the context of an interrogation is the process of convincing suspects that their best interests are served by making a confession. To achieve this objective the police may engage in a range of deception strategies.'[50] In communist Czechoslovakia, the regime considered confessions attained through psychological pressure more valuable in the preparation of public trials than those extracted through physical violence, which were thought more likely to be retracted during a trial.[51]

For prisoners, the interrogator was the main link to the Party, their family, and the outside world. As London explained, 'Every morning I asked to see an interrogator to inquire about my family.'[52] Interrogators could allow prisoners to receive letters or visits and controlled access to information from 'outside'. They could use these connections to manipulate the prisoner. London described how his interrogator threatened and lied to him. '[The interrogator] told me that my wife had repudiated me and asked for a divorce. So I had lost not only the Party, but my wife and children. . . . Only after my confession I was given the letters from my wife and children and discovered that I had been deceived.'[53]

London signed his first confession after psychological rather the physical torture. He described his interrogator, Vladimír Kohoutek, as a 'professional salesman': 'He was never coarse or brutal, either in words or acts, and showed no animosity. He went as far as to ask polite questions about my state of mind, my health and my family. I soon realized that he did not believe in his work and interpreted things with a crude cynicism.'[54] Few figures in the communist interrogation department represented continuities between communist and pre-communist interrogation practices (and undermined the impression that officials were driven only by ideology) more than Kohoutek, who began his career in the First Czechoslovak Republic and served in the Nazi Protectorate of Bohemia and Moravia, post-war National Front government, and Stalinist period. As his personnel file made clear, he was 'willing to serve any regime'.[55] London explained that Kohoutek made him feel trapped, as if there was no way out: 'When you realize that every effort is pointless, exhaustion gets the better of you. I began to think that my obstinacy was uselessly prolonging my ordeal.'[56]

Two psychological methods used by the interrogators were *argumentations* and *confrontations*. Both were adopted from the Soviet model. The practice of *argumentations* targeted defendants who had been members of the communist party. It aimed to encourage defendants to confess by appealing to their sense of duty toward the Party and USSR. The 'argument' was as follows: the Party has declared you guilty. For its sake it is necessary to admit to the charges.[57] According to London:

> To start with we did all we could to aid the Party by replying to every question in detail. . . . The years of struggle and discipline, all our past education, had taught us that the Party was never wrong, that the USSR was always right. We were prepared to criticize ourselves, to admit that we had made involuntary mistakes in our work which may have harmed the party.[58]

According to Doubek, this method was used when interrogators had no other evidence of a crime. It was used against Marie Švermová, a leading communist, after her arrest in 1951: 'Psychological methods were used [against Švermová]. . . . The interrogation was a means to oppress, humiliate, and insult Švermová . . . We gave her no room to breathe.'[59] As with the use of torture, evidence that argumentation had been used was removed from the final protocol.

Another psychological tactic was referred to as *confrontations*. In confrontations, prisoners, many of whom had known each other for years, were compelled to testify against one another. According to historian Igal Halfin, Soviet jurisprudence defined 'witness confrontations' as 'the simultaneous interrogation of two individuals concerning the same fact'.[60] But this definition does not capture the full extent of the practice. Confrontations instilled despair in defendants since 'guilt' was affirmed by friends, acquaintances and fellow party members. As London described: 'They fanned personal dislikes and old rancours. They mystified us: "So and so said this about you." "He can't have said that, the bastard!" . . . This was how they obtained the most defamatory evidence.'[61] Confrontations allowed interrogators to take incriminating material from one file and move it to another. It enabled them to use the defendants least able to withstand torture to incriminate others. It drew on connections between prisoners to cement guilt by association (referred to as 'objective guilt'). As London wrote of his association with other members of the International Brigades: 'Since my comrades from the International Brigades had signed confessions in which they admitted their guilt of various crimes against the state, I was "objectively guilty", since I was their superior.'⁶² Prisoners were overwhelmed by the evidence stacked against them: 'How', asked London, 'could you make people believe that not one, but dozens of signatures has been extorted? ... How could you fail to be crushed by the mountain of signatures confirming the negative side?'⁶³

Language and 'question protocols'

During his public trial in November 1952, Rudolf Slánský recited the following 'confession':

> First of all I wish to confess my guilt that, as the enemy of the Communist Party and people's democratic regime, I formed an Anti-State Conspiratorial Center of which I stood at the head for several years. In this center of ours I concentrated a number of capitalist and bourgeois-nationalist elements. My collaborators became agents of imperialist espionage services, that is, of the French, English, and particularly the American services, and carried out hostile activities serving the interests of the American and English imperialists, who aimed at liquidating the people's democratic order, restoring capitalism, and effecting a reorientation of Czechoslovak foreign policy in favor of the Western capitalist powers. I carried out hostile activities within the Czechoslovak Communist Party – in the economic, foreign, security, and other sectors.⁶⁴

This section examines the language of confessions. Part of the interrogators' violence, it argues, was to control the language of the final protocol, the existing record of a defendant's words, actions and intentions. Interrogators controlled which questions were asked, how questions were answered, and the facts of a defendant's life that entered the public record. The language they used to interpret the defendants' actions and intentions was heavily imbued with ideology. In preparing for show trials, national languages were 'translated' into what Bela Szász has described as the 'language of communism': 'It was not Hungarian they spoke, but an international language, the phraseology of communist seminar booklets, leading articles and pamphlets from which a multitude of political filters and chemicals had removed every individual color, taste, and shade.'⁶⁵

Interrogators' control over language – whether words, phrasings or formulations of guilt – was evident at every step of the process. As London described: 'undeterred by my presence [my interrogator] wrote entire pages of questions and answers. When he told me to sign them I protested indignantly about the importance of the charges and their new formulation although I had signed other "confessions" in the past.'⁶⁶ As Doubek confirmed of London's confession: 'its phrasing was more the work of [the interrogator] than of [London].'⁶⁷ Interrogators were instructed to fit defendants' words into linguistic formulations that presupposed guilt, as the training manual explained: 'We tend to use formulations that are accurate and correctly describe the defendant's criminal behaviour such as "our subversive organization", "my enemy connection", "my enemy activities", and so on.'⁶⁸ London gave an example of a question designed to prompt a self-incriminating answer (referred to in jurisprudence as a 'leading question'): 'When did you enter the American intelligence services directed by Allen Dulles? Who recruited you, and where? And with whom have you collaborated?'[69] The question was not 'were you an agent?' but rather *when* did you become an agent?', a phrasing that assumed a compromising answer.

In this system of 'question protocols', the interrogator formulated both the questions asked of the defendant and the answers they were likely to receive. As explained in the interrogators' training materials: 'Most protocols are written in the form of questions and answers. The questions must be clear and sharp. The answers must always address the question asked.'[70] Such an approach eliminated information from the protocol not considered 'relevant' to the question. It was introduced to Czechoslovakia by the Soviet advisers to replace 'chronological protocols' that recorded the events and actions leading up to a crime. Before the arrival of the Soviets, protocols in Czechoslovakia were written in a looser style that gave room to the defendant to explain his actions in his own words. They were free-form narratives only occasionally interrupted by the interrogator's questions.[71] The difference between Czech and Soviet protocols, and the amount of room defendants were given to explain their actions and movements, reflected differences between 'inquisitorial' interrogations, which aim to gather information about a person, and 'accusatorial' interrogations, which focus on proving guilt and obtaining confessions.[72]

The questions posed by the interrogators were unrelenting in assuming guilt. Defendants were only able to contest details or minor issues: 'Do not allow the defendant to lead the protocol in a different direction', interrogators were told.[73] They were instructed not to write down what the defendant said in his own words, but to rephrase what he said to fit prescribed ideological formulations: 'There are some views that when writing a protocol it is necessary to write down the words of the defendant as he says them. This view is incorrect.' It was necessary instead to rephrase the defendant's words in 'politically charged language'. Ambiguities were removed from protocols: 'Every answer by the defendant must be clear, concrete, and unambiguous (*jednoznačna*) so he cannot assert that he was poorly understood or meant something different.' This meant that defendants were rarely if ever able to explain that a particular action or situation was more complex than it seemed or had been misinterpreted. The resulting protocol was more the formulation of the interrogator, who became judge and arbiter of a defendants' words.

After the sentences were passed on the defendants in the Slánský trial – eleven death sentences and three sentences of long-term imprisonment – London described a remarkable scene. All of the defendants began to seek out their interrogators:

> My comrades who had been sentenced to death came out of the boxes and took the unknown warders by the arm: 'Where is my interrogator? Call my interrogator! Tell me where my interrogator is! I want to see my interrogator!' Their last chance of surviving was hidden in these officials who had grilled them hour after hour, day after day, month after month, year after year, but who also spoke to them, nourished them with hopes and promises, and acted as an intermediary between them and the outside world, the Party, and Gottwald. And suddenly

they no longer had this hope or this resort. No illusion. Nothing. Each man was alone with his death. When he asked for his interrogator he called for his link with the Party and Gottwald – with life. The interrogator represented the agony of the 'confessions,' the uninterrupted repetition of the reports, blackmail, infamy, and violence. But he also represented power.... The disappearance of the interrogators meant that all was over. All that remained were the 'confessions,' not the men who formulated them; the 'confessions' and the condemnation they carried with them. No more promises. The condemned men had kept their word to the last, but not the Party.[74]

This passage vividly demonstrates the power of interrogators over those they had destroyed. Interrogators were perceived of not only as tormentors, but also as representatives of the party, links with the outside world, and the ultimate deciders of the fate of the accused.

Conclusion

The confessions that interrogators spent months writing – and forcing defendants to sign and memorize through beatings, sleep deprivation, and torture – had many purposes in a communist state. With the opening of the archives in Eastern Europe, we can finally begin to understand how not only ideology, but also administrative practices and institutional structures influenced the self-understandings of Stalinist perpetrators and the nature of violence in early communist states. Certainly, confessions were also about ideology: about reformulating the words of defendants and interrogators to fit narrow and increasingly orthodox interpretations of Stalinist ideology. In Eastern Europe, this orthodox view of communist ideology pushed local officials to adhere more closely to Soviet practices and Stalinist interpretations of communist thought. It ran roughshod over the multiplicity of communist ideas that had been articulated during the period of national roads to socialism and mentally and physically destroyed the most important advocates of this way of thinking.

Confessions were also a way to Sovietize the Czechoslovak secret police and judiciary. Interrogations spread a new narrative about the state to the public, as well as to the victims and perpetrators of communist violence. As Richard Leo has pointed out in his history of police interrogations in the United States, 'virtually every criminal investigation is a richly textured narrative and morality play involving innocence and guilt, good and evil, and justice and injustice.'[75] The show trials, and the confessions that underpinned their message, produced a narrative in which defendants were transformed from complex people with difficult choices into caricatures of evil. They set in place important administrative practices and changes in Czechoslovakia by helping to create a new interrogation department and its jurisdiction and purpose. They helped form the self-conceptions of its newly recruited staff and set in place new standards of evidence for proving guilt. And success in attaining and writing confessions became the basis on which interrogators were selected, promoted and trained. Those most willing to go to any length to attain them, whether through torture, psychological manipulation, lies or threats, rose rapidly in the system. And many of these men remained in the interrogation department for years to come. Finally, they underpinned the show trials in which the newly created communist states asserted dominance over alleged enemies, as well as the previous elites, nonbelievers, and waverers, real and perceived.

Part Four

In Lieu of an Epilogue

10

Reckoning with the past: Stalin and Stalinism in Putin's Russia

James Ryan

It seemed a flippant question. 'So what?' President Vladimir Putin remarked about the Stalinist past, in a 2017 interview with the American film director Oliver Stone. After all, everyone and every society develops from that which existed before them. 'We all carry within us some birth-marks', Putin explained, with a slight chuckle.[1] And, after all, Russia lives with its 'totalitarian' Soviet past in plain sight, a history that includes almost unimaginable suffering and trauma. Symbols of the Soviet regime abound. Lenin streets and Lenin statues are still ubiquitous, and the monumental architecture of the Stalin and immediate post-Stalin years provide fulcra for major civic occasions and everyday routines. Millions travel the Moscow metro every day, many stations of which are resplendent with Socialist Realist depictions of Soviet socialism – what it was supposed to be like. And on any sunny summer weekend or holiday in the Russian capital, many thousands stroll through the triumphal gateway to Gorky Park, erected in 1955, directly across the Kryimskii Val thoroughfare from a popular open-air museum (the Muzeon) where busts and statues of Soviet leaders sit as silent witnesses to a turbulent century.

In Eastern Europe, the shadow of the twentieth century often seems only barely receded. The ongoing conflict in eastern Ukraine and the more general geopolitical tensions in the former western borderlands of the USSR provide graphic illustration that the consequences of Soviet power and control remain current. Besides, in any situation wherein national identities are re-configured, especially in fundamental ways, the past assumes particular significance as new national narratives are constructed.[2] For today's middle-aged and older generations of Russians, in particular, the loss of national identity with the Soviet collapse was acute.[3] And, in addition to the search for a collective national belonging, the enormously complicated experiences of twentieth-century dictatorship that these societies encountered need to be reckoned with, one way or another. Within states that occupy the spaces of the former Soviet Union and Eastern Bloc, those experiences are often engaged with in ways that illustrate clearly how the past is utilized for present-day political purposes. The challenge is to manage conflicting narratives and emotions of victimhood, guilt, and responsibility associated with the extraordinarily oppressive and repressive natures of both Soviet control and Nazi occupation, in order to create a cohesive sense of national identity and unity.[4]

Since the third presidential term of Vladimir Putin (from 2012 until his re-election in March 2018), numerous journalists, social commentators and scholars, in Russia and the West, have remarked upon a revival of Joseph Stalin's reputation. As evidence, they have cited statements from Russia's ruling elite that suggest a positive appraisal of the Stalin era and justification of Stalinist methods, and they have highlighted a dramatic rise in Stalin's popularity amongst Russian citizens. In fact, the term 're-Stalinization' has sometimes been used to account for these phenomena, as well as the state's authoritarian methods of rule and aggressive foreign policy.[5] The growth in Stalin's popularity has certainly been remarkable. Reputable opinion polls suggest that in 1998, 19 per cent of Russian citizens provided an overall positive appraisal of Stalin's role in Russian history. By 2016, that figure had grown to 54 per cent.[6] According to the March 2019 poll, 70 per cent of Russians possessed a positive view of Stalin's leadership, a rather stunning and unexpected exponential rise.[7] This is noteworthy, of course, because of the nature of Stalinist rule: an astonishingly violent dictatorship that pursued lethal policies of social upheaval and control in the name of socialist modernization, resulting in several millions of deaths in peacetime through execution or neglect and the suffering of many millions more.

This chapter examines and explains the views of Russians – both the ruling elite and ordinary citizens – on Stalin and Stalinism. In so doing, it considers the politics of history in Putin's Russia, representations of the Soviet past, and what these can tell us about the mindset of Russia's ruling elite and citizenry. The key question to be addressed is whether or not a distinct 'rehabilitation' of Stalin and Stalinism is occurring in contemporary Russia. By 'rehabilitation' in this context, I mean decisive action or a series of measures intended to restore largely to previous position or status the reputation and legacy of someone or something after a period of denigration, as well as a general popular attitudinal restoration of good repute.[8] There is by no means a consensus in scholarly writings that this is occurring. Indeed, the work of scholars such as historian Ekaterina Makhotina, anthropologist Aleksandra Arkhipova, and political scientists Thomas Sherlock and Ol'ga Malinova has provided nuanced readings of popular and elite appraisals of the Stalinist past that challenge forthright suggestions of the rehabilitation of Stalin and Stalinism.[9] This study builds on that work. It provides the fullest and most up-to-date analysis of the question following a notable boost in Stalin's popularity since 2014, with particular focus on the thorny issue of Stalinist repressions.

More generally, the chapter contributes to studies of collective memory and the uses of history through examination of the ways in which a society comes to terms with an extraordinarily complex, contradictory, and traumatic recent past. I reflect on the normative basis and validity of dominant assumptions about the need for public reckoning with, 'working through,' and 'overcoming' the past; how that should be conducted; and its consequences for a society's progression. To clarify, our concern here is with the question of a Russian *Vergangenheitsbewältigung* (coping with the past). An all-encompassing term that arose in the context of post-war West German confrontations with the Nazi regime, it has come to describe political, social and cultural reactions to troubling past events and eras that result in acknowledgement of and successful 'working through' that past.[10] As Mary Fulbrook has summarized, the Holocaust has 'become central to the identity and culture' of modern Germany, part of its 'moral fiber'.[11] The extent of societal introspection and acknowledgement of Nazi-era wrongdoing in Germany has assumed the standard form by which to measure a society's public reckoning with a brutal past; indeed, the German language has provided the very word used! But our interest here is also with the more precise concept *Vergangenheitspolitik*. Developed by historian Norbert Frei in reference to the West German Adenauer government's reintegration into society of former Nazis and collaborators, this refers to a top-down 'policy for the past' in the service of current political needs.[12]

Stalinism is a nebulous term that can mean different things to different people, although we have provided a working definition in the introduction to this volume (pp.6–7). As we will see, elite and popular attitudes towards Stalin and Stalinism in Russia are complex and resist simple categorization. The ruling elite has put forward a view of national history that stresses national unity and the historic necessity of a strong state, which can usefully be understood as a manifestation of 'great-powerness' or 'great power nationalism', with its focus the national state rather than ethnic national indicators.[13] Within that statist narrative there is certainly much space to accommodate the perceived achievements of Stalinism, especially victory over the Nazi war regime. However, the Putin administration has also been unambiguous in its condemnation of the unacceptable costs in human lives exacted by the Stalinist dictatorship. For that reason, the administration's *Vergangenheitspolitik* appears deliberately ambiguous and intricate. It is an attempt to meet the challenge of providing a unified historical narrative that addresses the need both for national pride and achievement, and at least some reconciliation with traumatic past legacies. Nonetheless, collective memory 'is a site of contestation for a wide range of different interest groups' and opinions, even in illiberal and authoritarian political systems.[14] In reality, it does not consist of a unitary set of beliefs, values and emotions that forms the basis of an indisputable collective identity. As will become clear, Russian citizens' assessments of Stalin's role in history reflect a manifold and divided society.

There is little appetite in Russia for a formalized process of state-instituted transitional justice that would prioritize the victims of Stalinism.[15] Nonetheless, a state-sponsored reckoning with the past is underway. How this is conducted, though, does not neatly reflect the conventional, liberal assumption that it is likely to be part of a process that results in defeat of illiberal and anti-democratic tendencies. That assumption is closely related to its inverse postulate: post-totalitarian societies that deny or restrict discussion of past repressions 'will continue to bear the signs of the regimes from which they emerge'.[16] What follows below does not refute that conventional wisdom as such, but it adds necessary complication to our understanding of the relationship between a repressive past and a society's future prospects. I demonstrate that recognition of the unacceptable crimes of a past regime is compatible with an illiberal polity in the present. We will see that it is a gross oversimplification as well as a historical inaccuracy to suggest that 're-Stalinization' is occurring in Russia, if that is understood in the literal sense of the worldview and behaviour of the state's leaders. Even 'symbolic re-Stalinization' in the sense of elite and popular rehabilitation of the reputation of Stalin and the Stalinist system is not a very accurate or adequate description of Russia's relationship, as a whole, with this period of its past. A significant deficit of political pluralism and democratic liberties – although to some extent 'signs' of an extraordinarily repressive past – does not signify re-iteration, rehabilitation, or repressed discussion of Stalinism. And, anticipating a Russia post-Putin, we simply do not know what that will look like.

Re-Stalinization of the ruling elite?

Under Putin, the Russian state has sought to craft a narrative of a 'usable' past that helps mobilize patriotic sentiment, construct a unified national identity, and legitimate the incumbent authorities.[17] There have been two core, intertwined motifs in the construction of the 'official' narrative of Russian history since the early 2000s: an integrative approach to the past that suggests an essential continuity from the imperial tsarist state through the Soviet era until the present day, and the crucial significance of a strong state in ensuring the integrity and progress of Russian national culture and national interests. Attempts to forge such an integrative narrative represent a significant discursive shift from the presidency of Boris El'tsin (Yeltsin) in the 1990s, with its emphasis on 'new' democratic Russia's break with the 'old' Soviet past, and indeed with much of the legacy of Imperial Russia.[18] These tropes of statist continuity were especially evident leading up to and during the tricky centenary of the Russian Revolution in 2017.[19]

The ruling elite is largely respectful of the independence of professional historians.[20] However, when it comes to the Great Patriotic War (Second World War), the state has attempted to police scholarship and wider public discussion. The reason is the close imbrication of wartime victory and post-Soviet Russian identity, and elite perception that attempts to besmirch that victory – especially through suggestions that the Stalinist USSR was just as terrible as the Nazi regime – serve a wider cultural strategy of Russophobia abroad. In 2009, after the European Parliament and the Parliamentary Assembly of the Organization for Security and Cooperation in Europe (OSCE) passed resolutions that implied a certain equivalence of the Soviet and Nazi regimes,[21] a notorious Presidential Commission to combat the 'falsification of history to the detriment of Russia's interests' was established, briefly, by then-president Dmitrii Medvedev. And in the context of the conflict in eastern Ukraine and the post-Soviet nadir in relations between Russia and Western powers since 2014, members of the ruling elite have actually declared national history a matter of 'national security'.[22] In practical terms, legislation was passed in 2014 that criminalizes intentional 'public distribution of lies' about the Soviet Union in the Great Patriotic War.[23]

The point is that during the Putin era, memory of victory in the Great Patriotic War – led by Stalin – has become the key, even sacred element of the symbolic infrastructure of patriotic national identity.[24] For the ruling elite it is much more significant and prominent than discussion of Stalin-era repressions, and this is the context within which Russian and foreign observers have perceived a rehabilitation of

Stalin and Stalinism. A selection of recent newspaper headlines in English is illustrative: 'Stalin rises from the ashes in Putin's Russia' (*The Moscow Times*, 2015); 'Stalin rises again over Vladimir Putin's Russia' (*Independent* [UK], 2016); and 'Stalin, Russia's New Hero' (*The New York Times*, 2016).[25]

The evidence for a good deal of rehabilitation seems compelling. Since 1998, at least 132 sculptural depictions of Stalin have appeared in Russia.[26] In 2007, the Kremlin oversaw production of controversial history textbooks that acknowledged the repressions of the Stalinist regime but suggested that these were unavoidable means of modernizing the country and preparing for war.[27] In Tver province, a new museum and monument to Stalin were unveiled in 2015. And in Perm the same year the Perm-36 Gulag museum was re-branded to showcase the contribution to the war effort of the local forestry industry, rather than document repressive forced labour.[28] The apparent restoration of Stalin's positive image and diminution of the horrors of his rule are usually explained as consequences of the increasing authoritarianism and arbitrariness of Putin's rule; Stalin's associations with military victory, 'empire' and strong leadership; and the search for a legitimating historical myth for the type of leadership that Putin projects.[29] But to what extent has Russia's ruling elite actually instituted a rehabilitation of Stalin's leadership?

In fact, Stalin and his rule occupy a position of considerable ambiguity in the elite imagination. Unsurprisingly, the source of this is the successful war effort, and realization of the consequences for the Slavic peoples if the Nazis had won. As noted in the volume's introduction, Putin explained the problem clearly at a meeting with young historians and history teachers in November 2014: 'It's just hard to say whether we could have won the war if the leaders had not been so cruel ... And what would the consequences have been if we'd lost? ... They [the Nazis] were going to physically exterminate the Slavic people, and not just ethnic Russians'.[30] In December 2009, when Prime Minister, Putin was more bullish in a televised question-and-answer session. Having raised the Stalin question himself, he averred that 'nobody can throw stones at those that organized and led the Victory'. However, Putin then proceeded to do precisely that, acknowledging that 'all' of the positives that resulted from the Stalin era were attained at an 'unacceptable' cost in human lives, and that the state committed 'mass crimes' against its own people.[31] Putin largely repeated those comments in interviews with Oliver Stone around 2016/2017.[32] Nonetheless, Putin is careful not to extend his criticism of Stalinism so far that it would undermine the legitimating myth of wartime victory. His preferred historical narrative is one that reconciles diverse, often discordant features of the Russian past through a message of state-centred historical continuity, what Thomas Sherlock describes as historical 'bricolage'.[33]

Sherlock has suggested that one of the reasons it is incorrect to refer to a policy of re-Stalinization on the part of the ruling elite is the lack of unity in their approach to national history.[34] The existence of relatively 'liberal' and 'conservative' strands within ruling circles seemed quite noticeable during the Medvedev presidency (2008–12). In an interview with a Russian newspaper in 2010, Medvedev condemned Stalin with a force exceeding that of his predecessor. There could be 'no forgiveness' for Stalin, he stated, and he described the Stalinist USSR as a totalitarian, economically ineffective dictatorship. What is also interesting is his reference to the fact that, for most people worldwide, Stalin generates 'no warm emotion'.³⁵ In other words, Medvedev implied the desirability of a certain harmonization of Russian and Western views of the Stalinist regime, which could be understood in the context of the Kremlin's attempts to ensure closer economic ties with the European Union following the financial crisis of 2008 and Russia's war with Georgia the same year.³⁶

Is there, then, a distinction between ruling factions on these matters? In the current geopolitical climate, does it serve the instrumental and ideological purposes of the Putin administration to permit, encourage and contribute to a certain revitalization of Stalinism? There has been a difference in stress and tone between the respective statements of Putin and Medvedev as president, and the ruling elite is certainly not monolithic; different institutions of state have different cultures and interests to defend. However, there does not appear to be much evidence of a clear-cut distinction between discrete factions in relation to historical controversies. It was, after all, under Medvedev's presidency that the infamous commission to combat 'historical falsification' was established. And since the mid-2010s, there has actually been increased attention to the victims of Stalinism in official pronouncements (see below).

What is demonstrable is that, although formally a constitutional parliamentary democracy, the Putin regime is to a considerable extent an illiberal 'managed democracy' that is quite often authoritarian and repressive. In addition, Putin has come to play a carefully scripted role as the personal embodiment of the nation's strength, values and unity, something not witnessed in this way in Russia since the time of Stalin.³⁷ Yet, even if one were to argue that Putin's Russia qualifies as an unambiguously authoritarian regime, authoritarianism – even Russian authoritarianism – is not synonymous with Stalinism. The latter had far greater pretensions to social transformation and can be considered truly 'totalitarian'.³⁸ The state under Putin, by contrast, has neither the ideological inclination nor the will to enforce as rigid or as repressive a control of the public sphere and economy as its Stalinist forebear. Furthermore, Russia is considerably more integrated into European and global economic, political, and cultural structures and conversations since the Stalin era. In this regard, it is significant that two new secondary school history textbooks approved by the Kremlin in 2015 are very different from the infamous productions of 2007. They present a rather more balanced view of Russia's twentieth century, and, despite intense international criticism of Russia's annexation of Crimea in 2014, they are not imbued with the anti-Western sentiment of the earlier texts.³⁹ Nevertheless, the narrative of triumphant Russian statehood still outweighs state-supported initiatives to reckon fully and in unpredictable fashion with the deep-seated, unmeasurable, traumatic legacies of the Soviet regime.

Re-Stalinization of Russian society?

There is often an assumption amongst political commentators that popular attitudes follow the messages emanating from the Kremlin.⁴⁰ In reality, the relationship between state and society is more interwoven than this suggests; the state, after all, may at times be projecting the inclinations of Russian society. Indeed, according to an insightful recent book recent book by Samuel Greene and Graeme Robertson, the nature of power in Russia actually rests upon a considerable amount of 'co-construction', or 'unprompted' (and sometimes prompted) popular support for the basic tenets and authoritative suppositions of Putin's political power, enacted in various ways.[41] In any case, we have seen that 'official' messages regarding the Soviet past are often quite intricate and confusing. Investigation of Russian citizens' views of Stalin and Stalinism further complicates the question of Russia's relationship with its recent history.

To begin with, it is necessary to take a close look at sociological surveys carried out by the Levada Center in Moscow, the internationally-renowned non-governmental sociological research centre. According to the Center, there have been three distinct periods that reflect changes in overall popular attitudes towards Stalin since Putin first became president in 1999. From 2001–2006, the predominant attitude towards Stalin was negative; from 2008–2012, the attitude was largely one of 'indifference' (*bezrazlichie*); and since 2014, views of Stalin have been largely positive.[42] The most detailed recent set of polls in March 2019 indicated that the percentage of respondents relating to Stalin with 'admiration', 'respect', or 'sympathy' was 51, and the percentage that considered him with 'dislike', 'fear', or 'hatred' was 14.[43]

However, the picture becomes more complicated when we consider responses to more specific queries. In response to the statement, 'whatever the mistakes and vices attributed to Stalin, most importantly, our people won the war', one sees the greatest and most consistent level of popular consensus. In 2018, 64 per cent of those polled agreed with it, 14 per cent disagreed, and 22 per cent could not or would not say. In 2016, 71 per cent agreed and 21 per cent disagreed.[44] But then we come to the proposition that Stalinist repressions were either criminal or historically justifiable. One would expect a majority to accept that the end justified the means, but Levada Center data indicate that in 2017, 39 per cent of respondents agreed with the statement that repressions were criminal, as opposed to 25 per cent that thought they were politically necessary and justifiable. In a 2019 poll that asked the more ambiguous question whether the sacrifices borne by the Soviet people during the Stalin era were justified by the results of that era (this would suggest or at least include wartime hardships and victory), 46 per cent of respondents declared the human sacrifices of that time justified to some extent, with 45 per cent resolute that nothing could justify them. In 2017, the corresponding figures were 36 per cent and 49 per cent respectively, and in 2011 as many as 61 per cent of respondents thought the sacrifices exacted under Stalinism could not be justified.[45]

This indicates a trend towards ever greater acceptance of historically justified hardships associated with Stalinism. However, when asked specifically about 'repressions', condemnation of the Stalinist state remains more likely. In 2017, the state-run sociological agency (VTsIOM) reported that 49 per cent of respondents thought Stalinist repressions constituted an unjustifiable 'crime against humanity', whereas 43 per cent suggested that they were necessary to maintain order.[46] Regarding attitudes towards Stalin specifically, the Levada Center has reported that in March 2018, 44 per cent (down from 62 per cent in 2016) agreed with the statement that he was a 'terrible, inhuman tyrant responsible for the destruction of millions of innocents', with 26 per cent in disagreement and 30 per cent not declaring either way.[47] Yet only

26 per cent thought that Stalin should be considered a state criminal, either categorically or to some extent.[48]

What sense can be made of all this? The Levada Center interviews approximately 1,600 people per survey, dispersed across age and location (and, presumably, gender). True, these polls cannot determine popular views with precision, although there are stable trends across this collection of figures over several years. But what is apparent is that the way questions are phrased, the particular terms used, are crucial; answers to questions that seek a general, overall impression can conceal a more multi-faceted and contradictory reality. A considerable majority of Russian citizens considers victory in the war to be the most important result of Stalinism. Asked about Stalin-era repressions, though, Russians are as yet more likely than not to consider that these were both unjustifiable and criminal.

Opinion polls also suggest that it is possible simultaneously to have a positive opinion of Stalin and a negative view of the Stalin era. This can help explain why a similar percentage of Russians considers Stalinist political repressions criminal and unjustifiable but rejects the proposition that Stalin should be considered criminally responsible. Yet in 2018, 44 per cent of respondents agreed that Stalin was an inhuman tyrant, whereas only 26 per cent disagreed! In fact, in 2016 Levada Center analysts published the remarkable observation that amongst those that considered Stalin an inhuman tyrant, 23 per cent nonetheless expressed positive feelings towards him.[49] In other words, it is possible simultaneously to have positive and negative views of Stalin as a leader.[50] According to Lev Gudkov, Levada Center director, the explanation for these paradoxical results is a political 'doublethink' characteristic of the legacy of 'totalitarianism' combined with the particularities of Russia's statist traditions.[51] National authority, in his view, is almost inconceivable without force and violence, however condemnable. Be that as it may (or not) for certain generations of Russians, there is surely more to this than the 'traumatized collective identity' that Gudkov identifies. The discordances of historical Stalinism, and elite political discourse that both valorizes and condemns the Stalinist regime, are intellectually challenging to negotiate.

Overall, the multiplicious and contradictory data from opinion polls make it impossible to conclude that a definitive process of popular rehabilitation of Stalin and Stalinism is occurring, certainly on a wide scale. The polls also expose deep divisions within Russian society. With the exception of victory in the war, there is little or no social consensus on basic questions of the Stalin era, although a broadly positive appraisal of Stalin has most recently become unmistakeable. Finally, there is also considerable popular indifference to, unawareness of, and unwillingness to comment on these issues.[52]

In order to create a more coherent picture, it is necessary to probe a little deeper. Inconsistent and conflicting views are held across social categories, but the typical 'Stalinist', according to the Levada Center, is elderly, without higher education, and resides outside of major cities and towns.[53] The generations that came of age during the Khrushchev and Brezhnev eras, and especially the former, are more likely to express positive views of Stalin. Correspondingly, the generations that grew up during and after *perestroika* tend to be disproportionately represented amongst those voicing indifference or lack of firm opinion.[54] Nonetheless, it would be incorrect to suggest that views of Stalin can be explained by any particular demographic indicator; as the social anthropologist Aleksandra Arkhipova has noted, it is not just pensioners that provide the support base for manifestations of Stalinist sentiment.[55]

There is a final but crucial observation to make. If Russia's leaders adopt an instrumental approach to the past, for present-day purposes, then so do many Russian citizens. An overall majority of respondents considers that Stalin played a positive role in Russian history, but, equally, an overall majority would not want to live under his rule.[56] Arkhipova and Ekaterina Makhotina have demonstrated that Stalin often serves less as a concrete historical figure and more as a symbolic representation of domestic order, economic justice, and anti-corruption, as well as geopolitical might and patriotic achievement.[57]

The rise in Stalin's popularity since 2014, then, can be explained by a number of factors. One, the sharp deterioration of relations between Russian and Western powers, and the imposition of economic sanctions on Russia, following the annexation of Crimea. Two, popular discontent with the current government, corruption and a perception of economic injustice. Resort to Stalin as a protest symbol suggests that citizens expect greater concern for their welfare from the state. For some it also reflects, perhaps, the persistence of a patriarchal conception of the role of the state and the leader.[58] Three, the fact that the *state* has formulated, propagated and permitted further expansion of a preferred historical narrative that incorporates the achievements of the Stalin era. To clarify, popular views are facilitated by state discourse but not determined by it;[59] as Arkhipova has noted, most recent monuments to Stalin have been paid for by private citizens without the support of local authorities. There is, however, a certain 'meeting of minds' between rulers and ruled on the Stalin question.[60]

Reckoning with repression

The reason that Stalin and Stalinism are controversial topics is, as mentioned, that the Stalinist regime was one of the bloodiest and most repressive in modern history, governed by a discredited communist ideology. The 1930s and 1940s witnessed waves of astonishing violence. Between 1930 and 1933, approximately three million peasants were arrested, shot, deported or forcibly resettled during the 'comprehensive collectivization' of agriculture.[61] Millions more suffered famine in Ukraine, Kazakhstan, and elsewhere. The apogee of mass violence came in the years 1937–8, when approximately 700,000 people were executed, the majority of victims 'ordinary' people and social marginals.[62] However, waves of violent deportations of particular Soviet ethnicities continued after 1938, including approximately half a million Chechens and Ingush expelled from the North Caucasus to Central Asia in 1944. In addition, a veritable colony of labour camps and special settlements, the Gulag, stretched across the vast expanses of Soviet territory by the time of Stalin's death, and close to 25 million people passed through those camps during his rule.[63] Unsurprisingly, few Russian family histories are not directly entwined with those repressions.

It was not possible truly to begin processing the maelstrom of Soviet state violence or to construct a 'memory infrastructure' around it until the era of *glasnost'* in the late

1980s.⁶⁴ But, although space was then opened for individuals and organizations to erect memorials and proffer narratives that would make sense of the short 'Soviet century', independent of the state, the Russian state itself failed to develop this further. Until very recently it has largely been silent in that regard, with little evidence of the inscription of the tragedies of Soviet-era repressions in what Aleksandr Etkind has termed 'hard memory': public monuments that typically require state support.⁶⁵ Unsurprisingly, then, a regular trope in critical commentary on contemporary Russia is the absence of serious, state-led reckoning with the brutal and traumatic Stalinist past that would strike with deep resonance into the Russian collective consciousness/conscience. The sub-title of a recent *Guardian* article read: 'Putin doesn't want the nation to address its guilt and ignorance'.⁶⁶ That headline could also apply to a moving and widely lauded book by Shaun Walker, former Moscow correspondent for the *Guardian*, published in 2018. Putin, according to Walker, has 'never' referred to Stalinist state terror as a 'crime', for to do so would undermine the triumphalism around Soviet victory in the war. Walker's conclusion is that the 'Russian case of forgetting' is on a 'different level' to that of most other countries.⁶⁷ And one of the most authoritative historians of Stalinist repressions, Nikita Petrov, has remarked that 'there is no place in the Kremlin's fine-tuned propaganda for an honest public discussion of Soviet-era political repression'.⁶⁸

Often in these writings there is a correlative suggestion of Russia's inability to develop fully as a society without undergoing its own process of *Vergangenheitsbewältigung*. According to Petrov's diagnosis, 'as long as Russia refuses to officially acknowledge the darkness in its past, it will be haunted by ideas that should have died long ago'.⁶⁹ Similarly, Alec Luhn, Moscow correspondent for the London-based *Telegraph*, has concluded that 'Russia won't be able to reform its increasingly authoritarian and corrupt government', a government that rejects '"Western" values like human rights and democracy', as long as it 'refuses to acknowledge the excesses of the most tyrannical government in its past'.⁷⁰ The assumption is that recognition of the crimes of Stalinism will constitute a necessary, if not sufficient, part of Russia's progression towards a more democratic and law-based polity, and there is also the assumption that most Russians must be 'ignorant' of the brutalities of Stalinism. These assertions and assumptions ought to be scrutinized.

Twenty-first century Russia continues to have a problematic relationship with its violent Soviet past. It is, however, important to remember that there are different institutional interests within the ruling elite, which are sometimes manifested in public pronouncements relating to their own histories. A case in point is the Federal Security Service (FSB), the successor to the Soviet political police (KGB). In an interview with the government newspaper in December 2017 to mark the centenary of its foundation, Aleksandr Bortnikov, head of the FSB and a former senior KGB official, appeared to defend not only his institution's role in the Stalinist USSR but the violent policies of the state more generally. According to Bortnikov, the threat of war required the deadly Stalinist policies of rapid industrialization and collectivization, and there was an evidentiary basis for a 'significant part' of the repressions of the late 1930s (despite the extensive role of falsified testimony and the disproportionate severity of most of the sentences). Bortnikov reserved his criticism for individual members of the Stalin-era security forces engaged in criminal activities.⁷¹

Bortnikov occupies one extreme of the opinion spectrum, although he is certainly not alone. Yet there are also powerful institutional and intellectual pressures to condemn Stalin-era repressions and perpetuate the memory of victims. Particularly significant in this regard is the stance of the Russian Orthodox Church. The Church is separate from the state and pursues its own interests, but their relationship is one of mutual benefit and support. In recent years political analysts and journalists have remarked upon a significant tendency toward Stalinist sympathies within the Church, even the existence of 'Orthodox [Church] Stalinists'.[72] However, according to Nikolai Mitrokhin, one of the most reliable experts on Orthodox matters, this is a 'marginal' trend. Although an active participant in the cult of the Great Patriotic War, the Church is also a principal bulwark against the 'spread of Stalinism', committed as it is to memorialization of the repressed – albeit primarily those repressed for their faith.[73] Particularly instructive is *how* the Church has managed to convert Stalinist repressions and their physical locations, such as the Butovo shooting field outside Moscow, into sacred 'sites of memory'.[74] As Zuzanna Bogumił has explained, through a language of Christian martyrdom and sacrifice the victims of Stalinism can be incorporated into a post-Soviet collective consciousness that harmonizes with a distinctively Russian national identity, of which Orthodoxy is partly constitutive. Suffering has (sacred) meaning, something better promises to come from it, and hence it is more readily absorbed within an overriding historical narrative of Russian state sovereignty.[75]

Returning to the ruling elite, it is categorically untrue that, taken as a whole, they have not acknowledged the unjustifiable nature of Stalinist repressions or engaged with their memory. In fact, in recent years they have done so in an increasingly meaningful way that has helped 'harden' memorialization of the victims. The reasons may be various, and it may be part of a deliberate strategy to appeal to liberal-minded citizens in the aftermath of major protests in 2011–13, but the steps taken have been significant. As early as 2001, the Gulag museum opened in central Moscow with the support of the city's Culture Department. Putin's televised comments in 2009, cited above, explicitly referred to the 'criminal' nature of Stalinist state violence. Then, on 15 August 2015, Medvedev as Prime Minister signed the Concept of State Policy to Perpetuate the Memory of the Victims of Political Repression, following recommendations of the Presidential Council for the development of civil society and human rights. The Concept acknowledges that perpetuation of the memory of victims of political repression is necessary for the development of civil society, the rule of law in Russia, and the country's 'moral leadership', albeit within an ideological framework of patriotic national unity and opposition to the divisiveness of revolution. A programme of education and public discussion is recommended until 2024.[76]

The culmination of this process of official recognition of the victims of the Soviet regime came on 30 October 2017. On that day, the Day of Remembrance for Victims of Political Repression, a state-funded national monument to victims of political repression in the USSR was finally unveiled in central Moscow by Putin. The chosen design, the sculptor Georgii Frangulian's 'Wall of Sorrow' (*Stena skorbi*), is a 32-metre-long curved wall containing a bas-relief of human figures, and several gaps that encourage visitors to feel at one with the victims. The wall was designed to 'become a warning to subsequent generations that the tragic consequences of authoritarianism affect everyone' and 'can recur'.[77] Speaking at the ceremony after the president, Vladimir Lukin, former human rights ombudsman, member of the Memorial Fund for victims of political repression, and member of the Federation Council (upper house of parliament), lamented that young generations know little of the tragedies of mass repression and Stalinist totalitarian dictatorship. Those terrible tragedies, he urged, should be 'part of our historical memory'.[78]

Putin, however, concluded his address at the 'Wall of Sorrow' with an admonition: it would be impermissible to agitate for a settling of old accounts in relation to the violence of the Soviet state, and nothing or nobody should 'push' society towards confrontation on that basis.[79] Indeed, as he appeared to intimate, the task for the incumbent authorities is to forge a national historical narrative that combines what Ol'ga Malinova terms 'two different models of memory politics'. These are acknowledgement of self-inflicted tragedy and trauma (and, to a lesser extent, that inflicted on other peoples through Soviet repressive policies), and a patriotic account of national triumph.[80] In his annual speech to the Federal Assembly in December 2016, Putin stated plainly that the lessons of national history are needed 'for reconciliation, for strengthening the social, political, civic consensus that we have today achieved'. 'We are one people', he noted, 'and we have one Russia'.[81]

This rhetoric of 'reconciliation' and 'consensus' is key to making sense of the state's approach to Stalinist repressions: it is important to acknowledge the tragedies of the past, but it is more important to 'move on' as a society, not dig too deeply, and focus on a positive rendering of national identity. There is, then, a certain symbolism to the monument's location within metres of the busy Garden Ring road, with its traffic hurtling and haltering and hollering. A complementary message to Putin's was conveyed in a 2019 primetime television programme by Dmitrii Kiselev, one of Russia's leading state broadcasters. Kiselev accepted that memory of Soviet repressions should remain always as a warning against their repetition, but he estimated that 70 per cent of Stalin's actions were beneficial.[82] This is the ideological context within which one can understand the tense relationship that currently exists between the state and Memorial, the internationally-renowned human rights organization that for almost thirty years has been at the forefront of attempts to memorialize the victims of Soviet mass violence. As Svetlana Boym observed at the outset of the Putin era, even then the 'recovery of memory' about the terrible tragedies of Soviet rule, which had assumed the form of a 'campaign' during the era of *glasnost*' and the post-Soviet transition, had given way to a widespread search for 'the imaginary ahistorical past'.[83]

To the next question: are Russians unaware of the true realities of Stalinism? The 2017 Levada Center poll on attitudes toward Stalinist repressions suggested that 44 per cent of respondents were familiar with their general outline, and a further 22 per cent were aware of them but with very little knowledge.[84] Hence, it is simply untrue that Russians are ignorant of Stalinist brutalities. Without doubt, there have been growing levels of unawareness amongst post-Soviet generations. Yet there are also many individuals and several groups within Russia that endeavour to educate society about the horrors of Stalinism, sometimes with considerable – even remarkable – success. A particularly notable example is a documentary film about the Kolyma Gulag camps made by the journalist and video-blogger Iurii Dud', released on his popular YouTube channel in April 2019. Created with the purpose of addressing lack of awareness of Stalinist repressions amongst Russian youth, within weeks the film had amassed over 12 million viewings.[85] Another illustration of the resonance of Stalinist repressions in contemporary Russian society is the success of the 2015 novel, *Zuleikha otkryivaet glaza* (published in English as *Zuleikha*), the debut work of Guzel Yakhina. A remarkably vivid and textured depiction of the deportation of 'kulaks' in 1930, with a focus on the resilience and transformation of the eponymous heroine Zuleikha, the work struck a deep chord – albeit not without controversy – with readers and literary critics alike. Amongst other awards it has earned the Russian Booker Prize, and a television adaptation is due to be aired on Russia's state-controlled Channel 1 in 2020.[86]

It remains to be seen what effects such phenomena will have on social impressions of the Stalin era. In any case, as Ekaterina Makhotina pithily observes, 'knowledge of mass repression does not stand in the way of admiration for Stalin'.[87] And it seems that knowledge and even condemnation of mass repressions do not necessarily lead to a desire for deep engagement with them. According to a 2017 Levada Center poll, 47 per cent thought it better to speak less of Stalin-era repressions and not 'stir' the past, whereas 38 per cent suggested that there should be 'active' discussion,[88] figures that suggest a certain harmonization of popular and elite attitudes. It is also instructive to consider that in late 2016, Memorial published an online database with brief information on over 40,000 political police cadres of special rank for the years 1935–9, the height of the purges. In response, some relatives of Stalinist perpetrators of violence objected bitterly to what they understood as an expectation that they should carry the shame of their grandparents' actions.[89]

This leads to the fascinating, complicated, perennial question whether a society can experience a surfeit of memory, whether a healthy society is better served by more memory or less. Writing about post-war West Germany, David Clay Large concluded that 'the appeal of *Vergangenheitsbewältigung* has always had to compete with the call for *Machtvergessenheit*: the "power to forget".[90] Most notably in recent European history, Spain's transition from the Franco dictatorship to a democratic polity in the 1970s and 1980s was predicated precisely on a political and social consensus of 'active forgetting'.[91] Furthermore, as a cognitive phenomenon those directly affected by traumatic occurrences often experience a psychological and emotional need to avoid communicating those experiences and confronting adversaries. It often takes decades for that to be possible.[92]

Societies, like history, are complex. There is no standard route along which any society will, or necessarily should, develop. Equally, there is no standard, rational way that a society will come to terms with its past. Russia provides an interesting perspective on managed memory, as well as the antipode to deliberate forgetfulness: a process of transitional justice. In a 2012 article, Nancy Adler warned that marginalization of victims' accounts of repression in Russia 'can cause the mechanisms of transitional justice to miscarry', because of impediments to the 'emergence of an inclusive post-repression narrative'.[93] However, we have seen that there is space (albeit unequal) for competing narratives about the past in Russia, including victims' perspectives. There is also, for the most part, official respect for the independence of the historical profession.

Additionally, there are particular intricacies involved with transitional justice in the case of today's Russia, at least with regard to the Stalin era.

This is not a country that has recently transitioned out of the brutal Stalinist system, although there should be no time-limit for reckoning with the past. That progression began officially, albeit fitfully, with Nikita Khrushchev's 'secret speech' in 1956. Today, the Stalinist past (wartime triumph notwithstanding) is less immediate and relevant for most Russians than is often the case in societies engaged in truth-and-reconciliation processes. Yet it should not be thought that this is a society for which the past is of little consequence. Rather than forgetfulness, Russia's present might better be characterized as 'oversaturated with the past', to the extent that diverse and highly divergent historical symbols and judgements exist simultaneously.[94] And, as anyone who has lived in the country recently knows, Russian political discussions are heavily imbued with references to the past. Besides, Stalinism is part of a larger and extraordinarily complicated Soviet experience that has bequeathed an ambiguous legacy difficult to condemn *in toto*. It was not for nothing that during the centenary of the Russian Revolution Putin and other members of the ruling elite referenced the 'powerful stimulus' provided by the Soviet welfare state for positive social developments in the modern world.[95]

In the political realm, who and what are remembered, how and to what extent, are ethical questions that all polities confront.[96] Nonetheless it is surely of great importance to acknowledge, condemn, and attempt to atone for past atrocities. The more seriously this is done and the more that governments, mass media and civic organizations promote the values of critical, collective, historical introspection, the more likely it is that a society will uproot the elements required to produce such actions and create favourable conditions for respectful and inclusive civic engagement. And the more likely it is that a society will be able to 'move on'. A policy of deliberate, selective forgetfulness can be a useful short-term strategy at a time of transition from a troubled era, but it is not likely to be compatible with the creation of a stable, shared collective identity capable of withstanding complex and open-ended examination of the past.[97] The legacies of the Franco regime, for example, continue to generate bitterness and political controversy in Spain.[98] What the example of Russia illustrates is that it is possible, to a considerable extent, to come to terms with a brutal past within an illiberal political structure that does not, as a consequence, shed its proclivities for authoritarian practices.[99] The profundity of that process is certainly questionable. Yet the fact that unambiguous acknowledgement and condemnation of Stalinist repressions have entered Russian public discourse will surely serve to remove some of the sharper edges of political controversy, as well as check any creeping 're-Stalinization' of the political sphere.

* * *

There is no suggestion here that Russia is somehow culturally disposed to some shade of authoritarian rule, condemned by the past to remain within its clutches. On the contrary, opinion polls consistently indicate that more respondents reject rather than accept the proposition that Russia requires a leader like Stalin, although that gap has recently reduced.[100] It is true that conviction in the necessity of a 'strong hand' (*sil'naia ruka*) at the country's helm remains a salient feature of Russian political thought, and yet, as employed in Levada Center polls, 'strong hand' is an ambiguous rhetorical construct.[101] It appears to imply concentration of power in the person of the ruler, but it is difficult to imagine any society overwhelmingly reject the bald suggestion that their elected representatives display strong leadership. In any case, Russian society appears to be undergoing gradual but significant transformation in political attitudes. Ekaterina Shul'man, a prominent Moscow-based political scientist, has demonstrated the decline of post-totalitarian legacies amongst Russia's largely urban, educated population, especially its younger generations. In particular, she has referenced sociological data from 2018 that indicate that a growing percentage of Russians considers that the country's future should be founded on 'social justice', human rights and democratic freedoms, and that these values are more important than a strong state power.[102]

Another way of putting this, as Shul'man suggests, is that paternalistic attitudes of dependency on the state seem to be in decline, even as popular expectations of a socially beneficent welfare state remain high. And another way of thinking about a historical tradition of authoritarian rule is to problematize the relationship between the past, the present and the future. Here we can learn from the multidisciplinary field of memory studies, which teaches us that there is no 'arrow' that points from the past to the future. Rather, in Michael Kontopodis's articulation of a non-linear conception of time, 'there are multiple ways of performing pasts, presents and futures by way of interrelating them'. In other words, there is considerable 'uncertainty' in the relationship of the past to the future, such that it is 'impossible to predict how pasts, presents and futures will relate to each other'.[103] This is not to deny that the past matters, or that it imparts structures and legacies, including traumatic ones, that help explain cultural configurations in the present. It is not to belie or belittle the contention of the historian Oleg Khlevniuk that the cruelty and arbitrariness of Stalin-era repressions helped habituate generations of Soviet (and post-Soviet) citizens 'to accept arbitrary and pernicious limitations' on their freedoms.[104] But it is to confront representations of the present and the future that are overdetermined by the past, and to re-position them. In Russia, Stalin represents a symbol around which competing and often contradictory values and narratives sometimes converge.[105] Nonetheless, the future of Russian politics and society is uncertain, and it will not necessarily depend on historical discourses. If democracy and civil liberties are truly to flourish in Russia, they will not result simply from greater acknowledgement of or engagement with the 'totalitarian' nature of Stalinism, although they would complement one another. Rather, they are likely to reflect the wider transformation of Russia's urban spaces, primarily, and the growth of confident and globalized generations of Russians for whom the forms, constraints and wider legacies of the country's past have increasingly limited hold. It is this that may lead to 'true de-Stalinization'.[106]

Conclusions

Stalinism was an evolving set of multi-faceted and contradictory ideas and practices, reflective of the deeply ironic fate of the Bolshevik Revolution. Under Stalin's rule, the Soviet Union at times seemed threatened with ruinous dysfunctionality, and yet it achieved victory over the gravest challenge in the twentieth century to humane, democratic, inclusive societies. Today, outside Russia especially, these complexities are frequently overlooked. Within Russia, however, the ruling elite and society more generally tend to imagine Stalin and Stalinism in ways that reflect their discordant historical legacies. But for many Western and liberal Russian observers, a rise in Stalin's popularity since Putin became president seems evidence of a growing rehabilitation of Stalin and Stalinism. We have seen that representations of Stalinism in Russia contain nuance and ambiguity as well as plain contradiction. It is precisely such nuances and inconsistencies that are usually overlooked in mainstream and popular commentaries on Russia's public memory, and it is all too common that the model of Stalinist dictatorship is the interpretive lens through which the Putin government is refracted. In response to our overarching question, it is greatly reductionist to assert that rehabilitation of Stalin and Stalinism is taking place, and it is not helpful to refer to the 're-Stalinization' of Russian politics.

Russian society is highly intricate. Stalin's 70 per cent approval rating in 2019 is a stunning statistic, and yet, apart from positive appraisal of victory in the Great Patriotic War, there is little firm consensus in assessments of Stalinism. When we examine sociological surveys, there are four principal observations to highlight. First, the importance of distinguishing Stalin as historical figure from Stalinism as political system. Second, the possibility of simultaneous expression of views that appear to be contradictory. Third, positive appraisals of Stalin and Stalinism amongst Russians, however distasteful, often convey a symbolic message of disaffection with present-day realities rather than serious suggestion of the desirability of life in the Stalin-era USSR. Fourth, it is significant that both the ruling elite and much of Russian society consider the enormity of Stalinist repressions unjustifiable.

Russia is engaged in a reckoning with its painful and traumatic past. How this has proceeded is surely insufficient and open to criticism, but it is undeniable that significant efforts have been made. Besides, the process of *Vergangenheitsbewältigung* cannot be predetermined in form or in consequence, and it is not necessarily helpful to establish Germany's profound confrontation with its Nazi past as the benchmark by which to judge. Although there is in fact much that is instructive about the German experience: the course to 'overcoming' the Nazi past in post-war West Germany and reunified Germany was controversial, convoluted and lengthy, rather than linear and swift. And even highly liberal societies struggle with the messiness and complexities of their histories, often preferring more palatable but mythologized notions of national identity. Conversely, illiberal and authoritarian power structures *are* capable of reckoning with the atrocities of a previous regime, without simultaneously rehabilitating it or reiterating its transgressions in form or extent. What is less clear is the consequences of reckoning with the past for Russia's political and social development. But it might not matter as much as is often thought. Maybe there is a touch of wisdom to Putin's apparently flippant remark.

Notes

Introduction

1. As a 'closed' session, the text was not included in the official publication of the Congress proceedings, although the title of Khrushchev's report was included. The speech is available online through various websites, and we have translated from the text available at http://www.coldwar.ru/hrushev/cult_of_personality.php (accessed 25 September 2019). It is available in English at https://www.marxists.org/archive/khrushchev/1956/02/24.htm (accessed 22 February 2019).
2. Polly Jones, *Myth, Memory, Trauma: Rethinking the Stalinist Past in the Soviet Union, 1953–1970* (New Haven, CT, and London: Yale University Press, 2013), 9. See also *The Dilemmas of De-Stalinisation: Negotiating Cultural and Social Change in the Khrushchev Era*, ed. Polly Jones (London: Routledge, 2005).
3. This was often a feature of the Cold War-era 'totalitarian' school of scholarship, but a more recent example is Robert Gellately's largely popular history, *Lenin, Stalin, and Hitler: The Age of Social Catastrophe* (London: Jonathan Cape, 2007).
4. Leon Trotsky, *The Revolution Betrayed: What is the Soviet Union and Where is it Going?* (1936), translated by Max Eastman, available at: https://www.marxists.org/archive/trotsky/1936/revbet/index.htm (accessed 19 February 2019).
5. See, for example, the preface to the 2017 volume of the British Socialist Register, wherein the authors accept that the legacy of the Russian Revolution is complex and requires 'critical reappraisal'. *Rethinking Revolution: Socialist Register 2017*, ed. Leo Panitch and Greg Albo (London: Merlin Press, 2016), ix.
6. On Stalinist 'developmental violence', see Christian Gerlach and Nicolas Werth, 'State Violence – Violent Societies', in *Beyond Totalitarianism: Stalinism and Nazism Compared*, ed. Michael Geyer and Sheila Fitzpatrick (New York: Cambridge University Press, 2009), 151. See also the editorial, 'What Was the Gulag?', in *Kritika: Explorations in Russian and Eurasian History* 16, no.3 (2015), 471.
7. Geoffrey Roberts, *Stalin's Wars: From World War to Cold War, 1939–1953* (New Haven, CT: Yale University Press), 2006, xiii.
8. See Roberts, *Stalin's Wars*.
9. On the complex and contradictory fate of the Russian Revolution, see especially *The Fate of the Bolshevik Revolution: Illiberal Liberation, 1917–1941*, ed. Lara Douds, James Harris and Peter Whitewood (London: Bloomsbury, 2020).
10. See James Ryan's chapter to this volume.
11. 'Meeting with young academics and history teachers', available at: http://en.kremlin.ru/events/president/news/46951 (accessed 25 April 2018).
12. Roberts, *Stalin's Wars*, xii.
13. For a good discussion on Stalin's absence and the historiography of Late Stalinism, see Juliane Furst, *Stalin's Last Generation: Soviet Post-War Youth and the Emergence of Mature Socialism* (Oxford: Oxford University Press, 2010), 22.
14. Furst, *Stalin's Last Generation*, 22–23.

15 Roberts, *Stalin's Wars*, 297.
16 Michael David-Fox, 'The Iron Curtain as Semipermeable Membrane: Origins and Demise of the Stalinist Superiority Complex', in *Cold War Crossings: International Travel and Exchange across the Soviet Bloc, 1940s–1960s*, ed. Patryk Babiracki and Kenyon Zimmer (Arlington, TX: A & M University Press, 2014), 19.
17 David-Fox, 'The Iron Curtain as Semipermeable Membrane', 19.
18 https://www.marxists.org/archive/khrushchev/1956/02/24.htm (accessed 19 March 2019).
19 Jan Plamper, *The Stalin Cult: A Study in the Alchemy of Power* (New Haven, CT: Yale University Press, 2012), xiv.
20 Plamper, *The Stalin Cult*, xviii.
21 E.A. Rees, 'Leader Cults: Varieties, Preconditions and Functions', in *Leader Cults in Communist Dictatorships: Stalin and Eastern Europe*, ed. B. Apor et al. (London: Palgrave Macmillan, 2004), 3.
22 Jonathan Waterlow, *It's Only a Joke, Comrade! Humour, Trust and Everyday Life Under Stalin* (CreateSpace, 2018), 62.
23 For further discussion of Late Stalinism, see Sheila Fitzpatrick, 'Conclusion: Late Stalinism in historical perspective', in *Late Stalinist Russia: Society Between Reconstruction and Reinvention*, ed. Juliane Furst (London: Routledge, 2006), 277.
24 Nina Tumarkin, *The Living and the Dead: The Rise and Fall of the Cult of World War II in Russia* (New York: Basic Books, 1994), 155–156.
25 According to Sheila Fitzpatrick, 'Stalinist and Soviet are overlapping concepts, the former representing both a maximalist version of the latter and its defining moment.' See Sheila Fitzpatrick, *Everyday Stalinism: Ordinary Lives in Extraordinary Times* (New York: Oxford University Press, 2000), 4. Graeme Gill has argued that the 'full-blown' Stalinist system was not actually established until after the apogee of violence in the late 1930s. See Graeme Gill, *The Origins of the Stalinist Political System* (Cambridge: Cambridge University Press, 1990), 4.
26 Some of the most reliable guides to Stalinism as a historical phenomenon include David Hoffmann, *The Stalinist Era* (New York: Cambridge University Press, 2018); Sarah Davies and James Harris, *Stalin's World: Dictating the Soviet Order* (New Haven, CT: Yale University Press, 2014); Svetlana Ushakova, *Ideologo-propagandistskie kampanii v praktike funktsionirovaniia stalinskogo rezhima: novyie podkhodyi i istochniki* (Moscow: ROSSPEN, 2013); Mark Edele, *Stalinist Society, 1928–1953* (New York: Oxford University Press, 2011); David Priestland, *Stalinism and the Politics of Mobilization: Ideas, Power, and Terror in Inter-war Russia* (Oxford: Oxford University Press, 2007); Fitzpatrick, *Everyday Stalinism*; Stephen Kotkin, *Magnetic Mountain: Stalinism as a Civilization* (Berkeley, CA: University of California Press, 1995); Erik van Ree, *The Political Thought of Joseph Stalin: A Study in Twentieth-century Revolutionary Patriotism* (London: Routledge, 2002); and Jochen Hellbeck, *Revolution on My Mind: Writing a Diary Under Stalin* (Cambridge, MA: Harvard University Press, 2006). A brilliant, almost encyclopedic study of Stalinist economic transformation, 1927–1939, is provided by the seven-volume *The Industrialization of Soviet Russia* (Basingstoke: Palgrave Macmillan, 1980–2018), written largely by R.W. Davies but also by Stephen G. Wheatcroft, Mark Harrison, and Oleg Khlevniuk. On the Soviet propaganda state, and its effectiveness, see Peter Kenez, *The Birth of the Propaganda State: Soviet Methods of Mass Mobilization, 1917–1929* (Cambridge: Cambridge University Press, 1985); David Brandenberger, *Propaganda State in Crisis: Soviet Ideology, Indoctrination, and Terror under Stalin, 1927–1941* (New Haven, CT: Yale University Press, 2011); and Ushakova, *Ideologo-propagandistskie kampanii*.

27 Oleg Khlevniuk, *Stalin: New Biography of a Dictator*, trans. Nora Seligman Favorov (New Haven, CT: Yale University Press, 2015), ix.
28 Hoffmann, *The Stalinist Era*, 1.
29 Lynne Viola, *Stalinist Perpetrators on Trial: Scenes from the Great Terror in Soviet Ukraine* (New York: Oxford University Press, 2017).
30 Waterlow, *It's only a Joke, Comrade!*.
31 Cynthia A. Ruder, *Building Stalinism: The Moscow Canal and the Creation of Soviet Space* (London: I.B. Tauris, 2018); Katherine Zubovich, 'The Fall of the Zariad'e: Monumentalism and Displacement in Late Stalinist Moscow', *Kritika: Explorations in Russian and Eurasian History* 21, no.1 (2020): 73–95, and Zubovich's forthcoming *Moscow Monumental: Soviet Skyscrapers and Urban Life under Stalinism* (Princeton, NJ: Princeton University Press, 2020).
32 Sarah Cameron, *The Hungry Steppe: Famine, Violence, and the Making of Soviet Kazakhstan* (Ithaca, NY: Cornell University Press, 2018), and Robert Kindler, *Stalin's Nomads: Power and Famine in Kazakhstan* (Pittsburgh, PA: University of Pittsburgh Press, 2018).
33 A particularly illuminating and personal insight into the challenges and controversies of Cold War-era American Sovietology is provided in Sheila Fitzpatrick, 'Revisionism in Retrospect: A Personal View', *Slavic Review* 67, no.3 (2008): 682–704.
34 Examples include Laura Engelstein, *Russia in Flames: War, Revolution, Civil War, 1914–1921* (New York: Oxford University Press, 2018); S.A Smith, *Russian in Revolution: An Empire in Crisis, 1890–1928* (Oxford: Oxford University Press, 2017); Mark D. Steinberg, *The Russian Revolution, 1905–1921* (New York: Oxford University Press, 2017); Andy Willimott, *Living the Revolution: Urban Communes and the Fate of Soviet Socialism, 1917–1932* (Oxford: Oxford University Press, 2017); *Rethinking the Russian Revolution as Historical Divide*, ed. Matthias Neumann and Andy Willimott (London: Routledge, 2017); and *The Fate of the Bolshevik Revolution*, ed. Douds, Harris, and Whitewood.
35 Bruno Bongiovanni, 'Totalitarianism: The Word and the Thing', *Journal of Modern European History* 3, no.1 (2005): 5–17.
36 For an overview, see David C. Engerman, *Know Your Enemy: The Rise and Fall of America's Soviet Experts* (New York: Oxford University Press, 2011).
37 Nathan Leites, *A Study of Bolshevism* (Glencoe, IL: The Free Press, 1953), 15–19; 285–286.
38 See, for example, the review by George Fischer in the *Western Political Quarterly* 7, no.3 (1954): 494–496.
39 Merle Fainsod, *How Russia is Ruled* (Cambridge, MA: Harvard University Press, 1963), 580.
40 Hannah Arendt, *The Origins of Totalitarianism* (Orlando, FL: Harcourt, 1968, xxv, xxxi–xxxii.
41 See, for example, Leszek Kołakowski's three-volume *Main Currents of Marxism: Its Rise, Growth, and Dissolution*, trans. P.S. Falla (Oxford: Clarendon Press, 1978).
42 Both approaches seem to have been favoured by Richard Pipes, a historian of late Imperial Russia but also a student of the early Soviet years. Pipes thought Lenin a tactician and a 'heartless cynic', a 'model' for Stalin; Richard Pipes, ed., *The Unknown Lenin: From the Secret Archive* (New Haven, CT: Yale University Press), 1. On the Russian antecedents and peculiarities of Soviet socialism, see in particular Merle Fainsod, *How Russia is Ruled* (Cambridge, MA: Harvard University Press, 1953). Robert Tucker examined the role of Stalin's personality in *Stalin as Revolutionary, 1879–1929: A*

Study in History and Personality (New York: Norton, 1973), and to a lesser extent in *Stalin in Power: The Revolution from Above, 1928-1941* (New York: Norton, 1990). According to Robert Conquest's highly influential study of the Stalin-era purges, the fundamental reason for this violent process was Stalin's 'personal and political drives'. See Robert Conquest, *The Great Terror: A Reassessment* (New York: Oxford University Press, 1990), 53. An insightful discussion of differences within the totalitarian model is provided in Abbott Gleason, 'The October Revolution: Invention and Reinvention, Ad Infinitum', *Journal of Modern History* 70, no.2 (1998): esp. 428–429.

43 A particularly influential model of totalitarianism for Sovietologists was provided by Carl Friedrich and Zbigniew Brzezinski, *Totalitarian Dictatorship and Autocracy* (Cambridge, MA: Harvard University Press, 1956).

44 See Lewis H. Siegelbaum, *Stuck on Communism: Memoir of a Russian Historian* (Ithaca, NY: Cornell University Press, 2019), 53.

45 See, for instance, R.W. Davies, *The Industrialization of Soviet Russia, Vol.1: The Socialist Offensive: The Collectivisation of Soviet Agriculture, 1929-1930* (London: Macmillan, 1980).

46 The most influential work of Cold War revisionism was William Appleman Williams, *The Tragedy of American Diplomacy* (Cleveland, OH: World Publishing Company, 1959).

47 These exchanges have been described in Sheila Fitzpatrick's memoir, *A Spy in the Archives: A Memoir of Cold War Russia* (London: I.B. Tauris, 2014), and Siegelbaum, *Stuck on Communism*, 50–54.

48 See here, Fitzpatrick, 'Revisionism in Retrospect': 682–704. In conventional historiographic terms, agenda-based revisionism is usually referred to as upper-case 'Revisionism', as distinct from lower-case 'revisionism' that represents, in effect, the task of all historical scholarship to revise and develop understandings of historical phenomena. However, it would be incorrect to suggest a neat distinction between Revisionism and revisionism in reference to the Soviet field. The Cold War-era outputs of Fitzpatrick and Stephen Cohen, for examples, while serving quite clearly to challenge the 'totalitarian' framework, nonetheless read as excellent works of scholarship that continue to merit attention.

49 *Stalinism: New Directions*, ed. Sheila Fitzpatrick (London: Routledge, 2000), 6.

50 Sheila Fitzpatrick, 'Impact of the Opening of Soviet Archives on Western Scholarship on Soviet Social History', *Russian Review* 74, no.3 (2015): 382.

51 See in particular, Lynne Viola, *The Best Sons of the Fatherland: Workers in the Vanguard of Soviet Collectivization* (New York: Oxford University Press, 1987).

52 Arendt, *The Origins*, 306–315; 323.

53 Sheila Fitzpatrick, *Education and Social Mobility in the Soviet Union, 1921–1934* (Cambridge: Cambridge University Press, 1979),

54 Ronald Grigor Suny, 'Toward a Social History of the October Revolution', *American Historical Review* 88, no.1 (1983): 31–52; S.A. Smith, *Red Petrograd: Revolution in the Factories, 1917-1918* (Cambridge: Cambridge University Press, 1983); Diane Koenker, *Moscow Workers and the 1917 Revolution* (Princeton, NJ: Princeton University Press, 1981); Diane Koenker and William G. Rosenberg, *Strikes and Revolution in Russia, 1917* (Princeton, NJ: Princeton University Press, 1990); and Alexander Rabinowitch, *The Bolsheviks Come to Power: The Revolution of 1917 in Petrograd* (New York: Norton, 1976).

55 Rabinowitch, *The Bolsheviks Come to Power*; Stephen F. Cohen, *Bukharin and the Bolshevik Revolution: A Political Biography, 1888-1938* (New York: Vintage, 1975); and

Robert V. Daniels, *The Conscience of the Revolution: Communist Opposition in Soviet Russia* (Cambridge, MA: Harvard University Press, 1960).
56 For an overview, see Priestland, *Stalinism*, 2–5.
57 Graeme Gill, *The Origins*, 6. Lest it be thought that Gill attributes little significance to ideology, see his more recent *Symbols and Legitimacy in Soviet Politics* (Cambridge: Cambridge University Press, 2011).
58 J. Arch Getty, *Origins of the Great Purges: The Soviet Communist Party Reconsidered, 1933–1938* (Cambridge: Cambridge University Press, 1985), and Roberta T. Manning, *Government in the Soviet Countryside in the Stalinist Thirties: The Case of Belyi Raion in 1937* (Pittsburgh, PA: The Carl Beck Papers, 1984).
59 J. Arch Getty, '"Excesses Are Not Permitted"! Mass Terror and Stalinist Governance in the Late 1930s', *The Russian Review* 61, no.1 (2002): 113–138.
60 Martin Malia's *The Soviet Tragedy: A History of Socialism in Russia, 1917–1991* (New York: The Free Press, 1994), is an example of a work written through the lens of the totalitarian, or a least neo-totalitarian, approach.
61 See here, Laura Engelstein, 'Culture, Culture Everywhere: Interpretations of Modern Russia, across the 1991 Divide', *Kritika: Explorations in Modern Russian and Eurasian History* 2, no.2 (2001): 363–393.
62 For an accessible introduction to poststructuralism and the historical profession, see Kevin Passmore, 'Poststructuralist and Linguistic Methods', in *Writing History: Theory and Practice*, 3rd edn, ed. Stefan Berger, Heiko Feldner and Kevin Passmore (London: Bloomsbury, 2020), 133–157. For an especially insightful reflection on the 'cultural turn', see Ronald Grigor Suny, *Red Flag Unfurled: History, Historians, and the Russian Revolution* (London: Verso, 2017), Ch. 1.
63 An important social-cultural study of the 1990s was Sarah Davies's unprecedently textured analysis of popular opinion in the 1930s: *Popular Opinion in Stalin's Russia: Terror, Propaganda and Dissent, 1934–1941* (Cambridge: Cambridge University Press, 1997).
64 See, for examples, Wendy Goldman, *Women at the Gates: Gender and Industry in Stalin's Russia* (Cambridge: Cambridge University Press, 2002); Lynne Attwood, *Creating the New Soviet Woman: Women's Magazines as Engineers of Female Identity, 1922–53* (Basingstoke: Macmillan, 1999); Elizabeth A. Wood, *The Baba and the Comrade: Gender and Politics in Revolutionary Russia* (Bloomington, IN: Indiana University Press, 1997); and Dan Healey, *Homosexual Desire in Revolutionary Russia: The Regulation of Sexual and Gender Dissent* (Chicago, IL: University of Chicago Press, 2001).
65 See John Lewis Gaddis, 'The Emerging Post-Revisionist Synthesis on the Origins of the Cold War', *Diplomatic History* 7, no.3 (1983): 171–190.
66 Katerina Clark, *Petersburg: Crucible of Cultural Revolution* (Cambridge, MA: Harvard University Press, 1995), ix–xii.
67 See here, S.A. Smith, 'Two cheers for the "return of ideology"', *Revolutionary Russia* 17, no.2 (2004): 119–135.
68 Igal Halfin and Jochen Hellbeck, 'Rethinking the Stalinist Subject: Stephen Kotkin's *Magnetic Mountain* and the State of Soviet Historical Studies', *Jahrbücher für Geschichte Osteuropas* 44, no.3 (1996): 456.
69 On the reception of ideology in inter-war Soviet society, and the failure and adaptation of the Soviet 'propaganda state', see David Brandenberger, *Propaganda State in Crisis: Soviet Ideology, Indoctrination, and Terror under Stalin, 1927–1941* (New Haven, CT: Yale University Press, 2011).

70 Kotkin, *Magnetic Mountain*, 2.
71 Kotkin, *Magnetic Mountain*, 229.
72 Halfin and Hellbeck, 'Rethinking the Stalinist Subject', 457.
73 See especially, Jochen Hellbeck, *Revolution on My Mind: Writing a Diary Under Stalin* (Cambridge, MA: Harvard University Press, 2006); Jochen Hellbeck, 'Working, Struggling, Becoming: Stalin-Era Autobiographical Texts', *Russian Review* 60, no.3 (2001): 340–359; and Igal Halfin, *Red Autobiographies: Initiating the Bolshevik Self* (Seattle, WA: University of Washington Press, 2011).
74 See, for example, Robert Thurston's review of Halfin's *Stalinist Confessions: Messianism and Terror in the Leningrad Communist University* (Pittsburgh, PA: University of Pittsburgh Press, 2009), in the *American Historical Review* 115, no.3 (2010): 918–919.
75 Eric Naiman, 'On Soviet Subjects and the Scholars Who Make Them', *Russian Review* 60, no.3 (2001): 314. A different picture of ordinary life in the Stalinist 1930s to that presented by the work of Hellbeck in particular is revealed in Orlando Figes, *The Whisperers: Private Life in Stalin's Russia* (London: Allen Lane, 2007).
76 See, for examples, Anna Krylova, 'Identity, Agency, and the "First Soviet Generation"', in *Generations in Twentieth-Century Europe*, ed. Stephen Lovell (Basingstoke: Palgrave, 2007), 103; Edele, *Stalinist Society*, 3–4; and Waterlow, *It's Only a Joke, Comrade!*, 6.
77 *Stalinism*, ed. Fitzpatrick, 11.
78 See in particular, Peter Holquist, *Making War, Forging Revolution: Russia's Continuum of Crisis, 1914–1921* (Cambridge, MA: Harvard University Press, 2002); David L. Hoffmann, *Cultivating the Masses: Modern State Practices and Soviet Socialism, 1914–1939* (Ithaca, NY: Cornell University Press, 2011); Daniel Beer, *Renovating Russia: The Human Sciences and the Fate of Liberal Modernity, 1880–1930* (Ithaca, NY: Cornell University Press, 2008); and Stephen Kotkin, 'Modern Times: The Soviet Union and the Interwar Conjuncture', *Kritika: Explorations in Russian and Eurasian History* 2, no.1 (2001), 111–164.
79 See, for examples, J. Arch Getty, *Practicing Stalinism: Bolsheviks, Boyars, and the Persistence of Tradition* (New Haven, CT: Yale University Press, 2013), and Terry Martin, 'Modernization or Neo-Traditionalism? Ascribed nationality and Soviet primordialism', in *Stalinism: New Directions*, ed. Sheila Fitzpatrick (London: Routledge, 2000), 355 ff
80 Michael David-Fox, 'Multiple Modernities vs. Neo-Traditionalism: On Recent Debates in Russian and Soviet History', *Jahrbücher für Geschichte Osteuropas* 55, no.4 (2006): 535–555.
81 Especially noteworthy are the damning biographies of Lenin and Stalin by the former Soviet colonel Dmitri Volkogonov. Volkogonov's biography of Stalin was originally published in two volumes in 1989 as *Triumf i tragediia: politicheskii portret I.V. Stalina* (Moscow: Novosti).
82 For background, see Igor Torbakov, 'History, Memory and National Identity: Understanding the Politics of History and Memory Wars in Post-Soviet Lands', in *Russian Nationalism, Foreign Policy, and Identity Debates in Putin's Russia: New Ideological Patterns after the Orange Revolution*, ed. Marlène Laruelle (Stuttgart: Ibid., 2012).
83 Information on the series is available at: https://rosspen.su/katalog/istoriya-stalinizma-/ (accessed 27 May 2020).
84 Indeed, important works focused on Stalin continued to appear in the 1990s and 2000s. See, for example, *Stalin: A New History*, ed. Sarah Davies and James Harris (New York: Cambridge University Press, 2005).

85 See here, 'The Call of the Vozhd' (editorial), *Kritika: Explorations in Russian and Eurasian History* 17, no.1 (2016): 1–4, and Stephen M. Norris, 'A Biographical Turn', ibid.: 163–179. Stalinist state-building is the focus of the special issue of *Europe-Asia Studies* 71, no.6 (2019).
86 See in particular, the two volumes already published of Stephen Kotkin's three-volume biography *Stalin* (London and New York: Penguin/Allen Lane, 2014, 2017); Christopher Read, *Stalin: From the Caucasus to the Kremlin* (London: Routledge, 2017); and Khlevniuk, *Stalin*, and Ronald Grigor Suny, *Stalin: Passage to Revolution* (Princeton, NJ: Princeton University Press, forthcoming 2020).
87 Philip Pomper, 'Stalin Biographies after the Fall', *Russian Review* 4, no.3 (2015): 478.
88 Oleg Khlevniuk, *Master of the House: Stalin and His Inner Circle* (New Haven, CT: Yale University Press, 2009), xiv.
89 Sheila Fitzpatrick, *On Stalin's Team: The Years of Living Dangerously in Soviet Politics* (Princeton, NJ: Princeton University Press, 2015), 2.
90 Timothy Snyder and Ray Brandon, eds, *Stalin and Europe: Imitation and Domination, 1928–1953* (New York: Oxford University Press, 2014).
91 Doubravka Olšáková, ed., *In the Name of the Great Work: Stalin's Plan for the Transformation of Nature and its Impact in Eastern Europe* (New York: Berghahn, 2016).
92 See, for examples, Alfred J. Rieber, S*talin and the Struggle for Supremacy in Eurasia* (Cambridge: Cambridge University Press, 2015); Alun Thomas, *Nomads and Soviet Rule: Central Asia under Lenin and Stalin* (London: I.B. Tauris, 2018); Cameron, *The Hungry Steppe*; Kindler, *Stalin's Nomads*; and Douglas Northrop, *Veiled Empire: Gender and Power in Stalinist Central Asia* (Ithaca, NY: Cornell University Press, 2004). Adeeb Khalid, *Making Uzbekistan: Nation, Empire, and Revolution in the Early USSR* (Ithaca, NY: Cornell University Press, 2015).
93 See here, Christopher Read, *Stalin: From the Caucasus to the Kremlin* (London: Routledge, 2017), 321.
94 Stephen Kotkin, *Stalin, Vol.1: Paradoxes of Power, 1878–1928* (New York: Penguin Press, 2014), xi.
95 See here, in particular, Paul Hagenloh, *Stalin's Police: Public Order and Mass Repression in the USSR, 1926–1941* (Washington, DC, and Baltimore, MD: Woodrow Wilson Center Press/Johns Hopkins University Press, 2009); David R. Shearer, *Policing Stalin's Socialism: Repression and Social Order in the Soviet Union, 1924–1953* (New Haven, CT: Yale University Press, 2009); and James Harris, *The Great Fear: Stalin's Terror of the 1930s* (Oxford: Oxford University Press, 2016).

Chapter 1

1 Christopher Read, *Stalin: From the Caucasus to the Kremlin* (London: Routledge, 2017).
2 Nina Tumarkin, *Lenin Lives: The Lenin Cult in Soviet Russia* (Cambridge, MA: Harvard University Press, 1997).
3 He called for the 'burning' of a book toting myths about his childhood in the following terms: 'The important thing resides in the fact that the book has a tendency to engrave on the minds of Soviet children (and people in general) the personality cult of leaders, of infallible heroes. This is dangerous and detrimental. The theory of "heroes" and the "crowd" is not a Bolshevik, but an SR [Socialist-Revolutionary] theory. The heroes

make the people, transform them from a crowd into people, thus say the SRs. The people make the heroes, thus reply the Bolsheviks to the SRs.' (*Voprosy istorii*, 11 [1953].)
4   Adrian Jones, *Late-Imperial Russia: An Interpretation: Three Visions, Two Cultures, One Peasantry* (Zurich: Peter Lang, 1997), 104.
5   Two very different influential works of the period were: Adam Ulam, *Stalin: The Man and His Era* (New York: Viking Compass, 1973) and Ronald Hingley, *Joseph Stalin: Man and Legend* (London: McGraw Hill, 1974).
6   Isaac Deutscher, *Stalin: A Political Biography* (Oxford: Oxford University Press, 1949), and many subsequent editions.
7   Ian Grey, *Stalin: Man of History* (London: Doubleday, 1979).
8   Alec Nove, *Was Stalin Really Necessary?* (London: Routledge, 1964).
9   *Pravda*, 14 February 1987.
10 Allister Heath, *Daily Telegraph*, 5 August 2015.
11 Robert H. McNeal, *Stalin: Man and Ruler* (New York: New York University Press, 1988); Robert C. Tucker, *Stalin as Revolutionary: 1879–1929* (New York: W.W. Norton, 1973); and Robert C. Tucker, *Stalin in Power: The Revolution from Above, 1928–1941* (New York: W.W. Norton, 1990).
12 Pipes's headstone modestly describes him as 'Architect of Cold War Victory', which says it all about this whole 'scholarly' trend.
13 Timothy Snyder, *Bloodlands: Europe between Hitler and Stalin* (New York: Basic Books, 2010).
14 To sample this intense debate, see: Robert Conquest 'Comment on Wheatcroft', *Europe-Asia Studies* 51, no.8 (1999): 1479–1483, and S.G. Wheatcroft, 'The Scale and Nature of Stalinist Repression and its Demographic Significance: On Comments by Keep and Conquest', *Europe-Asia Studies* 52, no.6 (2000): 1143–1159.
15 See Tucker, *Stalin as Revolutionary*, and Tucker, *Stalin in Power*.
16 See for example, Alexander Solzhenitsyn, *The First Circle* (New York: Harper and Row, 1968), chap. 18–21.
17 J. Arch Getty, *The Origins of the Great Purges: The Soviet Communist Party Reconsidered 1933–38* (Cambridge: Cambridge University Press, 1985).
18 The abridged English translation is Dimitrii Volkogonov *Stalin: Terror and Tragedy* (London: Weidenfeld and Nicolson, 1991).
19 Roy Medvedev, *Let History Judge: The Origins and Consequences of Stalinism* (New York: Columbia University Press, 1971).
20 Karl Marx, *The Eighteenth Brumaire of Louis Bonaparte*, Chapter 1 (1852), available online: https://www.marxists.org/archive/marx/works/1852/18th-brumaire/ch01.htm (accessed 17 October 2019).
21 Winston Churchill, 'Sinews of Peace', Speech at Westminster College, Fulton, Missouri, 5 March 1946, available online: https://www.cia.gov/library/readingroom/docs/1946-03-05.pdf (accessed 17 October 2019). One might speculate that historians of diplomacy and war, such as Geoffrey Roberts and Richard Overy in the West and Dmitrii Volkogonov in Russia, were among the first to portray a more rounded and credible picture of Stalin through their acquaintanceship with this material.
22 *The Nature of Stalin's Dictatorship: The Politburo 1924–1953*, ed. Arfon Rees (London: Palgrave, 2004). See also, Derek Watson, *Molotov: A Biography* (London: Palgrave, 2005).
23 For example, Mark Harrison, *Soviet Planning in Peace and War 1938–45* (Cambridge: Cambridge University Press, 1985).

24 Oleg Khlevniuk, *Stalin: New History of a Dictator* (New Haven, CT: Yale University Press, 2015).
25 J. Arch Getty and Oleg Naumov, *The Road to Terror: Stalin and the Self-Destruction of the Bolsheviks 1932–39* (New Haven, CT: Yale University Press, 1999).
26 Geoffrey Hosking, 'Cards on the Table Comrades', *The Times Literary Supplement*, 28 January 2000.
27 Erik van Ree, *The Political Thought of Joseph Stalin: A Study in Twentieth Century Revolutionary Patriotism* (London: Routledge, 2002).
28 Geoffrey Roberts, 'Joseph Stalin: Bloody Tyrant and Bookworm', *Irish Times*, 20 September 2016, and 'Overview of Stalin's Library, Guide to Fond 558 opis' 3, *Stalin Digital Archive*, available online: https://www.stalindigitalarchive.com/frontend/node/135125 (accessed 17 October 2019). Roberts is preparing a monograph on the subject.
29 David Brandenberger and Mikhail Zelenov, eds, *Stalin's Master Narrative: a Critical Edition of the Short Course on the History of the Communist Party (Bolsheviks)* (New Haven, CT: Yale University Press, 2019).
30 Robert Service, *Stalin: A Biography* (London: Pan Macmillan, 2004).
31 Stephen Kotkin, *Stalin: Paradoxes of Power: 1878–1928* (London: Penguin, 2015), and *Stalin: Waiting for Hitler 1928–1941* (London: Penguin, 2018).
32 Simon Montefiore, *The Young Stalin* (London: Weidenfeld and Nicolson, 2007); R. Suny, 'Beyond Psychohistory: The Young Stalin in Georgia', *Slavic Review* 50, no.1 (1991): 48–58. Alfred Rieber, 'Stalin: Man of the Borderlands', *The American Historical Review* 106, no.5 (2001):1651–1691.
33 Geoffrey Roberts, *Stalin's Wars: From World War to Cold War 1939–1953* (New Haven, CT: Yale University Press, 2006).
34 Jochen Hellbeck, *Revolution on my Mind: Writing a Diary under Stalin* (Cambridge, MA: Harvard University Press, 2009).
35 Yuri Slezkine, *House of Government: A Saga of the Russian Revolution* (Princeton, NJ: Princeton University Press, 2017).
36 Christopher Read, 'Writing the Life of Another: Structure, the Individual and Agency – Reflections of a Lenin Biographer', *Irish Slavonic Studies* 23 (2010): 1–16.
37 On the multiple problems of memoir sources in the Soviet era, see the excellent article by Claire Shaw, 'Soviet Memoir Literature: Personal Narratives of a Historical Epoch', in *Reading Russian Primary Sources*, ed. George Gilbert (London: Routledge, 2020 [forthcoming]).
38 The dark comedy film *Death of Stalin* manages to pull in an extraordinary number of such discredited clichés. *The Death of Stalin* (2017) [Film], Dir. Armando Iannucci, United Kingdom: eOne Films; France: Gaumont.
39 Sheila Fitzpatrick, *On Stalin's Team: The Years of Living Dangerously in Soviet Politics* (Princeton, NJ: Princeton University Press, 2015).
40 This has been recognized even by totalitarian-school historians like Tucker, but they often treated revolutionary commitment as a pathology.
41 For slightly more developed views of this apparent paradox, see Christopher Read, *Lenin: A Revolutionary Life* (London: Routledge, 2003), 212–219; and Christopher Read, *Stalin: From the Caucasus to the Kremlin* (London: Routledge, 2017), 165–166.
42 Trotsky confirms this in *Lenin* (1925), available online: https://www.marxists.org/archive/trotsky/1925/lenin/04.htm (accessed 17 October 2019).
43 See Suny, 'Beyond Pschohistory', and Rieber, 'Stalin'.
44 Read, *Stalin*, 221–222.

45 Ibid., 205–206.
46 See ibid., 259–293, and Roberts, *Stalin's Wars*, 245–253.

Chapter 2

1 Roger R. Reese, 'The Impact of the Great Purge on the Red Army: Wrestling with the Hard Numbers', *The Soviet and Post-Soviet Review* 19, no.1–3 (1992): 71–90; 'M.N. Tukhachevskii i "voenno-fashistskii zagovor"', *Voenno-istoricheskii arkhiv* (1998): 113–117.
2 A meeting of the Political Administration of the Red Army in August 1937 reported that 'Hundreds and thousands of eyes are now looking at the troops for the intrigues of enemies. The troops and commanders are writing hundreds, thousands of letters about faults, failures.' Rossiiskii gosudarstvennyi voennyi arkhiv (hereafter RGVA), f. 9, op. 29, d. 318, l. 11.
3 See for instance, Leonard Schapiro, 'The "great purge"', in *The Red Army*, ed. B.H. Liddell Hart (London: Weidenfeld & Nicholson, 1957); John Erickson, *The Soviet High Command: A Military-Political History* (London: Macmillan, 1962); Robert Conquest, *The Great Terror: Stalin's Purge of the Thirties* (London: Macmillan, 1968). For a more recent example, see E.A. Rees, *Iron Lazar: A Political Biography of Lazar Kaganovich* (London: Anthem Press, 2013), 202.
4 For more on the dossier, see Peter Whitewood, *The Red Army and the Great Terror: Stalin's Purge of the Soviet Military* (Kansas: University Press of Kansas, 2015), 4–6. The same objections apply to the version of the story that claims the Gestapo fabricated the dossier to fool Stalin into beheading his army.
5 Valentin Leskov, *Stalin i zagovor Tukhachevskogo* (Moscow: Veche, 2003). Only marginally more convincingly, Sergei Minakov argues there was a real military plot, but only to unseat head of the army, Kliment Voroshilov. *1937. zagovor byl!* (Moscow: Iauza; Eksmo, 2010).
6 Robert Service, *Stalin: a Biography* (Basingstoke: Macmillan, 2004); Oleg V. Khlevniuk, *Stalin: New Biography of a Dictator* (New Haven, CT: Yale University Press, 2015).
7 Rather than concentrate on the shorter-term proximate causes behind the Great Terror, other scholars see significance in longer-term patterns of state violence and in the efforts of the security apparatus to police the social order predating the turmoil of the 1930s. See David R. Shearer, *Policing Stalin's Socialism: Repression and Social Order in the Soviet Union, 1924–1953* (New Haven, CT: Yale University Press, 2009); and Paul Hagenloh, *Stalin's Police: Public order and Mass Repression in the USSR, 1926–1941* (Baltimore, MD: Johns Hopkins University Press, 2009). While recognizing the importance of longer-term trends, this chapter argues that contingent events are central to the outbreak of the military purge.
8 See in particular, Khlevniuk, *Stalin*, 150–162. For a recent interpretation of the Great Terror that emphasizes its longer roots, see James Harris, *The Great Fear: Stalin's Terror of the 1930s* (Oxford: Oxford University Press, 2016).
9 See Sarah Davies and James Harris, *Stalin's World; Dictating the Soviet Order* (New Haven, CT: Yale University Press, 2015).
10 See Lynne Viola, *Stalinist Perpetrators on Trial: Scenes from the Great Terror in Soviet Ukraine* (Oxford: Oxford University Press, 2018).

11 There was also criticism of a proposed people's militia, as the majority of the Russian population were peasants and not – more reliable – urban workers. Mark von Hagen, 'Civil-military Relations and the Evolution of the Soviet Socialist State', *Slavic Review* 50, no.2 (1991): 271.
12 A.G. Kavtaradze, *Voennye spetsialisty na sluzhbe respubliki sovetov, 1917–1920 gg.* (Moscow: Nauka, 1988), 224.
13 Leon Trotsky, *The Military Writings and Speeches of Leon Trotsky*, vol. 1, *1918: How the Revolution Armed* (London: New Park, 1979), 10.
14 Roger R. Reese, *The Soviet Military Experience: A History of the Soviet Army, 1917–1991* (London: Routledge, 2000), 22.
15 *Vos'moi s'ezd RKP(b), mart 1919 goda: protokoly* (Moscow: Gospolitizdat, 1919), 154.
16 V.I. Lenin, *Polnoe sobranie sochinenii*, vol. 39 (Moscow: Gosudarstvennoe izdatel'stvo politicheskoi literatury, 1969), 313.
17 See Orlando Figes, 'The Red Army and Mass Mobilisation during the Russian Civil War, 1918–1920', in *Warfare in Europe, 1919–1938*, ed. Geoffrey Jenson (Aldershot: Ashgate, 2008), 326.
18 V.P. Butt, *The Russian Civil War: Documents from the Soviet Archives* (Basingstoke: Macmillan, 1996), 104.
19 *F. E. Dzerzhinskii: predsedatel' VChK-OGPU 1917–1926: dokumenty*, ed. A.A. Plekhanov and A.M. Plekhanov (Moscow: MFD, Materik, 2007), 130–132.
20 I.V. Stalin, *Collected Works*, vol. 4 (Moscow: Foreign Languages Publishing House, 1953), 120; *Bol'shevistskoe rukovodstvo. perepiska, 1912–1927*, ed. A.V. Kvashonkin et al. (Moscow: Rosspen, 1996), 40.
21 Rossiiskii gosudarstvennyi arkhiv sotsial'no-politicheskoi istorii (hereafter RGASPI), f. 558, op. 11, d. 5410, l. 1.
22 RGASPI, f. 558, op. 11, d. 1139, l. 67.
23 Viktor Chebrikov, *Istoriia sovetskikh organov gosudarstvennoi bezopasnosti: uchebnik* (Moscow: KGB, 1977), 24.
24 *Arkhiv VChK: sbornik dokumentov*, ed. Vinogradov et al. (Moscow: Kuchkovo Pole, 2007), 131–133; *Dzerzhinskii*, ed. Plekhanov and Plekhanov, 133.
25 On White agents discovered in the army, see RGVA, f. 9, op. 28, d. 297, ll. 8–25; op. 9, d. 229, l. 272; Chebrikov, *Istoriia sovetskikh organov*, 13–101.
26 In 1920, the OO received one third of the Cheka's entire yearly budget. George Leggett, *The Cheka: Lenin's Political Police Force: The All-Russian Extraordinary Commission for Combating Counter-revolution and Sabotage (December 1917 to February 1922)* (Oxford: Clarendon, 1981), 207.
27 For cases of supposed foreign agents discovered in the army, see S.S. Voitikov, *Otechestvennye spetssluzhby i krasnaia armiia, 1917–1921* (Moscow: Veche, 2010), 71–77, 164, 289, 313, 362. Military specialists were also accused of working with foreign powers, see Aleksandr Zdanovich, *Organy gosudarstvennoi bezopasnosti i krasnaia armiia* (Moscow: Kuchkov Pole, 2008), 510–511.
28 For a fuller discussion, see James Harris, 'Intelligence and Threat Perception: Defending the Revolution, 1917–1937', in *The Anatomy of Terror: Political Violence under Stalin*, ed. James Harris (Oxford: Oxford University Press, 2013), 29–43.
29 Joshua Sanborn, *Drafting the Russian Nation: Military Conscription, Total War, and Mass Politics, 1905–1925* (Dekalb, IL: Northern Illinois University Press, 2003), 128.
30 Zdanovich, *Organy gosudarstvennoi bezopasnosti*, 493.

31 For espionage cases, see Boris Viktorov, *Bez grifa "sekretno": zapiski voennogo prokurova* (Moscow: Iurid. litra, 1990), 62, 66; Zdanovich, *Organy gosudarstvennoi bezopasnosti*, 606–613.
32 Zdanovich, *Organy gosudarstvennoi bezopasnosti*, 74–75.
33 The military procuracy made this danger clear in 1927. See RGVA, f. 4 op. 14, d. 70, ll. 1, 14–15.
34 Erickson, *Soviet High Command*, 191.
35 For such reports from the early 1920s, *Russkaia voennaia emigratsiia 20-kh-40-kh godov: dokumenty i materialy*, vol. 1, bk. 2, ed. V.A. Zolotarev et al. (Moscow: Geia, 1998), 87–89; Zdanovich, *Organy gosudarstvennoi bezopasnosti*, 337.
36 RGVA, f. 33987, op. 3, d. 186, ll. 34–35; *Krasnaia armiia v 1920-e*, ed. Sergei Kudriashov et al. (Moscow, 1997), 86.
37 *Russkaia voennaia emigratsiia*, vol. 4, ed. A.A. Kol'tiukov et al. (Moscow: RGGU, 2007), 815–817.
38 On White interest in Tukhachevskii as a 'Red Bonaparte', see Sergei Minakov, *Stalin i zagovor generalov* (Moscow: Eksmo, 2005), 71–98.
39 'M. N. Tukhachevskii i "voenno-fashistskii zagovor"', *Voenno-istoricheskii arkhiv* 1 (1997), 229–235.
40 For such an OGPU report on White interest in Tukhachevskii as a military dictator, see *Russkaia voennaia emigratsiia*, vol. 5, ed. A.A. Kol'tiukov et al. (Moscow: RGGU, 2010), 421–422.
41 RGVA, f. 33987, op. 3, d. 227, ll. 190–191; f. 33988, op. 3, d. 69, l. 133; RGASPI, f. 74, op. 2, d. 51, ll. 21–24.
42 The case was later discussed at the joint plenum of the Central Committee in October but no further action was taken. Iurii Fel'shtinskii and Georgii Cherniavskii, *Lev Trotskii. Kniga tret'ia. Oppozitsioner, 1923–1929 gg.* (Moscow: Tsentrpoligraf, 2012), 238, 267–268; Zdanovich, *Organy gosudarstvennoi bezopastnosti*, 320–322.
43 Michel Reiman, *The Birth of Stalinism: the USSR on the Eve of the "Second Revolution"* (Bloomington, IN: Indiana University Press, 1987), 125.
44 Ibid., 127.
45 Zdanovich, *Organy gosudarstvennoi bezopasnosti*, 325–326.
46 See RGVA, f. 9, op. 29, d. 178, l. 55; d. 16, l. 1; f. 37837, op. 10, d. 20, 11. 131–132; op. 21, d. 52, ll. 46, 48; d. 39, l. 32.
47 In 1928, Vitovt Putna, exiled as military attaché because of his support of Trotsky, received Stalin's enthusiastic support in returning to the central military apparatus. In a letter Stalin pressed that 'we will do everything possible' [to help Putna]. Voroshilov described him as 'one of the best of our commander-party men'. Putna was later arrested in 1936. RGASPI, f. 588, op. 11, d. 36, l. 17; f. 74, op. 21, d. 42, l. 91.
48 Primakov admitted in 1936 that he had secretly met with other former Trotskyists. 'Delo o tak nazyvaemoi "antisovetskoi trotskistskoi voennoi organizatsii" v krasnoi armii', *Izvetsiia TsK* 4 (1989), 44. Putna met with another former Trotskyist, Efim Dreister, in London. RGVA, f. 33987, op. 3, d. 872, l. 76.
49 On Trotskyist networks, see J. Arch Getty, *Origin of the Great Purges: The Soviet Communist Party Reconsidered, 1933–1938* (Cambridge: Cambridge University Press, 1991), 119–128.
50 Outside the minority of military Trotskyists, the Military Procuracy noted in 1927 that 'the infiltration of foreign agents into the RKKA is on an insignificant scale'. RGVA, f. 4, op. 14, d. 70, l. 1.

51 On the Red Army and collectivization, see in particular Nonna Tarkhova, *Krasnaia armiia i stalinskaia kollektivizatsiia, 1928–1933 gg.* (Moscow: Rosspen, 2010).
52 Iaroslav Tynchenko, *Golgofa russkogo ofitserstva v SSSR, 1930–1931 gody* (Moscow: Moskovskii obshchestvennyi nauchnyi fond, 2000,) 3.
53 'M. N. Tukhachevskii i "voenno-fashistskii zagovor"' (1997), 247. The evidence against Tukhachevskii was highly likely to have been obtained through torture.
54 RGASPI, f. 558, op. 11, d. 778, ll. 34, 38.
55 *Pis'ma I. V. Stalina V. M. Molotovu: 1925–1936 gg.: sbornik dokumentov*, ed. L. Kosheleva et al. (Moscow: Rossiia molodaia, 1995), 231.
56 For statistics on growing arrests for political crimes in the army in the mid-1930s from the Military Procuracy, see RGVA, f. 9, op. 29, d. 281, l. 144.
57 For Ezhov's September letter to Stalin, see Marc Jansen and Nikita Petrov, *'Stalinskii pitomets' – Nikolai Ezhov* (Moscow: Rosspen, 2008), 251; for his December comments, see 269.
58 Semen Budennyi wrote to Voroshilov in August 1936 calling for investigation of the army in light of the first show trial. See RGVA, f. 4, op. 19, d. 16, l. 265.
59 J. Arch Getty and Oleg Naumov, *Yezhov: the Rise of Stalin's "Iron Fist"* (New Haven, CT: Yale University Press, 2008), 182–184; Paul Hagenloh, *Stalin's Police: Public Order and Mass Repression in the USSR, 1926–1941* (Baltimore, MD: Woodrow Wilson Center Press, 2009), 230.
60 Ibid., 234–245.
61 William Chase, 'Stalin as Producer: The Moscow Show Trials and the Construction of Mortal Threats', in *Stalin: A New History*, ed. James Harris and Sarah Davies (Cambridge: Cambridge University Press, 2005), 226–248.
62 'Materialy fevral'skogo-martovskogo plenuma TsK VKP(b) 1937 goda', *Voprosy istorii* 3 (1995): 3–10.
63 Ibid., 13–14.
64 *Tragediia sovetskoi derevni: kollektivizatsiia i raskulachivanie: dokumety i materialy v 5 tomakh, 1937–1939*, vol. 5, bk. 1, ed. V. Danilov et al. (Moscow, 2004), 162–164; 'Materialy fevral'skogo-martovskogo plenuma TsK VKP(b) 1937 goda', *Voprosy istorii*, 4–5 (1992): 10.
65 'M. N. Tukhachevskii i "voenno-fashistskii zagovor"' (1997), 157.
66 Vladimir Khaustov and Lennart Samuelson, *Stalin, NKVD i repressii 1936–1938 gg.* (Moscow: Rosspen, 2010), 113.
67 'Delo o tak nazyvaemoi "antisovetskoi trotskistskoi voennoi organizatsii"', 45.
68 RGASPI, f. 4, op. 14, d. 1820, ll. 448–449.
69 RGVA, f. 9, op. 29, d. 319, l. 2.
70 'Delo o tak nazyvaemoi "antisovetskoi trotskistskoi voennoi organizatsii"', 61.
71 RGVA, f. 33987, op. 3, d. 965, ll. 65–81.
72 RGASPI, f. 558, op. 11, d. 203, ll. 62–88.

Chapter 3

1 For a basic introduction to Cold War interpretations of the Soviet role in Spain, see Paul Preston, 'War of Words: The Spanish Civil War and the Historians', in *Revolution and War in Spain*, ed. P. Preston (London: Methuen, 1984), 1–13; and, more recently, Paul Corthorn, 'Cold War Politics in Britain and the Contested Legacy of the Spanish Civil War', *European History Quarterly*, 44 (2014): 678–702. For the Left's broadly

negative interpretation of the Soviet role in Spain, the starting point is George Orwell, *Homage to Catalonia* (London: Secker and Warburg, 1938). Orwell believed the war triangulated between fascism, communism and democracy. He was witness to the Barcelona May Days, which saw the withering of Catalan anarchism and the destruction of the non-Stalinist POUM (Workers Party of Marxist Unification).

2   Michael Alpert, *A New International History of the Spanish Civil War* (London: St. Martin's, 1998), 215.
3   L.V. Ponomarieva, *Sovietskaia istoricheskaia nauka ot XX k XXII s"ezdu Komunisticheskoi partii Sovetskogo Soiuza. Istoriia stran Zapadnoi Evropii i Amerikii* (Moscow: Nauka, 1963), 210–216. A key mid-sixties work would be M.T. Meshcheriakov, 'Ispanskaia tema v rabotakh sovetskikh istorikov', *Vestnik Akademii Nauk SSSR* 5 (1965): 129–134.
4   Ibid., 132. Soviet veterans with whom Maiskii worked included Malinovskii, Voronov, Kuznetsov, Batov and Rodimtsev.
5   B.A. Kandel and E.A. Guterman, *Istoriia zarubezhnikh stran (Bibliografiia russkikh bibliografii)* (Moscow: Nauka, 1966).
6   L.M. Iurieva, *Natsionalno-revolutsionnaia voina v Ispanii i mirovaia literatura* (Moscow: Izdat. Nauka, 1973).
7   E.L. Gluzhinskaia, 'Sovetskie issledovaniia po istorii Ispanii (1917–1974)', *Problemy Ispanskoi istorii* (1975): 252–262. The same author produced an update the following decade: 'Sovetskie issledovaniia po istorii Ispanii (1975–1982)', *Problemy Ispanskoi istorii* (1984), 273–285. In all, Gluzhinskaia named 958 works on Spanish history produced in the Soviet Union between 1917 and 1984.
8   S.P. Pozharskaia, 'Sovetskaia istoriografiia antifashistskoi voiny v Ispanii (1936–1939)', *Novaia i noveishaia istoriia* (1987): 201–211. The result is broad in conception and minute in detail. One learns, for example, that two Soviet Hispanists died at the front in the Second World War.
9   *SSSR i fashistskaia agressiia v Ispanii: Sbornik dokumentov* (Moscow, 1937); *Dela Ispanii ni chastno dela ispantsev* (Moscow, 1937).
10 These publications, entitled *Voina v Ispanii*, appeared under the Defence Commissariat's own editorial, Voenizdat, between mid-1937 and the end of 1938. In all, twenty-six volumes were published. In recent years, several of these Voenizdat editions have been re-edited and published in, for example: B.M. Simonov, *Grazhdanskaia voina v Ispanii. Deystviia na tsentral'nom fronte. Oktiabr' 1936 aprel' 1937* (St Petersburg: Sankt-Peterburgskiy Universitet, 2006); and V.G. Goncharov, ed., *Voina v Ispanii. Tsentral'nyy front i Brunetskaia operatsiia Seriya* (Moscow: Veche, 2010).
11 *Vneshniaia politika SSSR: Sbornik dokumentov (1936–1943)*, Vol. IV (Moscow: Izdatel'stvo politicheskoi literatury, 1946), and *Dokumenty vneshnei politiki SSSR*, vols. XIX–XXI (Moscow: Izdatel'stvo politicheskoi literatury, 1974–77).
12 K.K. Shirinia, ed., *VII Kongress Kommunisticheskogo Internatsionala i bor'ba protiv fashizma i voiny (Sbornik dokumentov)* (Moscow: Politizdat, 1975), 440–465.
13 Dolores Ibárruri et al., *Voina i revoliutsiia v Ispanii, 1936–1939*, 4 vols. (Moscow: Progreso, 1966–71).
14 *Internatsional'naia solidarnost trudiiashikhsia zapadnoukrainskikh zemel s respublikanskoi Ispaniei: Sbornik dokumentov i materialov* (Kiev, 1988).
15 Mikhail Koltsov, *Ispanskii dnevnik* (Moscow: Sov. pisatel', 1957) was heavily redacted. A more complete version appeared three decades later: *Ispanskii dnevnik: Ispaniia v ognia*, ed. E.M. Tiper, 2 vols. (Moscow: Izd-vo politicheskoi literatury, 1987).

16 Ilya Erenburg, *Lyudi, gody, zhizn'* (Moscow: Sov. pisatel', 1990). An English translation has been published in four separate volumes, the second of which covers the war: Ilya Ehrenburg, *Memoirs: 1921–1941*, trans. Tatiana Shebunina and Yvonne Kapp (London: MacGibbon, 1963).
17 Ilya Ehrenburg, *Ispanskie reportazhi* (Moscow: Izd-vo Agenstva pechati Novosti, 1986). This work has never appeared in English, though a Spanish translation of a much older French version has just been issued: *Corresponsal en España,* trans. Javier Pérez (Barcelona: Editorial Prensa Ibérica, 1998).
18 For the most complete list of Soviet memoirs, see Novikov, *SSSR i Grazhdanskaia voina v Ispanii,* 18–38.
19 Ivan M. Maiskii, ed., *Iz istorii osvoboditel'noi voiny ispanskogo naroda* (Moscow: Akademiia Nauk SSSR, 1959). See also the same author's second such anthology: *Ispanskii narod protiv fashizma, 1936–1939 gg.; sbornik statei* (Moscow: Izd-vo Akademiia nauk SSSR, 1963).
20 Ivan M. Maiskii, *Ispanskii tetrady* (Moscow: Voennoe izdat., 1962). In English this first appeared as *Spanish Notebooks,* trans. Ruth Kisch (London: Hutchinson, 1966).
21 Ivan M. Maiskii, N.N. Voronov and I.N. Nesterenko, eds, *Pod znamenem ispanskoi respubliki: Vospominaniia sovetskikh dobrovol'tsev-uchastnikov natsional'no-revoliutsionnoi voiny v Ispanii, 1936–1939* (Moscow: Izdat. Nauka, 1965). This work was one of the few primary Soviet accounts of the war to be published by Moscow in a Spanish translation: *Bajo la bandera de la España Republicana* (Moscow: Progreso, 1965). Contributors included Batov, Krivoshein, Nesterenko, Rodimstev, Voronov, Malinovskii, Iakushin, Prokof'ev and Mezentsev.
22 D.P. Pritsker, ed., *Leningradtsy v Ispanii,* 3rd edn (Leningrad: Lenizdat, 1989).
23 L.L. Gorilovskogo, ed., *Vmeste s patriotami Ispanii: vospominaniia uchastnikov natsional'no-revoliutsionnoi voiny ispanskogo naroda* (Kiev: Izd-vo polit. lit-ry Ukrainy, 1986). *My internatsionalisty,* 2nd edn. (Moscow: Izdat. Politicheskoi Literatury, 1986).
24 In Russian, Kuznetsov's work has never gone out of print. The fourth edition of *Na dalekom meridiane* (Moscow: Veche) appeared in 2014, but the invaluable English edition of *Memoirs of Wartime Minister of the Navy* (Moscow: Progress, 1990) has appeared only once. In Spanish, there remains Kuznetsov's indispensible 'Con los marinos españoles en su guerra nacional-revolucionaria', in R. Ia. Malinovskii, ed., *Bajo la bandera de la España republicana* (Moscow: Progress, 1967), never re-issued.
25 Roman Karmen, *No Pasaran!* (Moscow: Izdatelstvo Sovetskaia Rossiia, 1972).
26 Ovadii Savich, *Dva goda v Ispanii, 1937–1939* (Moscow: Sovetskii Pisatel', 1981).
27 Adelina and Paulina Abramson, *Mosaico Roto* (Madrid: Compañía Literaria, 1995).
28 V.V. Kuleshova, *Ispaniia i SSSR: Kulturnye sviazi: 1917–1939* (Moscow: Izdat. Nauka, 1975).
29 Afanasii Arsen'evich Komshukov, 'Natsional'no-revoliutsionnaia voina ispanskogo naroda 1936–1939 gg. i sovetskaia obshchestvennost', Ph.D. diss. (Kharkov, 1979).
30 David Cattell, *Communism and the Spanish Civil War* (Berkeley, CA: University of California Press, 1955).
31 David Cattell, *Soviet Diplomacy and the Spanish Civil War* (Berkeley, CA: University of California Press, 1957), 132.
32 Robert L. Plumb, 'Soviet Participation in the Spanish Civil War', Ph.D. diss. (Georgetown, DC, 1956); David E. Allen, 'The Soviet Union and the Spanish Civil War, 1936–1939', Ph.D. diss. (Stanford, CA, 1952).
33 Only the last and most comprehensive need concern us here: Burnett Bolloten, *The Spanish Civil War* (Chapel Hill, NC: University of North Carolina Press, 1991).

34 George Orwell, *Homage to Catalonia* (London: Secker and Warburg, 1938).
35 Jonathan Haslam, *The Soviet Union and the Struggle for Collective Security in Europe, 1933–1939* (New York: St. Martin's, 1984); Jiri Hochman, *The Soviet Union and the Failure of Collective Security* (Ithaca, NY: Cornell University Press, 1984).
36 Hochman, *The Soviet Union and the Failure of Collective Security*, 172.
37 Geoffrey Roberts, 'Soviet Foreign Policy and the Spanish Civil War, 1936–1939', in *Spain in an International Context, 1936–1959*, ed. Christian Leitz and David J. Dunthorn (New York: Berghahn Books, 1999), 81–103.
38 Ibid., 96.
39 Ibid., 89.
40 Indeed, two of the main Western accounts of the 1950s, namely the Allen and Plumb dissertations, are primarily concerned with refuting the Nationalist-advanced thesis that the July uprising was a response to Soviet intervention in Spanish affairs.
41 Dolores Ibárruri et al., *Guerra y revolución en España 1936–1939*, 4 vols. (Moscow: Progreso, 1966).
42 Alba's books are too numerous to mention, though special attention should be drawn to *Historia del POUM* (Paris: Champ Libre, 1975); and *El marxismo en España: 1919–1939: Historia del BOC y del POUM*, 2 vols. (Mexico City: Costa-Amic, 1973).
43 Among Araquistain's publications, all of which repeat the same allegations, are 'La intervención de Rusia en la guerra civil española', *Cuadernos* 24 (1958); *La intervención de Rusia en el conflicto Español; Revelaciones de un Ex-Embajador de la Republica Española* (San José, Costa Rica, 1939); and *El comunismo y la guerra de España* (San José, Costa Rica, 1939).
44 See Juan García Durán, 'El hundamiento del "Komsomol"', *Tiempo de Historia* 3, no.34 (Sept. 1977): 34–37; and 'Por qué y cómo interveno Rusia en la guerra civil española', *Tiempo de Historia* 5, no.51 (Feb. 1979):10–25.
45 Among the only important works to emerge from Soviet scholars in the decade of the 1980s was M.T. Meshcheriakov, *Ispanskaia respublika i Komintern* (Moscow: Mysl', 1981). Meshcheriakov's work was the first to make use of the Party archive, now RGASPI, though his conclusions – very much a product of the time – cast the Moscow-based organization in far too charitable a light. Meshcheriakov's conclusions have largely been superseded by the more recent work of Elorza and Bizcarrondo, discussed below.
46 V.A. Tolmachaev, 'Sovetskii Soyuz i Ispaniia: Opyt i uroki internatsional'noi pomoshchi (1936–1939)', Ph.D. diss. (Leningrad, 1991). The author alleged that Kremlin officials fostered 'a suspicious, hateful atmosphere' in Spain (Ibid., 140).
47 M.V. Novikov, *SSSR, Komintern i grazhdanskaia voina v Ispanii 1936–1939*, 2 vols. (Iaroslav: Iaroslav gosud. universitet, 1995). The same author's previous *Grazhdanskaia voina v Ispanii, 1936–1939. Bibliograficheskii ukazatel' istochnikov i literatury, izdannykh v SSSR v 1936–1991* (Iaroslav: Iaroslav gos. universitet, 1994), became the indispensable bibliographical survey up to that point.
48 Iurii E. Ribalkin, 'Voennaia pomoshch' Sovetskogo Soiuza Ispanskomu narodu v natsional'no-revoliutsionnoi voine 1936–1939', Ph.D. diss. (Institute of Military History, Moscow, 1992); *Operatsiia 'X': Sovetskaia voennaia pomoshch' respublikanskoi Ispanii (1936–1939)* (Moscow: 'AIRO-XX', 2000); and (as Yuri Rybalkin) *Stalin y España* (Madrid: Marcial Pons, 2007).
49 S.P. Pozharskaya, ed., *Komintern i grazhdanskaia voina v Ispanii. Dokumenty Seriya: Dokumenty Kominterna* (Moscow: Nauka, 2001); Sergei Kudriashov, ed., *SSSR i Grazhdanskaia voina v Ispanii. 1936–1939 gody* (Moscow: Vestnik Arkhiv Presidenta

Rossiiskoi Federatsii, 2013); A.R. Efimenko, N.A. Myshov and N.S. Tarkhova, eds, *RKKA i Grazhdanskaia voina v Ispanii. 1936–1939 gody*. Tom 1: Sborniki № 1–15 (Moscow: Politicheskaia Entsiklopediia, 2019).
50 On Soviet air power in Spain, see V.V. Gagin, *Vozdushnaya voina v Ispanii (1936–1939)* (Moscow: Izdatel'skiy Literaturnyy Dom 'Voronezhskiy al'manakh', 1998); S.V. Abrosov, *V nebe Ispanii 1936–1939* (Moscow, 2003); and D. Degtev, Yu. Borisov and D. Zubov, *Ishak' protiv messera. Ispytanie voynoy v nebe Ispanii. 1936–1939* (Moscow: Tsentrpoligraf, 2012). On armour, see V. Shpakovskiy and S. Shpakovskaia, *Bronetekhnika grazhdanskoy voyny v Ispanii. 1936–1939 gg.* (Moscow: Poligon,1999). Recent works that provide analysis of the totality of Soviet advisers, technicians and their equipment include A.A. Izetdinov, *Voina v Ispanii. Khronika boevykh deystviy 1936–1939 godov* (Moscow: ArtKom, 2014).
51 V.V. Malay, *Grazhdanskaia voina v Ispanii 1936–1939 godov i Yevropa Avtor* (Moscow: Nauka, 2011).
52 O.V. Karimov and I.N Voloshenko, eds, *Iz Moskvy v stranu 'Iks'. Kniga pamyati sovetskikh dobrovol'tsev-uchastnikov grazhdanskoi voiny v Ispanii 1936–1939 gody*. 2 vols. (Moscow: GBU 'TsGA Moskvy', 2015).
53 See A.A. Pchelinov-Obrazumov, *Grazhdanskaia voina v Ispanii 1936–1939 gg. i rossiyskaya politicheskaya emigratsiya* (Moscow: BGNIU, 2015).
54 A.V. Shubin, V.V. Dam'e et al., *Grazhdanskaia voina v Ispanii: Izvestnoe i neizvestnoe* (Moscow: URSS Publications, 2018). Among the most intriguing chapters in the volume is K.K. Semyonov, 'K voprosu opredeleniia chislennosti russkikh dobrovol'tsev-emigrantov v armii Fransisko Franko' (193–200), whose subject is the so-called 'White Russian' volunteers for the Nationalist side.
55 Olga Volosiuk, Ekaterina Yuirchik y Vladimir Vediushkin, eds, *España y Rusia: diplomacia y diálogo de culturas. Tres siglos de relaciones* (Moscow: Indrik, 2018).
56 *Istoriia*, 2, no. 76 (2019), Ekaterina Grantseva and Georgy Filatov, eds.
57 Gerald Howson, *Arms for Spain: The Untold Story of the Spanish Civil War* (New York: Murray, 1998). Howson succeeds in bringing to light a number of important aspects of Soviet military assistance, though his emphatic claims that the Defence Commissariat overcharged the Republic for nearly all of the weapons supplied would not be entirely confirmed in subsequent studies that had deeper recourse to declassified Russian sources.
58 Rémi Skoutelsky, *L'espoir guidait leur pas: Les volontaires français dans les Brigades internationales, 1936–1939* (Paris: Bernard Grasset, 1998). The same author's more global approach would appear a few years later: *Novedad en el frente: Las Brigadas Internacionales en la guerra civil* (Madrid: Ediciones Temas de Hoy, 2006).
59 Steven J. Zaloga, 'Soviet Tank Operations in the Spanish Civil War', *Journal of Slavic Military Studies* 12, no.3 (Sept. 1999): 134–162. The most up-to-date account of Soviet armour in Spain is, again, Zaloga: *Spanish Civil War Tanks: The Proving Ground for Blitzkrieg* (Oxford: Osprey, 2010).
60 See Antonio Elorza and Marta Bizcarrondo, *Queridos Camaradas: La Internacional Comunista y España, 1919–1939* (Barcelona: Planeta, 1999). This work was the first non-Russian monograph to delve into Moscow's former party archive (RGASPI).
61 Mary Habeck and Ronald Radosh, *Spain Betrayed: The Soviet Union in the Spanish Civil War* (New Haven, CT: Yale University Press, 2001).
62 The author's first publication was a post-Soviet archival primer: see Daniel Kowalsky, 'Researching Spanish History in the Russian Federation', *Bulletin of the Society for Spanish and Portuguese Historical Studies* 23, no.3 (Autumn, 1998): 6–17. Monographs

by the author appeared several years later, first in Spanish and then in English: *La Unión Soviética y la Guerra Civil Española: Una Revisión Crítica* (Barcelona: Editorial Crítica, 2003), and a Gutenberg e-book that was published together with a soft cover version of the same: *Stalin and the Spanish Civil War* (New York: Columbia University Press, 2004). In the years that followed, the author published on various subthemes of the topic, including: 'The Soviet Union and the International Brigades, 1936–1939', *Journal of Slavic Military Studies* 19, no.4 (2006): 681–704; 'The Soviet Cinematic Offensive in the Spanish Civil War', *Film History* 19, no.1 (2007): 7–19; 'Las grandes campañas propagandísticas de la URSS', in *Los Rusos en la Guerra de España, 1936–1939*, ed. Ricardo Miralles (Madrid: Fundacion P. Iglesia, 2009), 59–65. More recently, the author has uncovered newly declassified Soviet materials and published them in a series of research articles: 'Operation X: Soviet Russia and the Spanish Civil War', *Bulletin of Spanish Studies* 91, no.1–2 (2014): 159–178; 'Exporting Soviet Commemoration: The Spanish Civil War and the October Revolution, 1936–1939', in *Echoes of October: International Commemorations of the Bolshevik Revolution, 1918–1990*, ed. Jean-François Fayet, Valerie Gorin, and Stefanie Prezioso (London: Lawrence and Wishart, 2017), 104–132; and 'From Marginalization to Mobilization: The Soviet Union and the Spanish Republic, 18 July–31 December 1936', in *Spain 1936: Year Zero*, ed. Raanan Rein and Joan Maria Thomas (Eastbourne: Sussex Academic Press, 2018), 152–173; 'Revisiting Operation X: Stalin and the Spanish Republic, 1936–1939', in *Desde la Capital de la Republic: Nuevas perspectivas y estudios sobre la guerra civil española*, ed. S. Valero Gómez and M. García Carrión (Valencia: Universitat de Valencia, 2018), 45–66. Finally, an entirely updated version of some 20 years of research will appear as *Decree and Power: The Soviet Union in the Spanish Civil War, 1936–1939* (London: Routledge, expected 2021).

63 Frank Schauff, *Der verspielte Sieg: Sowjetunion, Kommunistische Internationale und Spanischer Bürgerkrieg 1936–1939* (Frankfurt-Main: Campus Verlag, 2004); *La victoria frustrada: La Unión Soviética, la Internacional Comunista y la Guerra Civil Española* (Barcelona: Debate, 2008); *Proigrannaya pobeda. Sovetskiy Soyuz, Kommunistich. Internatsional i Grazhd. voina v Ispanii 1936–1939 gg* (Moscow: Politicheskaya entsiklopediya, 2017).

64 Angel Viñas, *La soledad de la república: el abandono de las democracias y el viraje hacia la Unión Soviética* (Barcelona: Crítica, 2006); *El escudo de la República: El oro de España, la apuesta soviética y los hechos de mayo de 1937* (Barcelona: Crítica, 2007), and *El honor de la República: Entre el acoso fascista, la hostilidad británica y la política de Stalin* (Barcelona: Crítica, 2008).

65 Ricardo Miralles, ed., *Los Rusos en la Guerra de España, 1936–1939* (Madrid: Fundacion P. Iglesia, 2009).

66 Those presenting research at the event, sponsored by the University of Pittsburgh, included William Chase, Immaculada Colomina, Daniel Kowalsky, Olva Novikova Monterde, Enrique Moradiellos, Josep Puigsech, Jonathan Sherry and Glennys Young.

67 For the niños, the interested reader is spoiled for choice. See Alicia Alted et al., *Los niños de la guerra de España en la URSS. De la evacuación al retorno (1937–1999)* (Madrid: Fundación Francisco Largo Caballero, 1999); Glennys Young, 'To Russia with "Spain": Spanish Exiles in the USSR and the *Longue Durée* of Soviet History', *Kritika: Explorations in Russian and Eurasian History* 15, no.2 (2014): 395–419; Rafael Moreno Izqueierdo, *Los niños de Rusia: La verdadera historia de una operación de retorno* (Barcelona: Critica, 2017). On the reception of Spanish culture in the USSR, see Olga Novikova, 'Las visiones de España en la URSS durante la guerra civil española',

Historia del Presente, no.11 (2008): 9–44. For Republican doctors in the USSR, see the recent Miguel Marco Igual, *Los médicos republicanos españoles en la Unión Soviética* (Barcelona: Flor del Viento, 2010). Also on Republican exiles, see Natalia Kharitonova, *Edificar la cultura, construir la identidad. El exilio republicana español de 1939 en la Unión Soviética* (Seville: Biblioteca del Exilio, 2014).

68 For example, Enrique Piquero Cuadros, *La guerra civil española a través de las crónicas de los corresponsales soviéticos* (Madrid: Miraguano, 2017).

69 Miguel Marco Igual, *La injusticia de un olvido. El mundo de Marcelino Pascua (1897–1977), médico y político* (Madrid: Universidad Nacional de Educación de Distancia, 2018).

70 See Stephen G. Marks, 'Cultural Migrations between Spain and Russia: Transnational Perspectives', *Cuadernos de Historia Contemporánea* 38 (2016), a special issue devoted to bilateral cultural ties, and see also the last monograph of the late Richard Stites: *The Four Horsemen: Riding to Liberty in Post-Napoleonic Europe* (Oxford: Oxford University Press, 2014).

71 Oleg Khlevniuk, *Stalin: New Biography of a Dictator,* trans. Nora Seligman Favorov (New Haven, CT: Yale University Press, 2015). Stephen Kotkin, *Stalin: Waiting for Hitler, 1928–1941* (London: Allen Lane, 2017). Kotkin uses no Spanish language sources, and he neglects all of the recent literature in French (Skoutelsky, for example).

72 Khlevniuk, *Stalin*, 153.

73 Kotkin, *Stalin*, 323.

74 For an enthralling socio-cultural study of the creation of the International Brigades, see Lisa A. Kirschenbaum, *International Communism and the Spanish Civil War: Solidarity and Suspicion* (Cambridge: Cambridge University Press, 2015). Still highly relevant, and never surpassed where the fate of the Brigaders is concerned, is David Wingeate Pike, *In the Service of Stalin: The Spanish Communists in Exile, 1939–45* (Oxford: Oxford University Press, 1993).

75 See Josep Puigsech, *Falsa leyenda del Kremlin: El consulado y la URSS en la Guerra Civil Española* (Madrid: Biblioteca Nueva, 2014). Since bursting on the scene less than fifteen years ago, the author has been prolific. Of equally great interest are Puigsech's *Entre Franco y Stalin:El difícil itinerario de los comunistas en Cataluña, 1936–1949* (Barcelona: El Viejo Topo, 2009); and, most recently, *La Revolució Russa I Catalunya* (Barcelona: Eumo Editorial SAU, 2017).

76 Jonathan Sherry, 'Stalinism on Trial: Spanish Republican Legality, the Soviet Union, and the Performance of Justice in the Spanish Civil War, 1936–1939' (Ph.D. dissertation, University of Pittsburgh, 2017). The same author's forthcoming monograph will no doubt become a standard reference in the field: *Stalinism on Trial: Communism and Republican Justice in the Spanish Civil War* (Eastbourne, UK: Sussex Academic Press, 2020).

77 Boris Volodarsky, *Stalin's Agent: The Life and Death of Alexander Orlov* (Oxford: Oxford University Press, 2015). Volodarsky's revisionist research supersedes the conclusions in canonical works of Slavic studies published throughout the Cold War, rendering obsolete, for example, Robert C. Tucker's hysterical discussion of a "multitude" of Stalinist agents, whose reign of terror handicapped the Republic's war effort, is characteristic of the deeply flawed analysis, supported by now-discredited sources. See *Stalin in Power: The Revolution from Above, 1928–1941* (New York: Norton, 1992), 510.

78 See Marcelino Pascua's notes of meeting with Stalin, Voroshilov and Molotov from 3.2.37, Archivo Histórico Nacional-Madrid, Archivo Marcelino Pascua, Legajo 2, Expediente 6.

Chapter 4

1. Melvyn C. Leffler, *For the Sake of Mankind: The United States, the Soviet Union and the Cold War* (New York: Macmillan, 2007), 55–56. Also cited online: https://www.quora.com/Who-is-more-ruthless-and-more-cunning-all-things-being-equal-Stalin-or-Putin (accessed 16 April 2019).
2. Office of the Historian US Department of State, *Milestones in the History of US Foreign Relations, 1937–1945, The Potsdam Conference 1945,* available online: https://history.state.gov/milestones/1937-1945/potsdam-conf (accessed 18 April 2019); *Berlin Experiences, The Potsdam Conference, 1945: Day-by-Day*. Compiled by Jim McDonough of the Berlin Guides Association, 5 August 2018, available online: https://berlinexperiences.com/potsdam-conference-1945/ (accessed 18 April 2019). Unpaginated, see 'Potsdam Conference Day 1: Tuesday, July 17, 1945 at Potsdam, Germany'.
3. Ibid., *Berlin Experiences*.
4. Geoffrey Roberts, *Stalin's Wars: from World War to Cold War, 1939–1953* (New Haven, CT: Yale University Press, 2005), 3.
5. K.E. Voroshilov, *Stalin and the Red Army* (Moscow: Foreign Languages Publishing House 1939), scanned as 1939_StalinandtheRedArmy_KEVoroshilov.pdf, available online: https://neodemocracy.blogspot.com/2019/03/stalin-and-red-army-tsaritsyn.html (accessed 19 April 2019).
6. Robert Argenbright, 'Red Tsaritsyn: Precursor of Stalinist terror', *Revolutionary Russia* 4, no.2 (1991): 157–158.
7. By the nineteenth century the Old Style (OS) Julian calendar had slipped twelve days behind the 'New Style' (NS) Gregorian calendar. The Russians used OS until 1917, by which time the difference was 13 days.
8. N. Markin, 'Appendix: Stalin and the Red Army', available online: https://www.marxists.org/archive/trotsky/1937/ssf/sf13.htm (accessed 22 April 2019).
9. Argenbright, 'Red Tsaritsyn: Precursor of Stalinist terror', 158, citing *Iz istorii grazhdanskoi voiny v SSSR, (From the History of the USSR Civil War)* Vol. 1 (Moscow: 1960), 290.
10. Ibid., Argenbright.
11. Ibid.
12. Ibid., 159–172. Makhrovskii was arrested again in 1921 and sentenced to death, later commuted to five years' imprisonment.
13. Phrase used by Professor Richard Holmes (1946–2011).
14. Markin, Appendix, p. 1, citing Trotsky, *My Life*, 486–450.
15. Voroshilov, *Stalin and the Red Army*, available online: https://www.marxists.org/reference/archive/stalin/biographies/1947/stalin/06.htm, Ch. VI, 2 (accessed 22 April 2019).
16. *15 October 1918 – the Battle of Tsaritsyn*, available online: https://www.stormfront.org/forum/t1260621/ (accessed 22 April 2019).
17. Cited in Markin, Appendix, p. 4, citing 'October 4, 1918. No.552. Trotsky', to Lenin.
18. Ibid., available online: https://www.stormfront.org/forum/t1260621/ (accessed 15 October 1918). Also, see the entry in the *Great Soviet Encyclopedia*, 3rd edn (1970–1979).
19. R.C. Raack, *Stalin's Drive to the West 1938–1945* (Stanford, CA: Stanford University Press, 1995).
20. Bruce C. Hopper, 'Narkomindel and Comintern: Instruments of World Revolution', *Foreign Affairs*, July 1941, available online: https://www.foreignaffairs.com/articles/

russian-federation/1941-07-01/narkomindel-and-comintern (accessed 19 February 2019).
21 See Jon Jacobson, *When the Soviet Union Entered World Politics* (Berkeley, CA: University of California Press: 1994).
22 Raack, *Stalin's Drive to the West 1938–1945,* 14–15.
23 Ibid.
24 Mikhail N. Tukhachevskii, *Izbrannye proizvedeniia*, 2 Vols, (Moscow: Voenizdat, 1964).
25 Aleksandr Svechin, *Strategiia* (2nd edn (Moscow: Voennyi Vestnik Press, 1927).
26 Marshal Vitalii Sokolovskii, *Voennaia strategiia* (Moscow: Voenizdat, 1962, 1963, 1968), trans. Harriet Fast Scott as *Soviet Military Strategy* (New York: Crane Russak & Co, 1984).
27 Nikolai N. Voronov, *Na sluzhbe voennoi* (Moscow: Voenizdat, 1963), 88, 165.
28 See Alvin D. Coox, *Nomonhan: Japan against Russia, 1939*, 2 vols. (Redwood, CA: Stanford University Press, 1988).
29 Willard C. Frank Jr, review of Jürgen Rohwer and Mikhail S. Monakhov, *Stalin's Ocean-Going Fleet: Soviet Naval Strategy and Shipbuilding Programmes, 1935–1953* (Portland, OR: Frank Cass, 2001), in *Naval War College Review* 56, no.3 (2003): 169–170. Emphasis added. Available online: https://digital-commons.usnwc.edu/nwc-review/vol56/iss3/17 (accessed 22 April 2019). Also https://digital-commons.usnwc.edu/cgi/viewcontent.cgi?referer=&httpsredir=1&article=2257&context=nwc-review; Robert W. Herrick, *Soviet Naval Theory and Policy: Gorshkov's Inheritance* (1989).
30 Frank review, 169.
31 P. Smirnov, People's commissar for the Navy from January 1938, '*Moguchii morskoi i okeanskii flot SSSR*' ('A mighty sea- and ocean-going fleet for the USSR', *Morskoi Sbornik (Naval Review)* 1/1938 pp. 10–17. Reference to Spain p. 11. Smirnov was executed in Stalin's great purge in 1939.
32 Ibid., 10.
33 Donald W Mitchell, *A History of Russian and Soviet Sea Power* (London: Andre Deutsch, 1974), 366.
34 Chairman Joseph Stalin – autograph note signed 01/13/1936 – HFSID 285910. *Raport*, PSA / JSA Authentication Guarantee. Available online: https://www.historyforsale.com/chairman-joseph-stalin-autograph-note-signed-01-13-1936/dc285910 (accessed 22 April 2019).
35 Ibid., 1.
36 This example is of renewed interest in the light of the recent Russian re-emphasis on 'hybrid' or, as the Russians prefer to call it, 'non-linear' or 'new -type' warfare. Vladimir Kvachkov, *Spetsnaz Rossii* (Moscow: Algoritm, 2015), 62.
37 Ibid., 63; see Christopher Andrew and Vasili Mitrokhin, *The Mitrokhin Archive: The KGB in Europe and the West* (London: Penguin Press History, 2000) for the evolution of Soviet and Russian State Security organizations.
38 Kvachkov, *Spetsnaz Rossii*, 66–67.
39 Ibid., 66.
40 Order No. 147, 'O naznachenii komissii dlia iz"iatiia politicheski vrednoi i ustarevshiI voennoi i voenno-politicheskoi literatury', in Ibid, 65–66, citing P. Sagaidak, A Tsyganok, 'Ispol'zovanie vozdushnykh desantov v Velikoi Otechestvennoi voine', *Voenno-Istoricheskiï* Zhurnal, 8/1960, 18 (emphasis added).
41 Kvachkov, *Spetsnaz Rossii*, 68–69.

42 Kvachkov, *Spetsnaz Rossii*, 69 citing (ref. 37, p. 235), the *War Diary* of the German Land Forces' Chief of Staff Friedrich Halder, Vol. 3 Book 2, translated into Russian, Moscow, 1972, 351.
43 Kvachkov, *Spetsnaz Rossii*, 70, 71, 76, 81.
44 Ibid., 81, citing No GKO-83ss of 10 July 1941.
45 Raack, *Stalin's Drive to the West, 1939-1945*, 11-36.
46 Robert Burns, *To a Mouse, On Turning up in Her Nest with the Plough*, November 1785, *Verse 7*, Lines 39-42, 'The best laid schemes o' Mice an' Men Gang aft agley'.
47 See Chris Bellamy, *Absolute War: Soviet Russia in the Second World War* (London: Pan Macmillan, 2007, 2009; New York: Knopf, 2008), 39-163. The correspondence relating to the Molotov-Ribbentrop Pact is in *SSSR-Germaniia 1939: Dokumenty i materialy o sovetsko-germansikh otnosheniyakh s aprelia po oktiabria 1939 g.* (Vilnius: Mosklas, 1989). Henceforward *SSSR-Germaniia*. See also Militärgeschichtes Forschungsamt (Research Institute for Military History), Potsdam, *Germany and the Second World War*, published in German by Deutsche Verlags-Anstalt GmbH, Stuttgart and in English by the Clarendon Press, Oxford (1996-2001).
48 *Germany and the Second World War*, Vol. IV, 119, 120-123, 125-125, 133, 136.
49 *Pravda* , 24 August 1939 has the seven open clauses of the Pact. Cited in *SSSR-Germaniia*, 60-62. The 'Secret Additional protocol' is Document 33, 62-64. The 28 September protocol is Document 56, 109-110.
50 Raack, *Stalin's Drive to the West 1938-1945*, 20-26.
51 See Harry Hinsley, 'British Intelligence and Barbarossa', in *Barbarossa: The Axis and the Allies*, ed. John Erickson and David Dilks (Edinburgh: Edinburgh University Press, 1994), 45, citing Joint Intelligence Committee (JIC) Report of 2 July 1940, UKNA, CAB 80/14.
52 Debate covered in Bellamy, *Absolute War*, 99-135.
53 People's Commissar of State Security of the USSR from 3 February 1941 until 20 July 1941, when the NKGB again fell under control of the NKVD as GUGB. From 1941 to 1943, Deputy People's Commissar of the NKVD. Head of the NKGB from 20 July 1943 until 1946.
54 The document, with Stalin's coarse comment tactfully redacted is in Lt Gen S.V. Stepashin, ed., *Organy Gosudarstvennoi Bezopasnost SSSR v Velikoi Otechestvennoi voine. Sbornik dokumentov*, Vol. 1 Nakanune, Bk. 2, 1 January 22 June 1941, (Moscow: FSK Academy, Russia, 1995), Document 251, *Soobshchenie Rezidenta NKGB SSSR v Berline o Srokakh Napadeniia Germanii na Sovetskii Soiuz*, 237-238. Original in Presidential Archive in the Kremlin, fond 3, 17 June 1941, No. 2279/sh 1170, Merkulov to Stalin and Molotov. Simon Sebag-Montefiore translates it in full and accurately in *Stalin: The Court of the Red Tsar* (New York: Knopf, 2003), 354.
55 Cited in Gabriel Gorodetsky (Gorodetskii), *Grand Delusion: Stalin and the German Invasion of Russia* (New Haven, CT: Yale University Press, 2005), 299.
56 Viktor Suvorov, *Icebreaker: Who Started the Second World War* (London: Hamish Hamilton, 1990), published in Russian as *Ledokol* (1992). V.A. Nevezhin, 'The Pact with Germany and the Idea of an "Offensive War (1939-1941)"', *Journal of Slavic Military Studies* 8, no.4 (1995): 809-843.
57 Vladimir Karpov, 'Marshaly Velikoï Otechestvennoï - Zhukov', *Kommunist Vooruzhënnykh Sil*, 5/1990, 62-68. Reported as 'Stalin's Plan to Cripple Germany', *Independent*, Saturday 14 April 1990, 12. Details of the plan and a map are in Bellamy *Absolute War*, 106-110.
58 See analysis in *Absolute War*, 104-110.

59 Ibid., 113–133.
60 Ibid., 116–117, 200. In the unexpurgated (2002) version of his memoirs, Rokossovskii recalls being ordered to open sealed orders at 04.00 Moscow time on the morning of 22 June, after the German attack. Although he did not then know that the Germans had attacked, and was suspicious, he opened them. His IX Mechanized Corps was ordered to move north-west, exactly as it would have done in Zhukov's 15 May plan. His corps was between 30 and 50 per cent strength and, he wrote, 'unready for military action as a mechanized formation in any form. There was no way that the Kiev Special Military District (KOVO) and the General Staff didn't know this'. This all suggests that the sealed orders were not intended for 22 June 1941 but maybe for the following year. K.K. Rokossovskii, *Soldatskii dolg*, revised and unexpurgated edition (Moscow: Olma Press, 2002), 30. This bit was cut from the original (Soviet) edition.
61 Stepashin, Vol. II, Bk. 1, Document 330. Stalin's appointments, 98.
62 Speech in Stepashin, Vol. II, Bk. 1. Doc. 282, 14–15.
63 Stepashin, Vol. II, Bk. 1, Document 330, 98–100, 105–106. Stalin's diary is published in full in Yuri Gor'kov, *Gosudarstvennyi Komitet Oborony Prikazivaet* (Moscow: Ol'ma Press, 2002).
64 Stepashin, Vol. II, Bk. 1, Document No. 293, '. . . o sozdanii stavki Glavnogo Komandovaniia Vooruzhënnykh Sil Soiuza SSR', 23 June 1941, 51–52.
65 Stepashin, Vol. II, Bk. 1, Document 340, 'Postanovlenie Prezidiuma Verkhovnogo Soveta SSSR Soveta Narodnykh Komissarov SSSR I Tsentral'nogo Komiteta VKP(b) ob obrazovanii Gosudarstvennogo Komiteta Oborony', 30 June 1941, 126–127.
66 Ibid., Document 305, '. . . o sozdanii Soveta po evakuatsii', 24 June 1941, 62. Quotation from commentary.
67 Stepashin, Vol. II, Bk. 1. Doc. 330, 101–103 and commentary, 106–109.
68 Anastas Mikoyan, 'V pervye mesiatsy Velikoi Otechestvennoivoiny', in *Novaia i noveishaia istoriia* 6 (1985), edited by his son, Stepan, in 'Barbarossa and the Soviet leadership: a Recollection, in Erickson and Dilks, *Barbarossa: the Axis and the Allies*, 128.
69 Constantine [Konstantin] Pleshakov, *Stalin's Folly. The Tragic First Ten days of World War II on the Eastern Front*. First published with subtitle, *The German Invasion of Russia June 1941* (2005; pbk., Boston and New York: Houghton Mifflin, 2006), 258.
70 Stepashin, Vol. II, Bk. 1, Document 355, *Vystuplenie po radio Predsedatelia Gosudarstvennogo Komitteta Oborony I. V. Stalina* 3 July 1941, 161.
71 Richard Rhodes, *Dark Sun: the Making of the Hydrogen Bomb* (New York: Simon and Schuster, 1995), 47–48, 60–61, citing an interview with Kaftanov in 1985.
72 Stalin's diary in Gor'kov, *GKO Prikazivaet,* 323.
73 https://nsarchive2.gwu.edu/nukevault/ebb525-The-Atomic-Bomb-and-the-End-of-World-War-II/documents/044.pdf No. 371 (accessed 23 April 2019). Letter from the USSR People's Commissar for State Security [Merkulov] to L.P. Beria on the preparation of atomic bomb test in the United States No. 4305/m July 10, 1945. Top Secret. Urgent. 'We have received information from several reliable USSR NKGB agent sources that in July of this year the U.S. has scheduled the first experimental explosion of the atomic bomb. The explosion is expected to take place on July 10th . . .' The report describes the implosion bomb tested in New Mexico and of the type later dropped on Nagasaki. The gun assembly bomb dropped on Hiroshima was so relatively simple it was not tested.
74 *Berlin Experiences, The Potsdam Conference, 1945: Day-by-Day*. Available online: https://berlinexperiences.com/potsdam-conference-1945/ (accessed 18 April 2019).

Chapter 5

1 Robert Tucker, *Stalin in Power: The Revolution from Above* (London: Norton, 1990), 3–9, 146–171. For interpretations that point to early Soviet cults' debt to Russian tradition, see: Nina Tumarkin, *Lenin Lives! The Lenin Cult in Soviet Russia* (Cambridge, MA: Harvard University Press, 1997); J. Arch Getty, *Practicing Stalinism: Bolsheviks, Boyars and the Persistence of Tradition* (New Haven, CT: Yale University Press, 2013), 86, 89–90, 95. For the Lenin Cult as a model for that of Stalin, see Graeme Gill, 'Political Myth and Stalin's Quest for Authority in the Party', in *Authority, Power and Policy in the USSR*, ed. T.H. Rigby, Archie Brown and Peter Reddaway (London: Macmillan, 1980), 80–117.

2 Balázs Apor, Jan C. Behrends, Polly Jones and E.A. Rees, eds, *The Leader Cult in Communist Dictatorship: Stalin in the Eastern Bloc* (Basingstoke: Palgrave Macmillan, 2004); Klaus Heller and Jan Plamper, eds, *Personality Cults in Stalinism – Personenkulte in Stalinismus* (Göttingen: V and R Unipress, 2004); Benno Ennker and Heidi Hein-Kirchner, eds, *Der Führer im Europa des 20. Jahrhunderts* (Marburg: Herder-Institut, 2010); Daniel Leese, *The Mao Cult: Rhetoric and Ritual in China's Cultural Revolution* (Cambridge: Cambridge University Press, 2011); Stephen Gundle, Christopher Duggan and Giulana Pieri, eds, *The Cult of the Duce: Mussolini and the Italians* (Manchester: Manchester University Press, 2013); Daniel Leese, 'Rituals, Emotions and Mass Mobilisation: the Leader Cult and Party Politics', in *The Palgrave Handbook of Mass Dictatorship*, ed. Paul Corner and Jie Hyun Lim (Palgrave Macmillan: London, 2016), 217–228; Balazs Apor, *The Invisible Shining: The Cult of Mátyás Rákosi in Stalinist Hungary 1945–1956* (Budapest: CEU Press, 2017); Kevin Morgan, 'Cults of the Individual', in *The Cambridge History of Communism. I. World Revolution and Socialism in One Country 1917–1941*, ed. Silvio Pons and S.A. Smith (Cambridge: Cambridge University Press, 2017), 551–572; Kevin Morgan, *Internationalism and the Cult of the Individual: Leaders, Tribunes and Martyrs under Lenin and Stalin* (London: Palgrave Macmillan, 2017). There were precursors in the nineteenth century: see Lucy Riall, *Garibaldi: Invention of a Hero* (New Haven, CT: Yale University Press, 2007); Jean Tulard, *Le Mythe de Napoléon* (Paris: Armand Colin, 1971).

3 The importance of the function of popular mobilization is argued also by C.A. Rees, 'Leader Cults: Varieties, Preconditions and Functions', in *Leader Cult*, ed. Apor et al., 17, 21; David Brandenberger, 'Stalin as Symbol: A Case Study of the Personality Cult and Its Construction', in *Stalin: A New History*, ed. Sarah Davies and James Harris (Cambridge: Cambridge University Press, 2005), 249–270; Andrea Orzoff, *Battle for the Castle: The Myth of Czechoslovakia in Europe 1914–1948* (Oxford: Oxford University Press, 2011), 119, 131.

4 A cult developed also around Miklós Horthy, the Regent of Hungary but does not seem to have involved comparable rites: see Ignác Romsics, 'Changing Images of Miklós Horthy', in *Cultic Revelations: Cult Personalities and Phenomena*, ed. Anssi Halmevirta (Tampere: Historietti Oy, 2011), 62–75. Thanks to Balázs Apor for this reference.

5 Boris Kolonitskii, 'Russian Leaders of the Great War and Revolutionary Era in Representations and Rumours', in *Russian Culture in War and Revolution 1914–1922. Book 2. Political Culture, Identities and Memory*, ed. Murray Frame, B.I. Kolonitskii, Steven G. Marks and Melissa Stockdale (Bloomington, IN: Slavica, 2014) 42; A.G. Golikov, 'Fenomenon Kerenskogo', *Otechstvennaya istoriya*, 5 (1992): 65.

6   Anna von der Goltz, *Hindenburg: Power, Myth and the Rise of the Nazis* (Oxford: Oxford University Press, 2009), 23–25; A. von der Goltz and Robert Gildea, 'Flawed Saviours: the Myths of Hindenburg and Pétain', *European History Quarterly* 39, no.3 (2009): 441–442.
7   R. Gerwarth and Lucy Riall, 'Fathers of the Nation? Bismarck, Garibaldi and the Cult of Memory in Germany and Italy', *European History Quarterly* 39, no.3 (2009): 388–413; Robert Gerwarth, *The Bismarck Myth: Weimar Germany and the Legacy of the Iron Chancellor* (Oxford: Oxford University Press: 2005), which examines the myth during the Weimar republic.
8   For a study of the Stalin cult in art, see Jan Plamper, *The Stalin Cult: A Study in the Alchemy of Power* (New Haven, CT: Yale University Press, 2012).
9   Wolfram Pyta, *Hindenburg: Herrschaft zwischen Hohenzollern und Hitler* (Berlin: Pantheon Verlag, 2009) 113, 120–121; von der Goltz, *Hindenburg*, 25–27, 118–120. Mussolini's press office played a major role in the production of photos and films of the leader and Mussolini intervened personally to shape his image, censoring those he did not like. About eight million postcards of him entered circulation and many artists and photographers applied for permission to paint or photograph him: Stephen Gundle, 'Mass Culture and the Cult of Personality', in *Cult of the Duce*, ed. Gundle et al., 82, 85.
10 Kerenskii, Lenin and Masaryk kitsch was also manufactured and, although postmortem, Atatürk's mausoleum has a souvenir shop stocked with all sorts of items (as do the souvenir shops at the World War II museum at Poklonnoe Gore and Gori, with the former holding a wide variety of Staliniana).
11 Faik Gur, 'Sculpting the Nation in Early Republican Turkey', *Historical Research* 86, no. 232 (2013): 346. Gur stresses the nation-building functions of Atatürk's monumental propaganda, whose analogies with that of Lenin are obvious.
12 Esra Özyürek, 'Miniaturizing Atatürk: Privatization of State Imagery and Ideology in Turkey', *American Anthropologist* 31, no.3 (2004): 377, 380.
13 Andrea Orzoff, *Battle for the Castle*, 59–61, observes that inter-war Czechoslovakia's 'adherence to democracy was in fact quite limited', as the President's political power challenged that of the parliament. I am indebted to J.P. Newman for pointing out the importance of the Legionaries to the Masaryk cult.
14 Andrea Orzoff, 'The Husbandman: Tomaš Masaryk's Leader Cult in Inter-War Czechoslovakia', *Austrian History Yearbook*, 39 (2008): 124, 127–128, 130. Both the Castle and citizens produced Masarykiana, including commemorative plates, cups and ashtrays adorned with his image, as well as printed ephemera.
15 Orzoff, 'Husbandman', 126, 129; Heidi Hein, *Der Piłsudski-Kult und seine Bedeutung für den polnischen Staat 1926–39* (Marburg: Herder-Institut, 2002), 301; Ian Kershaw, *The Hitler Myth: Image and Reality in the Third Reich* (Oxford: Oxford University Press, 1987), 59, 72; Ian Kershaw, 'Hitler and the Germans', in *Life in the Third Reich*, ed. Richard Bessel (Oxford: Oxford University Press, 1987), 47.
16 Orzoff, 'Husbandman', 130–133. Karel Čapek, *President Masaryk Tells his Story* (London: George Allen and Unwin, 1934), which was far more developed and personal than Stalin's official biography.
17 Hein, *Piłsudski-Kult*, 300–303, 306. The analogy with Hitler's *Mein Kampf* is obvious and possibly not fortuitous.
18 J. Devlin, 'The End of the War in Stalinist Film and Legend', in *The Fiction of History*, ed. Alexander Lyon Macfie (London: Routledge, 2014), 106–117.
19 Von der Goltz, *Hindenburg*, 104, 106–108, 112–113.

20 J. Devlin, 'A Case Study in Censorship: Stalin's Early Film Image', in *Central and East European Media under Dictatorial Rule and in the Early Cold War*, ed. Olaf Mertelsmann (Frankfurt-am-Main: Peter Lang, 2011), 27–48.
21 Kershaw, *Hitler Myth*, 69–70.
22 Özyürek, 'Atatürk', 384, 389 n.15; Sergei Yutkevich, *Sobranie sochinenii v trekh tomakh*, t.2 (Moscow: Iskusstvo,1991), 83–90: he and Zarkhi travelled to Turkey and were meant to make a full-length feature film about the fight for Turkish national liberation and Kemalism. There is no record in the Russian archives of Shub's film, which may have been lost or destroyed: see https://wfpp.cdrs.columbia.edu/pioneer/ccp-esfir-shub/#filmography. For cordial relations with the Soviet Union, especially between 1929 and 1935 and about these films, see Samuel Hirst, 'Anti-Westernism on the European Periphery: the Meaning of Soviet–Turkish Convergence in the 1930s', *Slavic Review* 72, no.1 (Spring 2013): 32–53, esp. 47–50.
23 David Brandenberger, 'Stalin as Symbol': 249–270; Kevin Morgan, *International Communism*, 261–262, 131–133, 282–285.
24 Ye. Dobrenko, 'Stalin's Writing: From the Romantic Poetry of the Future to the Socialist Realist Prose of the Past', in *Tyrants Writing Poetry*, ed. Albrecht Koschorke and Konstantin Kaminskij (Budapest, New York: Central European Press, 2017), 60–129.
25 Riall, *Garibaldi*, 148, 155–161, 196–200. Popular versions of Stalin's biography, especially those aimed at children, such as *Stalin i Khashim*, also deployed the stylistic and structural devices of romantic fiction.
26 For leaders' interventions, see Orzoff, 'Husbandman', 129–131; Hein, *Piłsudski-Kult*, 172, 300–307; von der Goltz, *Hindenburg*, 12, 107–113, 122. Mussolini also curated his image carefully: his first (best-selling) propagandistic biography was written by his mistress and presented him as a precocious and self-sacrificing leader, close to and beloved by the people, yet above them: Simona Storchi, 'Margarita Sarfatti and the invention of the Duce', in *Cult of the Duce*, ed. Gundle et al., 41–56.
27 Orzoff, 'Husbandman', 122–123; Hein, *Piłsudski-Kult*, 300–303; Özyürek, 'Atatürk', 377; Pyta, *Hindenburg*, 116; Leese, 'Rituals, Emotions and Mass Mobilisation', 224.
28 Hein, *Piłsudski-Kult*, 168–70; Özyürek,' Atatürk', 380; Orzoff, 'Husbandman', 127. For Soviet name changes see G.R.F. Bursa, 'Political Changes of Names of Soviet Towns', *Slavonic and East European Review* 63, no.2 (1985): 161–193; *Administrativno-territorial'noe delenie* (Moscow: Izdatel'stvo Vlast' Sovetov pri VTsIK, 1935), 461–466.
29 See Richard Wortman, *Scenarios of Power. 2: From Alexander II to the Abdication of Nicholas II* (Princeton, NJ: Princeton University Press, 2000), 19–91, for the recasting of Alexander's relationship with the Russian people.
30 Hein, *Piłsudski-Kult*, 217, 240–247. A cult also developed around Antanas Smetona, the authoritarian leader of Lithuania, whose 60th birthday in 1934 was celebrated with elaborate ceremonies: see Klaus Richter, 'Der Kult um Antanas Smetona in Litauen (1926–40). Funktionsweise und Entwicklungen', in *Der Führer im Europa*, ed. Ennker et al., 111–137.
31 Kershaw, *Hitler Myth*, 58; Richard Overy, *The Dictators: Hitler's Germany. Stalin's Russia* (London: Allen Lane, 2004), 122.
32 See J. Devlin, 'Soviet Power and its Images: Celebrating Stalin's Seventieth Birthday', in *War of Words: Culture and the Mass Media in the Making of the Cold War in Europe*, ed. J. Devlin and C. Müller (Dublin: UCD Press, 2013), 30–47.
33 Hein, *Piłsudski-Kult*, 246; Orzoff, *Battle for the Castle*, 123–124.

34 While alternative cults never emerged, after the incipient Trotsky and early Lenin cults, subordinate cults were tolerated. See: J. Arch Getty, 'Cults and Personalities, Politics and Bodies', in *Practicing Stalinism*, 86–89; Malte Rolf, 'The Leader's Many Bodies: Leader Cults and Mass Festivals in Voronezh, Novosibirsk and Kemerovo in the 1930s', in *Personality Cults*, ed. Heller et al, 197–206.

35 Orzoff, 'Husbandman', 124; Özyürek, 'Atatürk', 383. In a variation on this theme, Pétain acted as godfather to every fifteenth child in Vichy: von der Goltz and Gildea, 'Flawed Saviours', 451.

36 For letters, see: Orzoff, 'Husbandman', 127; von der Goltz, *Hindenburg*, 25, 105; Sarah Davies, 'The Cult of the *Vozhd'*: Representations in Letters 1934–41', *Russian History* 24, no.1–2 (Spring–Summer 1997): 131–147.

37 Boris Kolonitskii, *'Tovarishch Kerenskii': anti-monarkhicheskaya revoliutsiya i formirovanie kul'ta 'vozhdya naroda' mart-iiun'1917 goda* (Moscow: NLO, 2017), 335–336, for an effusion from Marina Tsvetaeva; von der Goltz, *Hindenburg*, 25 .

38 Orzoff, 'Husbandman', 124–125. Masaryk's birthday and death inspired poets, including the communist Nezval, who, echoing Mayakovsky, wrote: 'Our Masaryk has died. He only sleeps! No, he's no longer asleep [...]': see Robert B. Pynsent, 'Introduction', in *T.G. Masaryk (1850–1937): vol.2: Thinker and Critic*, ed. R. Pynsent (London: Macmillan, 1989), 1–2.

39 Orzoff, 'Husbandman', 125, 128. Newspapers featured the exploit of a wounded Legionary who allegedly walked on crutches from Brno to Prague Castle to wish Masaryk a happy 80th birthday: thanks to J.P. Newman for this observation.

40 Devlin, 'Stalin's Seventieth Birthday', 36–44; N.V. Ssorin-Chaikov, ed., *Dary vozhdyam* (Moscow: Pinakoteka, 2006) for a catalogue of gifts to all the Soviet leaders, including Stalin. Atatürk also received gifts, which were put on display after his death in the museum at Anitkabir: Leda Glyptis, 'Living up to the Father. The National Identity Prescriptions of remembering Atatürk; his homes, his grave, his temple', *National Identities* 10, no.4 (2008): 366.

41 For Gori, see Archive of Central Committee of Communist Party of Georgia (henceforth GPA): f.14: op.8: d.176: l.139 ob; RGASPI: f.17, op. 120, d. 172, l.1–14; Glyptis, 'Living up to the Father', 358–362.

42 Sofia Serenelli, 'A Town for the Cult of the Duce: Predappio as a Site of Pilgrimage', in *Cult of the Duce*, ed. Gundle et al., 93–109.

43 Hein, *Piłsudskii-Kult*, 212–214.

44 Glyptis, 'Living up to the Father', 366–367.

45 For Masaryk, Orzoff, *Castle*, 119, 131. The Garibaldi cult was taken up after his death by the political leaders of Italy in an attempt to claim his popularity and boost their legitimacy: see Christopher Duggan, 'Political cults in liberal Italy, 1861–1922', in *Cult of the Duce*, ed. Gundle et al., 17–18.

46 Hein, *Piłsudski-Kult*, 182–187, 189–200, 206.

47 Glyptis, 'Living up to the Father', 363–366, 368. For behaviour and comments in Gori: John Steinbeck, *A Russian Journey*, 1st edn 1948 (London: Penguin, 2000), 88; GPA: f. 8076, op.1, d. 17a for an early comment book, replete with reverential remarks.

48 Özyürek, 'Atatürk', 381.

49 See Polly Jones, 'From Stalinism to Post-Stalinism: De-Mythologising Stalin, 1953–56', in *Redefining Stalinism*, ed. Harold Shukman (London: Frank Cass, 2003), 130–141; J. Devlin, 'Stalin's Death and Afterlife', in *Death, Burial and Afterlife*, ed. Philip Cottrell and Wolfgang Marx (Dublin: Carysfort Press, 2014), 65–85.

50 Gur, 'Sculpting the Nation', 355–357: criticism was sharply repressed in Turkey.

Chapter 6

1. The same shop had another Orbán carving for sale in July 2019, but without a crown. This seems to support the argument that the crowned image was produced for the occasion of the national holiday.
2. Shmuel N. Eisenstadt, 'Multiple Modernities', *Daedalus* 129, no.1 (2000): 1–29.
3. For a summary of scholarship on the Leninist legacy see Jody LaPorte and Danielle N. Lussier, 'What is the Leninist Legacy? Assessing Twenty Years of Scholarship', *Slavic Review* 70, no.3 (2011): 637–654.
4. See for example, David L. Hoffmann, *Cultivating the Masses: Modern State Practices and Soviet Socialism, 1914–1939* (Ithaca, NY: Cornell University Press, 2011), and Michael David-Fox, *Crossing Borders: Modernity, Ideology, and Culture in Russian and the Soviet Union* (Pittsburgh, PA: University of Pittsburgh Press, 2015).
5. See for example, Terry Martin, 'Modernization or Neo-Traditionalism? Ascribed Nationality and Soviet Primordialism', in *Stalinism: New Directions*, ed. Sheila Fitzpatrick (London: Routledge, 2000), 348–367.
6. J. Arch Getty, *Practicing Stalinism: Bolsheviks, Boyars and the Persistence of Tradition* (New Haven, CT: Yale University Press, 2013), 288.
7. Getty, *Practicing Stalinism*, 95.
8. For extensive critical reflections on the book see David-Fox, *Crossing Borders*.
9. See for example, Archie Brown and Jack Gray, eds, *Political Culture and Political Change in Communist States* (New York: Holmes & Meier Publishers, 1979); and George Schöpflin, *Politics in Eastern Europe 1945–1992* (Oxford: Blackwell, 1993).
10. For overviews of post-communist legacies see Jan C. Behrends, 'Legacies of Communism: Comparative Remarks', in *The Cambridge History of Communism: Volume 3, Endgames? Late Communism in Global Perspective, 1968 to the Present*, ed. Juliane Fürst, Silvio Pons and Mark Selden (Cambridge: Cambridge University Press, 2017), 529–555; and Jason Wittenberg, 'Conceptualizing Historical Legacies', *East European Politics and Societies and Cultures* 29, no.2 (2016): 366–378.
11. Mark R. Beissinger, and Stephen Kotkin, eds, *Historical Legacies of Communism in Russia and Eastern Europe* (Cambridge: Cambridge University Press, 2014), 7.
12. Maria Todorova, 'Spacing Europe: What is a Historical Region?', *East Central Europe/ECE* 32 (2005): 59–78.
13. Vladimir Tismaneanu, *Fantasies of Salvation: Democracy, Nationalism, and Myth in Post-Communist Europe* (Princeton, NJ: Princeton University Press, 1999), 41.
14. Ibid., 21.
15. András Gerő, *Emperor Francis Joseph: King of the Hungarians* (Social Science Monographs, Boulder, Colorado, Center for Hungarian Studies and Publications, Inc., Wayne, NJ, Distributed by Columbia University Press, New York, 2001), 206. See also András Gerő, *Képzelt történelem. Fejezetek a magyar szimbolikus politika XIX-XX. századi történetéből* (Budapest: Eötvös Kiadó, PolgART, 2004), 83–109.
16. Gerő, *Emperor Francis Joseph*, 96.
17. Ibid., 206.
18. Ibid., 69.
19. Ibid., 152.
20. Ibid., 155.
21. Ibid., 156.
22. Ibid., 157–158.

23 On the cult of Elizabeth see Judith Szapor, 'From "Guardian Angel of Hungary" to the "Sissi Look-Alike Contest": The Making and Remaking of the Cult of Elizabeth, Queen of Hungary', in *Gender and Modernity in Central Europe: The Austro-Hungarian Empire and its Legacy*, ed. Agatha Schwarz (Ottawa: University of Ottawa Press, 2010), 235–250; Alice Freifeld, 'Empress Elizabeth as Hungarian Queen: The Uses of Celebrity Monarchism', in *The Limits of Loyalty: Imperial Symbolism, Popular Allegiances, and State Patriotism in the Late Habsburg Monarchy*, ed. Laurence Cole and Daniel Unowsky (New York: Berghan Books, 2007), 138–160; and Gerő, *Képzelt történelem*, 110–117.
24 Gerő, *Képzelt történelem*, 79.
25 Ágnes Deák, 'Deák, a magyarok Mózese (Deák Ferenc és a kortárs utókor, 1876)', *Holmi* 16, no.8. (2004): 935–946.
26 For overviews see Krisztián Ungváry, *A Horthy-rendszer mérlege – Diszkrimináció, szociálpolitika és antiszemitizmus Magyarországon* (Budapest: Jelenkor Kiadó, 2013); Gábor Gyáni and György Kövér, *Magyarország társadalomtörténete a reformkortól a második világháborúig* (Budapest: Osiris Kiadó, 2006); and Levente Püski, A Horthy-rendszer (Budapest: Pannonica Kiadó, 2006).
27 On the cult of Horthy, see Dávid Turbucz, *A Horthy-kultusz* (Budapest: MTA Bölcsészettudományi Kutatóközpont, 2016); Dávid Turbucz, 'A Horthykultusz kezdetei', *Múltunk* 54, no.4 (2009): 156–199; and Tibor Dömötörfi, A Horthy-kultusz elemei', *História* 12, no.12 (1990): 23–26.
28 Turbucz, *A Horthy-kultusz*, 63–64.
29 Ibid., 65; 87.
30 Ibid., 99–100.
31 Ibid., 120–121.
32 On the revisionist idea and the cult of irredentism see Miklós Zeidler, *A magyar irredenta kultusz a két világháború között* (Budapest: Teleki László Alapítvány, 2002); and Miklós Zeidler, *A revíziós gondolat* (Budapest: Osiris, 2001).
33 Turbucz, *A Horthy-kultusz*, 78; 85.
34 Ibid., 183–184, 192.
35 Ibid., 199–214.
36 Jan Bröker, '"Horthy is a Nobody" – Trials of lése-régent in Hungary 1920–1944' (MA dissertation, Central European University, 2011).
37 On the cult of Gömbös, see József Vonyó, 'Ki volt a vezér? Horthy és Gömbös: két kultuszteremtés Magyarországon', *Múlt-kor* 2, no.3 (2011), 94–97; Jenő Gergely, *Gömbös Gyula. Politikai pályakép* (Budapest: Vince, 2001), 262–266 and 309–315.
38 Such images were often evoked during the elections of 1935 by pro-Gömbös papers, such as *Új Magyarság* and *Függetlenség*.
39 Árpád Pünkösti, *Rákosi a hatalomért, 1945–1948* (Budapest: Európa, 1992), 112–113.
40 On the relationship of the Hungarian communists and national traditions, see Martin Mevius, *Agents of Moscow: The Hungarian Communist Party and the Origins of Socialist Patriotism 1941–1953* (Oxford: Oxford University Press, 2005); Miklós Lackó, 'A magyar kommunista mozgalom és a nemzeti kérdés 1918–1936', in *Gazdaság, társadalom, történetírás*, ed. Ferenc Glatz (Budapest: MTA Történettudományi Intézet, 1989), 255–272.
41 Árpád von Klimo, '"A Very Modest Man": Béla Illés or How to Make a Career through the Leader Cult', in *The Leader Cult in Communist Dictatorships: Stalin and the Eastern Bloc*, ed. Balázs Apor, Jan C. Behrends, Polly Jones and E.A. Rees (Basingstoke: Palgrave, 2004), 47–62.

42 On the cult of Rákosi, see Balázs Apor, *The Invisible Shining: The Cult of Mátyás Rákosi in Stalinist Hungary, 1945–1956* (New York: Central European University Press, 2017).
43 Apor, *The Invisible Shining*, 71–78.
44 Ibid., 18–23.
45 Ibid., 255–259.
46 Ibid., 318–319.
47 Ibid., 319–324.
48 Historians disagree on whether Kádár had a cult during his lifetime or not. One historian described the leader as 'a cult-less man': János M. Rainer, 'Kádár János: A kultusz nélküli ember', *Rubicon* 18, no.9 (2007): 42–49. A different work emphasizes the importance of manufactured leader images in the stabilization of the Kádár-regime: György Majtényi, *Vezércsel. Kádár János mindennapjai* (Budapest: Libri, 2012).
49 For an analysis of the role of corruption and nepotism in the consolidation of the new regime, see Bálint Magyar, *Post-Communist Mafia State: The Case of Hungary* (Budapest, Central European University Press, 2016).
50 István Povedák, 'Hősök és sztárok' (PhD dissertation, Eötvös Loránd Tudományegyetem, 2009), 165.
51 For an overview of Hungarian politics, including the shift towards authoritarian leadership, see András Körösényi, ed., *A magyar politikai rendszer – negyedszázad után* (Budapest: Osiris, 2015). For a biography of Viktor Orbán in English: Paul Lendvai, *Orbán: Hungary's Strongman* (Oxford: Oxford University Press, 2017).
52 Hajnalka Magyar, István Gulyás, János Kovács and Emma Világosi, 'Van egy magyar Magyarország' (16 June 2018). Available online: https://ia902806.us.archive.org/32/items/161189wA180616_201807/161189w_a_180616.pdf (accessed 6 October 2019).
53 'Orbán Viktor a helyszínen követte nyomon a mentési munkálatokat'. Available online: https://www.youtube.com/watch?v=ySMYexeZDbM (accessed 6 October 2019); 'Orbán Viktor megállította a Dunát', !!444!!!, 14 June 2013, https://444.hu/2013/06/14/orban-viktor-megallitotta-a-dunat (accessed 6 October 2019).
54 'National Consultation with Bözsi néni', 5 May 2017. Available online on Viktor Orbán's Facebook page: https://www.facebook.com/orbanviktor/videos/10155121921451093/ (accessed 6 October 2019); '"Hát ittunk egy kicsit" – mondta egy kukás Orbán Viktornak', !!444!!!, 21 February 2018: https://444.hu/2018/02/21/hat-ittunk-egy-kicsit-mondta-a-fideszes-kukas-orban-viktornak (accessed October 6 2019).
55 Turbucz, *A Horthy-kultusz*, 195.
56 'Virágzik az Orbán-póló biznisz', Index, 27 July 2019. Available online: https://index.hu/belfold/2019/07/27/orban_viktor_tusvanyos_beszed/legjobb_polok/ (accessed 6 October 2019).
57 'Kopók/Rangers', 27 November 2018, Viktor Orbán's Facebook page. Available online: https://www.facebook.com/orbanviktor/videos/897357740470458/ (accessed 6 October 2019).
58 "My Way – special edition," 9 July 2019, Viktor Orbán's facebook page. Available online: https://www.facebook.com/orbanviktor/videos/3549505681742107/ (accessed October 6, 2019)
59 'Orbán Viktor megkapta élete legnagyszerűbb ajándékát', !!444!!!, 18 February 2015. Available online: https://444.hu/2015/02/18/orban-viktor-megkapta-elete-legnagyszerubb-ajandekat/ (accessed 6 October 2019).
60 'Az összes megyei lap ugyanazzal a központi Orbán-interjúval jelent meg a választás előtti napon', !!444!!!, 7 April 2018. Available online: https://444.hu/2018/04/07/

az-osszes-megyei-lap-ugyanazzal-a-kozponti-orban-interjuval-jelent-meg-a-valasztas-elotti-napon (accessed 6 October 2019).
61 'A Volton sem marad le senki arról, hogy Orbán Viktor űzte ki a szovjeteket', Index, 26 June 2019. Available online: https://index.hu/belfold/2019/06/26/a_volt-on_sem_marad_le_senki_arrol_hogy_orban_viktor_uzte_ki_a_szovjeteket/ (accessed 6 October 2019).
62 'Menetel a Békemenet', !!444!!!, 13 October 2013. Available online: https://444.hu/2013/10/23/izgulnak-a-bekemenet-sztarjai (accessed 6 October 2019).

Chapter 7

1 See for example, the treatment of Stalin in Simon Sebag Montefiore, *Stalin: The Court of the Red Tsar* (London: Weidenfeld & Nicolson, 2003).
2 *The Death of Stalin* (2017), [Film] Dir. Armando Iannucci, United Kingdom: eOne Films; France: Gaumont. For the point about humour and the current view of Stalin, I am indebted to Professor Sheila Fitzpatrick and her comments at the BASSES Conference Cambridge, April 2019.
3 Martin Amis, *Koba The Dread. Laughter and the Twenty Million* (New York: Hyperion, 2002).
4 Andrei Kolesnikov, 'Why Russia is Making Stalin Great Again' (Moscow: Carnegie Moscow Center), 13 March 2019. Available online: https://carnegie.ru/2019/03/13/why-russi-is-making-Stalin-great-again-pub78590
5 Geoffrey Roberts, *Stalin's Wars: From World War to Cold War 1939–1953* (New Haven, CT: Yale University Press, 2006).
6 Caroline Kennedy-Pipe, *Stalin's Cold War: Soviet Strategies in Europe, 1943–1956* (Manchester: Manchester University Press, 1995).
7 George Orwell, 'You and the Atomic Bomb', *Tribune,* 19 October 1945.
8 D. Quentin Miller, *John Updike and the Cold War: Drawing the Iron Curtain* (Columbia, MI: University of Missouri Press, 2001).
9 'X' (George F. Kennan), 'The Sources of Soviet Conduct', *Foreign Affairs* (July 1947): 53–63.
10 Michael Cox, 'Why did we Get the End of the Cold War Wrong?', *The British Journal of Politics and International Relations* 11, no.2 (2009): 161–176.
11 John Lewis Gaddis, *The Long Peace: Inquiries into the History of the Cold War* (Oxford: Oxford University Press, 1987).
12 See for examples, Herbert Feis, *Churchill, Roosevelt, Stalin: The War They Waged and the Peace They Sought* (Princeton, NJ: Princeton University Press, 1957); and Louis J. Halle, *The Cold War As History* (New York: Harper & Row, 1967).
13 George F. Kennan, ed. Frank Costigliola, *Diaries* (New York: W.W. Norton and Co, 2014).
14 William Appleman Williams, *The Tragedy of American Diplomacy* (New York: Norton and Co., 1959).
15 J.A. Thompson, 'William Appleman Williams and the "American Empire"', *Journal of American Studies* 7, no.1 (1973): 91–104.
16 See, for example, Fred Halliday, *The Making of the Second Cold War* (London: Verso, 1983).
17 J.L. Gaddis, *The United States and the Origins of the Cold War, 1941–1947* (New York: Columbia University Press, 1972).

18 Michael Cox and Caroline Kennedy-Pipe, 'The Tragedy of American Diplomacy? Rethinking the Marshall Plan', *Journal of Cold War Studies* 7, no.1 (2005): 97–134.
19 J.L. Gaddis, *The United States and the Origins of the Cold War, 1941–1947* (New York: Columbia University Press, 1972).
20 Chen Jian, *Mao's China and the Cold War* (Chapel Hill, NC: University of North Carolina Press, 2001).
21 Gerald Stourzh and Wolfgang Mueller, *Cold War Over Austria: The Struggle for the State Treaty, Neutrality and the End of East-West Occupation, 1945–1955* (Lanham, MD: Lexington Books, The Harvard Cold War Book Series, 2018).
22 See for example, Sheila Fitzpatrick, *Everyday Stalinism: Ordinary Life in Extraordinary Times, Soviet Russia in the 1930s* (Oxford: Oxford University Press, 1999). See also, Jukka Gronow, *Caviar with Champagne: Common Luxury and the Ideals of the Good Life in Stalin's Russia* (Oxford: Berg, 2003).
23 John Lewis Gaddis, *We Now Know: Rethinking Cold War History* (Oxford: Clarendon Press, 1997).
24 Kathryn Weathersby, 'The Soviet Role in the Early Phase of the Korean War: New Documentary Evidence', *Journal of American-East Asian Relations* 2, no.4 (1993): 425–458.
25 John Lewis Gaddis, *Surprise, Security and the American Experience* (Cambridge, MA: Harvard University Press, 2004).
26 Tony Judt, 'The Cold War: A New History', *The New York Review of Books* 5 (23 March 2006).
27 Gar Alperovitz, *The Decision to Use the Atomic Bomb* (London: Harper Collins, 1995).
28 Odd Arne Westad, *Reviewing the Cold War: Approaches, Interpretations, Theory* (London: Frank Cass Publishers, 2000). See William Wohlforth, 'A Certain Idea of Science: How International Relations Theory Avoids Reviewing the Cold War', in Westad, *Reviewing the Cold War*, 126–148.
29 See Westad, *Reviewing the Cold War*, 2, 11; and see Kristan Ghodsee, *Second World, Second Sex: Socialist Women's Activism and Global Solidarity during the Cold War* (University Park, PA: Penn State University Press, 2019).
30 Paul Buhle, *William Appleman Williams: The Tragedy of Empire* (London: Routledge, 1995).
31 A.C. Grayling, *Among the Dead Cities: Is the Targeting of Civilians in War Ever Justified?* (London: Bloomsbury, 2006).
32 'Eisenhower Regrets Policy of Total Surrender; Asserts Roosevelt erred in his World War II goal: says fear of US Terms spared Nazis to Fight', *New York Times* (21 December 1964).
33 Gar Alperovitz, *The Decision to Use the Atomic Bomb and the Architecture of the American Myth* (London: Harper Collins,1995).
34 Sean Molloy, *Atomic Tragedy: Henry L. Stimson and the Decision to Use the Bomb against Japan* (Ithaca, NY: Cornell University Press, 2008).
35 Alperovitz, *The Decision to Use the Atomic Bomb*.
36 W.T.R. Fox, *The Super-Powers: The United States, Britain, and the Soviet Union – Their Responsibility for Peace* (New York: Harcourt Brace, 1944).
37 W.T.R. Fox, 'The Superpowers Then and Now', *International Journal* 35, no.3. (1980): 417–436.
38 R. Harrison Wagner, 'What was Bipolarity?' *International Organisation* 47, no.1 (1993): 77–106.
39 Wohlforth, 'A Certain Idea of Science'.

40 Geir Lundestad, '"Empire by Invitation" in the American Century', *Diplomatic History* 23, no.2 (1999): 189–217.
41 Florian Huber, *Promise Me You'll Shoot Yourself: The Downfall of Ordinary Germans* (London: Allen Lane, 2019).
42 Chris Bellamy, *Absolute War: Soviet Russia in the Second World War* (New York: Alfred A. Knopf, 2007). Antony Beevor, *Berlin: The Downfall, 1945* (London: Penguin, 1945).
43 Kennedy-Pipe, *Stalin's Cold War*.
44 Fraser Harbutt, *Yalta Europe and America at the Crossroads* (Cambridge: Cambridge University Press, 2010).
45 See Caroline Kennedy-Pipe, *Stalin's Danish Mystery* (Unpublished Manuscript).
46 Sven G. Holtsmark, 'The Limits to Soviet Influence: Soviet Diplomats and the Pursuit of Strategic Interests in Norway and Denmark, 1944–47', in *The Soviet Union and Europe in the Cold War, 1943–53*, ed. Francesca Gori and Silvio Pons (Basingstoke: Palgrave, 1996), 106–124.
47 Peter Ruggenthaler, *The Concept of Neutrality in Stalin's Foreign Policy* (Lanham, MD: Lexington Books, 2015). See also Holtsmark, 'The Limits to Soviet Influence'.
48 Harry S. Truman, *Memoirs* (Garden City, NY: Doubleday, 1955).
49 See David Holloway, *The Soviet Union and the Arms Race* (New Haven, CT: Yale University Press, 1983), and David Holloway, *Stalin & The Bomb: The Soviet Union and Atomic Energy 1939–1956* (New Haven, CT: Yale University Press, 1994).
50 See Kuross A. Somi, 'A Tale of Three Messages', in *Middle Eastern Studies* 23, no.1 (1987): 95–107.
51 Somi, 'A Tale of Three Messages'.
52 Isaac Deutscher, 'Has Stalin Stopped at the Middle East?' Source: *The Reporter*, 10 October 1950. Available online: https://marxists.org/archives/deutscher/1950/Stalin-Stopped.htm
53 Noel O'Sullivan, *Terrorism, Ideology & Revolution the Origins of Modern Political Violence* (Brighton: Wheatsheaf Books, 1986).
54 Tarak Barkawi and Mark Leffey, 'The Postcolonial moment in security studies', *Review of International Studies* 32, no.2 (2006): 329–352.
55 See for example, Fraser J. Harbutt, *Yalta 1945: Europe and America at the Crossroads* (Cambridge: Cambridge University Press, 2010).
56 Susan Butler, *My Dear Mr Stalin: The Complete Correspondence of Franklin D Roosevelt and Joseph V. Stalin* (New Haven, CT: Yale University Press, 2006).
57 For the twists and turns of how the British viewed Stalin during the years of war, see Martin Kitchen, 'Winston Churchill and the Soviet Union during the Second World War' *The Historical Journal* 30, no.2 (1987): 415–436.
58 A bust of Stalin was erected at the National D-Day memorial in Bedford, Virginia, in 2010 but subsequently removed.

Chapter 8

1 I. Kershaw, '"Working towards the Fuhrer": Reflections on the Nature of the Hitler Dictatorship', *Contemporary European History* 2, no.2 (1993): 117.
2 See G. Roberts, *Molotov: Stalin's Cold Warrior* (Washington, DC: Potomac Books, 2012), 16–18.
3 T. Hopf, *Reconstructing the Cold War: The Early Years, 1945–1958* (Oxford: Oxford University Press, 2012).

4   See my contribution to the H-Diplo/ISSF roundtable on Hopf's book, available online: https://issforum.org/roundtables/6-6-reconstructing-cold-war
5   On the early post-war history of the peace movement, see G. Roberts, 'Averting Armageddon: The Communist Peace Movement, 1948–1956', in *The Oxford Handbook of the History of Communism*, ed. S. Smith (Oxford: Oxford University Press, 2014); N. I. Egorova, *Narodnaia Diplomatiia Yadernogo Veka: Dvizhenie Storonnikov Mira i Problema Razoruzheniya 1955–1965 gody* (Moscow: Akvilon 2016); T.V. Raeva, 'Mirotvorchestvo "po-Sovetski"', in *Sovetskaya Kul'turnaya Diplomatiya v Usloviyakh Kholodnoi Voiny, 1945–1989*, ed. O.S. Nagornaia (Moscow: Rosspen, 2018); and V. Dobrenko, *Conspiracy of Peace: The Cold War, the International Peace Movement, and the Soviet Peace Campaign, 1946–1956* (Ph.D. diss., London School of Economics, 2016).
6   Rossiiskii Gosudarstvennyi Arkhiv Sotsial'no-Politicheskoi Istorii (hereafter: RGASPI) f. 17, op. 128, d. 1149, ll. 58–63. See also, Rossiiskii Gosudarstvennyi Arkhiv Noveishei Istorii (hereafter: RGANI) f. 3, op. 21, d. 2, l. 1. On the role of Polish intellectuals in the origin of the Wroclaw congress, see N. Jachec, 'The Polish Origins of Jean-Paul Sartre's "Questions of Method"', in S. Autio-Saramo and B. Humphreys (eds), *Winter Kept Us Warm: Cold War Interractions Reconsidered*, Aleksanteri Institute Cold War Series 1/2010.
7   RGANI ibid., ll. 5–6.
8   Arkhiv Vneshnei Politiki Rossiiskoi Federatsii (hereafter: AVPRF) f. 06, op. 10, Pap. 11, d. 11, ll. 4–6.
9   RGANI, f. 3, op. 21, d. 2, l. 1 12–13.
10 Ibid., ll. 19–31.
11 Fedoseev dropped out of peace movement activity after the Paris congress. His place as Fadeev's de facto partner was taken by Ehrenburg, whose memoir of his activities in the peace movement may be found in I. Ehrenburg, *Postwar Years, 1945–1954* (London: MacGibbon & Kee, 1966).
12 RGANI, f. 3, op. 21, d. 2, l.109.
13 The Nenni and Joliot-Curie speeches may be found in a special supplement of the congress published in Supplement to *New Times*, no.19 (1949). While in the context of the peace movement Nenni was a highly independent political figure, his Italian Socialist Party was in receipt of substantial Soviet funding. On a trip to Moscow in August 1949 (to attend the founding conference of the Soviet peace movement), Nenni wrote to Soviet party chief, G.M. Malenkov, thanking the Soviets for paying off his party's debts for 1949 but pointing out that a similar subsidy – to pay for press and propaganda work – would be needed for 1950. RGASPI, f. 17, op. 128, d. 1181 ll.141–144.
14 AVPRF, f. 197, op. 20, Pap. 125, d. 29, ll. 1–58. This file contains a detailed report (in French), dated December 1949, on the development of the peace movement after the Paris congress.
15 RGANI, f. 3, op.21, d. 2, ll.162–167.
16 On the Stalin Peace Prize, see *Stalinskie Premii: Sbornik Dokumentov* (Novosibirsk: Svin'in i Synov'ia, 2007). In 1956 the name of the prize was changed to the Lenin Peace Prize and all previous recipients' prizes were renamed accordingly.
17 RGANI, f. 3, op. 21, d. 2, ll. 47–70. The only other example of Stalin's direct involvement in the affairs of the peace movement is his editing of a draft speech by Fadeev to a peace congress in the United States in March 1949, which had been sent to him by Molotov. However, Stalin made minor changes to just one of its 12 pages and at the end he scrawled two additional concluding slogans: "Long live the struggle of

peoples for a lasting peace!" and "For peace in all the world!". RGASPI, F.558, Op.11, D.199.
18 AVPRF, f. 197, op. 20, Pap. 125, d. 29, l. 18.
19 J. Stalin, *Economic Problems of Socialism in the USSR* (Moscow: Foreign Languages Publishing House, 1952), 37–41.
20 RGANI f. 81. op. 1, d. 234, ll. 35–36.
21 *For a Lasting Peace, For a People's Democracy!*, 12 May 1950.
22 Stalin's corrections of Malenkov's draft speech may be found in RGANI, f. 592, op. 1, d. 6.
23 RGANI, f. 3, op. 21, d. 2, l.173, 184. The proposal to exclude the Yugoslavs came from Maurice Thorez, leader of the French Communist Party.
24 RGASPI, f.17, op. 166, d. 807, ll. 37–38.
25 See D. Watson, 'From "Fellow Traveller" to "Fascist Spy": Konni Zilliacus MP', *Socialist History* no.11 (1997): 59–87.
26 RGANI, f. 3, op. 21, d. 3, l. 54.
27 See G. Roberts, 'Science, Peace and Internationalism: Frédéric Joliot-Curie, the World Federation of Scientific Workers and the Origins of the Pugwash Movement', in *Science, (Anti-)Communism and Diplomacy*, ed. A. Kraft and C. Sachse (Leiden: Brill, 2019).
28 RGANI, f. 3, op. 21, d. 3, ll. 101–104.
29 Ibid., ll.107–110.
30 RGASPI, f. 17, op. 128, d. 1199, l. 61.
31 RGANI, f. 3, op. 21, d. 3, ll.122–129
32 RGANI, f. 3, Op. 21, d. 4, ll. 59–65.
33 Ibid., l. 72.
34 Ibid., ll.79–137.
35 Ibid., ll. 75–78.
36 See P. Deery, '"A Divided Soul"? The Cold War Odyssey of O. John Rogge', *Cold War History* 6, no.2 (2006): 177–204.
37 'Beseda s Korrespondentom *Pravdy*', 17 February 1951. The interview was published on the newspaper's front-page.
38 Bernal Papers, World Peace Council Box, Marx Memorial Library.
39 RGANI, f. 3, op. 21, d. 6, ll. 27–29. Austria and Vienna were at this time under Soviet and Western military occupation. Not until the Austrian State Treaty of 1955 did the country regain its independence.
40 Ibid., ll. 71–74.
41 Ibid., ll. 101–103.
42 See D. Lethbridge, 'Constructing Peace by Freedom: Jean-Paul Sartre, Four Short Speeches on the Peace Movement, 1952–1955', *Sartre Studies International* 18, no.2 (2012): 1–18. Sartre also attended and spoke at the Helsinki World Peace Assembly in 1955 and sponsored the World Congress on Disarmament and International Cooperation held in Stockholm in 1958.
43 *Na Prieme u Stalina* (Moscow: Novyi Khronograf, 2008), 553. The only other peace movement leader to meet Stalin was Nenni, in July 1952, when he, too, travelled to Moscow to collect his Peace Prize (ibid., 547). A Soviet record of Stalin's conversation with Nenni has yet to come to light but it seems they talked about the German question and Italy's role in international politics.
44 'Rech' Predsedatelya Soveta Ministrov Souza SSR Tovarishcha G.M. Malenkova', *Izvestiia*, 16 March 1953.

45 RGANI, f. 5, op. 128, d. 116, ll. 64–71.
46 RGANI, f. 5, op. 128, d. 33, l. 54.
47 See G. Roberts, *A Chance for Peace? The Soviet Campaign to End the Cold War, 1953–1955*, Cold War International Project Working Paper no.57 (2008).
48 RGANI, f. 5, op. 20, d. 356, ll.146–153.

Chapter 9

1 Artur London, *On Trial*, trans. Alastair Hamilton (London: Macdonald & Co. 1970), 179.
2 Nikita Khrushchev, 'Speech to the 20th Congress of the CPSU', 24–25 February 1956, available on Marxist internet archive, Marxists.org
3 David. L. Hoffmann, Book Review of Stalinist Confessions, *Slavic Review* 69, no.2 (2010): 451.
4 Igal Halfin, *Stalinist Confessions: Messianism and Terror at the Leningrad Communist University* (Pittsburgh, PA: University of Pittsburgh Press, 2009).
5 Amir Weiner and Aigi Rahi-Tamm, 'Getting to Know You: The Soviet Surveillance System, 1939–57', in *Kritika: Explorations in Russian and Eurasian History* 13, no.1 (2012): 13.
6 Lynne Viola, *Stalinist Perpetrators on Trial* (Oxford: Oxford University Press, 2017), 17.
7 Oleg Khlevniuk, 'Foreward', in Alexander Vatlin, *Agents of Terror: Ordinary Men and Extraordinary Violence in Stalin's Secret Police*, ed. and trans. Seth Bernstein (Madison, WI: University of Wisconsin Press, 2016), xiv.
8 In this sense, views of the Terror that attribute it to particular events, such as the assassination of Sergei Kirov, or the larger context of the time, such as the Spanish Civil War, or even to divides and disagreements within the Bolshevik leadership, appear questionable. J. Arch Getty, *The Road to Terror: Stalin and the Self-Destruction of the Bolsheviks* (New Haven, CT: Yale University Press, 1999); Oleg Khlevniuk, 'The Reasons for the Great Terror: The Foreign Political Aspect', in *Russia in the Age of Wars, 1914–1945*, ed. Silvio Pons and Andrea Romano (Milan: Feltrinelli, 1998), 163–165; Hiroaki Kuromiya, 'Accounting for the Great Terror', *Jahrbücher für Geschichte Osteuropas* 53, no.1 (2005): 86–101.
9 Edward Peters, *Torture* (Philadelphia, PA: University of Pennsylvania Press, 2018), 44.
10 Peter H. Solomon, *Soviet Criminal Justice under Stalin* (Cambridge: University of Cambridge Press, 1997), 363.
11 Peter H. Solomon, *Soviet Criminal Justice Under Stalin* (New York: Cambridge University Press, 1996), 363.
12 Elizabeth A. Wood, *Performing Justice: Agitation Trials in Early Soviet Russia* (Ithaca, NY: Cornell University Press, 2005).
13 Štěpán Plaček, 'K otázce centralisace a decentralisace ve státní bezpečnosti', 19 May 1950, in Jan Kalous, *Štěpán Plaček: Život zpravodajského fanatika ve službách KSČ*. Prague: Ústav pro studium totalitních režimů, 2010), 342.
14 London, *On Trial*, 81.
15 Ibid., 81–82.
16 Bohumil Doubek, 'StB o sobě: výpověd vyšetřovatele Bohumila Doubka' (Úrad dokumentace a vyšetrováni zločinů komunismu PČR, 2002), 101.

17 'Jak postupovat při výslechu zatčené osoby', 1952, ABS Prague, f. 310, ač. 310-39-24, non-paginated.
18 Doubek, *StB o sobě*, 51.
19 Ibid., 51.
20 'Jak postupovat při výslechu zatčené osoby', 1952, ABS Prague, f. 310, ač. 310-39-24, non-paginated.
21 Béla Szász, *Volunteers for the Gallows: The Anatomy of a Show Trial* (New York: Norton, 1971), 72.
22 Ibid.
23 The particularities of the conspiracy – who knew whom, its leaders, the main charges, and so on – were written and rewritten by the interrogators and the Soviet advisers throughout the investigations, a process reconstructed in great detail in Karel Kaplan, *Report on the Murder of the General Secretary* (Columbus, OH: Ohio State University Press, 1990).
24 London, *On Trial*, 77.
25 Ibid.
26 Ibid., 68.
27 Ibid., 91.
28 Gisli Gudjonsson, *The Psychology of Interrogations and Confessions: A Handbook* (New York: Bowker, 2003), 118.
29 Ibid., 120.
30 Nathan J. Gordon and William L. Fleisher, *Effective Interviewing and Interrogation Techniques*, 3rd edn (Burlington, MA: Academic Press, 2011), 28.
31 Aleksander Solzhenitsyn, *The Gulag Archipelago* (London: The Folio Society, 2005), 72.
32 Doubek, 'StB o sobě', 68–69.
33 Szász, *Volunteers for the Gallows*, 73.
34 Doubek, 'StB o sobě', 97.
35 London, *On Trial*, 108.
36 'Jak postupovat při výslechu zatčené osoby', 1952, ABS Prague, f. 310, ač. 310-39-24, non-paginated.
37 Viola, *Stalinist Perpetrators on Trial*, 40.
38 Ibid., 40.
39 Doubek, 'StB o sobě', 103.
40 Ibid., 55.
41 'Jak postupovat při výslechu zatčené osoby', 1952, ABS Prague, f. 310, ač. 310-39-24, non-paginated.
42 Doubek, 'StB o sobě', 54.
43 Ibid.
44 Doubek, 'StB o sobě', 54.
45 London, *On Trial*, 105–106.
46 Ibid., 105.
47 Szász, *Volunteers for the Gallows*, 60.
48 Ibid., 11.
49 Solzhenitsyn, *Gulag Archipelago*, 93.
50 Gudjonsson, *The Psychology of Interrogations and Confessions*, 8.
51 'Jak postupovat při výslechu zatčené osoby', 1952, ABS Prague, f. 310, ač. 310-39-24, non-paginated.
52 London, *On Trial*, 319.
53 Ibid., 132.

54 Ibid., 158–159.
55 'Zvláštní prověrka, Major Kohoutek Vladimír', ABS Prague, Vladimír Kohoutek: evidence PS 4049/12.
56 London, *On Trial*, 159.
57 Doubek, 'StB o sobě', 87.
58 London, *On Trial*, 58.
59 Ibid., 98
60 Halfin, *Stalinist Confessions*, 134.
61 London, *On Trial*, 117.
62 Ibid., 111.
63 Ibid., 214.
64 'Proceedings of the Slánský Trial', Prague, 20–27 November – 1952, broadcast by the Czechoslovak Home Service. Available from https://archive.org/details/ProceedingsOfSlanskyTrialPrague1952/mode/2up (accessed 29 May 2020).
65 Szász, *Volunteers for the Gallows*, 171.
66 London, *On Trial*, 241.
67 Doubek, 'StB o sobě', 241.
68 'Jak postupovat při výslechu zatčené osoby', 1952, ABS Prague, f. 310, ač. 310-39-24, non-paginated.
69 London, *On Trial*, 29.
70 'Jak postupovat při výslechu zatčené osoby', 1952, ABS Prague, f. 310, ač. 310-39-24, non-paginated.
71 Karel Kaplan's footnoted, in Doubek, 'StB o sobě', 76.
72 Gudjonsson, *The Psychology of Interrogations and Confessions*, 45.
73 Ibid.
74 London, *On Trial*, 313.
75 Richard Leo, *Police Interrogation and American Justice* (Cambridge, MA: Harvard University Press, 2008), 2.

Chapter 10

1 Quoted in Aleksandr Braterskii, 'Putinskii vzgliad na sovetskikh vozhdei', available online: https://www.gazeta.ru/politics/2017/06/17_a_10721567.shtml (accessed 25 April 2018). The interviews are accessible through Showtime, a subscription service available online: https://www.sho.com/the-putin-interviews#/closed (accessed 15 March 2020).
2 *Memory and Power in Post-War Europe: Studies in the Presence of the Past*, ed. Jan-Werner Müller (Cambridge: Cambridge University Press, 2002), 18.
3 See here, Shaun Walker, *The Long Hangover: Putin's New Russia and The Ghosts of the Past* (New York: Oxford University Press, 2018), 7–8.
4 See here, Igor Torbakov, 'History, Memory and National Identity: Understanding the Politics of History and Memory Wars in Post-Soviet Lands', in *Russian Nationalism, Foreign Policy, and Identity Debates in Putin's Russia: New Ideological Patterns after the Orange Revolution*, ed. Marlène Laruelle (Stuttgart: Ibid., 2012), 43–44; Olga Malinova, 'The Embarrassing Centenary: Reinterpretation of the 1917 Revolution in the Official Historical Narrative of Post-Soviet Russia (1991–2017)', *Nationalities Papers* 46, no.2 (2018): 275; Marci Shore, 'Poland Digs Itself a Memory Hole', *New York Times*, 4 February 2018, available online: https://www.nytimes.com/2018/02/04/

opinion/poland-holocaust-law-justice-government.html (accessed 10 February 2018); and *Memory and Theory in Eastern Europe*, ed. Uilleam Blacker, Alexander Etkind, and Julie Fedor (New York: Palgrave, 2013), esp. 1–11. On the uses and abuses of the past, and the pitfalls of 'memory' and 'forgetting', see also Paul Ricoeur, *History, Memory, Forgetting* (Chicago, IL: University of Chicago Press, 2004), esp. xv, 7, 57.

5   Examples include Paul R. Gregory, 'Russia's Re-Stalinization', 28 November 2018, available online: https://www.hoover.org/research/russias-re-stalinization (accessed 9 October 2019); Denis Volkov, 'Stalinskii vopros', *Levada-Tsentr*, 3 July 2017, available online: https://www.levada.ru/2017/07/03/stalinskij-vopros/ (accessed 22 April 2018); Eduard Galein, 'Reabilitatsiia stalinizma kak sredstvo utverzhdeniia putinskoi diktaturyi', *Petrimazepa*, 1 August 2017, available online: https://petrimazepa.com/stalinrehab.html (accessed 21 April 2018); and Dina Khapaeva, 'Triumphant memory of the perpetrators: Putin's politics of re-Stalinization,' *Communist and Post-Communist Studies* 49, no.1 (2016): 61–73.

6   'Rossiiane vse luchshe otnositsia k Stalinu, no zhit' pri nem ne khoteli byi', *Levada-Tsentr*, 25 March 2016, available online: https://www.levada.ru/2016/03/25/rossiyane-vse-luchshe-otnosyatsya-k-stalinu-no-zhit-pri-nem-ne-hoteli-by/ (accessed 21 April 2018).

7   Karina Pipiia, 'Dinamika otnosheniia k Stalinu', *Levada-Tsentr*, 16 April 2019, available online: https://www.levada.ru/2019/04/16/dinamika-otnosheniya-k-stalinu/ (accessed 16 April 2019).

8   Adapted from the *Oxford English Dictionary* definition of the word, 'rehabilitation, n.'. OED Online. December 2018. Oxford University Press. http://www.oed.com/view/Entry/161448?redirectedFrom=rehabilitation (accessed 31 January 2019).

9   See in particular, Ekaterina Makhotina, 'Nostalgia, Pride and Shame: The Many Faces of Stalin in Contemporary Russia', *Cultures of History Forum*, University of Jena, 23 January 2018, available online: http://www.cultures-of-history.uni-jena.de/debates/russia/nostalgia-pride-and-shame-the-many-faces-of-stalin-in-contemporary-russia/ (accessed 26 April 2018); Ol'ga Malinova, *Aktual'noe proshloe: Simvolicheskaia politika vlastvuiushchei elityi i dilemmyi Rossiiskoi identichnosti* (Moscow: ROSSPEN, 2015); Aleksandra Arkhipova, 'Stalin bez stalinizma', *Inliberty*, 29 June 2017, available online: http://old.inliberty.ru/blog/2616-Stalin-bez-stalinizma#f2b52bb99c5605c (accessed 24 April 2018); and Thomas Sherlock, 'Russian Politics and the Soviet Past: Reassessing Stalin and Stalinism under Vladimir Putin', *Communist and Post-Communist Studies* 49 (2016): 45–59.

10 The most thorough excavation and analysis of the ways by which Germany and Austria have reckoned with the Nazi past is Mary Fulbrook, *Reckonings: Legacies of Nazi Persecution and the Quest for Justice* (Oxford: Oxford University Press, 2018).

11 Fulbrook, *Reckonings*, 4.

12 Norbert Frei, *Adenauer's Germany and the Nazi Past: The Politics of Amnesty and Integration*, trans. Joel Golb (New York: Columbia University Press, 1997), esp. xi–xiv; and Devin O. Pendas, 'Seeking Justice, Finding Law: Nazi Trials in Postwar Europe', *Journal of Modern History* 81, no.2 (2009): 352–353. Most recently, James Pearce has referred to a 'Putin Agenda' in the Russian state's approach to the past. See James C. Pearce, *The Use of History in Putin's Russia* (Wilmington, DE: Vernon Press, 2020), xv.

13 See Marlène Laruelle, *Russian Nationalism: Imaginaries, Doctrines, and Political Battlefields* (London: Routledge, 2019), 9, and Laruelle's interview with Sean Guillory of 8 March 2019 on the SRB Podcast, available online: https://srbpodcast.org/2019/03/08/transcript-russian-nationalism/ (accessed 26 February 2020).

14 Chris Weedon and Glenn Jordan, 'Collective Memory: Theory and Politics', *Social Semiotics* 22, no.2 (2012): 144.
15 On transitional justice, see the website of the International Center for Transitional Justice, available online: https://www.ictj.org/about/transitional-justice (accessed 31 January 2019).
16 See here, Robert G. Moeller, 'What Has "Coming to Terms with the Past" Meant in Post-World War II Germany? From History to Memory to the "History of Memory"', *Central European History* 35, no.2 (2002): 226.
17 See Malinova, *Aktual'noe proshloe*, esp. 130–156; and also Olga Malinova, 'Constructing the "Usable Past": The Evolution of the Official Historical Narrative in Post-Soviet Russia', in *Cultural and Political Imaginaries in Putin's Russia*, ed. Niklas Bernsand and Barbara Törnquist-Plewa (Leiden: Brill, 2018), 88.
18 See here, Malinova, *Aktual'noe proshloe*, 139–143; 161
19 I have discussed this in James Ryan, 'The Politics of National History: Russia's Ruling Elite and the Centenary of 1917', *Revolutionary Russia* 31, no.1 (2018): 24–45.
20 See here Putin's remarks in 'Poslanie Prezidenta Federal'nomu Sobraniiu', 1 December 2016, available online: http://www.kremlin.ru/events/president/news/53379 (accessed 9 November 2017).
21 See https://www.oscepa.org/documents/all-documents/annual-sessions/2009-vilnius/declaration-6/261-2009-vilnius-declaration-eng/file, 48–49 (accessed 28 March 2018), and http://www.europarl.europa.eu/sides/getDoc.do?pubRef=-//EP//TEXT+TA+P6-TA-2009-0213+0+DOC+XML+V0//EN (accessed 28 March 2018).
22 See 'Predmet natsional'noi bezopasnosti', *Kommersant*', 5 April 2016, available online: https://www.kommersant.ru/doc/2956312 (accessed 24 March 2018).
23 See Mark Edele, 'Fighting Russia's History Wars: Vladimir Putin and the Codification of World War II', *History and Memory* 29, no.2 (2017): 90–124; and Aleksei I. Miller, 'Politika pamiati v Rossii: God razrushennyikh nadezhd', *Politia* 4 (75) (2014): 54.
24 On the Great Patriotic War and the politics of history in Putin's Russia, see Edele, 'Fighting Russia's History Wars', 90–124; Walker, *The Long Hangover*, 21–43; Elizabeth A. Wood, 'Performing Memory: Vladimir Putin and the Celebration of World War II in Russia,' *The Soviet and Post-Soviet Review* 38, no.2 (2011): 172–200; and Stephen M. Norris, 'Memory for Sale: Victory Day 2010 and Russian Remembrance,' *The Soviet and Post-Soviet Review* 38, no.2 (2011): 201–229.
25 David L. Hoffmann, 'Stalin Rises from the Ashes in Putin's Russia', *The Moscow Times*, 14 April 2015, available online: https://www.themoscowtimes.com/articles/stalin-rises-from-the-ashes-in-putins-russia-45743 (accessed 25 April 2018); Nadia Beard, 'Stalin Rises again over Vladimir Putin's Russia', *Independent*, 24 February 2016, available online: https://www.independent.co.uk/news/world/europe/stalin-rises-again-over-putins-russia-six-decades-after-his-death-a6893826.html (accessed 25 April 2018); Alec Luhn, 'Stalin, Russia's New Hero', *The New York Times*, 11 March 2016, available online: https://www.nytimes.com/2016/03/13/opinion/sunday/stalinist-nostalgia-in-vladimir-putins-russia.html (accessed 25 April 2018).
26 Arkhipova, 'Stalin bez stalinizma'.
27 See here, Sherlock, 'Russian politics', 48; and David Brandenberger, 'A New *Short Course*?: A.V. Filippov and the Russian State's Search for a "Usable Past"', *Kritika* 10, no.4 (2009): 825–833.
28 Galein, 'Reabilitatsiia stalinizma'; Mikhail Danilovich and Robert Coalson, 'Revamped Perm-36 Museum Emphasizes Gulag's "Contribution to Victory"', *Radio Liberty*,

28 25 July 2015, available online: https://www.rferl.org/a/russia-perm-gulag-museum-takeover-contribution-to-victory/27152188.html (accessed 24 April 2018).
29 See here, Igor' Iakovenko, 'Stalinizm – neizbezhnyi rezul'tat degradatsii putinizma', *Rossiiskaia politika*, 4 May 2015, available online: http://ruspolitics.ru/article/read/stalinizm--neizbezhnyj-rezultat-degradacii-putinizma.html (accessed 22 April 2018); Khapaeva, 'Triumphant Memory', e.g. 61; and Daniel Schearf, 'Stalin Gaining Popularity in Putin's Russia', *Voice of America*, 21 December 2015, available online: https://www.voanews.com/a/stalin-putin-russia/3112458.html (accessed 25 April 2018).
30 Available online: http://en.kremlin.ru/events/president/news/46951 (accessed 25 April 2018).
31 See Elena Zelinskaia, 'Putin nazval repressii Stalina "massovyimi prestupleniiami protiv sobstvennogo naroda"', 4 December 2009, available online: https://www.oprf.ru/ru/press/832/newsitem/8098?PHPSESSID=u31m2q4inaftqhcgkkb8sda4n6 (accessed 13 August 2019); and Roman Badanin and Aleksandr Artem'ev, 'Medvedev popravil Stalina', available at: https://www.gazeta.ru/politics/2010/05/07_a_3364297.shtml (accessed 25 April 2018).
32 Braterskii, 'Putinskii vzgliad na sovetskikh vozhdei'.
33 Sherlock, 'Russian politics', 45–46; 53.
34 Sherlock, 'Russian politics', 46.
35 Quoted in Badanin and Artem'ev, 'Medvedev popravil Stalina'.
36 Sherlock, 'Russian politics', 49.
37 See, in this regard, Wood, 'Performing Memory', 176.
38 A useful distinction between these two terms can be found in Juan J. Linz, *Totalitarian and Authoritarian Regimes* (Boulder, CO: Lynne Rienner Publishers, 2000), esp. 67, 159. In addition to a clear ideology, a single mass party, absence of political pluralism, lack of accountability, and the impossibility of peaceful, institutional means of replacing those in power, I consider as an essential characteristic of 'totalitarianism' the ethos and intention of total social transformation.
39 On the 2015 textbooks, see Sherlock, 'Russian politics', 48–53. On recent Russian school history teaching more generally, see in particular, Pearce, *The Use of History*, esp. 91–121.
40 This has also been observed by Aleksandra Arkhipova in 'Stalin bez stalinizma', *Inliberty*, 29 June 2017, available online: http://old.inliberty.ru/blog/2616-Stalin-bez-stalinizma#f2b52bb99c5605c (accessed 26 April 2018).
41 See Samuel A. Greene and Graeme B. Robertson, *Putin v. the People: The Perilous Politics of a Divided Russia* (New Haven, CT: Yale University Press, 2019), 2–13. Greene and Robertson do not mean by this that Russians actively support authoritarian rule; rather, support for Putin is insecure and contingent. See here also, Makhotina, 'Nostalgia, Pride and Shame'.
42 Karina Pipiia, 'Stalin v obshchestvennom mnenii', *Levada-Tsentr*, 10 April 2018, available online: https://www.levada.ru/2018/04/10/17896/ (accessed 27 April 2018).
43 Pipiia, 'Dinamika otnosheniia'.
44 'Rossiiane stali ravnodushnee k stalinu', *Levada-Tsentr*, 10 April 2018, available online: https://www.levada.ru/2018/04/10/rossiyane-stali-ravnodushnee-k-stalinu/ (accessed 28 April 2018).
45 See Pipiia, 'Dinamika otnosheniia', and 'Stalinskie repressii', *Levada-Tsentr*, 23 May 2017, available online: https://www.levada.ru/2017/05/23/stalinskie-repressii/ (accessed 28 April 2018).

46 'Bolee 40% rossian nazvali repressii Stalina "vyinuzhdennoi meroi"', *BBC Russian Service*, 5 July 2017, available online: https://www.bbc.com/russian/news-40460762 (accessed 23 January 2019).
47 'Rossiiane stali ravnodushnee k Stalinu'.
48 'Stalinskie repressii'.
49 'Rossiiane vse luchshe'.
50 Ibid.
51 Lev Gudkov, 'The Archetype of the Leader: Analyzing a Totalitarian Symbol', in Maria Lipman, Led Gudkov and Lasha Bakradze, ed. Thomas de Waal, *The Stalin Puzzle: Deciphering Post-Soviet Public Opinion* (Washington, DC: Carnegie Endowment for International Peace, 2013), 37.
52 See 'Rossiiane vse luchshe'.
53 Volkov, 'Stalinskii vopros'.
54 Pipiia, 'Stalin v obshchestvennom mnenii'.
55 Arkhipova, 'Stalin bez stalinizma'.
56 'Rossiiane vse luchshe'.
57 Arkhipova, 'Stalin bez stalinizma', and Makhotina, 'Nostalgia, Pride and Shame'. See also, Nika Golikova, 'Pochemy 70% rossiian liubiat Stalina?', *Afisha*, 19 April 2019, available online: https://daily.afisha.ru/relationship/11762-pochemu-70-rossiyan-lyubyat-stalina-rassuzhdayut-sociolog-istorik-kulturolog-i-zhurnalist/?fbclid=IwAR1Gf8KOHdAm1XZH3e8R36ePEx3YnDrCmBdV9z1iU-tP7Qzaf3jDbtysjU0 (accessed 26 April 2019).
58 See here especially, Arkhipova, 'Stalin bez stalinizma'.
59 See also, Sherlock, 'Russian politics', 107.
60 This has also been demonstrated in Seth Bernstein, 'Remembering War, Remaining Soviet: Digital Commemoration of World War II in Putin's Russia', *Memory Studies* 9, no.4 (2016): 422–436.
61 Michael Ellman, 'The Role of Leadership Perceptions and of Intent in the Soviet Famine of 1931–1934', *Europe-Asia Studies* 57, no.6 (2005): 828.
62 Estimates of executions in 1937–38 are provided in J. Arch Getty, '"Excesses Are Not Permitted"! Mass Terror and Stalinist Governance in the Late 1930s', *The Russian Review* 61 (2002): 113–114 (and n. 3), and Barry McLoughlin, 'Mass Operations of the NKVD, 1937–8: A Survey', in *Stalin's Terror: High Politics and Mass Repression in the Soviet Union*, ed. Barry McLoughlin and Kevin McDermott (Basingstoke: Palgrave, 2003), 141.
63 The death rate in the Gulag camps and their lethally-destructive nature are topics of considerable scholarly discussion and revision at the present time. See Golfo Alexopoulos, *Illness and Inhumanity in Stalin's Gulag* (New Haven, CT: Yale University Press, 2017), and Steven A. Barnes, *Death and Redemption: The Gulag and the Shaping of Soviet Society* (Princeton, NJ: Princeton University Press, 2011).
64 See here Zuzanna Bogumił, *Gulag Memories: The Rediscovery and Commemoration of Russia's Repressive Past* (New York: Berghahn Books, 2018).
65 Alexander Etkind, *Warped Mourning: Stories of the Undead in the Land of the Unburied* (Stanford. CA: Stanford University Press, 2013), 177, 193.
66 Sergey Parkhomenko, 'Russia Has Yet to Recover from the Trauma of the Stalin Era', *Guardian*, 7 March 2018, available online: https://www.theguardian.com/commentisfree/2018/mar/07/russia-stalin-putin-guilt-victims (accessed 29 April 2018).
67 Walker, *The Long Hangover*, 94.

68 Petrov, 'Don't Speak, Memory: How Russia Represses its Past', *Foreign Affairs* 97, no.1 (2018), available online: https://www.foreignaffairs.com/articles/russian-federation/2017-12-12/dont-speak-memory (accessed 14 March 2018)
69 Ibid.
70 Luhn, 'Stalin, Russia's New Hero'.
71 'FSB rasstavliaet aktsentyi', *Rossiiskaia gazeta*, 19 December 2017, available online: https://rg.ru/2017/12/19/aleksandr-bortnikov-fsb-rossii-svobodna-ot-politicheskogo-vliianiia.html (accessed 29 April 2018).
72 See, in particular, Andrei Desnitskii, 'Pravoslavnyi stalinizm: pochemu v RPTs poliubili Stalina', Moscow Carnegie Center, 24 December 2015, available online: https://carnegie.ru/commentary/62352 (accessed 14 August 2019).
73 See the interview with Mitrokhin of 2 November 2015, available online: https://www.currenttime.tv/a/27340093.html (accessed 14 August 2019). On the institutional commemorative rivalry that has developed between the Church and other civic organizations, mainly Memorial, see Zuzanna Bogumił, Dominique Moran and Elly Harrowell, 'Sacred or Secular? "Memorial", the Russian Orthodox Church, and the Contested Commemoration of Soviet Repressions', *Europe-Asia Studies* 67, no.9 (2015): 1416–1444, and Kathleen E. Smith, 'A Monument for our Times? Commemorating Victims of Repression in Putin's Russia', *Europe-Asia Studies* 71, no.8 (2019): 1318–1319.
74 See Pierre Nora, 'Between Memory and History: Les Lieux de Mémoire'. *Representations* 26 (1989): 7–24.
75 See the conclusion to Bogumił, *Gulag Memories*.
76 The text is available online: http://government.ru/docs/19296/ 18 August 2015 (accessed 7 September 2019); and see also, Sherlock, 'Russian politics', 54.
77 Mikhail Serafimov, 'Pamiatnik dolzhen predosteregat' ot koshmara', *Ogonëk*, 5 October 2015, available online: https://www.kommersant.ru/doc/2822233 (accessed 30 October 2019). On the monument, its significance, and its history, see Smith, 'A Monument for our Times?', esp.1333–1334.
78 Available online: https://www.novayagazeta.ru/articles/2017/10/30/74387-vladimir-putin-otkryl-memorial-stena-skorbi-zhertvam-bolshogo-terrora-v-tsentre-moskvy (accessed 27 August 2019).
79 '"Strashnoe proshloe nel'zia opravdat' nikakimi vyishimi tak nazyivaemyimi blagami naroda." Vladimir Putin otkryil "Stenu skorbi"', *Novaia gazeta*, 30 October 2017, available online: https://www.novayagazeta.ru/articles/2017/10/30/74387-vladimir-putin-otkryl-memorial-stena-skorbi-zhertvam-bolshogo-terrora-v-tsentre-moskvy (accessed 1 November 2017).
80 Malinova, 'Constructing the "Usable Past"', 88–89.
81 'Poslanie Prezidenta Federal'nomu Sobraniiu', 1 December 2016, available online: http://www.kremlin.ru/events/president/news/53379 (accessed 9 November 2017).
82 'Vesti nedeli: Kul'turnaia stranichka', 21 April 2019, available online: https://www.vesti.ru/doc.html?id=3139970# (accessed 9 May 2019).
83 Boym was writing here about popular nostalgia for the post-war and late Soviet era, but an 'imaginary' and 'ahistorical' past is a useful way of expressing what she terms 'deideologized' attitudes toward the past that normalize the extraordinary, minimize the tragic, and enfold the Soviet experience into the curt summation: 'It's all our history'. See Svetlana Boym, *The Future of Nostalgia* (New York: Basic Books, 2001), 57–58.
84 'Stalinskie repressii'.

85 'Kolyima – rodina nashego strakha', available online: https://www.youtube.com/watch?v=oo1WouI38rQ (accessed 27 August 2019).
86 See https://russia.tv/brand/show/brand_id/63217/ (accessed 16 March 2020).
87 Makhotina, 'Nostalgia, Pride and Shame'.
88 'Stalinskie repressii'.
89 See, for instances, Dmitrii Volchek, '"Myi tyichem palkoi v past' zveria." Razgovor s pravnykom chekista', *Radio Svoboda*, 17 March 2018, available online: https://www.svoboda.org/a/29101852.html (accessed 18 March 2018). The Memorial database is available online: https://nkvd.memo.ru/index.php/%D0%9D%D0%9A%D0%92%D0%94:%D0%93%D0%BB%D0%B0%D0%B2%D0%BD%D0%B0%D1%8F_%D1%81%D1%82%D1%80%D0%B0%D0%BD%D0%B8%D1%86%D0%B0 (accessed 3 March 2020).
90 David Clay Large, 'Reckoning without the Past: The HIAG of the Waffen-SS and the Politics of Rehabilitation in the Bonn Republic, 1950–1961', *Journal of Modern History* 59, no.1 (1987): 113.
91 See Carolyn P. Boyd, 'The Politics of History and Memory in Democratic Spain', *Annals of the American Academy of Political and Social Science* 617 (2008): 135
92 See here, Fulbrook, *Reckonings*, esp. 197–202.
93 Nancy Adler, 'Reconciliation with – or rehabilitation of – the Soviet past?,' *Memory Studies* no.3 (July 2012), 328.
94 Etkind, *Warped Mourning*, 10–11.
95 Ryan, 'Politics of National History', 11.
96 For useful reflections on the 'ethics of memory', see Müller (ed.), *Memory and Power*, 31–35.
97 See here also, Vladimir Tismaneanu, 'Democracy and Memory: Romania Confronts Its Communist Past', *Annals of the American Academy of Political and Social Science* 617 (2008): 168.
98 See Stephania Taladrid, 'Franco's Body Is Exhumed, as Spain Struggles to Confront the Past', *The New Yorker*, 26 October 2019, available online: https://www.newyorker.com/news/daily-comment/francos-body-is-exhumed-as-spain-still-struggles-to-confront-the-past (accessed 3 March 2020).
99 My argument here differs somewhat from Ol'ga Malinova's contention, in her 2015 book, that Russia's ruling elite is unwilling to confront 'difficult' aspects of modern Russian history. Malinova's book was published before significant symbolic acts such as Putin's opening of the Wall of Sorrow.
100 See here, 'Rossiiane stali ravnodushnee k Stalinu'.
101 See 'Gosudarstvennyi paternalizm', *Levada-Tsentr*, 25 February 2020, available online: https://www.levada.ru/2020/02/25/gosudarstvennyj-paternalizm/ (accessed 3 March 2020).
102 See here, '"Zapros est' takoi, chto zakruchennyie gaechki nemnogo potriakhivaet": Kakoi dolzhna byit' vlast' v Rossii i chego zhdet narod: lektsiia Ekaterinyi Shul'man', text available online: https://www.znak.com/2019-01-09/kakoy_dolzhna_byt_vlast_v_rossii_i_chego_zhdet_narod_lekciya_ekateriny_shulman (accessed 20 August 2019).
103 Michael Kontopodis, 'Editorial: Time. Matter. Multiplicity', *Memory Studies* 2, no.1 (2009): 6; and Michael Kontopodis, 'Documents' Memories: Enacting Pasts and Futures at the School for Individual Learning-in-Practice', *Memory Studies* 2, no.1 (2009): 23. In a short blog post for the American Historical Association, Michael David-Fox, one of the most thoughtful historians of modern Russia working today,

has wisely concluded that Russia observers should not overestimate the supposedly 'deep structure' of Russian history. See 'Is Today's Russia a Relic of the Past? A New Look at Contemporary Theories of Soviet History', 12 April 2016, available online: https://www.historians.org/publications-and-directories/perspectives-on-history/april-2016/is-todays-russia-a-relic-of-the-past-a-new-look-at-contemporary-theories-of-soviet-history (accessed 29 February 2020).

104 Oleg Khlevniuk (trans. Simon Belokowsky), 'The Gulag and the Non-Gulag as One Interrelated Whole,' *Kritika: Explorations in Russian and Eurasian History* 16, 3 (2015): 491, 498. 'People who've come out of socialism are both like and unlike the rest of humanity', writes Svetlana Alexievich, the Nobel Laureate. 'All of us come from the land of the gulag and harrowing war.' Svetlana Alexievich, *Secondhand Time: The Last of the Soviets. An Oral History*, trans. Bela Shayevich (New York: Random House, 2016), 3–4.

105 See here, Maria Lipman, 'Stalin is Not Dead: A Legacy that Holds Back Russia', in Lipman, Gudkov and Bakradze, *The Stalin Puzzle*, 22–24.

106 Ibid., 24.

Select Bibliography

(Published books and edited collections only)

Abramson, Adelina and Paulina. *Mosaico Roto.* Madrid: Compañia Literaria, 1995.
Alexievich, Svetlana. *Secondhand Time: The Last of the Soviets. An Oral History*, trans. Bela Shayevich. New York: Random House, 2016.
Alperovitz, Gar. *The Decision to Use the Atomic Bomb*. London: Harper Collins, 1995.
Alperovitz, Gar. *The Decision to Use the Atomic Bomb and the Architecture of the American Myth*. London: Harper Collins, 1995.
Alpert, Michael. *A New International History of the Spanish Civil War*. London: St. Martin's, 1998.
Alted, Alicia et al. *Los niños de la guerra de España en la URSS. De la evacuación al retorno (1937–1999)*. Madrid: Fundación Francisco Largo Caballero, 1999.
Amis, Martin. *Koba The Dread. Laughter and the Twenty Million*. New York: Hyperion, 2002.
Apor, Balazs. *The Invisible Shining: The Cult of Mátyás Rákosi in Stalinist Hungary 1945–1956*. Budapest: CEU Press, 2017.
Apor, Balazs, Behrends, Jan C., Jones, Polly and Rees, E.A. eds. *The Leader Cult in Communist Dictatorship: Stalin in the Eastern Bloc*. Basingstoke: Palgrave Macmillan, 2004.
Attwood, Lynne. *Creating the New Soviet Woman: Women's Magazines as Engineers of Female Identity, 1922–53*. Basingstoke: Macmillan, 1999.
Beer, Daniel. *Renovating Russia. The Human Sciences and the Fate of Liberal Modernity, 1880–1930*. Ithaca, NY: Cornell University Press, 2008.
Beevor, Antony. *Berlin: The Downfall, 1945*. London: Penguin, 1945.
Behrends, Jan C. 'Legacies of Communism: Comparative Remarks'. In *The Cambridge History of Communism: Volume 3, Endgames? Late Communism in Global Perspective, 1968 to the Present*, ed. Juliane Fürst, Silvio Pons and Mark Selden, 529–555. Cambridge: Cambridge University Press, 2017.
Beissinger, Mark R. and Kotkin, Stephen (eds). *Historical Legacies of Communism in Russia and Eastern Europe*. Cambridge: Cambridge University Press, 2014.
Bellamy, Chris. *Absolute War: Soviet Russia in the Second World War*. New York: Alfred A. Knopf, 2007.
Blacker, Uilleam, Etkind, Alexander, and Fedor, Julie (eds). *Memory and Theory in Eastern Europe*. New York: Palgrave, 2013.
Bogumił, Zuzanna. *Gulag Memories: The Rediscovery and Commemoration of Russia's Repressive Past*. New York: Berghahn Books, 2018.
Bolloten, Burnett. *The Spanish Civil War*. Chapel Hill, NC: University of North Carolina Press, 1991.
Boym, Svetlana. *The Future of Nostalgia*. New York: Basic Books, 2001.
Brandenberger, David. *Propaganda State in Crisis: Soviet Ideology, Indoctrination, and Terror under Stalin, 1927–1941*. New Haven, CT: Yale University Press, 2011.

Brandenberger, David. 'Stalin as Symbol: A Case Study of the Personality Cult and its Construction'. In *Stalin: A New History*, ed. Sarah Davies and James Harris, 249–271. Cambridge: Cambridge University Press, 2005.

Brown, Archie and Gray, Jack (eds). *Political Culture and Political Change in Communist States*. New York: Holmes & Meier Publishers, 1979.

Buhle, Paul. *William Appleman Williams: The Tragedy of Empire*. London: Routledge, 1995.

Butler, Susan. *My Dear Mr Stalin: The Complete Correspondence of Franklin D Roosevelt and Joseph V. Stalin*. New Haven, CT: Yale University Press, 2006.

Butt, V.P. *The Russian Civil War: Documents from the Soviet Archives*. Basingstoke: Macmillan, 1996.

Cameron, Sarah. *The Hungry Steppe: Famine, Violence, and the Making of Soviet Kazakhstan*. Ithaca, NY: Cornell University Press, 2018.

Cattell, David. *Communism and the Spanish Civil War*. Berkeley, CA: University of California Press, 1955.

Cattell, David. *Soviet Diplomacy and the Spanish Civil War*. Berkeley: University of California Press, 1957.

Chebrikov, Viktor. *Istoriia sovetskikh organov gosudarstvennoi bezopasnosti: uchebnik*. Moscow: KGB, 1977.

Cohen, Stephen F. *Bukharin and the Bolshevik Revolution: A Political Biography, 1888–1938*. New York: Vintage, 1975.

Conquest, Robert. *The Great Terror: Stalin's Purge of the Thirties*. London: Macmillan, 1968.

Coox, Alvin D. *Nomonhan: Japan against Russia, 1939*, 2 vols. Redwood, CA: Stanford University Press 1988.

Cuadros, Enrique Piquero. *La guerra civil española a través de las crónicas de los corresponsales soviéticos*. Madrid: Miraguano, 2017.

Daniels, Robert V. *The Conscience of the Revolution: Communist Opposition in Soviet Russia*. Cambridge, MA: Harvard University Press, 1960.

Danilov, V. et al. *Tragediia sovetskoi derevni: kollektivizatsiia i raskulachivanie: dokumety i materialy v 5 tomakh, 1937–1939*, vol. 5, bk. 1. Moscow, 2004.

David-Fox, Michael. *Crossing Borders: Modernity, Ideology, and Culture in Russia and the Soviet Union*. Pittsburgh, PA: University of Pittsburgh Press, 2015.

David-Fox, Michael. 'The Iron Curtain as Semipermeable Membrane: Origins and Demise of the Stalinist Superiority Complex'. In *Cold War Crossings: International Travel and Exchange across the Soviet Bloc, 1940s–1960s*, ed. Patryk Babiracki and Kenyon Zimmer, 14–39. Arlington, TX: A & M University Press, 2014.

Davies, R.W. *The Industrialization of Soviet Russia. Vol.1: The Socialist Offensive: The Collectivisation of Soviet Agriculture, 1929–1930*. London: Macmillan, 1980.

Davies, Sarah and Harris, James. *Stalin's World: Dictating the Soviet Order*. New Haven, CT: Yale University Press, 2015.

Devlin, J. 'Stalin's Death and Afterlife'. In *Death, Burial and Afterlife*, ed. Philip Cottrell and Wolfgang Marx, 65–85. Dublin: Carysfort Press, 2014.

Devlin, J. 'The End of the War in Stalinist Film and Legend', 106–117. In *The Fiction of History*, ed. Alexander Lyon Macfie. London: Routledge, 2014.

Devlin, J. 'Soviet Power and its Images: Celebrating Stalin's Seventieth Birthday'. In *War of Words: Culture and the Mass Media in the Making of the Cold War in Europe*, ed. J. Devlin and C. Müller, 30–47. Dublin: UCD Press, 2013.

Devlin, J. 'A Case Study in Censorship: Stalin's Early Film Image'. In *Central and East European Media under Dictatorial Rule and in the Early Cold War*, ed. Olaf Mertelsmann, 27–48. Frankfurt-am-Main: Peter Lang, 2011.

Dobrenko, Ye. 'Stalin's Writing: from the Romantic Poetry of the Future to the Socialist Realist Prose of the Past'. In *Tyrants Writing Poetry*, ed. Albrecht Koschorke and Konstantin Kaminskij, 60–129. Budapest, New York: Central European Press, 2017.

Edele, Mark. *Stalinist Society, 1928–1953*. New York: Oxford University Press, 2011.

Ehrenburg, I. *Postwar Years, 1945–1954*. London: MacGibbon & Kee, 1966.

Ehrenburg, I. *Memoirs: 1921–1941*, trans. Tatiana Shebunina and Yvonne Kapp. London: MacGibbon, 1963.

Ehrenburg, I. *Ispanskie reportazhi*. Moscow: Izd-vo Agenstva pechati Novosti, 1986.

Elorza, Antonio and Bizcarrondo, Marta. *Queridos Camaradas: La Internacional Comunista y España, 1919–1939*. Barcelona: Planeta, 1999.

Engelstein, Laura. *Russia in Flames: War, Revolution, Civil War, 1914–1921*. New York: Oxford University Press, 2018.

Engerman, David C. *Know Your Enemy: The Rise and Fall of America's Soviet Experts*. New York: Oxford University Press, 2011.

Ennker, Benno and Hein-Kirchner, Heidi (eds). *Der Führer im Europa des 20. Jahrhunderts*. Marburg: Herder-Institut, 2010.

Erickson, John. *The Soviet High Command: A Military-Political History*. London: Macmillan, 1962.

Etkind, Alexander. *Warped Mourning: Stories of the Undead in the Land of the Unburied*. Stanford. CA: Stanford University Press, 2013.

Fainsod, Merle. *How Russia is Ruled*. Cambridge, MA: Harvard University Press, 1953.

Feis, Herbert. *Churchill, Roosevelt, Stalin: The War They Waged and the Peace They Sought*. Princeton, NJ: Princeton University Press, 1957.

Fel'shtinskii, Iurii and Cherniavskii, Georgii. *Lev Trotskii. Kniga tret'ia. Oppozitsioner, 1923–1929 gg.* Moscow: Tsentrpoligraf, 2012.

Figes, Orlando. 'The Red Army and Mass Mobilisation during the Russian Civil War, 1918–1920'. In *Warfare in Europe, 1919–1938*, ed. Geoffrey Jenson. Aldershot: Ashgate, 2008.

Fitzpatrick, Sheila. *On Stalin's Team: The Years of Living Dangerously in Soviet Politics*. Princeton, NJ: Princeton University Press, 2015.

Fitzpatrick, Sheila. 'Conclusion: Late Stalinism in historical perspective', In *Late Stalinist Russia: Society between reconstruction and reinvention*, ed. Juliane Furst. London: Routledge, 2006.

Fitzpatrick, Sheila (ed.). *Stalinism: New Directions*. London: Routledge, 2000.

Fitzpatrick, Sheila. *Everyday Stalinism: Ordinary Life in Extraordinary Times, Soviet Russia in the 1930s*. Oxford: Oxford University Press, 1999.

Fitzpatrick, Sheila. *Education and Social Mobility in the Soviet Union, 1921–1934*. Cambridge: Cambridge University Press, 1979.

Fox, W.T.R. *The Super-Powers: The United States, Britain, and the Soviet Union – Their Responsibility for Peace*. Harcourt Brace, 1944.

Frei, Norbert. *Adenauer's Germany and the Nazi Past: The Politics of Amnesty and Integration*, trans. Joel Golb. New York: Columbia University Press, 1997.

Freifeld, Alice. 'Empress Elizabeth as Hungarian Queen: The Uses of Celebrity Monarchism'. In *The Limits of Loyalty: Imperial Symbolism, Popular Allegiances, and State Patriotism in the Late Habsburg Monarchy*, ed. Laurence Cole and Daniel Unowsky, 138–160. New York: Berghahn Books, 2007.

Friedrich, Carl and Brzezinski, Zbigniew. *Totalitarian Dictatorship and Autocracy*. Cambridge, MA: Harvard University Press, 1956.

Fulbrook, Mary. *Reckonings: Legacies of Nazi Persecution and the Quest for Justice.* Oxford: Oxford University Press, 2018.
Furst, Juliane. *Stalin's Last Generation: Soviet Post-War Youth and the Emergence of Mature Socialism.* Oxford: Oxford University Press, 2010.
Gaddis, John Lewis. *Surprise, Security and the American Experience.* Cambridge, MA: Harvard University Press, 2004.
Gaddis, John Lewis. *We Now Know: Rethinking Cold War History.* Oxford: Clarendon Press, 1997.
Gaddis, John Lewis. *The Long Peace: Inquiries into the History of the Cold War.* Oxford: Oxford University Press, 1987.
Gaddis, John Lewis. *The United States and the Origins of the Cold War, 1941–1947.* New York: Columbia University Press, 1972.
Gellately, Robert. *Lenin, Stalin, and Hitler: The Age of Social Catastrophe.* London: Jonathan Cape, 2007.
Gergely, Jenő. *Gömbös Gyula. Politikai pályakép.* Budapest: Vince, 2001.
Gerlach, Christian and Werth, Nicolas. 'State Violence: Violent Societies'. In *Beyond Totalitarianism: Stalinism and Nazism Compared*, ed. Michael Geyer and Sheila Fitzpatrick, 133–179. New York: Cambridge University Press, 2009.
Gerő, András. *Képzelt történelem. Fejezetek a magyar szimbolikus politika XIX–XX. századi történetéből.* Budapest: Eötvös Kiadó, PolgART, 2004.
Gerő, András. *Emperor Francis Joseph: King of the Hungarians.* Social Science Monographs, Boulder, Colorado, Center for Hungarian Studies and Publications, Inc., Wayne, NJ, Distributed by Columbia University Press, New York, 2001.
Gerwarth, Robert. *The Bismarck Myth: Weimar Germany and the Legacy of the Iron Chancellor.* Oxford: Oxford University Press: 2005.
Getty, J. Arch. *Practicing Stalinism. Bolsheviks, Boyars and the Persistence of Tradition.* New Haven, CT: Yale University Press, 2013.
Getty J. Arch and Naumov, Oleg. *Yezhov: the Rise of Stalin's 'Iron Fist'.* New Haven, CT: Yale University Press, 2008.
Getty, J. Arch. *Origins of the Great Purges: The Soviet Communist Party Reconsidered, 1933–1938.* Cambridge: Cambridge University Press, 1991.
Ghodsee, Kristen. *Second World, Second Sex: Socialist Women's Activism and Global Solidarity during the Cold War.* University Park, PA: Penn State University Press, 2019.
Gill, Graeme. *The Origins of the Stalinist Political System.* Cambridge: Cambridge University Press, 1990.
Gill, Graeme. 'Political Myth and Stalin's Quest for Authority in the Party'. In *Authority, Power and Policy in the USSR*, ed. T.H. Rigby, Archie Brown and Peter Reddaway, 80–117. London: Macmillan, 1980.
Goldman, Wendy. *Women at the Gates: Gender and Industry in Stalin's Russia.* Cambridge: Cambridge University Press, 2002.
Goncharov, V.G. (ed.). *Voina v Ispanii. Tsentral'nyy front i Brunetskaia operatsiia Seriia.* Moscow: Veche, 2010.
Gorilovskogo, L.L. (ed.). *Vmeste s patriotami Ispanii: vospominaniia uchastnikov natsional'no-revoliutsionnoi voiny ispanskogo naroda.* Kiev: Izd-vo polit. lit-ry Ukrainy, 1986.
Gor'kov, Yuri. *Gosudarstvennyi Komitet Oborony Prikazivaet.* Moscow: Ol'ma Press, 2002.
Grayling, A.C. *Among the Dead Cities: Is the Targeting of Civilians in War Ever Justified?* London: Bloomsbury, 2006.
Gronow, Jukka. *Caviar with Champagne: Common Luxury and the Ideals of the Good Life in Stalin's Russia.* Oxford: Berg, 2003.

Gudjonsson, Gisli. *The Psychology of Interrogations and Confessions: A Handbook.* New York: Bowker, 2003.
Gundle, Stephen, Duggan, Christopher and Pieri, Giulana (eds). *The Cult of the Duce: Mussolini and the Italians.* Manchester: Manchester University Press, 2013.
Gyáni, Gábor and Kövér, György. *Magyarország társadalomtörténete a reformkortól a második világháborúig.* Budapest: Osiris Kiadó, 2006.
Habeck, Mary and Radosh, Ronald. *Spain Betrayed: The Soviet Union in the Spanish Civil War.* New Haven, CT: Yale University Press, 2001.
Hagenloh, Paul. *Stalin's Police: Public Order and Mass Repression in the USSR, 1926-1941.* Baltimore, MD: Johns Hopkins University Press, 2009.
Halfin, Igal. *Red Autobiographies: Initiating the Bolshevik Self.* Seattle, WA: University of Washington Press, 2011.
Halfin, Igal. *Stalinist Confessions: Messianism and Terror at the Leningrad Communist University.* Pittsburgh, PA: University of Pittsburgh Press, 2009.
Halle, Louis J. *The Cold War As History.* New York: Harper & Row, 1967.
Halliday, Fred. *The Making of the Second Cold War.* London: New York, Verso, 1983.
Harbutt, Fraser J. *Yalta 1945: Europe and America at the Crossroads.* Cambridge: Cambridge University Press, 2010.
Harris, James. *The Great Fear: Stalin's Terror of the 1930s.* Oxford: Oxford University Press, 2016.
Harris, James. 'Intelligence and Threat Perception: Defending the Revolution, 1917-1937'. In *The Anatomy of Terror: Political Violence under Stalin*, ed. James Harris, 29–43. Oxford: Oxford University Press, 2013.
Haslam, Jonathan. *The Soviet Union and the Struggle for Collective Security in Europe, 1933-1939.* New York: St. Martin's, 1984.
Healey, Dan. *Homosexual Desire in Revolutionary Russia: The Regulation of Sexual and Gender Dissent.* Chicago, IL: University of Chicago Press, 2001.
Hellbeck, Jochen. *Revolution on My Mind: Writing a Diary Under Stalin.* Cambridge, MA: Harvard University Press, 2006.
Heller, Klaus and Plamper, Jan (eds). *Personality Cults in Stalinism – Personenkulte in Stalinismus.* Göttingen: V and R Unipress, 2004.
Hein, Heidi. *Der Piłsudski-Kult und seine Bedeutung für den polnischen Staat 1926-39.* Marburg: Herder-Institut, 2002.
Hochman, Jiri. *The Soviet Union and the Failure of Collective Security.* Ithaca, NY: Cornell University Press, 1984.
Hoffmann, David. *The Stalinist Era.* New York: Cambridge University Press, 2018.
Hoffmann, David L. *Cultivating the Masses: Modern State Practices and Soviet Socialism, 1914-1939.* Ithaca, NY: Cornell University Press, 2011.
Holloway, David. *The Soviet Union and the Arms Race.* New Haven, CT: Yale University Press, 1983.
Holloway, David. *Stalin & The Bomb: The Soviet Union and Atomic Energy 1939-1956.* New Haven, CT: Yale University Press, 1994.
Holquist, Peter. *Making War, Forging Revolution: Russia's Continuum of Crisis, 1914-1921.* Cambridge, MA: Harvard University Press, 2002.
Holtsmark, Sven G. 'The Limits to Soviet Influence: Soviet Diplomats and the Pursuit of Strategic Interests in Norway and Denmark, 1944-47'. In *The Soviet Union and Europe in the Cold War, 1943-53*, ed. Francesca Gori and Silvio Pons, 106–124. Basingstoke: Palgrave, 1996.

Hopf, T. *Reconstructing the Cold War: The Early Years, 1945-1958*. Oxford: Oxford University Press, 2012.

Howson, Gerald. *Arms for Spain: The Untold Story of the Spanish Civil War*. New York: Murray, 1998.

Huber, Florian. *Promise Me You'll Shoot Yourself. The Downfall of Ordinary Germans*. London: Allen Lane, 2019.

Ibárruri, Dolores et al. *Voina i revoliutsiia v Ispanii, 1936-1939*, 4 vols. Moscow: Progreso, 1966-71.

Iegorova, N. *Narodnaia Diplomatiia Yadernogo Veka: Dvizhenie Storonnikov Mira i Problema Razoryzheniia 1955-1956 gody*. Moscow: Akvilon 2016.

Igual, Miguel Marco. *La injusticia de un olvido. El mundo de Marcelino Pascua (1897-1977), médico y politico*. Madrid: Universidad Nacional de Educación de Distancia: 2018.

Iurieva, L.M. *Natsionalno-revolutsionnaia voina v Ispanii i mirovaia literature*. Moscow: Izdat. Nauka, 1973.

Izetdinov, A.A. *Voina v Ispanii. Khronika boevykh deystviy 1936-1939 godov*. Moscow: ArtKom, 2014.

Izqueierdo, Rafael Moreno. *Los niños de Rusia: La verdadera historia de una operación de retorno*. Barcelona: Critica, 2017.

Jansen, Marc and Petrov, Nikita. *'Stalinskii pitomets' – Nikolai Ezhov*. Moscow: Rosspen, 2008.

Jian, Chen. *Mao's China and the Cold War*. Chapel Hill, NC: University of North Carolina Press, 2001.

Jones, Polly. 'From Stalinism to Post-Stalinism: De-Mythologising Stalin, 1953–56'. In *Redefining Stalinism*, ed. Harold Shukman, 130–141. London: Frank Cass, 2003.

Jones, Polly. *Myth, Memory, Trauma. Rethinking the Stalinist Past in the Soviet Union, 1953–1970*. New Haven, CT: Yale University Press, 2013.

Jones, Polly (ed.). *The Dilemmas of De-Stalinisation: Negotiating Cultural and Social Change in the Khrushchev Era*. London: Routledge, 2005.

Kandel, B.A. and Guterman, E.A. *Istoriia zarubezhnikh stran (Bibliografiia russkikh bibliografii)*. Moscow: Nauka, 1966.

Karimov, O.V. and Voloshenko, I.N (eds). *Iz Moskvy v stranu 'Iks'. Kniga pamyati sovetskikh dobrovol'tsev-uchastnikov grazhdanskoi voiny v Ispanii 1936–1939 gody*. 2 vols. Moscow: GBU 'TsGA Moskvy', 2015.

Karmen, Roman. *No Pasaran!* Moscow: Izdatelstvo Sovetskaia Rossiia, 1972.

Kavtaradze, A.G. *Voennye spetsialisty na sluzhbe respubliki sovetov, 1917–1920 gg*. Moscow: Nauka, 1988.

Kennedy-Pipe, Caroline. *Stalin's Cold War: Soviet Strategies in Europe, 1943–1956*. Manchester: Manchester University Press, 1995.

Kershaw, Ian. *The Hitler Myth: Image and Reality in the Third Reich*. Oxford: Oxford University Press, 1987.

Kershaw, Ian. 'Hitler and the Germans'. In *Life in the Third Reich*, ed. Richard Bessel, 41–56. Oxford: Oxford University Press, 1987.

Khalid, Adeeb. *Making Uzbekistan: Nation, Empire, and Revolution in the Early USSR*. Ithaca, NY: Cornell University Press, 2015.

Khlevniuk, Oleg V. *Stalin: New Biography of a Dictator*. New Haven, CT: Yale University Press, 2015.

Khlevniuk, Oleg. *Master of the House: Stalin and His Inner Circle*. New Haven, CT: Yale University Press, 2009.

Kindler, Robert. *Stalin's Nomads: Power and Famine in Kazakhstan*. Pittsburgh, PA: University of Pittsburgh Press, 2018.
Kirschenbaum, Lisa A. *International Communism and the Spanish Civil War: Solidarity and Suspicion*. Cambridge: Cambridge University Press, 2015.
Koenker, Diane. *Moscow Workers and the 1917 Revolution*. Princeton, NJ: Princeton University Press, 1981.
Koenker, Diane and Rosenberg, William G. *Strikes and Revolution in Russia, 1917*. Princeton, NJ: Princeton University Press, 1990.
Kołakowski, Leszek. *Main Currents of Marxism: Its Rise, Growth, and Dissolution*, trans. P.S. Falla. Oxford: Clarendon Press, 1978.
Kolonitskii, Boris. *'Tovarishch Kerenskii': anti-monarkhicheskaya revoliutsiya i formirovanie kul'ta 'vozhdya naroda' mart-iiun'1917 goda*. Moscow: NLO, 2017.
Kolonitskii, Boris. 'Russian Leaders of the Great War and Revolutionary Era in Representations and Rumours'. In *Russian Culture in War and Revolution 1914-1922. Book 2. Political Culture, Identities and Memory*, ed. Murray Frame, B.I. Kolonitskii, Steven G. Marks and Melissa Stockdale. Bloomington, IN: Slavica, 2014.
Kol'tiukov, A.A. et al. *Russkaia voennaia emigratsiia*, vol. 5. Moscow: RGGU, 2010.
Kol'tiukov, A.A. et al. *Russkaia voennaia emigratsiia*, vol. 4. Moscow: RGGU, 2007.
Körösényi, András (ed.). *A magyar politikai rendszer – negyedszázad után*. Budapest: Osiris, 2015.
Kosheleva, L. et al. *Pis'ma I. V. Stalina V. M. Molotovu: 1925-1936 gg.: sbornik dokumentov*. Moscow: Rossiia molodaia, 1995.
Kotkin, Stephen. *Stalin: Waiting for Hitler, 1928-1941*. London: Allen Lane, 2017.
Kotkin, Stephen. *Stalin, Paradoxes of Power, 1878-1928*. New York: Penguin Press, 2014.
Kotkin, Stephen. *Magnetic Mountain: Stalinism as a Civilization*. Berkeley, CA: University of California Press, 1995.
Kowalsky, Daniel. 'From Marginalization to Mobilization: The Soviet Union and the Spanish Republic, 18 July–31 December 1936'. In *Spain 1936: Year Zero*, ed. Raanan Rein and Joan Maria Thomas, 152-173. Eastbourne: Sussex Academic Press, 2018.
Kowalsky, Daniel. 'Revisiting Operation X: Stalin and the Spanish Republic, 1936-1939'. In *Desde la Capital de la Republic: Nuevas perspectivas y estudios sobre la guerra civil española*, ed. S. Valero Gómez and M. García Carrión, 45-66. Valencia: Universitat de Valencia, 2018.
Kowalsky, Daniel. 'Exporting Soviet Commemoration: The Spanish Civil War and the October Revolution, 1936-1939'. In *Echoes of October: International Commemorations of the Bolshevik Revolution, 1918-1990*, ed. Jean-François Fayet, Valerie Gorin and Stefanie Prezioso, 104-132. London: Lawrence and Wishart, 2017.
Kowalsky, Daniel. 'Las grandes campañas propagandísticas de la URSS'. In *Los Rusos en la Guerra de España, 1936-1939*, ed. Ricardo Miralles, 59-65. Madrid: Fundacion P. Iglesia, 2009.
Kowalsky, Daniel. *Stalin and the Spanish Civil War*. New York: Columbia University Press, 2004.
Kowalsky, Daniel. *La Unión Soviética y la Guerra Civil Española: Una Revisión Crítica*. Barcelona: Editorial Crítica, 2003.
Krylova, Anna. 'Identity, Agency, and the "First Soviet Generation"'. In *Generations in Twentieth-Century Europe*, ed. Stephen Lovell. Basingstoke: Palgrave, 2007.
Kudriashov, Sergei (ed.). *SSSR i Grazhdanskaia voina v Ispanii. 1936-1939 gody*. Moscow: Vestnik Arkhiv Prezidenta Rossiiskoi Federatsii, 2013.

Kuleshova, V.V. *Ispaniia i SSSR: Kulturnye sviazi: 1917–1939*. Moscow: Izdat. Nauka, 1975.
Kvachkov, Vladimir. *Spetsnaz Rossii*. Moscow, Algoritm, 2015.
Kvashonkin, A.V. et al. *Bol'shevistskoe rukovodstvo. perepiska, 1912–1927*. Moscow: Rosspen, 1996.
Lackó, Miklós. 'A magyar kommunista mozgalom és a nemzeti kérdés 1918–1936'. In *Gazdaság, társadalom, történetírás*, ed. Ferenc Glatz, 255–272. Budapest: MTA Történettudományi Intézet, 1989.
Laruelle, Marlène. *Russian Nationalism: Imaginaries, Doctrines, and Political Battlefields*. London: Routledge, 2019.
Leese, Daniel. *The Mao Cult: Rhetoric and Ritual in China's Cultural Revolution*. Cambridge: Cambridge University Press, 2011.
Leese, Daniel. 'Rituals, Emotions and Mass Mobilisation: the Leader Cult and Party Politics'. In *The Palgrave Handbook of Mass Dictatorship*, ed. Paul Corner and Jie Hyun Lim. London: Palgrave Macmillan, 2016.
Leffler, Melvyn C. *For the Sake of Mankind: The United States, the Soviet Union and the Cold War*. New York: Macmillan, 2007.
Leggett, George. *The Cheka: Lenin's Political Police Force: The All-Russian Extraordinary Commission for Combating Counter-revolution and Sabotage (December 1917 to February 1922)*. Oxford: Clarendon, 1981.
Lendvai, Paul. *Orbán: Hungary's Strongman*. Oxford: Oxford University Press, 2017.
Leo, Richard. *Police Interrogation and American Justice*. Cambridge: Harvard University Press, 2008.
Leskov, Valentin. *Stalin i zagovor Tukhachevskogo*. Moscow: Veche, 2003.
London, Artur. *On Trial*, trans. Alastair Hamilton. London: Macdonald & Co. 1970.
Magyar, Bálint. *Post-Communist Mafia State: The Case of Hungary*. Budapest: Central European University Press, 2016.
Maiskii, Ivan M. (ed). *Iz istorii osvoboditel'noi voiny ispanskogo naroda*. Moscow: Akademiia Nauk SSSR, 1959.
Maiskii, Ivan M. *Ispanskii tetrady*. Moscow: Voennoe izdat., 1962.
Majtényi, György. *Vezércsel. Kádár János mindennapjai*. Budapest: Libri, 2012.
Malay, V.V. *Grazhdanskaia voina v Ispanii 1936–1939 godov i Yevropa Avtor*. Moscow: Nauka, 2011.
Malinova, Olga. 'Constructing the "Usable Past": The Evolution of the Official Historical Narrative in Post-Soviet Russia'. In *Cultural and Political Imaginaries in Putin's Russia*, ed. Niklas Bernsand and Barbara Törnquist-Plewa. Leiden: Brill, 2018.
Malinova, Ol'ga. *Aktual'noe proshloe: Simvolicheskaia politika vlastvuiushchei elityi i dilemmyi Rossiiskoi identichnosti*. Moscow: ROSSPEN, 2015.
Manning, Roberta T. *Government in the Soviet Countryside in the Stalinist Thirties: The Case of Belyi Raion in 1937*. Pittsburgh, PA: The Carl Beck Papers, 1984.
Martin, Terry. 'Modernization or Neo-Traditionalism? Ascribed Nationality and Soviet Primordialism'. In *Stalinism: New Directions*, ed. Sheila Fitzpatrick, 348–367. London: Routledge, 2000.
McLoughlin, Barry. 'Mass Operations of the NKVD, 1937–8: A Survey'. In *Stalin's Terror: High Politics and Mass Repression in the Soviet Union*, ed. Barry McLoughlin and Kevin McDermott. Basingstoke: Palgrave, 2003.
Meshcheriakov, M.T. *Ispanskaia respublika i Komintern*. Moscow: Mysl', 1981.
Mevius, Martin. *Agents of Moscow: The Hungarian Communist Party and the Origins of Socialist Patriotism 1941–1953*. Oxford: Oxford University Press, 2005.

Miller, D. Quentin. *John Updike and the Cold War: Drawing the Iron Curtain*. Columbia, MI: University of Missouri Press, 2001.
Minakov, Sergei. *Stalin i zagovor generalov*. Moscow: Eksmo, 2005.
Miralles, Ricardo (ed.). *Los Rusos en la Guerra de España, 1936–1939*. Madrid: Fundacion P. Iglesia, 2009.
Molloy, Sean. *Atomic Tragedy: Henry L. Stimson and the Decision to Use the Bomb against Japan*. Ithaca, NY: Cornell University Press, 2008.
Montefiore, Simon Sebag. *Stalin: The Court of the Red Tsar*. London: Weidenfeld & Nicolson, 2003.
Morgan, Kevin. 'Cults of the Individual'. In *The Cambridge History of Communism. I. World Revolution and Socialism in One Country 1917–1941*, ed. Silvio Pons and S.A. Smith, 551–572. Cambridge: Cambridge University Press, 2017.
Morgan, Kevin. *Internationalism and the Cult of the Individual: Leaders, Tribunes and Martyrs under Lenin and Stalin*. London: Palgrave Macmillan, 2017.
Müller, Jan-Werner (ed). *Memory and Power in Post-War Europe: Studies in the Presence of the Past*. Cambridge: Cambridge University Press, 2002.
Neumann, Matthias and Willimott, Andy (eds). *Rethinking the Russian Revolution as Historical Divide*. London: Routledge, 2017.
Northrop, Douglas. *Veiled Empire: Gender and Power in Stalinist Central Asia*. Ithaca, NY: 2004.
Novikov, M.V. *Grazhdanskaia voina v Ispanii, 1936–1939. Bibliograficheskii ukazatel' istochnikov i literatury, izdannykh v SSSR v 1936–1991*. Iaroslav: Iaroslav gosud. universitet, 1994.
Novikov, M.V. *SSSR, Komintern i grazhdanskaia voina v Ispanii 1936–1939*, 2 vols. Iaroslav: Iaroslav gosud. universitet, 1995.
Olšáková, Doubravka (ed.). *In the Name of the Great Work: Stalin's Plan for the Transformation of Nature and its Impact in Eastern Europe*. New York: Berghahn, 2016.
Orwell, George. *Homage to Catalonia*. London: Secker and Warburg, 1938.
Orzoff, Andrea. *Battle for the Castle: The Myth of Czechoslovakia in Europe 1914–1948*. Oxford: Oxford University Press, 2011.
O'Sullivan, Noel. *Terrorism, Ideology & Revolution the Origins of Modern Political Violence*. Brighton: Wheatsheaf Books, 1986.
Overy, Richard. *The Dictators. Hitler's Germany. Stalin's Russia*. London: Allen Lane, 2004.
Panitch, Leo and Albo, Greg (eds). *Rethinking Revolution: Socialist Register 2017*. London: Merlin Press, 2016.
Pchelinov-Obrazumov, A.A. *Grazhdanskaia voina v Ispanii 1936–1939 gg. i rossiyskaia politicheskaia emigratsiia*. Moscow: BGNIU, 2015.
Peters, Edward. *Torture*. Philadelphia, PA: University of Pennsylvania Press, 2018.
Pike, David Wingeate. *In the Service of Stalin: The Spanish Communists in Exile, 1939–45*. Oxford: Oxford University Press, 1993.
Plamper, Jan. *The Stalin Cult: a Study in the Alchemy of Power*. New Haven, CT: Yale University Press, 2012.
Plekhanov, A.A. and Plekhanov, A.M. (eds). *F. E. Dzerzhinskii: predsedatel' VChK-OGPU 1917-1926: dokumenty*. Moscow: MFD, Materik, 2007.
Ponomarieva, L.V. *Sovietskaia istoricheskaia nauka ot XX k XXII s"ezdu Komunisticheskoi partii Sovetskogo Soiuza. Istoriia stran Zapadnoi Evropii i Amerikii*. Moscow: Nauka, 1963.
Pozharskaya, S.P. (ed.). *Komintern i grazhdanskaia voina v Ispanii*. Dokumenty Seriya: Dokumenty Kominterna. Moscow: Nauka, 2001.

Preston, Paul. 'War of Words: The Spanish Civil War and the Historians'. In *Revolution and War in Spain*, ed. P. Preston, 1–13. London: Methuen, 1984.
Priestland, David. *Stalinism and the Politics of Mobilization: Ideas, Power, and Terror in Inter-war Russia*. Oxford: Oxford University Press, 2007.
Pritsker, D.P. (ed.). *Leningradtsy v Ispanii,* 3rd edn. Leningrad: Lenizdat, 1989.
Pünkösti, Árpád. *Rákosi a hatalomért, 1945–1948*. Budapest: Európa, 1992.
Püski, Levente. *A Horthy-rendszer*. Budapest: Pannonica Kiadó, 2006.
Pyta, Wolfram. *Hindenburg: Herrschaft zwischen Hohenzollern und Hitler*. Berlin: Pantheon Verlag, 2009.
Rabinowitch, Alexander. *The Bolsheviks Come to Power: The Revolution of 1917 in Petrograd*. New York: Norton, 1976.
Raeva, T.V. 'Mirotvorchestvo "po-Sovetski"'. In *Sovetskaia Kul'turnaia Diplomatiia v Usloviiakh Kholodnoi Voiny, 1945–1989*, ed. O.S. Nagornaia. Moscow: Rosspen, 2018.
Read, Christopher. *Stalin: From the Caucasus to the Kremlin*. London: Routledge, 2017.
Rees, E.A. *Iron Lazar: A Political Biography of Lazar Kaganovich*. London: Anthem Press, 2013.
Reese, Roger R. *The Soviet Military Experience: A History of the Soviet Army, 1917–1991*. London: Routledge, 2000.
Reiman, Michel. *The Birth of Stalinism: The USSR on the Eve of the 'Second Revolution'*. Bloomington, IN: Indiana University Press, 1987.
Rhodes, Richard. *Dark Sun: The Making of the Hydrogen Bomb*. New York: Simon and Schuster, 1995.
Riall, Lucy. *Garibaldi: Invention of a Hero*. New Haven, CT: Yale University Press, 2007.
Ricoeur, Paul. *History, Memory, Forgetting*. Chicago, IL: University of Chicago Press, 2004.
Rieber, Alfred J. *Stalin and the Struggle for Supremacy in Eurasia*. Cambridge: Cambridge University Press, 2015.
Roberts, G. 'Science, Peace and Internationalism: Frédéric Joliot-Curie, the World Federation of Scientific Workers and the Origins of the Pugwash Movement'. In *Science, Peace and Communism*, ed. A. Kraft and C. Sachse. Leiden: Brill, 2019.
Roberts, G. 'Averting Armageddon: The Communist Peace Movement, 1948–1956'. In *The Oxford Handbook of the History of Communism*, ed. S. Smith. Oxford: Oxford University Press, 2014.
Roberts, G. *Molotov: Stalin's Cold War*. Washington, DC: Potomac Books, 2012.
Roberts, G. *Stalin's Wars: From World War to Cold War 1939–1953*. New Haven, CT: Yale University Press, 2006.
Roberts, G. 'Soviet Foreign Policy and the Spanish Civil War, 1936–1939'. In *Spain in an International Context, 1936–1959*, ed. Christian Leitz and David J. Dunthorn, 81–103. New York: Berghahn Books, 1999.
Romsics, Ignác. 'Changing Images of Miklós Horthy'. In *Cultic Revelations: Cult Personalities and Phenomena*, ed. Anssi Halmevirta. Tampere: Historietti Oy, 2011.
Ruggenthaler, Peter. *The Concept of Neutrality in Stalin's Foreign Policy*. Lanham, MD: Lexington Books, 2015.
Sanborn, Joshua. *Drafting the Russian Nation: Military Conscription, Total War, and Mass Politics, 1905–1925*. Dekalb, IL: Northern Illinois University Press, 2003.
Savich, Ovadii. *Dva goda v Ispanii, 1937–1939*. Moscow: Sovetskii Pisatel', 1981.
Schapiro, Leonard. 'The "great purge"'. In *The Red Army*, ed. B.H. Liddell Hart. London: Weidenfeld & Nicholson, 1957.
Schauff, Frank. Proigrannaia pobeda. Sovetskiy Soyuz, Kommunistich. Internatsional i Grazhd. voina v Ispanii 1936–1939 gg. Moscow: Politicheskaia entsiklopediia, 2017.

Schauff, Frank. *La victoria frustrada: La Unión Soviética, la Internacional Comunista y la Guerra Civil Española*. Barcelona: Debate, 2008.
Schauff, Frank. *Der verspielte Sieg: Sowjetunion, Kommunistische Internationale und Spanischer Bürgerkrieg 1936–1939*. Frankfurt- am- Main: Campus Verlag, 2004.
Schöpflin, George. *Politics in Eastern Europe 1945–1992*. Oxford: Blackwell, 1993.
Service, Robert. *Stalin: A Biography*. Basingstoke: Macmillan, 2004.
Shearer, David R. *Policing Stalin's Socialism: Repression and Social Order in the Soviet Union, 1924–1953*. New Haven, CT: Yale University Press, 2009.
Shirinia, K.K. (ed.). *VII Kongress Kommunisticheskogo Internatsionala i bor'ba protiv fashizma i voiny (Sbornik dokumentov)*. Moscow: Politizdat, 1975.
Shubin, A.V., Dam'e, V.V. et al. *Grazhdanskaia voina v Ispanii: Izvestnoe i neizvestnoe*. Moscow: URSS, 2018.
Simonov, B.M. *Grazhdanskaia voina v Ispanii. Deystviya na tsentral'nom fronte. Oktyabr' 1936 aprel' 1937*. St Petersburg: Sankt-Peterburgskiy Universitet, 2006.
Skoutelsky, Rémi. *L'espoir guidait leur pas: Les volontaires français dans les Brigades internationales, 1936–1939*. Paris: Bernard Grasset, 1998.
Smith, S.A. *Russia in Revolution: An Empire in Crisis, 1890–1928*. Oxford: Oxford University Press, 2017.
Smith, S.A. *Red Petrograd: Revolution in the Factories, 1917–1918*. Cambridge: Cambridge University Press, 1983.
Snyder, Timothy and Brandon, Ray (eds). *Stalin and Europe: Imitation and Domination, 1928–1953*. New York: Oxford University Press, 2014.
Sokolovskii, Marshal Vitalii. *Voennaia strategiia*. Moscow: Voenizdat, 1962, 1963, 1968. Trans. Harriet Fast Scott as *Soviet Military Strategy*. New York: Crane Russak & Co; Reprint edition, 1984.
Solomon, Peter H. *Soviet Criminal Justice under Stalin*. Cambridge: University of Cambridge Press, 1997.
Ssorin-Chaikov, N.V. (ed.). *Dary vozhdiam*. Moscow: Pinakoteka, 2006.
Steinberg, Mark D. *The Russian Revolution, 1905–1921*. New York: Oxford University Press, 2017.
Stourzh, Gerald and Mueller, Wolfgang. *Cold War Over Austria: The Struggle for the State Treaty, Nejutrality and the End of East-West Occupation, 1945–1955*. Lanham, MD: Lexington Books, The Harvard Cold War Book Series, 2018.
Svechin, Aleksandr. *Strategiia*. 2nd edn. Moscow: Voennyi Vestnik Press, 1927.
Szapor, Judith. 'From "Guardian Angel of Hungary" to the "Sissi Look-Alike Contest": The Making and Remaking of the Cult of Elizabeth, Queen of Hungary'. In *Gender and Modernity in Central Europe: The Austro-Hungarian Empire and Its Legacy*, ed. Agatha Schwarz, 235–250. Ottawa: University of Ottawa Press, 2010.
Szász, Béla. *Volunteers for the Gallows: The Anatomy of a Show Trial*. New York: Norton, 1971.
Tarkhova, Nonna. *Krasnaia armiia i stalinskaia kollektivizatsiia, 1928–1933 gg*. Moscow: Rosspen, 2010.
Thomas, Alun. *Nomads and Soviet Rule: Central Asia under Lenin and Stalin*. London: I.B. Tauris, 2018.
Tismaneanu, Vladimir. *Fantasies of Salvation: Democracy, Nationalism, and Myth in Post-Communist Europe*. Princeton, NJ: Princeton University Press, 1999.
Torbakov, Igor. 'History, Memory and National Identity: Understanding the Politics of History and Memory Wars in Post-Soviet Lands'. In *Russian Nationalism, Foreign Policy, and Identity Debates in Putin's Russia: New Ideological Patterns after the Orange Revolution*, ed. Marlène Laruelle. Stuttgart: Ibid., 2012.

Tucker, Robert. *Stalin in Power: The Revolution from Above*. London: Norton, 1990.
Tucker, Robert. *Stalin as Revolutionary, 1879–1929: A Study in History and Personality*. New York: Norton, 1973.
Tulard, Jean. *Le Mythe de Napoléon*. Paris: Armand Colin, 1971.
Tumarkin, Nina. *Lenin Lives! The Lenin Cult in Soviet Russia*, enlarged edn. Cambridge, MA: Harvard University Press, 1997.
Tumarkin, Nina. *The Living and the Dead: The Rise and Fall of the Cult of World War II in Russia*. New York: Basic Books, 1994.
Tynchenko, Iaroslav. *Golgofa russkogo ofitserstva v SSSR, 1930–1931 gody*. Moscow: Moskovskii obshchestvennyi nauchnyi fond, 2000.
Ungváry, Krisztián. *A Horthy-rendszer mérlege – Diszkrimináció, szociálpolitika és antiszemitizmus Magyarországon*. Budapest: Jelenkor Kiadó, 2013.
Ushakova, Svetlana. *Ideologo-propagandistskie kampanii v praktike funktsionirovaniia stalinskogo rezhima: novyie podkhodyi i istochniki*. Moscow: ROSSPEN, 2013.
Vatulescu, Cristina *Police Aesthetics: Literature, Film, and the Secret Police in Soviet Times*. Stanford, CA: Stanford University Press, 2010.
Viktorov, Boris. *Bez grifa "sekretno": zapiski voennogo prokurova*. Moscow: Iurid. litra, 1990.
Viñas, Angel. *El honor de la República: Entre el acoso fascista, la hostilidad británica y la política de Stalin*. Barcelona: Crítica, 2008.
Viñas, Angel. *El escudo de la República: El oro de España, la apuesta soviética y los hechos de mayo de 1937*. Barcelona: Crítica, 2007.
Viñas, Angel. *La soledad de la república: el abandono de las democracias y el viraje hacia la Unión Soviética*. Barcelona: Crítica, 2006.
Vinogradov et al. *Arkhiv VChK: sbornik dokumentov*. Moscow: Kuchkovo Pole, 2007.
Viola, Lynne. *Stalinist Perpetrators on Trial: Scenes from the Great Terror in Soviet Ukraine*. Oxford: Oxford University Press, 2018.
Viola, Lynne. *The Best Sons of the Fatherland: Workers in the Vanguard of Soviet Collectivization*. New York: Oxford University Press, 1987.
Voitikov, S.S. *Otechestvennye spetssluzby i krasnaia armiia, 1917–1921*. Moscow: Veche, 2010.
Volosiuk, Olga, Yuirchik, Ekaterina and Vediushkin, Vladimir (eds). *España y Rusia: diplomacia y diálogo de culturas. Tres siglos de relaciones*. Moscow: Indrik, 2018.
Von der Goltz, Anna. *Hindenburg: Power, Myth and the Rise of the Nazis*. Oxford: Oxford University Press, 2009.
Voronov, N.N. *Na sluzhbe voennoi*. Moscow. Voenizdat, 1963.
Walker, Shaun. *The Long Hangover: Putin's New Russia and The Ghosts of the Past*. New York: Oxford University Press, 2018.
Waterlow, Jonathan. *It's Only a Joke, Comrade! Humour, Trust and Everyday Life Under Stalin*. Scots Valley, CA: CreateSpace, 2018.
Westad, Odd Arne. *Reviewing the Cold War: Approaches, Interpretations, Theory*. London: Frank Cass Publishers, 2000.
Whitewood, Peter. *The Red Army and the Great Terror: Stalin's Purge of the Soviet Military*. Kansas: University Press of Kansas, 2015.
Williams, William Appleman. *The Tragedy of American Diplomacy*. New York: Norton and Co, 1959.
Willimott, Andy. *Living the Revolution: Urban Communes and the Fate of Soviet Socialism, 1917–1932*. Oxford: Oxford University Press, 2017.
Wood, Elizabeth A. *Performing Justice: Agitation Trials in Early Soviet Russia*. Ithaca, NY: Cornell University Press, 2005.

Wood, Elizabeth A. *The Baba and the Comrade: Gender and Politics in Revolutionary Russia*. Bloomington, IN: Indiana University Press, 1997.
Wortman, Richard. *Scenarios of Power, 2 From Alexander II to the Abdication of Nicholas II*. Princeton, NJ: Princeton University Press, 2000.
Yutkevich, Sergei. *Sobranie sochinenii v trekh tomakh*, t.2. Moscow: Iskusstvo, 1991.
Zaloga, Steven J. *Spanish Civil War Tanks: The Proving Ground for Blitzkrieg*. Oxford: Osprey, 2010.
Zdanovich, Aleksandr. *Organy gosudarstvennoi bezopasnosti i krasnaia armiia*. Moscow: Kuchkov Pole, 2008.
Zolotarev, V.A. et al. *Russkaia voennaia emigratsiia 20-kh-40-kh godov: dokumenty i materialy*, vol. 1, bk. 2. Moscow: Geia, 1998.

Geoffrey Roberts Select Bibliography

(scholarly books and articles only)

Books

Inside Stalin's Library: An Intimate History of a Dictator and His Books (forthcoming, with Yale University Press).
Churchill and Stalin: Comrades-in-Arms during the Second World War. Barnsley: Pen & Sword Books, 2019 (with Martin Folly and Oleg Rzheshevsky).
Marshal of Victory: The Autobiography of General Georgy Zhukov. Barnsley: Pen & Sword Books, 2014.
Stalin's General: The Life of Georgy Zhukov. New York: Random House, 2012.
- Also published in *Swedish* (Stockholm: Historiska Media, 2012), *Finnish* (Helsinki: Tammi, 2013), *Estonian* (Tallinn: Tanapaev, 2013), *Russian* (Moscow: AST, 2013), *Japanese* (Tokyo: Hakusuisha, 2014); *Polish* (Kracow: Znak, 2014), *Chinese* (Beijing: Social Sciences Academic Press, 2015), *Turkish* (Istanbul: Kalkedon, 2016) and *Romanian* (Bucharest: Corint, 2019).

Molotov: Stalin's Cold Warrior. Washington, DC: Nebraska University Press/Potomac Books, 2012.
- Also published in *Russian* (Moscow: AST, 2014).

Stalin's Wars: From World War to Cold War, 1939–1953. New Haven, CT: Yale University Press, 2006.
- Also published in *Czech* (Prague: PZH, 2008), *German* (Dusseldorf: Patmos, 2008), *Polish* (Warsaw: Swiat Ksiazki, 2010), *Chinese* (Beijing: Social Sciences Academic Press, 2013), *Russian* (Moscow: AST, 2014) and *French* (Paris: Editions Delga, 2014).

Victory at Stalingrad: The Battle that Changed History. London: Longman, 2002.
- Also published in *Russian* (Moscow: URSS, 2003) and *Chinese* (Beijing: CIP, 2005).

The Soviet Union in World Politics: Coexistence, Revolution and Cold War, 1945–1991. London: Routledge, 1999.
The Soviet Union and the Origins of the Second World War. New York: St. Martin's Press/London: Macmillan, 1995.
The Unholy Alliance: Stalin's Pact with Hitler. Bloomington, IN: Indiana University Press/London: I.B. Tauris, 1989.

Edited Volumes

Stalin – His Times and Ours. Dublin: Irish Association for Russian and East European Studies, 2005.
The History and Narrative Reader. London: Routledge, 2001.
- Also part published in *Persian* (Imam Sadiq University Press: Tehran 2011).

Ireland and the Second World War: Politics, Society and Remembrance (co-edited with B. Girvin). Dublin: Four Courts Press, 2000.

Journal Articles

'A League of their Own: The Soviet Origins of the United Nations', *Journal of Contemporary History* 54, no.2 (2019): 1–25.

'Long Shadow, Wrong Shadow: World War II Perceptions of the Great War', *Mir Istorii* (2018), available online: http://www.historia.ru/2018/01/2018-01-roberts.htm

'An Autobiographical Pact: The Memoirs of Marshal Georgy Zhukov', *Moving the Social: Journal of Social History and the History of Social Movements*, 51 (2014): 73–94.

'The Cold War as History', *International Affairs* 87, no.6 (2011): 1475–1484.

'Moscow's Cold War on the Periphery: Soviet Policy in Greece, Iran, and Turkey, 1943–1948', *Journal of Contemporary History* 46, no.1 (2011): 58–81.

'A Chance for Peace? The Soviet Campaign to End the Cold War, 1953–1955', *Cold War International History Project* Working Paper No.57 (2008).

'Shans Dlia Mira? Sovetskaia Kampaniia v Pol'zu Zaversheniia "Xholodnoi Voini", 1953–1955gody', *Novaia i Novesihaia Istoriia* (2008): 35–75.

'J.H. Hexter: Narrative History and Common Sense', *Chronicon* 3 (2007): 36–43, http://www.ucc.ie/chronicon/3/roberts.pdf.

'Stalin at Tehran, Yalta and Potsdam', *Journal of Cold War Studies* 9, no.4 (2007): 6–40.

'History, Theory and the Narrative Turn in IR', *Review of International Studies* 32 (2006): 703–714.

'Sexing up the Cold War: New Evidence on the Molotov–Truman Talks of April 1945', *Cold War History* 4, no.3 (2004): 105–125.

'Stalin, the Pact with Nazi Germany and the Origins of Postwar Soviet Diplomatic Historiography: A Research Note', *Journal of Cold War Studies* 4, no.3 (2002): 93–103.

'Litvinov's Lost Peace, 1941–1946', *Journal of Cold War Studies* 4, no.2 (2002): 25–56.

'Sfery Vliniya i Sovetskaya Vneshnyaya Politika v 1939–1945gg: Ideologiya Raschet i Improvizatsiya', *Novaia i Noveishaia Istoriia* 5 (2001): 75–91.

'Stalin and the Grand Alliance: Public Discourse, Private Dialogues, and the Political Direction of Soviet Foreign Policy, 1941–1947', *Slovo* 14 (2001): 1–15.

'Ideology, Calculation and Improvisation: Spheres of Influence and Soviet Foreign Policy, 1939–1945', *Review of International Studies* 25, no.4 (1999): 655–673.

'The Limits of Popular Radicalism: British Communism and the People's War, 1941–1945', *Chronicon: An Electronic History Journal* 1 (1997): paras 1–92, http://www.ucc.ie/chronicon/robfra.htm.

'Postmodernism versus the Standpoint of Action', *History and Theory* 36, no.2 (1997): 249–260.

'The Alliance that Failed: Moscow and the Triple Alliance Negotiations, 1939', *European History Quarterly* (1996): 383–414.

'Narrative History as a Way of Life', *Journal of Contemporary History* 31, no.1 (1996): 221–228.

'Soviet Policy and the Baltic States, 1939–1940: A Reappraisal', *Diplomacy & Statecraft* 6, no.3 (1995): 672–700.

'Moscow and the Marshall Plan: Politics, Ideology and the Onset of the Cold War, 1947', *Europe-Asia Studies* 46, no.8 (1994): 1371–1386.

'A Soviet Bid for Peaceful Coexistence with Nazi Germany, 1935–1937: The Kandelaki Affair', *International History Review* 16, no.3 (1994): 466–490.

'Military Disaster as a Function of Rational Political Calculation: Stalin and 22 June 1941', *Diplomacy & Statecraft* 4, no.2 (1993): 313–330.

'The Fall of Litvinov: A Revisionist View', *Journal of Contemporary History* 27, no.4 (1992): 639–657.

'The Soviet Decision for a Pact with Nazi Germany', *Soviet Studies* 44, no.1 (1992): 55–78.

'Infamous Encounter? The Merekalov–Weizsacker Meeting of 17 April 1939', *The Historical Journal* 35, no.4 (1992): 921–926.

Book Chapters

'Working towards the *Vozhd*'? Stalin and the Peace Movement, 1948–1956'. In *Revisioning Stalin and Stalinism*, ed. J. Ryan and S. Grant. London: Bloomsbury Academic, 2020.

'Science, Peace and Internationalism: Frederic Joliot-Curie, the World Federation of Scientific Workers and the Origins of the Pugwash Movement'. In *Science, (Anti-) Communism and Diplomacy*, ed. A. Kraft & C. Sachse. Leiden: Brill 2019, 43–79.

'Impossible Allies? Soviet Views of France and the German Question in the 1950s'. In *France and the German Question*, ed. F. Bozo and C. Wenkel. New York: Berghahn Books, 2019, 72–89.

'Antipodes or Twins? The Myths of Yalta and Potsdam'. In *Das Potsdamer Abkommen 1945–2015. Rechtliche Bedeutung und historische Auswirkungen*, ed. C. Koch. Frankfurt-am-Main: Peter Lang, 2017, 215–233.

'From World War to Cold War'. In *The Oxford Illustrated History of World War Two*, ed. R. Overy. Oxford: Oxford University Press, 2015, 402–432.

'Cherchil', Ruzvel't i Stalin: Rol' Lichnostnogo Faktora v Uspekhakh i Neudachakh Velikogo Al'yansa'. In *The Co-operation of the Anti-Hitler Coalition*. Moscow: Military Leaders Club of the Russian Federation, 2014, 173–196.

'Georgii Zhukov'. In *Oxford Bibliographies in Military History*, ed. D. Showalter. New York: Oxford University Press, 2014.

'Averting Armageddon: The Communist Peace Movement after World War II'. In *The Oxford Handbook of the History of Communism*, ed. S. Smith. Oxford: Oxford University Press, 2014, 322–338.

'Stalin's Wartime Vision of the Peace'. In *Stalin and Europe: Imitation and Domination, 1928–1953*, ed. T. Snyder and R. Brandon. New York: Oxford University Press, 2014, 233–263.

'Molotov'. In *Encyclopedia of the Cold War*, ed. R. van Dink et al. London: Routledge, 2008, 594–596.

'The Yalta Conference'. In *Encyclopedia of the Cold War*, ed. R. van Dink et al. London: Routledge, 2008, 967–969.

'Irlandiia, Velikobritaniia i Nurnbergskogo Protsesa' (Ireland, Great Britain and the Nuremberg Process). In *Nurnbergskii Protsess: Uroki Istorii*, ed. N.S. Lebedeva and V.V. Ishchenko. Moscow: Institute of General History, Russian Academy of Sciences, 2007, 174–181.

'Grande Alleanza'. In *Dizionario del comunismo*, ed. S. Pons and R. Service. Einaudi: Turin, 2006, 347–351.

- (also published in *English* in 2010 by Princeton University Press).

'Conferenza di Jalta'. In *Dizionario del comunismo*, ed. S. Pons and R. Service. Einaudi: Turin, 2006, 456–459.
- (Also published in *English* in 2010 by Princeton University Press).

'Stalin and the Katyn Massacre'. In *Stalin – His Times and Ours*, ed. G. Roberts. Dublin: IAREES, 2005, 191–202.

'Neutrality, Identity and the Challenge of the "Irish Volunteers"'. In *Ireland in World War Two*, ed. D. Keogh and M. O'Driscoll. Cork: Mercier Press, 2004, 274–284.

'The History and Narrative Debate, 1960–2000'. In *The History and Narrative Reader*, ed. G. Roberts. London: Routledge, 2001, 1–21.

'Geoffrey Elton: History and Human Action'. In *The History and Narrative Reader*, ed. G. Roberts. London: Routledge, 2001, 130–134.

'Cherchil' i Stalin: Epizody Anglo-Sovetskikh Otnoshenii (Sentiabr' 1939-Iun' 1941) (Stalin and Churchill: Episodes from Anglo-Soviet Relations)'. In *Voina i Politika 1939-1941*, ed. R.O. Chubari'an and G. Gorodetskii. Nauka: Moscow, 1999, 141.

Index

Abramson, Paulina and Adelina, 54
'absolute truth,' 146
absolutism, 98
Academy of Sciences of the USSR, 52, 54
access to historical Soviet documents
   background and overview, 7, 24, 26–7
   on Cold War, 114, 116
   on Spanish Civil War, 51, 52, 57–8, 62
   for Stalin biographies, 27–30, 33, 180 n.21
accusatorial interrogations. *See* interrogations
Adler, Nancy, 169
agency, individual, 30, 109
aircraft carriers, 68
Alba, Victor, 57, 188 n.42
Allen, David E., 55, 188 n.40
Alliluyeva, Nadezhda, 34
Amis, Martin, 113
Anka, Paul, 107–8
Ankara, Heart of Turkey (Yutkevich and Arnshtam), 85
Anti-Comintern Pact, 48
Apor, Balázs, 17
Araquistáin, Luis, 57, 188 n.43
Arendt, Hannah, 8–9, 10
argumentation interrogation method, 150
Arkhipova, Aleksandra, 158, 165
armed forces, development of Soviet, 67–70
Arms for Spain (Howson), 59, 189 n.57
Arnshtam, Leo, 85
Árpád, Captain, 101, 103
Atatürk, Mustafa Kemal, 17, 83–6, 88–90, 197 n.10, 199 n.40
atomic bombs. *See* nuclear weapons
Attlee, Clement, 77
Austria, 116, 207 n.39
Austro-Hungarian Empire, 98, 100
authoritarianism
   leader cults, 106

Putin, 97, 161, 162, 213 n.41
   reckoning with Stalinism, 166, 167–8, 170–1, 172
   re-Stalinization, 158, 161
   Stalin, 65

balance of power, 118–19
Baltic States, 71, 121
Barbusse, Henri, 86, 131
Basque children evacuees, 54, 60, 61
battlecruisers, 68
Battle of Khalkin-Gol, 67–8
Beissinger, Mark, 97
Belarus, 71
Bellamy, Chris, 16
Beneš, Edvard, 84
Beria, Lavrentii, 33, 73–5, 76
Berlin, race for, 120
Berlin Appeal, 137
Bessarabia, 71
Bethlen, István, 102
big three conferences, 63, 77, 121
biographies on Stalin, 21–37
   breakdown of binary discourse, 23–6
   considerations for writing, 30–7
   cult of personality, 21–3, 85–6, 198 n.25
   historical document access, 26–30, 180 n.21
   revisionary, 113
   Spanish Civil War, 58, 61
   See also specific biographies
biography genre, 14, 31
bipolarity, 114, 119
Bizcarrondo, Marta, 59, 188 n.45, 189 n.60
Black Book of Communism, The, 32
Bloodlands (Snyder), 25
Bloom, Molly, 31
Bogumił, Zuzanna, 167
Bolloten, Burnett, 55, 59
Bolloten-Orwell thesis, 55

Bolsheviks
 modernization, 95
 Red Army purge, 40, 41–4, 183 n.11
 Tsaritsyn, 64–6
Bolshevism
 ideology, 12–13
 Stalin and, 35
Bornholm, 121–2
Bortnikov, Aleksandr, 166–7
Boym, Svetlana, 168, 215 n.83
Brandenberger, David, 29
Brandon, Ray, 15
Brest-Litovsk, treaty of, 34, 42
Breumelberger, Werner, 85
Brezhnev era, 6
Britain
 peace movement, 135, 136, 137
 Spanish Civil War, 54, 56
 Stalin, 71, 76
 as a superpower, 118–19
British Peace Committee (BPC), 135
Brittain, Vera, 118
Brodie, Bernard, 120
Budënny, Semen, 70, 74, 185 n.58
Building of the State, 84
Bukharin, Nikolai, 23, 34–5, 66
bureaucratization, 24, 36, 45

Cairncross, John, 77
calendars, 192 n.7
Cameron, Sarah, 7
Čapek, Karel, 84, 88
capitalism, 3, 12, 66, 123, 133–4
Carr, E.H., 27–8
Cattell, David, 54
ceremonies and celebrations, 87–8, 91, 99, 101, 103, 104, 108, 198 n.30
Chamberlain, Neville, 54
Chase, William, 60, 190 n.66
Cheka, 43, 183 n.26
children
 Basque evacuees, 54, 60, 61
 leader cults, 87, 88, 107
China, 5, 133
Chinese Communist Party, 23, 133
Churchill, Winston
 Iron Curtain speech, 4, 27
 Stalin, 27, 34, 76, 77, 119, 123
Clark, Katerina, 12

coexistence between capitalism and socialism, 133–4
Cohen, Stephen, 10, 176 n.47
Cold War, 113–25
 background and overview, 4–5, 113–15
 broader landscape of, 123–4
 conclusions, 124–5
 historiography, 7–12, 33, 115–17
 moralism, 123, 124
 novelty, 117–20, 122–3
 peace movement of (*See* peace movement)
 realpolitik, 121–3
Cold War, The (Gaddis), 117
collective identity, 159, 164, 170
collective security, 3, 51, 55–6
collectivization, 2, 37, 46, 127, 165, 166
Comintern, 52, 54, 59–60, 66–7, 71
communism
 historical legacies, 96–7
 historiography, 116–17
 in Hungary, 93, 102–5, 202 n.48
 'language' of, 151
 modernity, 95
 Spanish Civil War, 54, 55
 Stalin and Stalinism, 5, 24–5, 32, 72, 123
 See also Communist Party
Communism and the Spanish Civil War (Cattell), 54
'communist kingdom,' 93
Communist Party
 Chinese, 23, 133
 peace movement, 130–1, 135
 psychological torture, 150–1
 Spanish, 54
 Stalin, 2, 23
 See also communism
Compromise of 1867, Hungarian, 98, 100
Concept of State Policy to Perpetuate the Memory of Victims of Political Repression, 167
confession constructing, 141–54
 background and overview, 141–4
 conclusions, 153–4
 interrogation department, 142, 143, 144–7, 209 n.23
 language of, 151–3
 torture, 147–51
confrontation interrogation method, 150

Congress of Peoples for Peace, 137–8
Conquest, Robert, 24, 25, 176 n.41
'consent and evade,' 65
conspiracy
    Czechoslovakian interrogation and, 145–6, 209 n.23
    Red Army purge and, 39, 40, 41, 46–8
Containment Doctrine, 119
Conversations with Masaryk (Čapek), 84
coping with the past, 158–9, 166, 169, 172
counter attacks on Germany, 72–3, 76
counter-cult of personality for Stalin, 22–3
counterintelligence, 44–5
Crimea, 73, 113, 165
crisis as a political theme, 106–7
cult of personality of Stalin, 21–6
    background and overview, 5–6, 91
    binary discourse breakdown, 23–6
    counter cult, 22–3, 199 n.34
    Hungary, 104–5
    iconography, 82–4, 94
    patrimonial rule, 95–6
    post mortem, 90, 105
    rituals and practices, 87, 88–9
    Stalin biographies, 21–3, 84, 85–6, 198 n.25
    Stalin's dislike of, 22, 179–80 n.3
cults, leader, 81–91
    background and overview, 81, 196 n.4
    biography and history, 84–6
    conclusions, 90–1
    in Hungary (*See* cults in Hungary, leader)
    iconography, 82–4, 100–1, 197 n.9–10
    persistence, change, and legacy, 94–7
    post-mortem, 89–90, 199 n.45
    rituals and practices, 86–9, 91, 98, 101, 103–4, 106, 198 n.35
    See also cult of personality, Stalin's
cults in Hungary, leader, 93–109
    background and overview, 93–7
    communism, 102–5, 202 n.48
    conclusions, 108–9
    monarchy and nationalism, 98–102
    post-communist, 105–8
culture, political
    Hungarian, 93–4, 96, 97–8, 100–2, 103
    Stalin cult, 81, 91
culture and social structures, 11

culture of honour, 32, 35
Czechoslovakia, confession in. *See* confession constructing

Daily Telegraph, 24
Daniels, Robert, 10
David-Fox, Michael, 5, 13–14, 216 n.103
Davies, R. W., 9, 28
Day of Remembrance for Victims of Political Repression, 167–8
D-Day anniversary snub, 113
Deák, Ferenc, 100, 101
Death of Stalin, The, 37, 113, 181 n.38
decision-making of Stalin, 127–9
Defence Commissariat
    Spanish Civil War, 52, 57, 58, 186 n.10, 189 n.57
    war operations, 70
Degtiiarev, Georgii, 77
Denmark, 71, 121–2
deportations, 2–3, 165, 169
de-Stalinization, 6, 171
Deutscher, Isaac, 21, 23, 61, 122
developmental violence, 3
development of Soviet armed forces, 67–70
Devlin, Judith, 16–17
diversionary operations, 47, 69–70
Dobrenko, Yevgeny, 86
documentary films, 84–5, 168–9, 198 n.22
documents, access to historical Soviet. *See* access to historical Soviet documents
Donne, John, 31
dossier of evidence of military conspiracy, 40, 182 n.4
Doubek, Bohumil, 143, 144–5, 146–7, 148, 150, 151
Dreister, Efim, 184 n.48
Duď, Iurii, 168–9
Dumas, Alexandre, 86
Dva goda v Ispanii (Savich), 54
Dzerzhinskii, Feliks, 43

Eastern Europe and Stalinist ideology
    background and overview, 2, 5, 15
    historiography, 115
    leader cults, 95–7, 102–5, 109
    reckoning, 157

Economic Problems of the USSR (Stalin), 133, 134
Eden, Anthony, 125
Ehrenburg, Ilya, 53, 131, 132, 135, 136, 137–9, 187 n.16–17, 206 n.11
Eighth Party Congress, 42
Einstein, Albert, 131
Eisenhower, Dwight D., 118, 120, 136
Eisenstadt, Schmuel, 17, 95
Elorza, Antonio, 59, 188 n.45, 189 n.60
El'tsin, Boris, 116, 160
Estonia, 71, 121
Etkind, Aleksandr, 166
European Parliament, 160
Evacuation Soviet, 75
Ezhov, Nikolai, 47–8

Fadeev, Aleksandr, 131–2, 136, 206 n.17
Fainsod, Merle, 8, 10
famine, 7, 24, 25, 165
Farkas, Mihály, 104
father figures
  leader cults, 88, 90, 99, 101, 104, 107
  Stalin as, 1, 21
Federal Security Service (FSB), 166
Fedoseev, P.N., 131–2, 203 n.11
Feleségverseny (Spíró), 93–4
FIDESZ, 106, 108
Filatov, Georgy, 59
films
  Death of Stalin, 37, 113, 181 n.38
  on Gulag camps, 168–9
  leader cults, 84–6, 198 n.22
  Spanish Civil War, 53, 61
Finland, 121
Fitzpatrick, Shelia, 9–10, 13, 14, 33, 174 n.25, 176 n.47
five-power pact campaign, 137, 138
Five-Year Plans, 66
Flërov, Georgii, 77
For a Lasting Peace, For a People's Democracy!, 133–4
foreign infiltration of Red Army, 40–1, 43, 44, 46–7, 48–9, 184 n.50
Foreign Policy Commission, 129, 135, 137–8
forgetfulness, 169–70
Forward Steps in the Turkish Revolution (Shub), 85
Fox, William T.R., 118

France, 54, 71, 76, 116, 120, 135, 137
Frangulian, Georgii, 167–8
Franquista theories of Spanish Civil War, 56, 188 n.40
Frei, Norbert, 159
FSB (Federal Security Service), 166
Fulbrook, Mary, 159
Fundación Pablo Iglesias, 60

Gaddis, John Lewis, 115, 116–17
Gamarnik, Ian, 39, 49
Garibaldi, Giuseppe, 86, 199 n.45
genre of biography, 14, 31
geopolitical strength of Soviet Union, 2, 5, 165
Germany
  coping with the past, 158–9, 169, 172
  defeat of, 117–18, 120
  leader cults, 82, 84–5, 91
  Lenin, 41–2
  Nazis and Nazism, 25, 55
  peace movement, 136
  Red Army infiltration, 48, 49
  Soviet Union attack, 70, 71–6
  Stalin, 36, 54, 55, 56, 71–6, 120, 195 n.60
Gerő, András, 98
Getty, J. Arch, 11, 26, 28, 33, 95–6
Gill, Graeme, 10, 174 n.25
GKO, 74–5
Glyptis, Leda, 89, 90
Gömbös, Gyula, 102
Gorbachev, Mikhail, 24, 26, 113
GPU, 44–5
Grantseva, Ekaterina, 59
Great Patriotic War
  big three conferences, 63, 77, 121
  policing scholarship on, 160
  pre-war armed forces development, 67–70
  revisioning the Cold War and, 117–23, 124
  Stalin, 3–4, 6, 16, 66, 71–8, 113, 172
Great Terror
  confession and torture, 141–2, 147, 208 n.8
  cult performance, 91
  historiography, 24
  See also purge of the Red Army; purges

Great Terror, The (Conquest), 24
Greene, Samuel, 163, 213 n.41
Grey, Ian, 23
Guardian, 166
Gudkov, Lev, 164
Guerra y revolución en España, 57
guilt by association, 145, 150–1
Gulag Archipelago (Solzhenitsyn), 146
Gulag camps, 165, 168–9, 214 n.63
Gulag museum, 161, 167

Habeck, Mary, 59–60
Habsburg monarchy, 99, 100
Halfin, Igal, 12–13, 150
Haller, Jozsef, 88
Harriman, Averill, 63
Harrison, Mark, 28
Haslam, Jonathan, 55–6
Hein, Heidi, 84, 88, 90
Hellbeck, Jochen, 12–13, 30
Helsinki World Peace Assembly, 139, 207 n.42
Hindenburg, Paul von, 82–5, 86, 87, 88
Hiroshima bombing, 118, 195 n.73
Historia 16, 57
historical document access. *See* access to historical Soviet documents
historical legacies, 93–7, 100, 102–6, 107, 108–9, 170–2
historical materialism, 11
history as national security, 160
History of Foreign Countries (Kandel and Guterman), 52
History of Stalinism, 14
History of the USSR (Davies), 28
Hitler, Adolf
    compared to Stalin, 127–8, 139
    cult of personality, 83, 84, 85, 86, 87
    Molotov-Ribbentrop Pact, 71
    simplification of, 33
    Spanish Civil War, 51
    Stalin and, 4, 25, 36
Hitler Day, 87
Hochman, Jiri, 55–6
Hoffman, David, 7, 13, 142
Holloway, David, 118, 122
Holocaust, 159
Holquist, Peter, 13
Homage to Catalonia (Orwell), 55, 186 n.1

Hopf, Ted, 129–30
Horthy, István, 102
Horthy, Miklós, 93, 94, 100–3, 107, 109, 196 n.4
Hosking, Geoffrey, 28
House of Government (Slezkine), 30
How Russia is Ruled (Fainsod), 8
Howson, Gerald, 59, 189 n.57
Hungary
    leader cults (*See* cults in Hungary, leader)
    revolution of 1956, 105
    torture methods, 149

Iagoda, Genrikh, 43
Ibárruri, Dolores, 56–7
Icebreaker (Rezun), 72
iconography, 82–4, 88, 90–1, 94, 197 n.9–10
identity
    collective, 159, 164, 170
    national, 4, 157–8, 160, 164, 167, 168, 172
ideology
    in historical documents, 27, 28–9
    interpretation schools of thought, 8, 9, 10, 12, 14
    interrogations and confession, 142, 143, 146, 151, 152, 153
    leader cults, 97, 109
    moralism, 117, 123, 124
    Spanish Civil War, 56, 61–2
    US, 115, 117, 123
ILC (International Liaison Committee of Intellectuals for Peace), 131–2
Imperial Army, 42
individuality and biography writing, 30–1, 33
industrialization, 2–3, 37, 66, 166
inevitability of war, 133–4, 137
Ingush, 165
inquisitorial interrogations, 152
Institute of Marxism-Leninism, 22, 52
Institute of Marxism-Leninism-Stalinism, 22
Intelligence and Reconnaissance Directorate, 70
International Liaison Committee of Intellectuals for Peace (ILC), 131–2

International Relations studies, 114, 117–19
International Solidarity with the Spanish Republic (Academy of Sciences of the USSR), 54
interrogations
   background and overview, 141, 143
   Czech interrogation department, 142, 143, 144–7, 209 n.23
   torture, 147–51
interrogators, 143, 144–7, 149, 152–4
Iran, 113, 122
Iron Curtain speech of Winston Churchill, 4, 27
Iron Hindenburg, 84–5
Ispanskaia respublika i Komintern (Meshcheriakov), 188 n.45
Ispanskie reportazhi (Ehrenburg), 53, 187 n.17
Ispanskii dnevnik (Koltsov), 53, 186 n.15
Ispanskii tetrady (Maískii), 53, 187 n.20
Istoriia, 59
Istoriia stalinizma, 14
Istoriia zarubezhnikh stran (Kandel and Guterman), 52
Italian Socialist Party, 132, 206 n.13
Iurieva, L.M., 52

Japan, 32, 48, 67–8, 115–16, 117–18, 120, 124
Joliot-Curie, Frédéric, 132, 134–5
Jones, Adrian, 23
Jones, Polly, 2
Joseph, Franz, 98–100, 102, 109
Judt, Tony, 117
justice for Stalinism victims, 159

Kádár, János, 93, 94, 105, 202 n.48
Kaftanov, Sergei, 77
Kaganovich, Lazar, 74
Kalashnikov, Mikhail, 77
Kamenev, Lev, 25
Karatygin, P.A., 69
Karmen, Roman, 53–4
Kazakhstan, 7, 165
Kazbegi, Aleksandr, 35
Kennan, George F., 114, 115, 119, 121
Kennedy-Pipe, Caroline, 17, 113–14, 124
Kerenskii, Aleksandr, 82, 88, 197 n.10
Kershaw, Ian, 18, 127–8, 139

Khlevniuk, Oleg, 7, 14, 28, 61, 171
Khrushchev, Nikita
   de-Stalinization, 6
   secret speech, 1–2, 3, 5, 22, 23, 141, 170, 173 n.1
   Stalin as a war leader, 74
   totalitarianism, 8
Kindler, Robert, 7
Kirov, Sergei, 40, 47, 87
Kiselev, Dmitrii, 168
Kitchlew, Saifuddin, 138
kitsch, 82, 197 n.9–10, 197 n.14
Koba the Dread (Amis), 113
Kohoutek, Vladimír, 149–50
Koltsov, Mikhail, 53, 186 n.15
Komshukov, A.A., 54
Konigsberg, 121
Kontopodis, Michael, 171
Korean War, 124, 136
Kossuth, Lajos, 99, 101, 103
Kotkin, Stephen, 12, 15, 29, 61, 97, 191 n.71
Kowalsky, Daniel, 60, 189–90 n.62
Kozma, Andor, 99
Krasnaia Zvezda, 76
Krasnov, Pëtr, 65
Kuleshova, V.V., 54
Kuznetsov, Nikolai, 53, 73, 74, 186 n.4, 187 n.24

language
   of interrogations, 151–2
   leader cults, 22, 88
Laos, 124
Large, David Clay, 169
Latvia, 71, 121
leader cults. *See* cult of personality, Stalin's; cults, leader; cults in Hungary, leader
leadership role of Stalin, 3–4
Leites, Nathan, 8
Lenin, Vladimir
   Khrushchev on, 1, 2
   leader cults, 21, 22, 83, 86, 89, 197 n.10
   New Left, 24
   revolution, 34, 36, 66–7
   Soviet army, 42–3
   Stalin, 22, 29, 34, 64–5, 96
   totalitarian school of thought on, 8

Leningradsty v Ispanii (Pritsker), 53
Leninism, 2, 12, 22, 97
Lenin Peace Prize, 206 n.16
Leo, Richard, 153
Levada Center, 163–4, 168, 169, 171
Lih, Lars, 27
Lithuania, 71, 121
Litvinov, Maxim, 55–6
Liudi, gody, zhizn (Ehrenburg), 53, 187 n.16
London, Arthur, 141, 143, 144, 145, 148–53
Luhn, Alec, 166
Lukin, Vladimir, 168

Magnetic Mountain (Kotkin), 12
Maiskii, Ivan M., 52, 53, 186 n.4, 187 n.20–1
Makhotina, Ekaterina, 158, 165, 169
Makhrovskii, K.A., 65, 192 n.12
Malay, V.V., 58
Malenkov, Georgii, 74–5, 134, 138
Malinova, Ol'ga, 158, 168, 216 n.99
Manhattan Project, 76–7
Manning, Roberta, 11
Markin, n., 64
Marks, Stephen, 61
Marshall Plan, 4, 37, 116, 119
Marx, Karl, 9, 27
Marxism, 5, 11, 134
Masaryk, Tomáš Garrigue, 83–4, 86–8, 90, 197 n.10, 197 n.13–14, 197 n.16, 199 n.38–9
McCullough, David, 63, 77
mediocrity myth of Stalin, 28, 36
Medvedev, Dmitrii, 160, 161–2, 167
Medvedev, Roy, 26
Mekhlis, Lev, 73
memoirs of Soviets in Spanish Civil War, 52–4
memorials and monuments, 83, 90, 108, 157, 161, 165–6, 167–8
memory, 158–9, 160, 165–6, 167–9, 171–2
Menzhinskii, Viacheslav, 45–6, 47
Merkulov, Vsevolod, 72, 74, 77, 194 n.53, 195 n.73
Meshcheriakov, M.T., 52, 188 n.45
Mikoyan, Anastas, 74–5
Military Archive (RGVA), 59

Military Council of the Northern Caucasus Military District, 65
military operations, 64, 67, 69–70, 76
  See also specific operations
Military Opposition, 42
military specialists *(voenspets)*
  in Red Army purge, 42–3, 44, 46–7, 183 n.27
  Stalin at Tsaritsyn and, 65
Military Strategy (Sokolovskii), 67
military-technological development, 76–7
Minakov, Sergei, 182 n.5
Minin, Sergei K., 43, 65
Mitrokhin, Nikolau, 167
modernity
  in Hungary, 98
  leader cults, 17, 83, 91, 95, 98
  in Soviet Union, 13–14, 95
Molotov, Polina, 129
Molotov, Viacheslav
  morality, 32
  peace movement, 129, 131–2, 206 n.17
  Red Army purge, 49
  Stalin, 28, 35, 68, 73–5, 129
Molotov-Ribbentrop Pact, 71
monarchical symbols, 93, 94, 102, 106, 109
Monarchist Union of Central Russia, 45
monarchy and Hungary, 98–102
Monroe Doctrine, 119, 123
Montefiore, Simon Sebag, 29
monuments and memorials, 83, 90, 108, 157, 161, 165–6, 167–8
mood reports. *See* public opinion
moralism, 17, 31–2, 114, 117, 123, 124
moral judgement and biography, 31–2
Mosaico Roto (Abramson), 54
Moscow, 157
museums and leader cults, 88–9, 90, 104
Mussolini, Benito
  leader cult, 82, 83, 89, 197 n.9, 198 n.26
  Spanish Civil War, 51
  totalitarianism school of thought on, 7
My First Struggles (Piłsudski), 84
My internatsionalisty, 53
myths, historical
  leader cults, 83–4, 85, 90, 97, 103, 107
  Putin and, 161
  Spanish Civil War, 60, 62
  Stalin and, 29–30, 33, 37

Nagasaki bombing, 118, 195 n.73
Naiman, Eric, 13
name day celebrations, 87–8
naming after leaders, 86–7
narratives
  leader cult, 83, 85–6, 90–1
  Russian history, 157, 159–62, 165, 167, 168, 169, 171
national identity, 4, 157–8, 160, 164, 167, 168, 172
nationalism, 102, 109, 159
National Peace Council (NPC), 135
national unity, 159, 167
NATO, 116, 119, 125, 132
Navy, Soviet, 68, 73
Nazis, 127–8, 158–9, 160, 161, 172
Nazism and communism, 25
Nazi-Soviet Pact, 34
Nenni, Pietro, 132, 137, 138, 206 n.13, 207 n.43
Neo-Revisionists on Cold War, 115–17
neo-traditionalism, 13–14, 95
New Economic Policy (NEP), 6, 9
New Left, 9, 24, 115
Nikolaev, Leonid, 47
Niños de Guerra, 54
Nitti, Giuseppe, 138
Nixon, Richard, 115
NKVD
  about, 69
  purge of Red Army, 39–40, 41, 47–9, 50
  Spanish Civil War, 62
  war operations, 70
Nolte, Ernst, 25
Non-Intervention Agreement, 51
Non-Intervention Committee (NIC), 52, 54, 58
No Pasaran (Karmen), 53–4
No Pasarán! slogan, 62
Norris, Chuck, 107
Northern Iran, 122
Nove, Alec, 23
Novikov, M.V., 57
NPC (National Peace Council), 135
nuclear weapons
  Cold War historiographies, 115, 117
  dropping of, 32, 118, 120, 195 n.73
  peace movement, 129, 132, 133, 134–5, 137, 138–9

proxy wars, 124
Soviet development, 5, 120, 122
Soviet vulnerability, 118, 120, 121, 122
US development, 76–7

objective guilt, 145, 150–1
October Revolution, 2, 25
OGPU, 44–7, 69
Olšáková, Dubravka, 15
On Trial (London), 141, 143, 144, 145, 148–53
operational art, 64, 67
Operation Barbarossa, 73, 127
Operation Springtime, 47
Operation X, 51, 58, 61, 62
opinion polls, 4, 105, 158, 163–5, 168–9, 170–1
Orbán, Viktor, 94, 97, 106–8, 109, 200 n.1
Order GKO-83 ss, 70
Order Number 147, 69–70
Origins of Totalitarianism (Arendt), 8–9, 10
Orkán, Akeràl, 93–4, 95, 105, 109
Orwell, George, 55, 59–60, 61, 114, 186 n.1
Orzoff, Andrea, 84, 88
Osbye otdely (OO), 43, 183 n.26
OSCE (Parliamentary Assembly of the Organization for Security and Cooperation in Europe), 160
O'Sullivan, Noel, 123
output system of interrogation, 146–7
Özyürek, Esra, 85

Parliamentary Assembly of the Organization for Security and Cooperation in Europe (OSCE), 160
Partisans for Peace, 132, 135
partisan warfare, 69–70
Partizanstvo (Karatygin), 69
Pascua, Marcelino, 61
paternalism, 96, 107, 108, 171
  See also father figures
patriarchal rule, 7, 165
patrimonial rule, 93, 95–6, 97, 108
Pavlov, Grigor'evich, 70
PCPP (Permanent Committee of Partisans of Peace), 132, 133, 134–6

peace movement, 127–40
  after Stalin, 138–9
  background and overview, 127–9
  conclusions, 139–40
  emergence, 130–2
  foreign policy, 129–30
  Stalin, 133–4, 206 n.17
  Stockholm Appeal, 134–6
  Vienna peace congress, 137–8
  World Peace Council, 136–7
peace prizes, 131, 133, 138, 206 n.16, 207 n.43
People's Commisariat for Defence, 69, 73–4
people's militia, 41, 183 n.11
Perm-36 Gulag museum, 161
Permanent Committee of Partisans of Peace (PCPP), 132, 133, 134–6
persistence and change, 95–7
Peters, Edward, 142
Petrov, Nikita, 166
photography and leader cults, 82–4, 197 n.9
physical violence and confession, 147–8, 149
Piłsudski, Jozef
  coup planning, 44, 45
  leader cult, 83, 84, 86–8, 89, 90
Pipes, Richard, 9, 24, 175 n.41, 180 n.12
Plumb, Robert Lee, 55, 188 n.40
Podliubnyi, Stephan, 30
Pod znamenem Ispanskoi respubliki (Maiskii, et al), 53, 187 n.21
poetry and leader cults, 22, 88, 99, 104, 199 n.38
Poland
  espionage, 44, 46
  Lenin's attack on, 66–7
  Molotov-Ribbentrop Pact, 71
  Nazi occupation of, 72, 127
  peace movement, 130–1
  Piłsudski and, 83, 84, 86–7, 88, 90
  Soviet interest in, 121
Political Administration of the Red Army (PUR), 45, 182 n.2
political symbolism, 81, 94, 97, 99–103, 106
Political Thought of Stalin, The (van Ree), 28

polluted sources, 33
popular frontism, 56, 62, 136
popularity of Stalin, 4, 158, 163–5, 172
portraits and leader cults, 82–4, 88, 197 n.9
Poskrebyshev, A.N., 137
post-Communist society features, 96–7
post-mortem leader cults, 89–90, 199 n.45
post-revisionist school of thought, 11–14
Potsdam big three conference, 63, 77
POUM (Workers Party of Marxist Unification), 55, 57, 62
power of Stalin, 36–7, 40, 50
Pozharskaia, Svetlana, 52, 58, 186 n.8
Practicing Stalinism (Getty), 95–6
Pravda
  Spanish Civil War, 53
  Stalin, 49, 82, 137, 207 n.37
Presidential Archive, 27, 58
Primakov, Vitalii, 39, 46, 47, 184 n.48
Pritsker, D.P., 53
Problemy ispanskoi istorii (Gluzhinsskaia), 52
proxy wars, 124
psychological torture, 147–51
Psychology of Interrogations and Confessions, 149
public opinion, 4, 105, 158, 163–5, 168–9, 170–1
Pucci, Molly, 18
Puigsech, Josep, 61–2, 191 n.75
PUR (Political Administration of the Red Army), 45, 182 n.2
purge of the Red Army
  background and overview, 39–41, 50, 182 n.2, 182 n.4–5, 182 n.6
  civil war and military vulnerabilities, 41–3
  Great Terror and, 46–50, 184 n.50
  1920's threats, 43–6, 184 n.33
purges
  morality, 24
  Spanish Civil War and, 62, 191 n.77
  totalitarian view on, 24
  victims, 25–6, 30, 39, 69, 165, 182 n.2
  See also purge of the Red Army
Puskás, Ferenc, 108
Putin, Vladimir
  as an authoritarian leader, 97, 161

D-Day anniversary snub, 113
Future and, 125
on Great Patriotic War, 4, 161
Stalinism, 18, 157, 159–63, 166, 167, 168, 170, 172
Putna, Vitovt, 39, 47, 184 n.47–8
Pyta, Wolfram, 82

question protocols of interrogation, 151–2

Raack, R.C., 71
Rabinowitch, Alexander, 10
Radosh, Ronald, 59–60
Rákosi, Mátyás, 94, 103–5, 109
Raport, 68–9
Read, Christopher, 15–16
realpolitik, 114, 121–3
reckoning with Stalin and Stalinism, 157–72
  background and overview, 157–60
  conclusions, 171–2
  repression and, 165–71
  re-Stalinization of Russian society, 162–5
  re-Stalinization of the ruling elite, 160–2
Reconnaissance and Intelligence Directorate, 69
Red Army
  foreign infiltration, 43, 44, 46–7, 48–9, 184 n.50
  purge of (*See* purge of the Red Army)
  Stalin as a war leader, 69–70
  at Tsaritsyn, 65
Rees, Arfon, 28
rehabilitation of Stalinism. *See* re-Stalinization
Reid Technique, 146
Reno, William, 124
repression
  public opinion on, 163–4
  purges (*See* purges)
  reckoning and rehabilitation, 160–1, 165–71
re-Stalinization
  background and overview, 18, 158, 159–60
  ruling elite, 160–2
  Russian society, 162–5

Reviewing the Cold War (Westad), 117
revisionism, 9, 101, 176 n.47
revisionist school of thought
  Cold War, 115–17, 122, 123
  purge, 26, 118
  Stalinism, 9–11, 12, 14
Rezun, Vladimir, 72
RGASPI, 59
RGVA (Military Archive), 59
Riall, Lucy, 86
Ribalkin, Iurii, 57, 58
Rieber, Alfred, 29, 35
Riefenstahl, Leni, 85
rituals, 86–9, 91, 98, 101, 103–4, 106, 198 n.35
Roberts, Geoffrey, 17–18, 28–9, 113, 120
  Spanish Civil War, 56
  Stalin's Wars, 3, 4, 29–30, 63
Robertson, Graeme, 163, 213 n.41
Rogge, O. John, 136–7
Rokossovskii, Konstantin, 73, 76, 195 n.60
Rome-Berlin Axis, 48
Roosevelt, Franklin D., 77, 117–18, 120, 123, 124–5
Rosefielde, Stephen, 25
'royal cult,' 93–4
Ruder, Cynthia, 7
ruling elite and Stalin and Stalinism, 158, 159–62, 166, 167, 170, 172, 216 n.99
'Rusos en la Guerra de España, Los,' 60
Russian Orthodox Church, 167
Russian Political Encyclopedia (ROSSPEN), 14
Russo-German pact of 1939, 54
Ryan, James, 18

Saint Stephen, King, 94, 99, 106
Sartre, Jean-Paul, 138, 207 n.42
Savich, Ovadei, 54
'scenario of love,' 87, 88
Schauff, Frank, 60
second front in Great Patriotic War, 63, 76, 122
Second World, 116
Second World War. *See* Great Patriotic War
secret speech of Khrushchev, 1–2, 3, 5, 22, 23, 141, 170, 173 n.1
security, collective, 3, 51, 55–6

security threats to Soviet military, 16, 40–1, 46, 50
Service, Robert, 29
Sherlock, Thomas, 158, 161
Sherry, Jonathan, 62, 191 n.76
Short Course, 29, 86
show trials
  Czech, 141, 142, 145, 151, 153–4
  Soviet, 25, 35, 47, 48, 62, 142, 185 n.58
Shpagin, Georgii, 77
Shub, Esfir, 85, 198 n.22
Shulman, Marshal D., 130
Shul'man, Ekaterina, 171
simplification of Russian politics, 33, 115, 159
Skoutelsky, Rémi, 59, 189 n.58
Slánský, Rudolf, 141, 151, 152–3
sleep deprivation, 141, 148–9
Slezkine, Yuri, 30
Smetona, Antanas, 198 n.30
Smirnov, P., 193 n.31
Snyder, Timothy, 15, 25
socialism
  capitalism's coexistence with, 133–4
  Czech, 143
  leader cults, 103, 104, 105
  reckoning with, 157, 217 n.104
  Spanish Civil War, 56
  Stalinism, 3, 4, 6, 12, 34, 66–7, 71
'socialism in one country,' 34, 66–7, 71
Sokolovskii, Vitalii, 67
Solomon, Peter, 142
Solzhenitsyn, Aleksander, 25–6, 143, 146, 149
Soong Ching-ling, 133
'Sovetskaia istoriografiia antifashistkoi voiny v Ispanii' (Pozharskaia), 52, 186 n.8
Soviet Academy of Sciences, 52
Soviet advisers to Czech interrogators, 141, 143, 144–5, 146–9, 152, 209 n.23
Soviet Diplomacy and the Spanish Civil War (Cattell), 54
sovietization, 103–4, 143, 153
'Soviet Participation in the Spanish Civil War' (Plumb), 55
"Soviet Union and the Failure of Collective Security" (Hochman), 55–6

'Soviet Union and the Spanish Civil War, The' (Allen), 55
Soviet Union and the Struggle for Collective Security in Europe (Haslam), 55–6
Spain Betrayed (Habeck and Radosh), 59–60
Spanish Civil War
  about, 51
  collective security, 51, 55–6
  reckoning with, 170
  Soviet support and participation, 51, 54–7, 59–62, 67, 68, 69
  See also Spanish Civil War historiography
Spanish Civil War historiography, 51–62
  background and overview, 51–2, 62, 186 n.1
  non-Russian post Cold War, 59–62
  Russian language post Cold War, 57–9
  USSR 1936-1991, 52–4, 186 n.7, 188 n.45
  Western countries 1936-1991, 54–7
'Spanish Civil War's Impact on Spanish and Soviet Political Cultures, The' (Chase), 60, 190 n.66
Spanish Communist Party (PCE), 54
Spanish Notebooks (Maiskii), 53, 187 n.20
Spanish Republican Army, 69
Special Departments, 43, 183 n.26
Special Forces, 69
Specialist Diversionary Department, 70
Spíró, György, 93–4
spy infiltration of Red Army, 40–1, 43, 44, 46–7, 48–9, 184 n.50
Stalin, Joseph
  background and overview, 2–4
  Cold War, 4, 118, 119, 120, 121, 122, 123–5
  compared to Hitler, 127–8, 139
  cult of personality (*See* cult of personality of Stalin)
  decision-making, 127–9
  early years, 22, 34, 35–6
  Germany, 36, 54, 55, 56, 71–6, 120, 195 n.60
  July 3, 1941 speech, 76
  Khrushchev's secret speech, 1–2, 3, 5, 22, 23, 141, 170, 173 n.1
  mediocrity myth, 28, 36

motivation, 33–4, 181 n.40
'normal' personality, 34–6
peace movement, 129–30, 137, 138, 139–40, 207 n.43
popularity, 4, 158, 163–5, 172
power, 36–7, 40, 50
reckoning with (*See* reckoning with Stalin and Stalinism)
Red Army purge, 39–40, 41, 43, 46–50
revolutionary convictions, 2, 34, 66, 71
Spanish Civil War, 51–2, 54, 61–2
torture, 147
as a villain, 124–5, 205 n.58
See also Stalin as a war leader
Stalin and Europe (Snyder and Brandon), 15
Stalin as a war leader, 63–78
  background and overview, 63–4
  development of armed forces, 67–70
  geopolitics and geostrategy, 66–7
  Germany's attack on Soviet Union, 71–6, 195 n.60
  international relations, 76, 77–8
  military-technological development, 76–7
  romance with Germany, 71–3
  at Tsaritsyn, 64–6
Stalinism
  background and overview, 5–7, 15, 174 n.25
  confessions, 142–3, 153
  cult leaders, 103–4, 107
  post-revisionist school of thought on, 11–14
  reckoning with (*See* reckoning with Stalin and Stalinism)
  rehabilitation of (*See* re-Stalinization)
  revisionist school of thought on, 9–11, 12, 14
  term of, 22, 159
  totalitarian school of thought on, 7–9, 10, 24–6, 175–6 n.41
'Stalino-fascist baroque,' 97
Stalin Peace Prizes, 131, 133, 138, 206 n.16, 207 n.43
Stalin's Cold War (Kennedy-Pipe), 113–14, 124
Stalin's Foreign Policy Reappraised (Shulman), 130

Stalin's Wars (Roberts), 3, 4, 29–30, 63
Starshina, 72
Stavka, 66, 74–5
Steel Division, 66
Steinbeck, John, 90
Stites, Richard, 61
Stockholm Appeal, 134–6, 137
Stone, Oliver, 157, 161
Strana Sovetov, 68
strategic bombing, 118
Strategy (Svechin), 67
'strong hand,' necessity of, 170–1
Sudoplatov, P.A., 70
Suny, Ronald Grigor, 10, 29, 35
superpowers, 17, 78, 115–16, 118–19, 122
Suslov, Mikhail, 133, 139
Suvorov, Victor, 72
Svechin, Aleksandr, 67
Švermová, Marie, 150
symbolic politics, 81, 94, 97, 99–103, 106
Sytin, Pavel, 43
Szász, Béla, 143, 145, 147, 149, 151

Talashova, V.A., 54
tanks, 59, 61, 67–8
Tannenberg, 85
Taylor, A.J.P., 131
Tehran big three conference, 63, 77
Tenth Army, 65
tëplopelengator, 68–9
terror
  in East Europe, 142, 208 n.8
  Soviet Great Terror (*See* Great Terror)
textbooks, history, 84, 161, 162
theory of confessions, 146
thermal direction finders, 68–9
Third International, 52, 54, 59–60, 66–7, 71
Third World, 116
Thurston, Robert, 25, 33
Tiempo de Historia, 57
Tiflis bank robbery, 35
Timoshenko, Semën, 70, 72, 73–4
Tismaneanu, Vladimir, 97
Tito, Josip Broz, 134, 136–7
Todorova, Maria, 97
Together with Spanish Patriots, 53
Tolmachaev, Vladimir, 57, 188 n.46
torture, 39, 141, 142, 147–51, 153

totalitarianism, 7–9, 81, 162, 164, 213 n.38
totalitarian school of thought
   cult of personality, 24–6
   Stalin biographies, 28, 30
   Stalinism, 7–9, 10, 173 n.3, 175–6 n.41–42
Traditionalists, 115, 117, 124–5
training manuals on interrogation, 144–5, 147, 151–2
trains, armoured, 65, 66
transitional justice, 169–70
treasures, Soviet, 75
Treaty of Brest-Litovsk, 34, 42
Treaty of Trianon, 101, 102
Triumph of the Will, 85
Trotsky, Leon
   purges, 26, 42–3, 44, 45–6, 48
   Stalin and Stalinism, 2, 22–4, 28, 36, 65–6, 67
Trotskyites, 45–8, 49, 50, 61
Truman, Harry S., 63, 77–8, 118, 119, 122, 123, 125
Truman Doctrine, 4
Trust Operation, 45
Tsaritsyn, 43, 64–6
Tucker, Robert, 24, 25, 191 n.77
Tukhachevskii, Mikhail
   about, 67, 69
   purge of Red Army, 39, 40, 44–5, 47, 48, 49–50, 182 n.4
Twentieth Party Congress, 22, 23
two-camps doctrine, 4–5, 130, 132
Two Years in Spain (Savich), 54

Uborevich, Ieronim P., 39, 69
Ukraine
   famine in, 24, 165
   Molotov-Ribbentrop Pact, 71
   partisan warfare, 69
   Soviet power, 157
   Spanish Civil War, 52
Unconditional Surrender doctrine, 117–18
Under the banner of the Spanish republic (Maiskii, et al), 83, 187 n.21
uninterrupted interrogations, 145–6, 148
United Nations, 37
Updike, John, 114
US Naval War College Review, 68
USSR collapse, 113–14, 116, 157

van Ree, Eric, 28
Vasilevskiĭ, Aleksandr, 53, 72, 76
Vatsetis, Ioakhim, 42–3
Vatutin, Nikolai, 74
vergangenheitsbewältigung, 158–9, 166, 169, 172
Vergangenheitspolitick, 159
victims
   of Communism and Imperialism, 32
   confession and, 141–2, 143
   of purges, 25–6, 30, 39, 69, 165, 182 n.2
   reckoning with the past, 159, 162, 165, 167–8, 169
   See also specific victims
Victory of Belief (Riefenstahl), 85
Vienna Awards, 101–2
Vienna peace congress, 137–8, 139
Vietnam War, 9, 124
Viñas, Angel, 58–9, 60
Viola, Lynne, 7, 18, 147
Vmeste s patriotami Ispanii, 53
voenspets. *See* military specialists
Voina i revoliutsiia v Ispanii, 52
Voina v Ispanii, 52, 186 n.10
Volkogonov, Dmitri, 26, 61, 178 n.80
Volodarsky, Boris, 62, 191 n.77
Von der Goltz, Anna, 84, 85, 88
Voronov, Nikolai, 53, 67, 73, 186 n.4, 187 n.21
Voroshilov, Kliment
   purge of Red Army, 43, 44, 46, 48–50, 182 n.5, 184 n.47
   Stalin as a war leader, 64, 65, 70, 74, 76
Voznesenskii, Nikolai, 74–5
VTsIOM, 163

Walker, Shaun, 166
Wallace, Henry, 131
'Wall of Sorrow' (Frangulian), 167–8
War Cabinet, 74–5
War of Independence, Hungarian, 99–100
Waterlow, Jonathan, 7
We Internationalists (Gorilovskogo), 53
We Now Know (Gaddis), 116
Westad, Odd Arne, 117, 124
Wheatcroft, Stephen, 25

White Armies, 42–5, 64–5
Whitewood, Peter, 16
Williams, William Appleman, 115, 117, 176 n.45
Wohlforth, William, 119
women
    Cold War, 117
    peace movement, 132, 136
Workers Party of Marxist Unification (POUM), 55, 57, 62
World Congress of Intellectuals for Peace, 130–1
World Congress of Partisans of Peace
    in Paris, 132, 133
    in Warsaw, 135–6
World Federation of Scientific Workers, 134–5
World Peace Council (WPC), 135–7, 138–9
world revolution, 2, 34, 43, 66–7, 71
World War II. *See* Great Patriotic War
Wortman, Richard, 87
Wroclaw congress, 130–1

XIV Partisan Corps, 69

Yakhina, Guzel, 169
Yakir, I.E., 69
Yalta big three conference, 63, 77, 121
Yeltsin, Boris, 116, 160
Yugoslavia, 4, 104, 134, 136–7
Yutkevich, Sergei, 85

Zaloga, Steven, 59
Zhdanov, Andrei, 4–5, 130, 132
Zhdanovshchina, 4
Zhigarev, Pavel, 74
Zhloba, Dmitrii Petrovich, 66
Zhukov, Georgii, 33, 68, 72–4, 76
Zilliacus, Konni, 134, 135
Zubovich, Katherine, 7
Zuleikha otkryivaet glaza (Yakhina), 169